In this rigorous investigation of the staging of Shakespeare's plays, Alan Dessen wrestles with three linked questions: (1) what did a playgoer at the original production actually see? (2) how can we tell today? and (3) so what? His emphasis is upon images and onstage effects (e.g. the sick-chair, early entrances, tomb scenes) easily obscured or eclipsed today. The basis of his analysis is his survey of the stage directions in the approximately 600 English professional plays performed before 1642. From such widely scattered bits of evidence emerges a vocabulary of the theatre shared by Shakespeare, his theatrical colleagues, and his playgoers, in which the terms (e.g. *vanish*, *as in* ..., *as from* ..., "*Romeo opens the tomb*") often do not admit of neat dictionary definitions but can be glossed in terms of options and potential meanings. To explore such terms, along with various costumes and properties (keys, trees, coffins, books), is to challenge unexamined assumptions that underlie how Shakespeare is read, edited, and staged today.

RECOVERING SHAKESPEARE'S THEATRICAL VOCABULARY

RECOVERING SHAKESPEARE'S THEATRICAL VOCABULARY

ALAN C. DESSEN

Peter G. Phialas Professor of English
University of North Carolina, Chapel Hill

Published by the Press Syndicate of the University of Cambridge
The Pitt Building, Trumpington Street, Cambridge, CB2 1RP
40 West 20th Street, New York, NY 10011–4211, USA
10 Stamford Road, Oakleigh, Melbourne 3166, Australia

First published 1995
Reprinted 1996

Printed in Great Britain by Antony Rowe Ltd, Chippenham, Wilts.

A catalogue record for this book is available from the British Library

Library of Congress cataloguing in publication data

Dessen, Alan C., 1935–
Recovering Shakespeare's theatrical vocabulary / Alan C. Dessen.
p. cm.
Includes bibliographical references and index.
ISBN 0 521 47080 3
1. Shakespeare, William, 1564–1616 – Dramatic production.
2. Theater – England – Production and direction – Terminology.
3. English language – Early modern, 1500–1700 – Semantics. 4. Drama – Technique – Terminology. 5. Stage directions – History. I. Title.
PR3091.D47 1995 792.9–dc20 94-16507 CIP

ISBN 0 521 47080 3 hardback

TAG

To the memory of Bernie Beckerman (1921–1985)

“*The best in this kind are but shadows*”

Contents

Preface *page* xi
Note on texts and old spelling xii

1 The problem, the evidence, and the language barrier 1
2 Lost in translation 19
3 Interpreting without a dictionary 39
4 Juxtapositions 64
5 Theatrical *italics* 88
6 Sick chairs and sick thrones 109
7 Much virtue in *as* 127
8 The vocabulary of "place" 150
9 "*Romeo opens the tomb*" 176
10 *Vanish* and vanishing 196
Conclusion: So what? 216

Notes 225
Plays and editions cited 269
Index 277

Preface

This project has evolved over many years, a process greatly abetted by a Fall 1990 fellowship at the Institute for the Arts and Humanities at the University of North Carolina, Chapel Hill, and a Spring 1991 National Endowment for the Humanities Senior Fellowship at the Folger Shakespeare Library. Along that tortuous path a treatment of keys in *The Merchant of Venice* that became a part of chapter 8 appeared in *Shakespeare Bulletin* (1985); some material now in chapters 1 and 2 appeared in *Word and Image* (1988); a discussion of *Romeo and Juliet*, 5.3 that now frames chapter 9 was published in *Shakespeare and the Sense of Performance*, edited by Marvin and Ruth Thompson (1988); and an early version of chapter 4 appeared in *Renaissance Papers 1991*. I wish to thank the editors of those journals and the University of Delaware Press for their permission to incorporate such materials here. In addition, parts of this argument have been presented to various groups, so for helpful comments my thanks are due to my graduate students in a 1992 seminar and to colleagues at several seminars of the Shakespeare Association of America, a 1991 seminar of the New York Shakespeare Society, the 1991 Southeastern Renaissance Conference, and the 1992 Ohio Shakespeare Conference. Of the many people who have been generous in sharing insights and offering criticisms, I would like to single out Homer Swander, Andrew Gurr, Robert Hapgood, George Walton Williams, G. B. Shand, Steven Urkowitz, John Astington, Cary Mazer, D. F. Rowan, William Long, Lena Orlin, Catherine Belsey, E. Pearlman, Peter Blayney, Leslie Thomson, and June Schlueter. I am also grateful for the help provided by Todd Stabley and by Betsy Walsh and her staff at the Folger Shakespeare Library.

Note on texts and old spelling

Unless otherwise noted, quotations from Shakespeare are taken from *The Complete Pelican Shakespeare*, general editor Alfred Harbage. Elsewhere, I have relied heavily upon facsimiles of the earliest texts (as with the Tudor Facsimile series, The Norton First Folio, and the Huntington Shakespeare Quartos), diplomatic editions (as with the reprints provided by the Malone Society), and the early printed texts themselves (thanks to the resources of the Folger Shakespeare Library). I use only those nineteenth- and twentieth-century editions that faithfully reproduce both the wording and placement of the original stage directions (e.g., the six-volume 1874 edition of Thomas Heywood) and, in many instances, have checked relevant passages in these modern editions against the original texts.

To avoid a cumbersome apparatus, I have not provided a footnote or endnote for each of the myriad stage directions that constitute the bulk of my evidence but instead have included line, signature, or page numbers in my text and then listed the plays cited and editions used at the end of the book. When a multi-volume edition does include line numbers (as with Peele, Dekker, and Massinger), I do not provide the volume number in my citation. When line numbers are not provided, however (as with Heywood, Fletcher, Brome, and Davenant), I cite volume and page numbers (for example, Heywood, *2 The Iron Age*, III, 413).

Since Shakespeare is almost always read in modern spelling, I have chosen to modernize the spelling of non-Shakespearean passages. To avoid some obvious inconsistencies in my own text, moreover, I have also regularized the use of italic and roman type in my presentation of stage directions and expanded some abbreviations. Any minor distortions caused by such changes are more than offset by the added ease for some readers and, in symbolic terms, the presentation of Shakespeare and his contemporaries as orthographic equals (as opposed to "modern" Shakespeare versus "primitive" Heywood).

CHAPTER I

The problem, the evidence, and the language barrier

"You speak a language that I understand not"
The Winter's Tale, 3.2.79

The terms invoked in this book's title trail with them various problems. To concentrate upon *recovering* X from the past, especially the theatrical past, is to set in motion a process that makes some readers and many theatrical professionals uncomfortable, even hostile. Admittedly, historically oriented scholars attuned to such disciplines as philology, iconography, and "ideas-of-the-time" contextual interpretation will find my goals and methods familiar, even self-evident. Such scholars will agree with John Shearman who, in his study of Mannerism, notes that "contemporary standards" of our age not only "do not give the right guidance to understanding a past age" but, in fact, can be "a positive hindrance." Rather, he argues: "In decoding messages from the other side we get more meaningful results if we use their code rather than ours," for "wherever possible a work of art should be interpreted by throwing it back into the nest of ideas in which it was born."[1]

As practiced for several generations, however, the invocation and application of a Renaissance "nest of ideas" or "code" in Shakespeare studies has led to many oversimplified formulations and interpretations, so that post-structuralists attuned to indeterminacy, free play, and the death of the author may understandably be dubious when confronted with claims about "recovery." Similarly, theatrical professionals hostile to "museum theatre" are justifiably suspicious of scholarly accounts that use purported Elizabethan stage practice to set up strictures about what should and should not be done in today's productions. For both communities, to focus upon recovering the theatrical practice of the past is to send up danger signals.

Nonetheless, some actors and directors *are* interested in the onstage rationale behind the Shakespeare playscripts with which they wrestle – even though they do not feel bound to reproduce such effects. Historical or historicist interpretations, moreover, are much in fashion of late in scholarly journals, especially in English Renaissance studies, so that a reinvestigation of the tangled evidence at the roots of what we know (or think we know) about the staging of plays at the Theatre, the Globe, and the Blackfriars would seem to be relevant to various projects that build upon the interactions between the play-as-event and the playgoer (e.g., the concept of negotiations or circulation of social energy advanced by Stephen Greenblatt).[2] To what were the original playgoers responding or reacting? How can we tell today? What difference do (or should) such findings make for our interpretations on the page, on the stage, or in the classroom?

In the chapters that follow, moreover, I do not offer an interpretation of Shakespeare's plays in terms of "the ideas-of-the-time." In his critique of these and other interpretations linked to "context," Richard Levin notes in passing the value of the contextual material "supplied for us by the footnotes in modern scholarly editions of works of the past," annotations that provide "the knowledge necessary to construe the very meaning of the words of the text and understand the social customs and institutions, the proverbial lore, the beliefs, and the like that these words allude to." Such material, he observes, "should probably be considered an extension of the very general context of 'language'" and therefore "a necessary preliminary to any interpretation." The use of such "linguistic" contexts, he concludes, is "preinterpretive," for "the interpreter does not have to decide whether or not to apply it (although he may certainly be ignorant of it)." Rather, "like the language itself, it precedes the contexts that present him with conscious choices."[3]

My goal in this book is to recover or reconstitute comparable preinterpretive materials that, ideally, "like the language itself," should form the basis for would-be historical or historicist interpretations of Shakespeare's plays. My project is therefore analogous to that of a philologist, an iconographer, or an archaeologist (or a student of discursive and signifying practices) but with a focus not upon words, icons, or lost artifacts (or theatres) but upon theatrical strategy and techniques taken for granted by Shakespeare, his player-colleagues, and his playgoers. My emphasis will therefore fall upon some building blocks (analogous to nouns, verbs, and prepositions), particularly those alien to our literary and theatrical ways of thinking today and hence likely to be blurred or filtered out by editors, readers, and theatrical professionals. Whether or not the "author" as agency is dead, someone or some group in the 1590s and early 1600s made choices that led to something being acted out on the stage. My concern is with that something – what the original playgoers saw or might have seen.

To recover or reconstitute elements in those original performances, however, is to confront formidable, at times insurmountable, problems. The participial form that begins my title is therefore important to my formulation, for this book is, at best, a beginning, the start of an ongoing process that can only be advanced by future editors, bibliographers, critics, theatre historians, historicists of many stripes, and theatrical professionals (groups that, unfortunately, do not speak the same languages). My goal is to provide a book with implications for all those who interpret these plays (and, as in my earlier book on stage conventions, I include editors in the category *interpreters*), but, as in that earlier study, I am less concerned with individual readings (which, at times, I cannot resist suggesting) than with the larger process. Indeed, one of my major agendas is to expand the options for interpreters, whatever their medium (production, edition, essay, lecture) and whatever their professed or unacknowledged ideology. No proposition or project, we are constantly reminded, is ideology-free, especially the appeal to so-called "common sense" (so that my own assumptions about history and authority are already evident), but, in spite of the difficulties with a "dictionary" approach set forth in chapter 3, I have sought whenever possible to model my procedures, categories, and invocation of examples on entries in the *OED* or an iconographical handbook. What use others make of my findings or options is not (and should not be) under my control.

Behind my title, moreover, lurks a series of linked assumptions, so, to reduce the level of mystification at the outset, let me begin by singling out two basic propositions. First, in putting quill to paper Shakespeare was crafting not *literary texts* (to be read and interpreted by readers) but *theatrical scripts* (to be bodied forth by actor-colleagues, with whom he was in close contact, and then interpreted by playgoers). In one form or another, this proposition has been widely promulgated in recent decades, to the point that it has spawned a so-called "performance" criticism approach to Shakespeare's plays and, more recently (and inevitably), some shrewd revisionist critiques (both from sympathizers and opponents).[4] No surprises here.

Few of those in this ongoing performance-oriented debate, however, are much concerned with a second (and to me equally crucial) proposition: that Shakespeare designed those playscripts for players, playgoers, and playhouses that no longer exist. Ay, there's the rub. The thirty-seven playscripts (a number that includes *Pericles* and *Henry VIII* but excludes *The Two Noble Kinsmen*) *do* survive (in whatever altered state or multiple versions) in the form of the early quartos (nineteen plays, all save *Othello* in print during the author's lifetime) and the 1623 First Folio (where eighteen plays appear for the first time seven years after the author's death). Most of us know them, however, insofar as they have been filtered through the editorial tradition that started in the eighteenth century and has culminated in our generation in the New Arden series, the Wells–Taylor Oxford editions, and several other impressive volumes or sets of volumes (including excellent facsimiles of the original quartos and First Folio). Nonetheless, the players who enacted those scripts (presumably with the playwright at hand and, for part of his career, in the cast) are gone, leaving behind little evidence about their technique or style of performance. Moreover, the original playgoers who supported this highly competitive commercial theatre are also gone (despite the efforts of Ann Jennalie Cook and Andrew Gurr to characterize them) as are all of the playhouses of the period (in contrast to the situation in Spain).[5]

Sam Wanamaker's project (along with his team of scholars, architects, and other experts) to reconstruct the Globe Theatre near its original site is an attempt to recover or reconstitute the second of those four components (to join the extant playscripts). But even if we accept the authenticity of that reconstruction, the would-be theatrical historicist should not lose sight of the obvious: at the original Globe, the playwright, players, and playgoers would have shared what I am terming a theatrical vocabulary (linked, in large part, to what could and could not be done on their stage) that is lost or blurred today. The process of playing the original scripts (as opposed to today's editorial text) in that reconstructed Globe *may* lead to the recovery or rediscovery of signifiers in that shared vocabulary that Shakespeare, his colleagues, and his audience took for granted. Even in this potential laboratory or testing ground, however, such a process of investigation is highly vulnerable to contamination by post-Elizabethan theatrical thinking wherein actors and directors instinctively translate the original onstage logic into our 1990s idiom (a process that can produce exciting productions for today's audiences but nonetheless interferes with any quest for recovery).

Behind my overall formulation and especially my second proposition therefore lies the assumption (reinforced again and again over many years of wrestling with such problems) that we no longer speak the same theatrical language as did Shakespeare and his contemporaries.[6] Rather, my working model or paradigm is: in reading one of the early printed texts of a Shakespeare play, we enter into the middle of a conversation – a discourse in a language we only partly understand – between a dramatist and his actor-colleagues, a halfway stage that was completed in a performance now lost to us. Although we will never reconstitute that performance, we may be able to recover elements of that vocabulary and hence better understand that conversation. To recover that lost vocabulary, however, requires a fresh, uncompromised look at the only plentiful evidence, the extant scripts. The alternative is the situation engendered by Leontes, to whom Hermione can say: "You speak a language that I understand not" (3.2.79).

By this point the reader not attuned to the many forays into Elizabethan theatres and theatrical practice (and perhaps familiar with various straightforward handbook formulations) may be puzzled (this author doth protest too much, methinks). Why should an attempt to recover what the original playgoers actually saw pose so many problems and challenges? The answers to that question are fundamental to this book and are the focus for this chapter. To begin a journey towards recovery and discovery by calling attention to the many potholes, detours, and unmapped roadways may appear unventuresome to some readers, particularly those who prefer bold formulations, but the murkiness of the terrain demands caution. In Brutus' terms, such a situation "craves wary walking" (2.1.15).

The most important reason for the difficulties in recovering Shakespeare's theatrical vocabulary is painfully simple. Most of the relevant evidence, including many things so obvious to players and playgoers in the 1590s and early 1600s as to be taken for granted, has been lost – as much as ninety percent, perhaps even more. Having written a book on the performance history of *Titus Andronicus*, I am more aware than most scholars of the difficulty of reconstituting a twentieth-century production I have not seen, even when photographs, print reviews, and interviews with participants are available. For the study of the performances of Elizabethan–Jacobean plays, however, almost no external evidence is available (and the few eyewitness accounts or other documents that *have* survived are often unreliable or hard to interpret – most notably, the drawing of the Swan Theatre). As a result, the primary, often sole evidence for the recovery of stage practice and theatrical vocabulary lies in the many surviving printed texts of plays, the extant manuscripts (at least sixteen with links to the playhouses), the "plots" or "plats," and a few other relevant documents (e.g., Philip Henslowe's papers).[7] Missing so much basic information about performance and playhouse practice, scholars and theatre historians have generated formulations composed of varying combinations of facts, inferences, and hypotheses, with those inferences and hypotheses often hardening into facts after years of use and application. The surprises occasioned by the evidence unearthed at the site of the Rose Theatre are only the latest of many such chastening revelations that have bumped up against long received opinions. And thereby hangs my tale.

Not only theatre historians but editors too must regularly confront such problems. Consider the useful terms and distinctions provided by Philip Gaskell in his revealing treatment of Tom Stoppard's *Travesties*. In this formulation, a work "intended to be communicated primarily by spoken performance rather than by a written text characteristically goes through three textual stages." First comes "the script, the written version of what was originally intended to be said." Second comes "the performance text, what is actually said in one or more performances." Finally comes "the reading text, the version subsequently published by author or editor as a record of what might or should have been said." As Gaskell notes, "anyone who has written a lecture, has delivered it, and has published it, will recognize these three textual stages; and they are especially apparent in plays, in which the second stage, the performance text, is developed not by the author alone but by the director and the actors as well."[8]

Gaskell's three categories pertain as well to manuscripts and printed texts in the age of Shakespeare. Ben Jonson and Sir William Berkeley reclaimed their plays from the players and self-consciously prepared reading texts unconstrained by the limitations (or "contamination") of the playhouse (so that for most of Jonson's plays any sense of the original performance text has been blurred if not lost). The extant playhouse manuscripts form a category comparable to Gaskell's performance texts (although the differences between these documents and nineteenth or twentieth-century prompt-books often are more revealing than the similarities). When dealing with one group of Shakespeare's plays, editors regularly refer to the dramatist's "foul papers" or fair copy, terms that denote authorial scripts that would have been presented to an Elizabethan theatrical company. Yet, with the possible exception of a fragment of *Sir*

Thomas More, no Shakespeare manuscript has survived, so that, even though much has been inferred from painstaking analysis of the printed quartos and the First Folio, scholars have no empirical evidence about Shakespeare's working practices in his scripts or authorial drafts (whether "foul" or "fair" papers or, as is likely, some mixture of the two). The nature of the manuscript copy that lies behind a printed text is of crucial importance to an editor (so that inferences about that printer's copy take up considerable space in most textual introductions), but, despite the long accepted, even hallowed, terms and distinctions set up by bibliographical giants such as R. B. McKerrow, W. W. Greg, and Fredson Bowers, the various litmus tests for making such determinations are not reliable (and recently have come under attack).[9]

A related area of contention or puzzlement arises from varying views about the presence and role of "the author" or "authorial intention." For many readers, to invoke Shakespeare's name in my title is merely to place this book in that larger realm of "Shakespeare studies" (and therefore to add to the already overcrowded shelves), but, in some circles, to invoke Shakespeare as "author" or unitary agent responsible for the extant texts is to move onto contested ground. In recent years, strong arguments have been advanced against transhistorical meaning and "essentialism," particularly as applied to the great-minded Swan of Avon who so well understood the human heart that his plays stand as paradigms not for an age but for all time. In another arena, attacks have been mounted against the long-standing editorial goal of providing a text as close as possible to the "author's intentions."[10] To posit a Shakespearean theatrical vocabulary available to be recovered is then to run afoul of some vigorous theoretical and bibliographical arguments.

These arguments cannot be lightly dismissed. As a confirmed pluralist, I too am uncomfortable with a monistic approach to interpretation that seeks to recover the author's "intention" or unitary meaning, "true" both then and now and evident to the discerning reader. As both a theatrical historian and an inveterate playgoer, moreover, I am also conscious of the collaborative nature of theatrical practice in which the dramatist is a major but not the only contributor to what eventually happens onstage. In addition, I am aware of the tangled editorial and bibliographical problems generated by the early printed texts of "Shakespeare's" plays wherein what the dramatist originally wrote or approved or what was presented in the first productions is very much in doubt (the Hecate scenes in *Macbeth* can serve as one chastening example). Not only has much evidence been lost, but the primary evidence that has survived carries with it many attendant problems and perplexities.

To apply Gaskell's distinctions to the early printed editions of Shakespeare's plays is therefore to confront a series of knotty problems with which every editor must contend. Those editorial problems, in turn, are comparable to but not always identical with the equally difficult problems confronting the theatre historian who must build edifices upon the same evidence, the early printed texts. For an excellent introduction to both sets of problems, consider the lucid formulation provided by Gary Taylor. The original manuscripts of Shakespeare's plays (Gaskell's *scripts*), as Taylor notes, "were not written for that consortium of readers called 'the general public'" but "were written instead to be read by a particular group of actors, his professional colleagues and personal friends, who would in turn communicate the plays through performance to a wider public." Shakespeare could therefore "rely on this first special readership to 'edit' his manuscript, at least mentally and perhaps physically, as they read it"; and, more important to the theatre historian, "he could also rely on those readers to bring to the reading much specialist knowledge about the conditions and working practices of the contemporary theatre, and the circumstances of the specific company to which they and he belonged."

Shakespeare's ability to rely upon his colleagues, in turn, has significant implications for any attempt at "recovery" today, for, as Taylor goes on to observe: "The written text of any such manuscript thus depended upon an unwritten para-text which always accompanied it: an invisible life-support system of stage directions, which Shakespeare could either expect his first readers to supply, or which those first readers would expect Shakespeare himself to supply orally." The problem for the editor and especially the theatre historian, then, is that "the earliest editions of the plays all fail, more or less grossly, to supply this unwritten text." Subsequent editors (including Taylor and Stanley Wells in their Oxford edition) have sought "to rectify the deficiency, by conjecturally writing for him the stage directions which Shakespeare himself assumed or spoke but never wrote," but, as Taylor admits, "to fill such lacunae is necessarily hazardous: necessary, if we are to relish the texts as scripts for theatrical performance, but hazardous, because the filling which modern editors concoct might not always be to Shakespeare's taste."[11]

Taylor's formulation is geared towards the editorial practice in a monumental project, a practice that involves a distinctive and controversial approach to stage directions.[12] In such a project, the filling in of lacunae is understandable, perhaps inevitable, for, as Jerome J. McGann has noted, "the pursuit of textual studies has been carried out by people whose practical concerns are circumscribed by their editorial aims or by that subset of related, largely technical problems that bear upon editorial method (e.g., the preoccupation in recent years with the problem of copy text)." McGann argues, however, "that textual criticism is a field of inquiry that supervenes the narrower issues that concern editors, and that textual criticism is a pursuit incumbent upon anyone who works with and teaches literary products." In this formulation, "textual criticism does not meet its fate in the completion of a text or an edition of some particular work" but rather "is a special method that students of literature must and should use when they examine, interpret, and reproduce the works we inherit from the past."[13]

To McGann's students of literature should be added students of performance or theatrical vocabulary. Indeed, given the often differing goals of the theatre historian and the editor, the former cannot build upon the latter's text, especially a text that "necessarily" fills in theatrical lacunae, even when that filling in is done by editors as astute about performance as Wells and Taylor. Rather, would-be theatrical historians must themselves become textual critics in McGann's terms capable of dealing with the puzzling and often frustrating documents that constitute the primary evidence for the process of recovery or discovery.

What makes Shakespeare special (and the recovery process so difficult) is the absence of what Taylor terms the "para-text" and the blurring of what I am terming the shared theatrical vocabulary. As an attached or in-house dramatist for most of his career, Shakespeare did not have to spell out onstage procedures for his colleagues – a great advantage for him but a severe disadvantage for the theatre-oriented reader today. As Taylor notes, much information important to our understanding would have been self-evident to the Lord Chamberlain's or King's Men (or would have been conveyed orally) and is therefore missing from the printed texts. Equally problematic, some of the performance-oriented signals that *have* survived (e.g., the placement of various stage directions) have seemed anomalous or inaccurate to scholars and have therefore been adjusted or ignored in our editions, so that extant signals that may have been meaningful then can be lost or blurred today. To these two categories, moreover, must be added a third (familiar to iconographers) wherein a distinctive onstage configuration may no longer carry the same shared meanings.

The reader of the early printed editions is therefore left with many gaps and puzzles. To unravel these various threads requires a combination of skills (editor–textual critic, bibliographer, theatre historian, theatrical professional, historical scholar), but these figures, each expert in his or her own arena, do not speak the same languages (ay, there's another rub). To seek to recover a lost theatrical vocabulary is therefore to confront a language barrier that stands both between us and the age of Shakespeare and between groups of academic and theatrical interpreters today.

The would-be theatrical historian is therefore left with a series of dilemmas. The primary evidence for answering many questions is to be found in the early printed editions, but the links between those texts and "Shakespeare" have been repeatedly challenged. The so-called "good" quartos (e.g., *Love's Labor's Lost*, *Much Ado*, *Richard II*, 1 and 2 *Henry IV*, *The Merchant of Venice*, *Hamlet* Q2) *may* stand at one remove from Shakespeare's initial script, the draft he delivered to his fellow players, the beginning of what I am terming his conversation with his colleagues that eventually resulted in a production. The so-called "bad" quartos (e.g., the first printed editions of 2 *Henry VI*, 3 *Henry VI*, *Romeo*, *Merry Wives*, *Henry V*, and *Hamlet*) *may* reflect a performance of some version of the play as remembered by one or more actors (and, if so, provide valuable evidence about the end of that conversation). Other printed texts (e.g., Folio *Hamlet*, Folio *Lear*) *may* correspond to the performance text, an approximation of the words actually included in a performance. Other Folio texts (e.g., *The Tempest*, *Measure*, *Merry Wives*, *The Winter's Tale*, *Two Gentlemen*) probably give us the play as transcribed (and perhaps edited or "improved") by scrivener Ralph Crane. All of these printed texts have to some degree been edited or mediated by the compositors in the various printing shops, especially Jaggard's notorious Compositor B whose emendations are now impossible to distinguish from "Shakespeare." Particularly with a play such as *Macbeth* that appears for the first time in the Folio, today's interpreter cannot with any confidence distinguish "Shakespeare" from his collaborators.

Comparable problems arise from our ignorance about the stages in the process by which an Elizabethan play moved from script to actual performance. Clearly, the few surviving "plots" or "plats" are back-stage documents used to control aspects of a performance, but none survives from Shakespeare's company nor, despite astute analyses by Bernard Beckerman and David Bradley, is their function altogether clear. The limited information (and many apparent errors and inconsistencies) that survive in the extant playhouse manuscripts suggest that these documents too may not have played as significant a role in a given performance as today's scholar may expect. Perhaps then the key document would not have been the playhouse book but rather the actor's part (or side), presumably copied at some point from the author's script or some subsequent transcription (and the presence and character of such "intermediate copies," a category defined and championed by Fredson Bowers, is a matter of some dispute). In writing his script, moreover, Shakespeare presumably had a good idea who would be playing a given part, how the roles in general would be assigned (so, in his draft, he could take into account the necessary doubling or tripling of parts), and what physical resources he could draw upon (e.g., costumes, flying machinery, doors, traps), but most of that information about the give-and-take between author–actor–sharer and his actor colleagues is lost to us. All that we know for certain is that at some point Shakespeare wrote out his play, and at some later point that play was put on a stage to be viewed by playgoers. But the theatrical historian today lacks that originating script, has little information about that performance, and cannot be certain about the path or process that carried "the play" from script to performance.

Since no undisputed, unmediated version of "what Shakespeare wrote" or "what Shakespeare intended" has survived, today's interpreter is left with many gaps and questions. One possible conclusion is to acknowledge the existence of "bibliographic matters that have unmoored the Shakespearian texts from the authorial hand" and therefore to posit "the radical instability" of those printed texts which "cannot be assimilated to an authorial intentionality."[14] My choice, in my search for that lost theatrical vocabulary, is to accept the extant quartos and Folio texts as relevant and useful evidence about stage practice and theatrical vocabulary, regardless of whether a given text is based upon (1) a manuscript that shows the pre-production concept of the author; (2) a manuscript (authorial or otherwise) lightly annotated for a performance; (3) a manuscript recopied and perhaps "improved" by a scribe; or (4) a manuscript compiled by one or more actors involved in a given production. Certainty about the author's intentions in the originating script or about the nature of the actual performance text may be impossible, but since a shared theatrical vocabulary does not depend upon authorial agency alone, for my purposes evidence from supposed authorial scripts and supposed performance texts is equally valid. Rather, to recover elements of Taylor's para-text and my conversation in that lost or blurred theatrical language, *any* part of the playwright–player dialogue is relevant and worthy of our attention.[15]

Therefore, although aware of the dangers of oversimplification, I am going to retain the authorial agency announced in my title and treat the surviving evidence in the quartos and Folio as primary evidence, regardless of editorial inferences about authorial drafts and "prompt-books." Many hands other than Shakespeare's may have contributed to the manuscript that lies behind the Folio text of *Macbeth*, but I am going to assume that most of that printed text and most of the text of a supposedly "good" quarto such as *Much Ado* do reflect Shakespeare's design or strategy. In Gaskell's terms, both the script and the performance text of a Shakespeare play can only be inferred, not seen directly, but, proceeding with caution, I hope to build upon the vestiges of both to learn more about the theatrical vocabulary in which they are conceived and the conversation that we may be overhearing.

Other problems and choices also need to be acknowledged. Thus, I have chosen not to focus upon that shared language of icons and emblems prominent in paintings, emblem books, and such performed works as masques and pageants. The study of such materials can be rewarding, but those practitioners who invoke such learned traditions in their treatments of Shakespeare's plays rarely take into account the evidence of what the original playgoers actually saw and sometimes blur the distinction between an "image" on canvas or the page (where anything is possible) and an "image" on the stage (where what the spectator witnesses is heavily conditioned by what the players are able to present). For similar reasons, I have not built upon the plentiful evidence about the Jacobean masques, for those no-expense-spared productions with their one-time-only effects tell us little about the exigencies of professional repertory theatre in the 1590s and 1600s where any onstage devices or choices within the confines of the wooden O had to be practical and repeatable.[16]

Other seemingly related areas have also been sidestepped.

Obviously, I am not the first scholar to comb through the extant plays for clues about stages and staging, but many of those who *have* pored over such materials have been guided by a different set of questions. In particular, I am not concerned in this book with the size, shape, and facilities of individual playhouses, an area to which my research has nothing new to contribute. For that reason I have not limited my exploration of the extant evidence to the plays known to have been staged in any one theatre (a practice essential to a series of valuable studies of the Red Bull, the Globe, and other venues) nor to any one segment of the long sweep of Elizabethan–Jacobean–Caroline drama. I will not argue that staging procedures stayed the same in all theatres between the 1580s and the early 1640s, but the fact that a host of playwrights (that includes such seasoned professionals as Shakespeare, Heywood, Dekker, Fletcher, Massinger, Shirley, and Brome) in many theatres over many decades appear to be using the same shared language strikes me as important.

Furthermore, although this book is not designed as an exercise in explication, I do not refrain from offering interpretations of some of the scenes with which I am dealing, interpretations that inevitably are conditioned by my own formalist reflexes and by my interest in images, analogical links, and anomalies. My goal, however, is to present such readings not as ends in themselves (so as to persuade the reader of "my" interpretation) but rather as exemplary readings that can demonstrate the implications of my findings or hypotheses for *any* interpretation of a given play. My larger purpose therefore is not to solve the mystery of Hamlet (or *Hamlet*) but to tease out the "text" or phenomena that would have been the basis for interpretations by the original audiences. To invoke again Richard Levin's distinction, my emphasis whenever possible is upon "preinterpretive" materials that would presumably have been shared by playwright, players, and playgoers rather than upon interpretations of what Shakespeare "meant" or how playgoers, then or now, should interpret a given passage or scene. For example, readers of chapter 6 may not accept my formulation of the political issues at stake in *Richard II* or *2 Henry IV*, but my primary concern is with the onstage presence in the same play of a sick-chair and a throne, a conjunction that, once recognized, should be basic to any interpretation. Similarly, in chapter 5 and elsewhere my concern is more with the concept of "theatrical *italics*" and with various italicized moments than with a specific interpretation of a given scene or image.

In the chapters that follow I will therefore place more emphasis upon evidence and upon recovery of theatrical vocabulary than upon explication. Whenever possible, I have sought to place signifiers in that vocabulary in the widest possible context, but, even though I have looked at a very large number of plays (with an eye especially on their stage directions), I make no claims about completeness. Rather, the more I revisit the hundreds of available plays, the more relevant information I find (e.g., a new set of questions or yardsticks elicits fresh insights); another scholar (with different questions in mind) looking at the same materials might generate different results. I can attest, however, that many of my findings (e.g., about early entrances, sick-chairs, and *vanish*) resulted not from any preconceived notions but from a growing awareness, after looking at hundreds of scenes, of an emerging pattern or phenomenon. Inevitably, what is presented here cannot be separated from my tastes and assumptions (e.g., about "minimalism" and the role of the playgoer's imagination), but I have done my best to keep an open mind on a range of questions and let the results be driven by the evidence.

In ranging widely for that evidence I have not excluded examples that may appear anomalous, illogical, even bizarre to today's reader. Since so much information obvious to the original playgoers has been lost, I feel strongly that whatever evidence that *has* survived should be prized, especially the apparent anomalies. If Shakespeare's theatrical vocabulary does indeed differ significantly from ours, those differences will surface (or various windows will open up) when the reader nurtured on Ibsen, O'Neill, and the fourth wall convention collides with something that clearly does not fit with the theatre of naturalism or psychological realism. For the historian, those collisions are to be welcomed, not avoided, for they can generate valuable insights into onstage practice then versus now. Attention to the anomalous, the unexpected, even the seemingly illogical or perverse will then be a recurrent feature of the chapters that follow.

As indicated by the many problems and qualifications enunciated in this chapter, to focus upon *recovering* and upon *theatrical* (as opposed to literary or strictly philological) *vocabulary* is to become enmeshed in some messy editorial, historical, theatrical, and procedural problems for which neat solutions are not forthcoming. For the philologist or iconographer, to solve a puzzle or to define a word or icon may involve an immense amount of reading or looking, but a wealth of evidence *is* there for the intrepid scholar. To define accurately or meaningfully signifiers in an onstage vocabulary is similarly to range through many plays, so that (to cast as wide a net as possible) I have looked at the stage directions in every English professional play from the 1400s through the early 1640s (and consulted as well a large batch of Restoration plays as a control group). All this effort, however, cannot yield "definitive" results. Indeed (to be only partly facetious), the pay-off is far less than would be gained from access to a video-cassette version of the original production of any Elizabethan–Jacobean play.

Unfortunately, no such tangible theatrical evidence survives. Rather, the student of onstage theatrical vocabulary must tease out inferences about potential meanings from the extant stage directions, dialogue, and that rare external account. Five playgoers who saw the original performance of *Twelfth Night* might have come away with five different interpretations of the play's "meaning," but (allowing for variations in their attentiveness and placement in the theatre) they would have seen the same onstage choices and practices and would have been in tune with both the spoken and the fuller theatrical language. The reliance upon inferences from printed texts (of playscripts not of our age) rather than upon the in-the-theatre experience of the original playgoers is at the heart of the problems confronted in this book.

In conclusion, let me return to the three linked questions noted at the outset of this chapter: (1) to what were the original playgoers responding or reacting? (2) how can we tell today? (3) what difference do (or should) such findings make for our interpretations on the page, on the stage, or in the classroom? Without that magical videotape, responses to the first question must be at best provisional. Evidence and procedures *are* available to deal with the second question, but the road to recovery or rediscovery is rocky, not smooth. As to the third question (what I think of as the "so what?" response), only the reader of this book can assess the gains from assaulting various language barriers by teasing out the implications buried in hundreds of stage directions.

CHAPTER 2

Lost in translation

> "The literature of the past is a foreign literature. We must either learn its language or suffer it to be translated."[1]
>
> Harley Granville-Barker

To attempt to recover Shakespeare's theatrical vocabulary is then to wrestle with the early printed editions, the primary evidence for how the plays were staged in the 1590s and early 1600s and our major point of entry into the conversation between the playwright and his player-colleagues. To categorize these texts (and the manuscripts or other copy that stands behind them) scholars have developed various terms and concepts (e.g., *foul papers*, *memorial reconstruction*, *good* and *bad quartos*) and have fashioned appropriate strategies for creating differing editions for differing clienteles. These editions (some of them major works of scholarship in their own right) in turn have become the basis for subsequent scholarship (so that each generation is to some extent characterized by its editing of Shakespeare). In the 1980s and 1990s, for example, one subgroup of such editions exhibits a performance orientation by including accounts of production choices, photographs, stage history, additional stage directions, and other ancillary material to enhance a reader's awareness of the theatrical dimension that extends beyond the printed page.

Such editions, however, whether scholarly or performance-oriented, are often of little help to the project pursued in this book. In making such a statement I do not wish to denigrate such ongoing projects (which have considerable value for their implied audiences), but rather to note that, in the search for Shakespeare's theatrical vocabulary, the editorial process is often part of the problem rather than part of the solution. In making hundreds of decisions about words, punctuation, stage directions, locale, speech prefixes, and other elements, editors (often unconsciously) invoke their sense of what is logical or realistic or "Shakespearean" and in that process filter out many particles. Eliminated by that editorial filter, along with obvious errors and inconsistencies, are various items essential to this book. In addition, as noted by Gary Taylor, the interpolation of many necessary stage directions (especially exits) absent from the original printed texts can also complicate matters, for to insert such signals today is to introduce an editorial or theatrical logic that may or may not be in tune with the original vocabulary (or para-text in Taylor's terms). To bypass such editions, then, is not to resolve the many problems in the recovery process but at least to eliminate one possible source of intervention.

The lost or blurred signifiers in that theatrical vocabulary fall into various categories. One group consists of signals that do survive but are treated by editors and other interpreters as errors or inconsistencies (in one formulation, *accidental* as opposed to *substantive* matters). Sometimes, however, even the most minuscule of changes or adjustments can have significant implications in the theatre. Consider the presence or absence of one typographical space in *A Midsummer Night's Dream*. Thus, in modern editions (including the Wells–Taylor Oxford old spelling edition), in her final interchange with her ass-headed lover Titania tells Bottom: "Sleep thou, and I will wind thee in my arms," and then tells her attendants: "Fairies, be gone, and be all ways away" (4.1.39–40). The Arden editor then glosses "be all ways away" as "Be off in every direction" (p. 88). Wanting to be alone, this Titania sends her fairies off every which way – presumably using all the available stage doors or exits.

But in all the quartos and all the folios Titania's line reads: "Faieries be gon, and be alwaies away" (Q1, F3r). When spoken, the sound of the two alternative phrases, of course, is the same; the difference apparently is a mere space on the page (as seen most clearly in the Oxford old-spelling rendition of "al waies" – 1481). But in Homer Swander's 1990 Santa Barbara production the actress playing Titania delivered the line with great force so as to convey that she meant not "in every direction" but *always–forever*, for this Bottom had permanently superseded Mustard, Cobweb, and the others. This interpretation of the line was then reinforced by the shocked expressions on the faces of the exiting fairies as they made a hasty and disorganized departure. Titania's "dotage" was therefore more extreme in this production than in any other I have seen, a strong theatrical choice that in turn set in motion other effects to follow in this scene. The same sounds may be linked to both the Quarto and the emended line, but the theatrical options encouraged by "alwaies" are lost when the original word (and potential signal) is screened out by the editor (and the recent New Cambridge Edition does not list this change in its textual notes – see p. 106).

A comparable problem is to be found in the deposition scene of *Richard II*. Except in old-spelling editions (see Wells–Taylor, 2023), in today's texts Richard's response to Bolingbroke's "Are you contented to resign the crown?" reads: "Ay, no; no, ay; for I must nothing be; / Therefore no no, for I resign to thee" (4.1.200–2). But in the two late quartos (where this sequence first appears) and in the Folio the passage actually begins: "I, no; no, I" (TLN 2122). Admittedly, throughout the period *ay* often *is* printed as *I*; as with *alwaies–all ways*, moreover, the words as spoken sound the same. But is a yes–no–no–yes rendition on the page an accurate transcription or is it a translation? Especially with the first *I*, an actor then or now could easily signal the first person I–me by a gesture, even an intonation, a signal that in turn can affect much of the major speech of unkinging that follows (with its strong emphasis upon "I"). As with *alwaies–all ways*, to make this seemingly self-evident change is, perhaps, to close down a valid theatrical option.

The problems posed by the signals that survive in the early printed editions are not limited to spaces and spelling. For example, consider the so-called "bad" quartos, printed texts that, according to one prevailing theory, are based not upon a Shakespeare manuscript but upon a manuscript put together by one or more actors who drew upon their memories of a specific production. The differences, however, between supposedly "bad" and "good" versions can often be instructive. Thus, the "good" (and presumably "authorial") Folio version of *3 Henry VI* directs the dying Clifford to enter "*Wounded*" (TLN 1281), but the "bad" 1594 octavo text (which differs in many interesting ways from the Folio version) includes the detail (also found in Holinshed) "*with an arrow in his neck*" (C3V). Does the absence of such a striking detail from the "good" text indicate that the arrow was not a regular part of the play as performed? Or does it suggest that Shakespeare, as an in-house dramatist for his theatrical company, did not feel compelled to stipulate every such detail in his manuscript if he was to be present at the early rehearsals? In this instance, the availability of the "bad" version (perhaps based upon the memory of one or more actors involved in a 1590s production) has preserved the arrow, but quartos – good, bad, or indifferent – survive for only half of Shakespeare's plays. Here as elsewhere, details or effects highly visible, even striking for the original spectators may have melted into air, into thin air, because they were not written down by playwrights or were omitted by scribes and compositors.

The absence of this particular detail in the "good" Folio text means that some editors will omit it from their editions. But for the interpreter concerned with the script as realized onstage, such a detail can be crucial, for the theatrical *image* that emerges for a spectator (here a dying figure pierced by an arrow) can be more memorable than any *words* spoken during the scene. Moreover, at least two subsequent scenes in this play (3.1, 4.4) involve figures who carry bows (e.g., "*Enter two Keepers with crossbows in their hands*" – 3.1.0.s.d.). This memorable onstage image may then be part of an iterative sequence but a sequence not available to readers of some editions.

For a comparable example from a better known play, consider Ophelia's lute. For her first appearance after Hamlet's departure, the "good" second quarto and the Folio supply no distinctive details, but the first or "bad" quarto calls for Ophelia's entrance "*playing on a Lute, and her hair down singing*" (G4V). To the New Arden editor, "the lute, uncalled for in the text and incongruous with the ballad snatches Ophelia spontaneously breaks into, looks like an actor's embellishment" (p. 348); he therefore buries this "bad" stage direction in his textual notes. But, as elsewhere in Shakespeare, the presence of a musical instrument can add to a spectator's sense of harmony violated (as signaled also by Ophelia's disheveled hair or by her terms earlier: "sweet bells jangled, out of time and harsh" – 3.1.158). The image or concept of such an instrument, moreover, has already been orchestrated by Hamlet, first in his praise of those men like Horatio "whose blood and judgment are so well commeddled / That they are not a pipe for Fortune's finger / To sound what stop she please" (3.2.66–8) and later in the same scene, with a recorder in his hand, in his critique of Guildenstern ("you would play upon me, you would seem to know my stops" – 350–1). A lute in Ophelia's hand, whether played skillfully or played discordantly or not played at all, could be a meaningful image for a spectator, then or now. But did or did not the Lord Chamberlain's or King's Men incorporate that lute into performances based upon the play as scripted in the "good" quarto or the Folio?

The problems of recovering that lost or blurred vocabulary are therefore inextricably entwined with the editorial tradition. Again, the issue often is not one of right versus wrong but rather of keeping various options open, options that might seem negligible to an editor but could be of considerable interest to another interpreter, whether in the theatre or on the page. Consider one of the best-known comic moments in all of Shakespeare, the entrance of a smiling Malvolio in yellow stockings and cross-gartered (*Twelfth Night*, 3.4). Except for the Riverside Shakespeare, all the modern editions I have consulted place that entry just before Olivia's "How now, Malvolio?" (15), so that she and the playgoer see the entering figure at the same time. In the Folio, however, Malvolio is directed to enter two lines earlier (TLN 1535), just after Olivia's "Go call him hither," so that in the only authoritative early printed text of this comedy Malvolio is onstage for her "I am as mad as he, / If sad and merry madness equal be" (13–14).

To some readers the difference may seem unimportant; to most editors, apparently, the Folio placement appears illogical or impractical. Given the preferred staging today, moreover, to follow the Folio is to run the risk of drowning Olivia's lines in the audience laughter at Malvolio's new look and bizarre behavior. But this Folio placement is but one of many that fall into the category of what I term "early" entrances (to be discussed in chapter 4) in which the original printed text brings in a figure one or two or even ten lines before he or she actually speaks or is noticed by those already onstage. Some of these early entrances may be the result of errors or sloppiness (by author, scribe, bookkeeper, or compositor); many (like this one) have been filtered out of the editions we use.

But what happens if we take this placement as seriously as any other bit of evidence in the Folio *Twelfth Night* (a clean orderly text that has no other such anomalous placements)? For example, what would be the effect upon Malvolio if at his entrance he overhears Olivia talking about her own madness? Could such words reinforce in his mind the evidence gained from the letter in 2.5 and therefore serve as another building block for the cross-purposes and comic delusion that follow? Or would a playgoer who sees Malvolio enter while at the same time hearing Olivia talk of her own malady be more likely to see an analogy between the two instances of comic madness or self-delusion? In procedural terms, should not this apparent anomaly at such a rich moment be field-tested in the theatre as opposed to being rejected out of hand? I have no desire to be prescriptive (i.e., to state categorically: now all productions *must* do it this way), but should not a director at least know of the option, particularly if this moment is but one example of a larger family of comparable entrances scattered throughout the canon?

Titania's "always," Richard II's "I," Clifford's arrow, Ophelia's lute, and Malvolio's early entrance represent one category: possible clues or theatrical signals (or signifiers) in the early printed editions not prized by later editors and often screened out of their texts (and therefore unavailable to the many critics and directors who do not read the textual notes). Even easier to miss or ignore are the many moments when no stage directions or other clear signals survive at all. Admittedly, some onstage effects can be inferred from the dialogue, but those inferences are easily shaped by unstated assumptions (e.g., about "realism" or "dramatic illusion") not in tune with the original logic of presentation. Rather, readers can easily pass over effects important for understanding a given scene or an iterated image without realizing that importance. Indeed, what needs continual emphasis, especially for those who have not worked with the extant evidence, is how often the theatre historian must struggle, sometimes in vain, to discover what would have been so obvious as not to need observing in the 1590s. Those who have wrestled with the shape and design of the early playhouses are well aware of the problem, but the difficulties are as great if not greater in the attempt to recover what happened *within* those buildings and *upon* those stages.

Consider something as mundane as the use of the two or three stage doors in a given playhouse. Given the demanding repertory system with up to six different plays performed per week (according to Henslowe's records), did the players have to keep track of which door to use for entrances and exits (something rarely noted in the extant manuscripts and printed texts unless the situation calls for some special effect)? Or was there some less cumbersome, more efficient approach? For example, Bernard Beckerman, assuming the availability of two stage doors, proposes "that standard usage was for actors to enter regularly through one door and exit through the other," with the practice being so commonplace "that directions for these regularized entrances were minimal." According to this hypothesis, "where the actors varied their entrances for theatrical purposes, the variations were noted in the Plot to remind them of the special arrangement," but otherwise the practice would go unnoted. Beckerman thereby tentatively posits a convention shared by players and playgoers by which "it was understood that entrances were made at one conventionally designated door and exits at the other unless the actor was specifically instructed otherwise." If true, this practice would have been part of a theatrical vocabulary known then but only dimly discernible today.[2]

For a comparable effect perhaps obvious then but invisible today, consider the possibility of what I term conceptual casting. Shakespeare had only a limited number of actors to handle the speaking parts in his plays (scholarly estimates vary from eleven to sixteen), a theatrical exigency that occasioned much doubling and tripling of roles. For example, in *Julius Caesar* only four figures (Brutus, Cassius, Antony, and Lucius) reappear after the assassination (five if one counts Caesar's ghost), so that the many speaking parts after 3.1 had to be taken by the actors who had played the conspirators, Cicero, Artemidorus, the soothsayer, Portia, Calphurnia, and others. On what basis, then, was the decision made as to who came back as whom? Would the players have allotted the roles? Or are we to assume that when Shakespeare killed off a major figure (and hence a major actor) early or midway in a script (e.g., Caesar, Polonius, Duncan) that he somehow planned for the return of that actor?

Scholars have advanced varying formulations about how such necessary doubling or tripling was assigned or conceived.[3] Some of these formulations have been generated by textual oddities (as with the presence of Peto rather than Poins to pick Falstaff's pockets at the end of *1 Henry IV*, 2.4, or the presence of Caius Ligarius but not Cassius in *Julius Caesar*, 2.2). Other proposed doubles or triples, however, whether on the page or on the stage, arise from conceptual rather than logistical concerns. For example, in his 1988 Shakespeare Santa Cruz production of *Julius Caesar*, director Michael Edwards had the same actor who had played Julius Caesar reappear not as Octavius (one available hypothesis) but first as Pindarus, then as Strato. In this interpretation, Brutus was correct in more ways than one when he stated: "O Julius Caesar, thou art mighty yet! / Thy spirit walks abroad and turns our swords / In our own proper entrails" (5.3.94–6), for the Caesar actor, if not Caesar himself, held the swords that killed Cassius and Brutus.

Speculation today about the meaningful use of the same actor for several roles in a Shakespeare play can therefore lead to some suggestive (albeit unprovable) links. What has not been noted, however, is that some (admittedly limited) evidence in support of such conceptual casting does survive. Thus, the 1598 Quarto of *Mucedorus* provides a breakdown so that "Eight persons may easily play it"; the 1610 Quarto, which contains some additions, then adjusts this list for "ten persons." In both lists, as one might expect, primary weight is given to the leading man (Mucedorus), the heroine (Amadine), the villain and rival lover (Segasto), and the clown (Mouse), none of whom is required to double. Of particular interest, however, are the roles allotted to the fifth actor on the list (call him Actor E) who plays Envy, Tremelio, and Bremo. As Envy, he enters in the Induction with "*his arms naked besmeared with blood*," threatening repeatedly to turn Comedy's "mirth into a deadly dole: / Whirling thy pleasures with a peal of death" and challenging Comedy to "send thy actors forth / And I will cross the first steps of their tread: / Making them fear the very dart of death" (A2r–A3r). This same actor then reappears as Tremelio, the victorious captain who is hired by Segasto to murder the comic hero or, in Envy's terms, "cross the first steps" of Mucedorus "with the very dart of death" but who is instead killed by his intended victim. The actor then appears a third time as Bremo, the wild man, who is the primary threat to Mucedorus and Amadine in the second half of the play but who again is finally subdued by the comic hero.

Since both Tremelio and Bremo are tools or extensions of Envy and threats to Comedy, the three parts played by this actor exhibit a clear continuity, so that the tripling, if recognized, *does* become one means of calling attention to structural or thematic analogies. The evidence here is therefore limited but firm: the play (apparently) *was* (or could be) cast this way (whether for eight or ten actors); the apportioning of roles *does* make sense and *can* be meaningful (insofar as anything in this frothy romance can be said to be "meaningful"). Nothing is lost if the tripling goes unnoticed, but something may be gained if a playgoer at some point becomes conscious of the continuity of the actor's identity beneath the three disparate parts. Mucedorus' defeat of Tremelio and then his far more difficult triumph over Bremo epitomize that larger triumph of Comedy over Envy that frames the entire play.[4]

Investigation of the *Mucedorus* casting list does not provide any startling discoveries (ingenious critics and directors have offered far more provocative doublings and triplings) but does supply at least some evidence that the doubling necessitated by theatrical exigency could have a thematic or conceptual pay-off, even in such a lightweight comedy as *Mucedorus*. I am not arguing that critical ingenuity as applied to casting-doubling must be limited to linking the enemies of Comedy, but such a procedure *has* emerged as a strategy that can actually be documented from a printed casting list attached to a 1590s play. Conceivably, conceptual doubling could have served as one signifier in a theatrical vocabulary shared by Elizabethan playwrights, players, and playgoers, a strategy therefore available to an experienced dramatist who knew well his actor-colleagues, his audience, and his craft in the playhouse. As with Beckerman's hypothesis about the use of stage doors, however, what may have been standard practice then can only be conjectured today.

As a third (and more concrete) example of an effect that may have disappeared from the printed text, consider the theatrical and imagistic potential if Othello in 2.3 confronts the brawling Cassio and Montano wearing a nightgown. Initially, such a suggestion may sound extraneous, even silly, but, as I have demonstrated elsewhere,[5] such nightgowns are specified in a large number of Elizabethan plays. Thus, in a theatre without access to variable lighting, the nightgown, along with candles or torches, was used to signal night or to denote a figure roused from sleep. Other relevant associations are to be found in stage directions that call for figures to enter "*unready*" or, as in *1 Henry VI*, "*half ready and half unready*" (2.1.38.s.d.).

In *Othello*, the Folio stage directions mention no nightgowns, but the 1622 Quarto has Brabantio first appear in the opening scene "*at a window*" (B2r) and then enter to Roderigo "*in his night gown*" accompanied by servants "*with Torches*" (B3r). The nightgown and the torches confirm that the scene takes place at night, a fact already established in the dialogue. More important, Shakespeare is here setting up a Brabantio "*as newly come out of Bed*" (*A Woman Killed With Kindness*, II, 141) or "*as newly risen*" (*Dick of Devonshire*, 1286), with the awakening of this "unready" figure caused by a plot set up by Iago (and using Roderigo as a tool) that leads to accusations against Desdemona and her lover, Othello.

No equivalent stage direction survives for 2.3, but, as a result of Cassio's brawling, Othello (rather than Brabantio) is awakened from sleep, again as part of a plot instigated by Iago with Roderigo as a tool, a plot that soon leads to accusations against Desdemona and a supposed lover, this time Cassio, with the willing ear being lent not by Brabantio but by Othello. Although neither the Quarto nor the Folio specifically calls for a nightgown, when Desdemona enters, Othello remarks: "Look if my gentle love be not raised up!"; then tells her: "All's well now, sweeting; come away to bed"; and concludes at his exit: "Come, Desdemona, 'tis the soldiers' life / To have their balmy slumbers waked with strife" (2.3.240–8). Brabantio's sleep, interrupted and poisoned by Iago, has now become Othello's interrupted wedding night, again affected by Iago's pestilence, with the two moments linked (perhaps) by both the nightgown and, equally important, by the associations that garment carries – here unreadiness, vulnerability.

For, like figures in other plays who failed to "watch" properly, Othello clearly is unready, unprepared. Moreover, the violation of sleep and the marriage bed (offstage here, onstage in 5.2) is a paradigm for the larger, deeper violation yet to come. The best gloss on the larger metaphor is provided a few scenes later when Iago first notes that "the Moor already changes with my poison" and then adds: "Not poppy nor mandragora, / Nor all the drowsy syrups of the world, / Shall ever med'cine thee to that sweet sleep / Which thou owedst yesterday" (3.3.325, 330–3). If Othello in 2.3 enters wearing a nightgown, the spectator has already seen such a violation of "sweet sleep," a violation that apparently was offset by Othello's ordering of Cyprus and the brawl but was actually a first step towards the larger tragedy. The stage configuration of

2.3 (with a recently awakened sleeper, clearly unready for what is to come, functioning as a supposed figure of order and authority) epitomizes on various levels the tragic hero's vulnerability and helps to establish key images and links for the rest of the play, especially if Othello and Desdemona are wearing such nightgowns in the final scene on and around the marriage bed.

But, to return to the problem of evidence, this potential series of linked images that *may* have been visible and hence readily available to the original spectators is lost to the modern imagist. Brabantio's nightgown survives in only one of the two early printed texts, Othello's nightgown in neither. Admittedly, citing comparable situations from other plays cannot prove the presence of such a garment in 2.3, but a survey of contemporary plays confirms that in such situations nightgowns did serve as a means to denote night, unreadiness, and interrupted sleep and therefore constituted one item or signifier in an available theatrical vocabulary shared by playwrights, players, and playgoers. Such an effect for Othello's appearance in 2.3 is therefore likely, even probable. Here, then, is a potentially meaningful image screened out not by editors or text-oriented readers but by the passage of time that has eroded elements of that theatrical language taken for granted by Shakespeare and his actor-colleagues.

Some of the best examples of the erosion of that lost vocabulary can be seen in the collision between Elizabethan and later approaches to "place" and locale (a collision to be explored in chapters 8 and 9). As an instructive example, consider the final appearance of the dying Henry IV in *2 Henry IV*. Editors divide this sequence into two scenes, 4.4 and 4.5, but that division (not to be found in either the Quarto or the Folio) helps to mask a distinctive effect. First, the ailing king enters to get reports (about Prince Hal and victories over the rebel forces) and then swoon. When he recovers, Henry instructs: "I pray you, take me up, and bear me hence / Into some other chamber" (4.4.131–2), at which point the Pelican editor, in keeping with editorial tradition, indicates a new scene and adds a bracketed stage direction: "*They bear him to another place.*"

What follows is well known: the placing of the crown upon the pillow; Prince Hal's taking of that crown; the king's chastising of his son; and the reconciliation and final advice. At the end of the sequence, the king asks Warwick: "Doth any name particular belong / Unto the lodging where I first did swoon?" and gets the reply: "'Tis called Jerusalem, my noble lord." Henry IV's final words then close the scene:

> Laud be to God! Even there my life must end.
> It hath been prophesied to me many years
> I should not die but in Jerusalem,
> Which vainly I supposed the Holy Land.
> But bear me to that chamber; there I'll lie.
> In that Jerusalem shall Harry die. (4.5.232–40)

Presumably, the group of figures then exeunt through the appropriate stage door, with Shallow, Falstaff, and others entering at another door to begin 5.1.

Note what happens, however, when an interpreter sidesteps post-Elizabethan assumptions about scene divisions and chambers. If not already seated, Henry would collapse into a sick-chair (a property to be discussed in chapter 6) around line 110. At his command ("take me up, and bear me hence / Into some other chamber") the king in his chair would be carried to another part of the large platform stage and in this "other chamber" (as defined by this physical displacement or visible onstage movement) would have his interview with Prince Hal. A sense of a second room or chamber would therefore be provided without any clearing of the stage.

Given such a staging, consider the added effect for a playgoer in the 1590s of the scene's closing lines devoted to Jerusalem. The king's query about "the lodging where I first did swoon" makes good literal sense to the reader but can have a greater impact upon a spectator, especially if a gesture from either the king or Warwick ("'Tis called Jerusalem") to that part of the stage vacated when Henry was carried to "some other chamber" reminds that spectator of the close proximity of "Jerusalem." In my reconstruction, however, what the playgoer would see is a king who orders "bear me to that chamber" so to die "in Jerusalem" but then is carried not to the place where he "first did swoon" but rather to an adjacent stage door and off the stage. The playgoer is not shown or told whether or not Henry IV achieves his "Jerusalem." Rather, the king is seen taken off in a direction away from the area now, *ex post facto*, defined as "Jerusalem"; as a result, we recognize that, moments earlier, he had been where he most wanted to be but did not know it. Post-Elizabethan notions of scene division and "place," however, can blur or eliminate this potentially meaningful image with its ironic, even deflationary comment upon the career of this distinctive figure.

As a final example of the erosion of that lost vocabulary, consider the problem that faces any director staging a Shakespeare script today: where to place the intermission (USA) or interval (UK). So far as we can tell, throughout most of his career Shakespeare would have seen his plays performed continuously, from start to finish, with no breaks between acts or scenes. Around 1610, however, the fashion changed, so that performances in the public theatres gradually began to follow the practice of the private theatres in having brief pauses, with musical interludes, between the acts. Elizabethan and Jacobean audiences would therefore have been comfortable with either procedure (continuous flow or act pauses) but would have been surprised by the single fifteen-minute break today's playgoer takes for granted (again, "you speak a language that I understand not"). As a result, the imposition of such a break upon a dramatic strategy predicated upon a continuous flow of action will of necessity introduce changes and sometimes a new set of problems. For example, in making such a decision today's director must not only be concerned with where to stop (some kind of climactic moment) but also where to start up again, for the Elizabethan dramatist, who was not thinking in terms of such a decisive stop and start, did not provide that director with a scene that would re-engage an audience once again settling into their seats after a chat and a drink.

In making their choices directors today often take practical considerations into account. For example, several plays have busy ensemble scenes midway in the action that entail much onstage furniture that then can be removed during such a break; thus, *1 Henry IV* is often divided after thc big tavern scene (2.4), *Macbeth* after the banquet scene (3.4), and *As You Like It* after 2.7 where, again, an onstage banquet can be cleared away. But such choices have consequences. For example, to break the action with Prince Hal surveying a sleeping Falstaff at the close of 2.4 is to gain a potentially strong climactic image but also to diminish strongly the contrapuntal effect in which the Hotspur–Glendower relationship in 3.1 comments upon Hal–Falstaff and then the Hal–Henry IV confrontation (3.2) comments upon both. The three scenes are scripted as one continuous sequence, but that sequence is blurred if not eclipsed by the break. In such instances, our playgoing reflexes (that take for granted an intermission–interval) have superseded the original theatrical vocabulary predicated upon narrative continuity, juxtaposition, and counterpoint.[6]

A third category includes scenes wherein theatrical signals do survive and in turn are included in our editions, but, owing to the language barrier, these signals are difficult to interpret today. Since such problems in translation are central to the chapters that follow (e.g., chapter 6 is devoted to one such major image – the sick chair – with its built in analogy to the sick-throne), I will limit myself here to two examples.

First, consider the moment in *King John* when young Arthur, determined to escape or die, enters "*on the walls*" (4.3.0.s.d.), has an eight-line speech, and then leaps to his death. As used here (and in many comparable situations) "*on the walls*" is a signal equivalent, in "fictional" terms, to the more purely "theatrical" stage direction "*enter above*," an effect clarified by Arthur's opening lines ("The wall is high, and yet will I leap down, / Good ground, be pitiful and hurt me not!"). In simplest terms, Shakespeare presents us with a figure above, a leap, and a death.

What complicates this effect is that, according to the dialogue, Arthur has put on a distinctive costume, for, as he tells us: "This ship-boy's semblance hath disguised me quite" (4.3.4). Such a disguise is not to be found in Shakespeare's sources, including the comparable scene in *The Troublesome*

Reign, and has received little attention from editors and critics. An appropriate question for the student of theatrical vocabulary is therefore: would the presence of a "ship-boy" above have set up a significant image or effect for a playgoer in the 1590s?

The answer is: possibly, yes. Given the exigencies of the Elizabethan open stage, dramatists seldom present scenes on board a ship. Perhaps the most elaborate example is to be found in *Fortune by Land and Sea* (VI, 410–18) where, in alternating scenes, Heywood presents a battle between two ships at sea by means of such theatrical signals as sound effects ("*a great Alarum and shot*," "*a piece goes off*"), appropriate properties (e.g., "*Sea devices fitting for a fight*"), and distinctive nautical figures (a captain, mariners). One of those distinctive figures is a boy who, here as in comparable scenes, is sent "*above*" or "*aloft*" to serve as lookout and who then calls down news of an approaching vessel.

What then if the purpose of Arthur's seemingly irrelevant disguise is to set up a stage picture that calls to mind a ship? The image may seem strange to us, but spectators in the 1590s would, at least for a moment, have received the signal that they were seeing a ship-boy or lookout in his position "*aloft.*" Nor does the image end here. Rather, in a comparable moment at the end of the play, the dying King John welcomes the Bastard with the lines: "The tackle of my heart is cracked and burnt, / And all the shrouds wherewith my life should sail / Are turned to one thread, one little hair" (5.7.52–4). John, moreover, is here surrounded by many of the same figures (the Bastard, Pembroke, Salisbury) who stood around the body of Arthur after his fall in 4.3; the Bastard reports, moreover, not of a shipwreck but of the fate of his forces "in the Washes all unwarily / Devoured by the unexpected flood" (63–4).

To push the ship or shipwreck image of 4.3 too hard may be to strain the evidence; nonetheless, Shakespeare *did* include the ship-boy disguise and *did* provide a comparable verbal image in John's last speech. The link between these two moments is not evident to the reader or even to the modern playgoer, but, given the theatrical vocabulary of the 1590s, such a image could have been signaled in Arthur's death scene and then recapitulated or developed at John's death. An "image" and resulting network visible or available in the 1590s may now be lost or blurred by the passage of time.

For a second more complex example, consider the penultimate "monument" scene of *Much Ado About Nothing* (5.3) which begins: "*Enter Claudio, Prince, and three or four with tapers.*" Although not noted, to my knowledge, in any edition, this stage direction contains what is probably an error (or, given the putative "foul papers" copy for this printed text, an unrevised first thought), for the introduction of *tapers* (slender candles) would normally signal an indoor scene as opposed to the use of *torches*, the appropriate lighting implement for outdoors (presumably Iago would carry a torch in 5.1 but Othello would carry a taper in 5.2). According to one possible explanation, at the outset of the scene Shakespeare was thinking of a monument or tomb indoors (for which tapers would be appropriate), but by the end, with Don Pedro's reference to sunrise, had moved his thoughts outdoors (hence "put your torches out" – 5.3.24). As with several other inconsistencies in the Quarto (e.g., the two early references to Leonato's wife, Innogen – 1.1.0.s.d, 2.1.0.s.d.), *tapers* appears to be a vestige of Plan A that has been superseded by Plan B but not edited out.

The issue of tapers versus torches is part of a larger set of problems linked to properties and stage business in this scene. For example, some object is required upon which the epitaph for Hero is written, so that the Arden and Pelican editors insert "*reads from a scroll*" before the epitaph is read and "*Hangs up the scroll*" after line 8 (before "Hang thou there upon the tomb ..." so that the subject of "Praising her when I am dumb" is this scroll). The introduction of such a property, however, raises the question: what then happens to this scroll at the end of the scene? That question in turn is linked to yet another: what kind of "tomb" or "monument" did or should a spectator see: an elaborate physical structure as in most productions today? Or, in contrast, something left largely to the playgoer's imagination? If one assumes the presence of an elaborate tomb, the scroll could easily be removed along with it. If the tomb is a stage door, the scroll could be hung and then a curtain pulled to cover it for the final scene. But if the tomb is represented by a stage post, the scroll (and hence some sense of "the tomb") conceivably could still be visible *during* the final scene (so as to overlap with such lines as "One Hero died defiled; but I do live" and "She died, my lord, but whiles her slander lived" – 5.4.63, 66).

The latter possibility does not concern the Arden editor who envisages "a monument out of doors" rather than "a church" (in keeping with torches rather than tapers); he adds: "wherever situated, an impressive tomb (a stage-property, as in *Romeo and Juliet*) is essential, to symbolize the gravity of death and the purgatorial nature of Claudio's reverence." To this reader: "Short though the scene is, a conviction of religious grief and awe is to be evoked, creating depth and dignity of emotion more by non-verbal than by verbal means" (p. 210).

Maybe, maybe not. "An impressive tomb" may indeed be "essential" to this interpretation but is not "essential" for staging this moment (or *Romeo and Juliet*, 5.3) in the 1590s. Rather, much depends upon how the interpreter reconstructs those verbal and non-verbal signals. Yes, some kind of stage-property tomb could have been introduced, here or in *Romeo* 5.3, but, given the exigencies faced by the Lord Chamberlain's Men, that notion may equally well be a canard. Something *is* there for the "scroll" to hang upon ("hang thou there upon the tomb..."), but that something, whatever it is, is neatly established by the opening line ("Is this the monument of Leonato?"). For the playgoer, whatever Claudio gestures to at his *this* in effect "becomes" the monument. Another clue is provided by the song in which the mourners for Hero "with songs of woe, / Round about her tomb they go" (14–15). If taken literally, these lines signal a circling of the tomb, a ritual that could be performed around a stage property thrust onto the stage but could also be easily accomplished by a circling of a stage post (that could be identified as the tomb by the opening line and further reinforced by the hanging of the scroll).

Such a reconstructed staging, though practical and economical, is no more definitive than the postulation of an impressive tomb. To complicate matters further, a major theatrical image in the scene (a possible punch line so to speak) has gone unnoticed. Thus, after "yearly will I do this rite" Don Pedro and Claudio share the remaining ten lines (24–33) in which the former calls attention to the coming dawn ("and look, the gentle day ... / Dapples the drowsy east with spots of grey"), both say farewell to their companions (who may depart through different doors – "Each his several way"), and finally the two nobleman determine to "put on other weeds" and proceed to Leonato's house. Omitted from this cursory summary of these ten lines is the simple direction contained in line 24: "Good morrow, masters. Put your torches out."

With modern productions in mind, this moment is unremarkable (perhaps no more than a bit of necessary filler), for in our terms the coming of "the gentle day" in "the drowsy east" is easily signaled by a lighting change (so that the putting out of no longer necessary torches is perfunctory). But what would have happened when this moment was performed in a theatre in which the players could not control the onstage illumination during the course of the performance? In their terms, the new day is signaled not by an effect generated by a computerized lighting board but by the words spoken by Don Pedro and by the putting out of the torches (so that the coming of new light is linked to the *elimination* of artificial lights). "Dawn's coming," as the Arden editor notes may be "imaginatively appropriate to the plot's emergence from the shadows of evil and grief" (p. 212), but, especially given the play's iterated emphasis upon sight, eyes, misprision, and noting-nothing, Don Pedro's "put your torches out" may provide an alternative effect for those who may be less sanguine about Claudio's actions and repentance. Thus, in other plays of the period such putting out of candles, lanterns, or torches (in night scenes where such implements are supposedly the only source of light) serves as a theatrical signal that the playgoer is to imagine a plunge into total darkness.[7] For that 1590s playgoer, the initial effect of "Put your torches out. / The wolves have preyed ..." *may* have been a sense of impenetrable night (at least until conditioned by subsequent references to "the gentle day" and "spots of grey").

The possibility of even a momentary sense of deeper darkness (at least in terms of a 1590s theatrical vocabulary) generates a series of related questions. Since the original playgoer at the Theatre or Globe would have witnessed no change in the onstage daylit illumination (other than a possible slight darkening when the torches were put out), is the movement (with now extinguished torches) from the tomb to the wedding a movement from darkness to dawn–light (the romantic–optimistic interpretation offered by the Arden editor and readily reinforced by our sense of light–lighting)? Or, conversely, would the original playgoer have sensed an ironic movement from physical darkness to another, subtler form of darkness–misprision (that may or may not be resolved when Hero unmasks moments later)? Put simply, in psychological, moral, or symbolic terms, does the end of this scene bring light or continued darkness?

The fact that what may be an outright error (the taper in 5.3.0.s.d.) has not been recognized as such provides a chastening reminder of our level of expertise in reading Elizabethan playscripts. As noted in my epigraph from one of the shrewdest of twentieth-century scholar–directors, "the literature of the past is a foreign literature," so that "we must either learn its language or suffer it to be translated." When reading the early printed texts of Shakespeare's plays, we regularly confront a theatrical shorthand murky to us but accessible to the original players and playgoers. In interpreting these plays, some degree of "translation" is then inevitable (and, in the case of today's productions, may be healthy and fruitful). But at what point do the losses of potential meanings and effects in such translation outweigh the gains?

CHAPTER 3

Interpreting without a dictionary

"There's a double meaning in that."

Much Ado About Nothing, 2.3.237

To return to my basic assumptions, in putting quill to paper Shakespeare was crafting theatrical scripts rather than literary texts; the stage directions and other signals in those scripts were directed not at us but at players, playgoers, and readers who shared a language of the theatre easily lost or obscured today. As a result, what to an editor's eye may appear an error or an inconsistency (Malvolio's early entrance, Titania's *always*, Richard II's "I, no; no, I"), to a theatrical eye (then or now) may provide a potentially meaningful option. The many silences, moreover – whether about the use of the stage doors, conceptual doubling, or patterned costuming (as with Othello's possible nightgown in 2.3) – may also cloak images or effects highly visible in the original productions.

To recover or reconstitute those images and effects today, however, can be difficult, sometimes impossible. As an instructive paradigm, consider the even greater hurdles that confront the scholar who seeks to recover what the original playgoers saw at a performance of a Greek tragedy (for which no stage directions survive). At the moment when the messenger from Corinth tells Oedipus about his true origins, how did the (male) actor (wearing a mask) act out Jocasta's presumably silent reaction (she has no lines until later in the episode) in front of 10,000 spectators sitting outdoors in the daylight on a hillside? Was Jocasta silent and unmoving so that the playgoer is to imagine her state of mind (assuming "state of mind" is a relevant concept in this culture)? Would music or other sound effects have accompanied (and somehow enhanced) this moment? To signal her reaction, would the masked actor playing Jocasta have provided some stylized movement or gesture (e.g., a slow turn of the head) or some distinctive sound? When watching a modern production (e.g., Don Taylor's 1986 rendition for BBC Television) the viewer can zero in upon the face of the actress (in this instance, Claire Bloom) so as to chart Jocasta's growing horror, for the scene or effect *can* readily be translated into our theatrical idiom. The expressive face of an actress and the television–cinema close-up, however, were not part of Sophocles' arsenal in a theatre geared to masks, daylight, and many far-distant spectators. What then does or should constitute a scholarly–historical performance-oriented approach to this moment?

The problems in dealing with the Elizabethan–Jacobean staging of Shakespeare's plays are less formidable than those occasioned by Greek tragedy but are substantial nonetheless. Regardless of those difficulties, scholars throughout this century have provided a series of reconstructions: of Shakespeare's theatres, audiences, and theatrical practice, and, more generally, of his "world picture," ideology, and culture. Studies that constitute the latter group, although of considerable interest, lie far beyond the province of this book. Similarly, the work of Ann Jennalie Cook and Andrew Gurr has taught us much about Shakespeare's playgoers,[1] but only occasionally can such research shed light upon what those playgoers actually witnessed. Investigations of the physical features and dimensions of Shakespeare's theatres have grown increasingly sophisticated, with the complex issues recently brought to a head by the archaeological evidence unearthed at the Rose and Globe sites,[2] but the evidence from drawings, documents, and archaeological excavations has revealed little about the interiors of such theatres and even less about what happened upon such stages.

More relevant to the focus of this book are the many studies specifically devoted to Shakespearean or Elizabethan staging, theatrical practice, or stage conventions (three terms that sometimes mean the same thing). Some of the earliest such studies (by scholars who had read widely in the extant plays) can still be valuable, even though they are at times undermined by assumptions about "the triumph of realism," "the inner stage," and other such narratives or hypotheses now discredited.[3] As to stage conventions and stage practice, M. C. Bradbrook's pioneering work has exerted a considerable influence upon subsequent studies (including my own 1984 book), as has the excellent chapter on staging in Bernard Beckerman's book on the Globe.[4] More recently, a series of scholars (working primarily with Shakespeare's plays) have, in different ways, extracted and organized information about properties, costumes, and general procedures.[5] In short, there is no shortage of scholarly books on what is variously termed Shakespeare's staging, stagecraft, orchestration, or theatrical practice.

All this work has been useful and fruitful. Nonetheless, the language barrier and the problems in translation cited in chapters 1 and 2 persist so as to bedevil such scholars and qualify the value of such studies. Although theatre historians are aware of the many gaps between then and now, with few exceptions (Beckerman is one) the powerful desire for clear formulations and unequivocal findings (that will make immediate sense to today's interpreters) can take precedence over the often tangled evidence. From such studies a "Shakespeare our contemporary" can emerge in theatrical rather than ideological terms, a Shakespeare whose "stagecraft" or "theatrical practice" bears a remarkable resemblance to that of today's actor, director, editor, or teacher (and the practices of other dramatists of the period play a minor part at best in such studies). In discussions of staging (as in other areas) the questions posed and the evidence adduced can generate self-fulfilling prophecies wherein the investigator "discovers" what he or she assumed would be there.[6]

By concentrating upon "theatrical vocabulary" and by casting as wide a net as possible, I am attempting to break out of this hermeneutic circle so as to recover some of those shared meanings easily obscured by both the passage of time and post-1642 assumptions. In so doing, I will inevitably revisit some terrain already covered by others or even by myself. In my pursuit of such signifiers, moreover, I will invoke some categories or materials that might more properly be classified as stage conventions (as with the use of stage doors, conceptual casting, or intervals–intermissions noted in chapter 2). In particular, in chapters 4 and 5 I shall concentrate upon two techniques (juxtapositions and theatrical *italics*) that may not fit snugly under the rubric of "vocabulary." This latter choice I have deemed necessary so as to establish some building blocks and key terms for the chapters that follow.

The evidence I have collected from hundreds of plays does help to illuminate some dark areas (as I hope to demonstrate), but at the same time that evidence generates new questions and problems. Most readers of this book (understandably) would prefer more space devoted to illumination and less to problems, pitfalls, and anomalies. Indeed, most attractive to such readers would be a dictionary or a handbook comparable to the *OED* that would define both stock terms and less familiar usages so as to facilitate interpretation.

Consider possible entries for such a dictionary for several verbs or verb phrases:

[*enter*] *to him* [or *to them*]: enter during an on-going action so as to join (and usually immediately address or be addressed by) one or more figures already onstage; this usage is regularly found in the "plots"

exeunt: the plural of *exit*, hence a direction for two or more figures to leave the stage; compare *manet* and *manent* for the singular and plural form of the direction for one or more figures to remain when others depart

offers to go: makes a movement or gesture as if to exit but is prevented or forestalled; for a Latin version, *Exiturus*, see Chapman's plays (e.g., *The Widow's Tears*, 4.2.179.s.d.); *offers to* ... or some equivalent is used for other actions as well as in *offers to kill himself* (Chettle, *The Tragedy of Hoffman*, 921–2)

discover: as a transitive verb, to part a curtain or otherwise reveal to the playgoer (and often to onstage figures) something hitherto unseen: "*Here Prospero discovers Ferdinand and Miranda playing at chess*" (5.1.171.s.d.); regularly used as a passive verb ("*Hell is discovered*" – Marlowe, *Dr. Faustus*, B-text, 2017), often with *is* omitted ("*King Priam discovered kneeling at the Altar*" – Heywood, 2 *The Iron Age*, III, 390); what is parted or drawn may sometimes be a curtain around a bed rather than an arras covering a stage door

As in the *OED*, fuller entries for such verbs might record first usages, changes in meaning over time, and variations (e.g., *exeunt severally*, *going*, *draws a curtain*).

Other comparable details linked to costumes or properties could be glossed accordingly. Consider:

enter booted: a widely used signal to denote a figure who has recently completed a journey or is about to undertake one – hence often associated with haste or weariness; other comparable items are also specified (spurs, riding wands, riding-cloaks, safeguards) as in *The Merry Devil of Edmonton* (B1r) which calls for "*the men booted, the gentlewomen in cloaks and safe-guards*"; for a rich use of such associations by Falstaff see *2 Henry IV*, 5.3.128–32 and 5.5.13–27

enter muffled: enter hiding one's face in a garment (e.g., a cloak or a hat) – hence enter surreptitiously or in conspiratorial fashion; in *Julius Caesar*, 2.1 Lucius describes the offstage conspirators: "Their hats are plucked about their ears / And half their faces buried in their cloaks, / That by no means I may discover them / By any mark of favor" (73–6)

enter with a halter: either enter prepared to commit suicide (as in Peele's *Edward I*: "*Enter ... David with a halter ready to hang himself*" – 2108.s.d.) or, equally common, enter in an abject position as if to say "my life is in your hands" as in *2 Henry VI*, 4.9.9.s.d. where the former followers of Jack Cade appear before Henry VI "*with halters about their necks*" (Clifford glosses the gesture: "all his powers do yield, / And humbly thus, with halters on their necks, / Expect your highness' doom of life or death" – 10–12)

enter with her hair about her ears or *with her hair disheveled*: a signal (particularly if the woman has been seen previously with a decorous coiffure) that the entering figure is distraught with madness, shame, extreme grief, or the effects of recent violence; in the latter category, disheveled hair can be one way of signaling *enter ravished* – as in *Dick of Devonshire* (687–9), Massinger's *The Unnatural Combat* (5.2.185.s.d.), and Arthur Wilson's *The Swisser* (4.1.0.s.d.) and perhaps with Lavinia in *Titus*, 2.4.0.s.d.; for examples from Shakespeare's plays see, for grief, Folio *Richard III* (2.2.33.s.d., TLN 1306) and, for madness, Q1 *Hamlet* (4.5.20.s.d., G4v) and Folio *Troilus* (2.2.100.s.d., TLN 1082–3); to gain the effect, a boy actor playing the role need only have changed his wig

enter in a nightgown: this ubiquitous item of costume can signal (depending upon the context) (1) time of day (night or early morning – as in Heywood's *The English Traveller*, IV, 70: "*in a night-tire, as coming from Bed*"), (2) place (a bedroom or some other domestic space – as in Webster's *The White Devil*, 2.2.23.s.d.: "*in her nightgown as to bed-*

ward"), or, more generally, (3) unreadiness, a troubled conscience, or sleeplessness (as with Henry IV in *2 Henry IV*, 3.1); the nightgown regularly appears in a sexual or romantic context but can equally well be linked to major political figures such as Henry IV ("uneasy lies the head that wears the crown") or Julius Caesar (in 2.2)

Here then is the most straightforward way to deal with a theatrical vocabulary, whether key verbs, properties, or items of costume.[7] In subsequent chapters I will therefore explore several comparable terms or signifiers: *enter sick* or *enter in a chair*; enter *in his study* or *in a shop*; keys; *vanish*.

My putative dictionary of theatrical signifiers would indeed be useful, especially for readers not familiar with a wide range of plays. As anyone who has struggled to learn a second language knows, however, to master dictionary definitions (or elementary vocabulary) is at best a first step, one that can take the beginner only a short distance. Rather, the fuller language contains irregularities, nuances, and idioms not easily codified in a handbook, a situation that pertains to theatrical language as well. In addition (as I have repeatedly stressed), important signifiers in the original theatrical vocabulary have been blurred or lost so as to make the process of recovery even more difficult. Indeed, the more I wrestle with the extant evidence, the less confident I become about my understanding of even such relatively straightforward terms as those listed above.

One difficulty in glossing terms arises from unique or unusual usages. Dictionary definitions are linked to shared meanings, but what happens when a word or phrase turns up only once (as with Caliban's *scamels* – 2.2.168)? For example, in *The Pilgrim* to enhance a sense of the forest Fletcher first calls for "*Music and Birds*" and then "*Music afar off. Pot Birds*" (v, 221). William J. Lawrence cites with approval an earlier German scholar who "very shrewdly maintains that 'pot birds' signifies that well-known device, so alluring to all well-ordered boyhood, of producing warbling sounds by blowing into a bowl of water through a pipe."[8] Lawrence may well be correct, but the absence of supporting evidence from contemporary playscripts (or other sources) prevents any definitive glossing of this term.

From Shakespeare's plays a comparable curious usage is to be found in *All's Well That Ends Well*: "*Enter a gentle Astringer*" (TLN 2601, 5.1.6.s.d.). Many editors emend this signal and have it read instead "*enter a gentleman*" or "*enter a gentleman, a stranger.*" The *OED*, however, cites *astringer* (or *austringer* or *ostringer*) as "a keeper of goshawks" – in short, a falconer. Such falconers are called for in *2 Henry VI* where the Folio brings on a hunting party "*with Falconers halloaing*" (TLN 716, 2.1.0.s.d.); the equivalent signal in the Quarto (C1v), moreover, calls for the same group to enter "*as if they came from hawking*" and specifies that Queen Margaret is to enter "*with her Hawk on her fist.*" Such a falcon was introduced into Terry Hands's 1977–78 Royal Shakespeare Company production of *2 Henry VI*; similarly, in Sir Peter Hall's 1992–93 RSC production of *All's Well* actor Griffith Jones (as the astringer) and two others carried in three hooded falcons in 5.1. In the 1992 Oregon Shakespeare Festival production, however, the astringer was eliminated; rather, his lines in both 5.1 and 5.3 were given to the Countess's steward, Rinaldo.

As will be demonstrated in subsequent chapters, ranging widely in the plays of the period can enable the scholar (like the lexicographer or iconographer) to collect repeated usages of a signal so as to explore its potential meaning. Such a procedure cannot work, however, whether for "*Pot Birds*" or "*Enter a gentle Astringer*," when no such context can be adduced. Fletcher's signal may be written off as an oddity, but the identification of the figure who meets Helena in 5.1 could be significant. Is the Folio stage direction to be deemed an error (as perhaps with "*Pot Birds*") and therefore emended (as often happens)? Or is the astringer (with or without a hooded falcon) somehow part of the onstage vocabulary of 5.1 (and perhaps of 5.3 as well when he reappears to deliver his message)?[9]

Consider as well the second appearance of the ghost in the second quarto of *Hamlet*, where Horatio says "I'll cross it though it blast me" and the marginal stage direction reads: "*It spreads his arms*" (B3r). The Pelican editor changes this signal to "*He spreads his arms*" (1.1.127.s.d.) so that (presumably) the gesture is made by Horatio, not by the ghost. Q2's *It*, however, leaves open the possibility of a reaction from the ghost (perhaps in response to Horatio's "stay illusion"), an option less likely to be noted or explored given the emendation.

Although the matter may not seem consequential to a reader of the scene today, a spreading of arms by the actor playing the ghost may have been a meaningful signifier in an Elizabethan theatrical vocabulary. Thus, after Horatio's injunctions for the ghost to speak, "*The cock crows*" (138.s.d.), at which point "it started, like a guilty thing / Upon a fearful summons" (148–9). At Horatio's command, Marcellus and Bernardo strike at the departing figure with their partisans, but they are unable to affect it ("'Tis here. / 'Tis here. / 'Tis gone" – 140–2). As will be demonstrated in chapter 10, the staging of such a ghostly departure or vanishing, without access to variable lighting, poses various interpretative problems, with (in cases such as this) few opportunities for the kind of verisimilar staging today's interpreter takes for granted. Although apparently anomalous today, "*It spreads his arms*" may have been an onstage signifier then to denote that the ghost was visible or accessible to Horatio. If the signal is read this way, at the crowing of the cock this ghost would then have repositioned its arms to denote that it had faded from sight and was therefore invulnerable to the sentinels' partisans. Here as in other instances involving supernatural vanishings or departures, we do not know enough about Elizabethan theatrical practice to dismiss "*It spreads his arms*" as an error rather than accepting it as a valid theatrical signifier worthy of investigation. The absence (to my knowledge) of comparable signals elsewhere in the period, however, makes such a claim problematic.

The notion of a dictionary of theatrical terms or signifiers therefore remains attractive but elusive. Consider another area of concern. Mid way between the silences about how to stage a given moment and the signals that can (apparently) be glossed lie the ellipses or what I think of as theatrical shorthand, an argot readily adopted when one professional (e.g., an attached dramatist such as Shakespeare or Heywood) addresses another.

Not all such situations need be cryptic today. For example,

near the end of *Richard III*, 1.2 the body of Henry VI is carried off the stage, but the actual stage direction in the Folio reads: "*Exit Corse*" (TLN 423). No one, to my knowledge, interprets this signal as "*The corpse rises and exits*"; rather the Pelican editor, for one, expands this elliptical statement to read: "*Exit* [*Guard with Bearers and*] *corse*" (1.2.226.s.d.). A comparable locution involves halberds carried by officers guarding a prisoner or performing some ceremonial function. For example, three times in Folio *Richard III* figures are directed to enter "*with halberds*": "*Enter the Corse of Henry the sixth with Halberds to guard it, Lady Anne being the Mourner*" (TLN 173–4, 1.2.0.s.d.); "*Enter Sir Richard Ratcliffe, with Halberds, carrying the Nobles to death at Pomfret*" (TLN 1933–4, 3.3.0.s.d.); "*Enter Buckingham with Halberds, led to Execution*" (TLN 3371–2, 5.1.0.s.d.). Here and elsewhere[10] "*with halberds*" clearly means that X should enter accompanied by soldiers or officers carrying such weapons.

Nonetheless, despite the glosses above, even such simple terms as *exit* and *exeunt* can prove opaque rather than transparent, elliptical rather than informative. For example, a scene-ending *exeunt* in a quarto or the First Folio (that would appear to direct two or more figures to leave the stage together) can function as an on-the-page shorthand that cloaks a series of separate exits or some other complex effect. A straightforward example is provided by the departure of the four lovers in *A Midsummer Night's Dream*. The passage as printed below (taken from the Pelican text) is typical of both modern editions and modern productions:

LYSANDER: Now follow, if thou dar'st, to try whose right,
Of thine or mine, is most in Helena.
DEMETRIUS: Follow? Nay, I'll go with thee, cheek by jowl.
[*Exeunt Lysander and Demetrius.*]
HERMIA: You, mistress, all this coil is long of you.
Nay, go not back.
HELENA: I will not trust you, I,
Nor longer stay in your curst company.
Your hands than mine are quicker for a fray;
My legs are longer, though, to run away.
HERMIA: I am amazed, and know not what to say.
Exeunt [*Helena and Hermia*]. (3.2.336–44)

Most readers of the dialogue would infer that Lysander and Demetrius depart together ("cheek by jowl") followed a beat later by Helena and Hermia (some editors give the two women separate exits). As indicated by the Pelican editor's square brackets, however, the only stage direction provided by the Quarto (FIr) is an *Exeunt* to the right of Hermia's final line (curiously, the Folio adds "*Exit Lysander and Demetrius*" at the appropriate point [TLN 1378] but omits the *Exeunt* for the two women). Although in this instance the staging is not in doubt, here (as at the end of *Much Ado*, 5.3) the Quarto's *Exeunt* conceals a rich effect that cannot be conveyed adequately by a dictionary entry.

For a more complex example, consider the end of *Macbeth*, 2.4:

ROSS: Will you to Scone?
MACDUFF: No, cousin, I'll to Fife.
ROSS: Well, I will thither.
MACDUFF: Well, may you see things well done there. Adieu,
Lest our old robes sit easier than our new!
ROSS: Farewell, father.
OLD MAN: God's benison go with you, and with those
That would make good of bad, and friends of foes. (35–41)

The Folio stage direction then reads "*Exeunt omnes*" (TLN 979) followed by "*Enter Banquo*" (TLN 981) to begin 3.1.

The simplest (and perhaps the correct) interpretation of this *Exeunt omnes* is that all three figures (Macduff, Ross, and the old man) go off either together or in sequence through the same stage door (with perhaps Macduff delivering his couplet upstage while Ross says his farewell to the old man). Such a reading of this *exeunt* would be in keeping with the procedure suggested by Bernard Beckerman (noted in chapter 2) "that entrances were made at one conventionally designated door and exits at the other unless the actor was specifically instructed otherwise." No more than two stage doors would therefore be required, for three figures would depart through door B and Banquo would enter at door A.

But despite the Folio's *Exeunt omnes*, a close reading of these lines could suggest a sequence of *exits*, not a group *exeunt*, in three different directions: Macduff to Fife (after a couplet that provides some sense of closure), Ross to Scone, and the old man (who provides another couplet) to wherever. A literalist could then use this scene as evidence for the presence of four stage doors so that an exiting Macduff would not be tripping over an entering Banquo. If three doors are available, Macduff could be out door A and out of sight by the time Banquo enters (the Macduff couplet would then be a way of conveying "I'm out of here" so that Banquo could use that door), leaving doors B and C for Ross and the old man. With only two doors, the three exiting figures could go out in sequence through door B (with the old man lingering or, in his age, moving more slowly) or Macduff could, as suggested above, go off earlier through door A a beat before Banquo enters.

My goal here is not to "solve" the problem but rather to suggest how even a straightforward on-the-page term such as *Exeunt* can be insufficient or puzzling. At the least the definition cited earlier ("a direction for two or more figures to leave the stage") may have to be adjusted so as to include "usually together but sometimes separately and a few lines apart." To deal solely with terms or signifiers in Shakespeare's theatrical vocabulary (or to deal with them in rigorous lexigraphical fashion) is rarely sufficient (though to do so can be a fruitful point of departure). For this reason chapter 4 and especially chapter 5 will move onto more general terrain so as to deal with two useful principles (juxtaposition and theatrical *italics*) relevant to many such vocabulary items.

The limitations of a dictionary-oriented approach to theatrical vocabulary are well illustrated by the problems posed when defining *aside*. Consider the following entry:

> *aside*: as a noun, words spoken by an actor which other performers onstage are supposed not to hear; as a stage signal, usually to be taken as an adverb; hence [*speak*] *aside* directs an actor to direct his words to the playgoer or to another onstage figure so as to maintain the fiction that those words are not overheard by others onstage

The *OED* supports both usages, but provides no examples of *aside* as a noun before the eighteenth century.

And thereby hangs my tale (or at least part of it). Readers today know (or think they know) what an *aside* is, just as they know (or think they know) what a *morality play* is (a term that comes into use in the eighteenth century to bolster a now discredited view of the development of drama) or that the Forest of Arden demands visible onstage trees (an assumption to be discussed later in this chapter). But the actual use of the term by Elizabethan playwrights and playhouse annotators sometimes does not conform to such expectations, a disparity that can generate interpretative problems, particularly with Shakespeare. A summary account of the evidence and the problems can therefore be informative – and chastening – for those who would settle for neat dictionary definitions.

Even though the noun *aside* is rare, use of the term as part of an implicit verb phrase ([*speak*] *aside*)[11] is widespread in plays of this period, including manuscripts and printed texts annotated for performance. A good example is provided by *The Two Noble Ladies*, a manuscript play from the 1620s with extensive playhouse annotations, where (along with other stage directions) the many asides (usually spelled *asside*) are carefully marked in the right margin; moreover, many are boxed so as to make them more visible.[12] In addition to the term standing alone, other variations include "*aside to Cyprian*" and the response "*aside to Lysander*" (427–8). This playhouse manuscript provides ample and clearly marked evidence for the usage taken for granted by today's reader.

Such a consistent and clearly marked use of *aside*, however, is not characteristic of the 1590s and early 1600s (although many designated asides *can* be adduced). In particular, such is not the case for the Shakespeare quartos and First Folio. Admittedly, the dialogue in the canon provides plentiful use of "aside." Noteworthy, moreover, are the many spoken commands that use the word to call for movement, most notably "stand aside" (fourteen examples) but also "walk aside" (3), "step aside" (2), "take him aside" (1), "turn aside" (1), and "aside, aside" (2).[13]

Three of the stage directions that invoke the term accord with this usage, for, as with the fourteen examples of "stand aside" in the dialogue, in these instances *aside* is linked not to speech but to physical movement. First, in *Coriolanus*, when Menenius turns his attention from the two tribunes to the three entering women, the Folio stage direction reads: "*Bru. and Sic. Aside*" (2.1.89, TLN 992). The tribunes remain "*Aside*" as silent observers for roughly one hundred lines, so as used here the term refers to physical spacing, not to any special mode of address. The same is true in the complex eavesdropping scene in *Love's Labor's Lost* where first Berowne "*stands a side*" as Navarre enters (4.3.17, Quarto E2v); and then, when Longaville enters, "*The King steps a side*" (4.3.39, Quarto E3r). The Folio provides the same two signals but spells the term *aside* rather than *a side* (TLN 1353, 1376). By 1623 *aside* is the preferred spelling, but given the infrequency of the term in Shakespeare's stage directions, the Quarto's *a side* (with its possible meaning of *on a side* or *move to a side of the stage*) should not be completely dismissed.

In contrast to these three examples, hundreds of speeches that seem obvious *asides* to editors and actors are not marked as such in the quartos and the Folio. The two exceptions are to be found in scenes usually not linked directly to Shakespeare's hand. First, Folio *Merry Wives* has no asides (indeed, it has almost no stage directions), but the Quarto (a text classified as a "bad" quarto and hence usually not linked to a Shakespeare manuscript) does provide one. Thus, just before Falstaff gets into the basket (E1r, equivalent to 3.3.121–2) Mrs. Page speaks to him "*Aside*" to chide him ("Fie sir *John* is this your love? Go to"). The on-the-page usage here does correspond to what a reader today would consider normative, but few scholars would argue that Q1 *Merry Wives* provides direct evidence of Shakespeare's practice in writing out his manuscripts. The only other "standard" *asides* signaled as such come in *Pericles*, indeed, twice during the same Simonides speech (2.5.74.s.d., 78.s.d., D4v), a part of the play usually attributed to a hand other than Shakespeare's. The only examples in the Shakespeare canon of what today is deemed the normative use of *aside* therefore are to be seen in (1) a suspect part of *Pericles* and (2) a "bad" quarto.

My point is not that asides (in our sense) did not occur in

performances of Shakespeare's plays or those of his contemporaries (some of whom did use the term in a fashion readily recognized today).[14] The phenomenon (or something closely akin to it) did exist, but Shakespeare apparently did not use the term as part of his working vocabulary. What he (and some of his contemporaries) did use (in lieu of *aside*) varies.

As with many comparable situations, the norm in the early printed texts is silence, no signal whatsoever, even for what seem obvious *aside* situations (so that the implementation was left to the actor). Thus, speakers such as Aaron, Hamlet, and Iago (who seem masters of this mode of address) have no speeches specifically designated as asides.[15] Another such figure, Richard of Gloucester, also has plentiful aside situations in both *3 Henry VI* (e.g., 5.7.33–4) and *Richard III* (e.g., 3.1.79, 82–3), but only one such speech is singled out in any way. Thus, in *Richard III* the Folio (but not the Quarto) directs that for one speech Richard "*speaks to himself*" (1.3.317, TLN 792). A comparable locution turns up in *The Merchant of Venice*: "*A Song the whilst Bassanio comments on the caskets to himself*" (3.2.62, E4r). These two examples of "*to himself*" are from supposedly "good" texts (and correspond to locutions used by other dramatists as well).[16]

The evidence outside the Shakespeare canon is too diverse to be summed up neatly (and I have not attempted the daunting task of logging every aside in the period). For example, plentiful in Shakespeare and his contemporaries are directions for a figure to whisper, but such situations almost always involve not an aside but rather a conversation that is not heard by the playgoer.[17] Occasionally, insights into the delivery of some asides are provided by the reactions of other figures on stage. For example, in *Macbeth*, 1.3 the Folio designates no asides for Macbeth, so that the Pelican editor adds such signals for lines 116–17, 118–20 ("*Aside to Banquo*"), 127–9, 130–42, 146–7, and 153–5 (again, "*Aside to Banquo*"). During one such sequence Banquo tells Ross and Angus "Look how our partner's rapt" and "Worthy Macbeth, we stay upon your leisure" (142, 148), so in this instance Macbeth's detachment is noted, not concealed (and hence he may be distanced somehow from the other three onstage). Other moments can also be cited where someone onstage does not hear the content of an aside but is aware of the non-attention of the aside speaker.[18]

The term *aside* as used in stage directions of this period can therefore have at least three related yet discrete meanings:

[*to stand*] *aside* (or, as in Quarto *Love's Labor's Lost*, *a side*): to move to a side of the stage so as to observe other figures or carry on some surreptitious activity

[*to speak*] *aside* [*to X*]: to direct a speech so as to have it heard by another onstage figure and by the playgoer; usually to be distinguished from *whispers* [*to X*] wherein the speech is not heard by the playgoer

[*to speak*] *aside* [*to the playgoers*]: to direct a speech so as (somehow) to maintain the fiction that it cannot be heard by other onstage figures

Examples of all three situations are readily found in Shakespeare's plays, but I know of no convincing evidence that *aside* as denoting a spoken speech was indeed part of his working vocabulary.[19]

A second major problem linked to the aside (in any period of drama) arises from the *somehow* in option three above. Were the speeches spoken aside, whether to another onstage figure or to the audience, signaled by some physical action or spacing no longer evident today? Attempts to recover or approximate that original onstage delivery, in turn, can be compromised by today's assumptions about naturalism or verisimilitude. Thus, several scholars have challenged modern "realistic" assumptions about the aside. For example, Bernard Beckerman notes that "many asides give the actor neither time nor motivation for creating verisimilitude." Although readers often assume that, to deliver an aside, a Richard III or Hamlet must be distanced from the other figures on stage, Beckerman (drawing upon examples from *Pericles* and *Othello*) argues that "the Globe players, in the staging of asides, did not think in terms of creating an illusion of actuality but of relating the crucial elements of the narrative to each other."[20] Or, as Ernest L. Rhodes has noted, "the important thing was not the distance but the signal for the 'aside,' regardless of whether it was given by a movement on the stage, a gesture, by a special tone of the voice, or by all of these."[21] The modern sensibility may expect some visible separation between the speaker and potential listeners, but if the deliverer of the aside is close to the other actors, the emphasis may fall not upon his deceptive speaking but rather upon their faulty listening, an effect demonstrably present in many moral interludes and used adroitly for sardonic comic purposes repeatedly in *Volpone*. Is, then, the gap between aside speaker and potential listener verisimilar, conventional, or symbolic?

As noted by Beckerman and Rhodes, many asides even today can be delivered by an actor staying in place but somehow turning to the playgoers to signal such a special communication. To cite one suggestive example, the Folio version of *The Taming of the Shrew* provides no marked asides, but in the equivalent to 2.1 in the 1594 Quarto, *The Taming of a Shrew*, Kate protests to her father about the betrothal to her mad-cap wooer, but then "*she turns aside and speaks*," saying: "But yet I will consent and marry him" (B3r). To *turn aside* (as opposed to *stand aside* or *move aside*) could involve no more than a movement in place of head and body so as to provide a signal to the playgoer.

The reader or scholar who accepts the aside phenomenon (even though Shakespeare may not have used the term itself) and is aware of the choice between verisimilar and non-verisimilar delivery is still (despite the apparent simplicity of a dictionary entry) left with the problem of what is and is not to be labeled as an *aside* in a modern edition. E. A. J. Honigmann, for one, has argued: "Modern editions of Shakespeare contain many more asides than are found in the Folio and quartos, as often as not a legacy from eighteenth-century editors who maimed and deformed where they undertook to cure." Honigmann then uses examples from *1 Henry IV*, *Timon*, and *Hamlet* to argue shrewdly against the assumptions that lurk beneath many editorial choices. For example, he notes that by inserting *aside* an editor "often implies that the speaker would not have dared to utter the same words openly," but "if the situation includes an impudent speaker or an inattentive listener the case for an aside is weakened." Thus, for Honigmann Hamlet's "A little more than kin, and less than kind!" (1.2.65) "expresses the riddling impudence that is characteristic of all of his exchanges with Claudius before Act 5"; why then "assume that he would not have dared to speak out loud, and that the only alternative is an aside?" Another alternative is "that Hamlet, the arch-soliloquizer, not infrequently mutters to himself and cares not a rap whether or not others catch his words," but "such opportunities are lost if the editor prints '*aside*'."[22]

My own pet example is to be found at the end of the cauldron scene where Macbeth, although onstage with Lennox, devotes twelve lines (4.1.144–55) to his plans against the Macduffs and his innermost thoughts. Most editors treat this passage as an aside and have Macbeth address Lennox again only in the final line and a half of the scene – a choice that does work effectively in today's productions. But, as with Honigmann's Hamlet, Macbeth by this point may not care who knows what he is thinking or planning or, as an alternative, may be so rapt in his little world of man (as in 1.3) that he is momentarily unaware of Lennox's presence. As with Honigmann's examples, to mark this speech as an *aside* is to enforce upon the unsuspecting reader one choice at the expense of other equally interesting (and perhaps revealingly Jacobean) options.

To sum up the moral of this section: the dictionary entries for *aside* proposed at the outset and then subsequently refined can be useful and rewarding, especially for that reader unfamiliar with stage practice in general and Elizabethan stage practice in particular. But such neat on-the-page definitions do not stand up well against the varied evidence (e.g., Shakespeare's usage or non-usage of the term) or, equally telling, the lack of evidence. As to the latter, the many silences (especially in the Shakespeare quartos and Folio) lend special importance to the role of the editor whose often unstated sense of what is or is not an aside can condition the response of varied readers.

Another obstacle to a dictionary approach to Shakespeare's theatrical vocabulary is epitomized in Richard Hosley's distinction between *theatrical* and *fictional* signals. For Hosley, *theatrical* signals "usually refer not to dramatic fiction but rather to theatrical structure or equipment" (e.g., *within*, *at another door*, *a scaffold thrust out*), whereas *fictional* signals "usually refer not to theatrical structure or equipment but rather to dramatic fiction" (e.g., *on shipboard*, *within the prison*, *enter the town*).[23] The same onstage event can therefore be signaled by both *enter above* and *enter upon the walls* [of a city], with the second locution the "fictional" version of the first.

To see this distinction most clearly consider the extremes in each category. The most decidedly "theatrical" signals are practical in-the-tiring-house directions about properties and personnel. The left margin of the playhouse manuscript of Massinger's *Believe as You List* is unusually rich in such signals: "*Table ready: and six chairs to set out*" (654–6); "*the great book: of Accompt ready*" (982–4); "*Gascoine: and Hubert below: ready to open the Trap door for Mr Taylor*" (1825–31); "*Antiochus – ready: under the stage*" (1877–9); "*Harry: Wilson: and Boy ready for the song at the Arras*" (1968–71). Such practical stage directions survive in printed texts as well: "*two Torches ready*" (Fletcher, *Love's Cure*, VII, 205); "*Whil'st the Act plays, the Footstep, little Table, and Arras hung up for the Musicians*" (Massinger, *The City Madam*, 4.4.160.s.d).

At the other extreme are those "fictional" directions in which a dramatist slips into a narrative or descriptive style seemingly more suited to a reader facing a page than an actor on the stage. To read "*The Romans are beat back to their trenches*" (*Coriolanus*, 1.4.29.s.d.) is to conjure up a vivid image more appropriate to a cinematic battle scene than an onstage effect at the Globe. Some of these "fictional" signals show the dramatist thinking out loud in the process of writing (so that the details anticipate what will be evident in the forthcoming action): "*Parolles and Lafew stay behind, commenting of this wedding*" (*All's Well*, 2.3.182.s.d.); "*The King suddenly enters having determined what to do*" (Chapman, *Tragedy of Byron*, 4.2.164.s.d.); "*Enter two sergeants to arrest the scholar George Pyeboard*" (*The Puritan*, E1r); "*Enter two Intelligencers, discovering treason in the Courtier's words*" (Fletcher, *The Woman Hater*, X, 102). Such stage directions can be valuable insofar as they provide evidence about the dramatist's thought processes or his sense of the narrative, but often tell us little about what the playgoers saw.

Various complications can arise, however, when (as in *Much Ado*, 5.3) the interpreter cannot be certain if the signal is "theatrical" (and therefore calls for a significant property such as a tomb or a tree) or "fictional" (so that a sense of a tomb or forest is to be generated by means of language, hand-held properties, and appropriate actions in conjunction with the imagination of the playgoer). Chapter 9 will be devoted to the problems linked to one such stage direction: "*Romeo opens the tomb.*" To read such a signal as "fictional" as opposed to "theatrical" can yield a very different sense of the relationship between player and playgoer.

Such complications are further compounded by the presence in a wide range of stage directions (as will be documented in chapter 7) of an explicit or implicit *as* or *as if*. A seemingly straightforward "fictional" signal such as "*Enter Marius solus from the Numidian mountains, feeding on roots*" (Lodge, *Wounds of Civil War*, 1189–90) initially may appear to tell the story rather than provide a signal to an actor. Nonetheless, a starving Marius who has been alone in exile could enter "[*as if*] *from the Numidian mountains*" so that the actor will use "*feeding on roots*" (as in *Timon of Athens*), along with disheveled costume and hair, to signal his mental and physical state. Similarly: "*Enter Sanders' young son, and another boy coming from school*" (*A Warning for Fair Women*, F4r) may be merely a telling of the story, but, if construed as "[*as if*] *coming from school*," the two boys could be dressed in distinctive costumes and carrying books. Again: "*Enter old M. Chartly as new come out of the Country To inquire after his Son*" (Heywood, *The Wise Woman of Hogsdon*, V, 340) tells the mission of the old man in narrative terms but may also signal some "country" costume or other property (e.g., a staff, a basket). A "fictional" signal such as "*enter on the walls*" requires only that the figure enter *above* or *aloft*; other seemingly "fictional" signals (e.g., "*coming from school*") may in contrast convey some practical instructions albeit in an Elizabethan code or argot.

In this context, consider the most innocuous of terms, the preposition *to*, as used in scenes that depict an onstage council or parliament. Most of these scenes (as is typical for the period) merely call for a group of figures to *enter*. Some, however, follow the procedure found in 2 *Henry VI*, 3.1.0.s.d. where both the

Quarto (D3r) and the Folio (TLN 1292–4) have the king and his entourage enter "*to the Parliament.*" Similarly, at 3.4.0.s.d. Quarto *Richard III* (G1r) has "*Enter the Lords to Council,*" although the Folio (TLN 1964–6) has the same group enter "*at a Table.*"

Should an entrance "*to Council*" or "*to the Parliament*" be read as "fictional" (and hence a part of the narrative) or read as "theatrical" (and hence a coded instruction for a particular onstage effect)? In this instance, the latter option is supported by a few signals in which an implicit *as* [*if*] is made explicit, most notably in Folio *Richard II* where at 4.1.0.s.d. a group is directed: "*Enter as to the Parliament*" (TLN 1921). The *as*, however, is not to be found in Quarto *Richard II* ("*Enter Bullingbrook with the Lords to parliament*" – G4r). Compare as well Caesar's entrance "*with his Council of War*" (*Antony and Cleopatra*, 5.1.0.s.d., TLN 3108–9) and two Caroline signals: enter "*as at a council of war*" (Shirley, *The Cardinal*, 2.1.0.s.d.); "*Enter Lords as to Council*" (Denham, *The Sophy*, p. 18).

Other more explicit stage directions suggest how "*as to Council*" could be staged or conceived. As already noted, the Folio calls for the council figures in *Richard III*, 3.4 to enter "*at a Table*"; similarly, in Quarto *Othello* the Venetian council scene begins: "*Enter Duke and Senators, set at a Table with lights and Attendants*" (C1r, 1.3.0.s.d.). In *King John and Matilda* (2.4.0.s.d., p. 29) Davenport provides: "*A Chair of state discovered, Tables and Chairs responsible, a Guard making a lane,*" so that King John, Pandulph, and the lords "*enter between them*"; in a later scene, after "*A Table and Chairs set out,*" Davenport instructs: "*Sit to Council*" (3.4.0.s.d., p. 47). Even more elaborate is *Henry VIII*, 5.3.0.s.d. (TLN 3035–41): "*A council table brought in with chairs and stools, and placed under the state. Enter Lord Chancellor, places himself at the upper end of the table on the left hand, a seat being left void above him, as for Canterbury's seat.*" Five figures "*seat themselves in order on each side. Cromwell at lower end, as secretary*"; a few lines later "*Cranmer approaches the council table*" (5.3.7.s.d., TLN 3055).

The elaborate description of the council scene in *Henry VIII*, 5.3 is far removed from enter "*at a table*" or "*Sit to Council*" and even farther from "*Enter the Lords to Council,*" but all four signals can be encompassed within the simple "*enter to*..." formula. Again, today's reader is eavesdropping on a conversation carried out in an elliptical theatrical language that we only partly understand. Dealing with such ellipses will therefore be a continuing concern in this book.

The difficulty of distinguishing today between fictional and theatrical signals is one major source of confusion in recovering Shakespeare's theatrical vocabulary. A different yet related set of problems is generated by the scholar's inability to determine what in the original productions was presented in a verisimilar manner versus what was left to the imagination of the playgoer. Both in *Much Ado*, 5.3 (as noted in chapter 2) and *Romeo and Juliet*, 5.3 (to be discussed in chapter 9), the presence or absence of a significant verisimilar property to serve as "the tomb" or "the monument" can have major implications for the imagery and potential meanings of a given scene. As a result, in subsequent chapters I will focus upon such questions as: how much is required in the Elizabethan theatrical vocabulary to present a forest, a shop, a study, or a tomb? Wherein lies the evidence for such distinctive places or effects? What are the implications for interpretation today, especially if the interpreter takes seriously the possibility that many such effects were keyed to the imagination of the playgoer rather than to the skills of a property master?

A good illustration of both the kinds of evidence available and the difficulty of interpreting that evidence is provided by the problems linked to onstage trees. From the many comedies and romances for which "forest scenes" are essential to the narrative emerge few stage directions other than *enter*; the few detailed signals that do survive usually call for portable properties such as weapons or hunting horns and for items of costume (often green) associated with the hunt or the woods).[24] Occasionally, a generic signal *does* turn up, as with "*Enter Timon in the woods,*" "*Enter a Soldier in the woods, seeking Timon*" (*Timon of Athens*, 4.3.0.s.d., 5.3.0.s.d.), or "*Enter Albert in the woods*" (*The Hog Hath Lost His Pearl*, 1177); occasionally, a figure *is* discovered along with a stage property (presumably linked to the moss-bank noted in Henslowe's inventory): "*Curtains open, Robin Hood sleeps on a green bank, and Marian strewing flowers on him*" (Munday, *The Downfall of Robert Earl of Huntingdon*, 1490–1). But, as will be discussed in chapter 7, other signals clearly build upon the playgoer's imagination in the spirit of *as if*, as with "*Andrugio, as out of the woods, with Bow and Arrows, and a Cony at his girdle*" (Whetstone, *Promos and Cassandra*, K4r). What is not to be found in the extant printed texts and manuscripts, moreover, including those with playhouse annotations, is evidence for the introduction of property trees to convey a sense of "*in the woods*."

Given the few signals and the many silences, scholars have varied widely in their assessment of the presence and use of onstage trees. In the most extensive discussion of such scenes, Werner Habicht stresses the atmospheric advantages of trees and related effects, but in the process he assumes a great deal about what would have been visible (especially in Shakespeare's forest scenes) without offering any evidence other than the dialogue.[25] Similarly, in his edition of Lyly's plays Carter A. Daniel infers from the dialogue and plot of *Gallathea*: "The forest area of the stage must have been thickly wooded, since on six separate occasions characters hide on the stage and watch the actions of others, and the hiding places are referred to as 'thickets' or 'yonder woods'."[26] Many if not most of the scenes cited by both scholars could have been played with no visible trees. In contrast, Ernest Rhodes argues that property trees (rather than stage posts) would have been used "when the trees were thrust up through the trap, taken away through the trap, ... brought onto the stage, climbed, their fruit picked ... , or torn down and stripped of leaves," but with reference to less ambitious effects he concludes: "I am inclined to believe that when a stage post or a fictive tree could have served it did indeed serve."[27] In general, as Bernard Beckerman succinctly observes: "it is difficult to distinguish when prop trees are used and when stage posts."[28]

Evidence for the availability of such properties is firm; without doubt, Shakespeare and his contemporaries could if they desired bring property trees onto the stage (and Henslowe's inventory lists "1 bay tree," "1 tree of golden apples," and "Tantalus' tree").[29] In the actual extant stage directions, however, such trees are brought or raised onto the stage primarily in dumb shows and other moments that involve special, often spectacular effects rather than normal forest or woods scenes that are part of the flow of the play. For example: "*The Magi with their rods beat the ground, and from under the same riseth a brave Arbour*" (Lodge and Greene, *A Looking Glass for London and England*, 522–3); "*Hereupon did rise a Tree of gold laden with Diadems and Crowns of gold ... The Tree sinketh*" (Peele, *The Arraignment of Paris*, 456.s.d., 462.s.d.); "*Here Bungay conjures and the tree appears with the dragon shooting fire ... Here he begins to break the branches ... Exit the spirit with Vandermast and the Tree*" (Greene, *Friar Bacon and Friar Bungay*, 1197–8, 1214, 1280); "*Here the hind vanishes under the altar and in the place ascends a rose-tree, having one rose upon it*" (*The Two Noble Kinsmen*, 5.1.162.s.d.). In Dekker's *Old Fortunatus* Vice is to "*bring out a fair tree of Gold with apples on it*" and Virtue "*bring a tree with green and withered leaves mingled together, and little fruit on it*"; onstage figures then "*set the trees into the earth*" (1.3.0.s.d., 19.s.d.).[30]

At the other extreme from such clear use of property trees are the many situations in which the dialogue calls for a tree but a stage post would prove not only adequate but more efficient. Often the fictive situations have nothing to do with forests or green worlds. Rather, the "tree" is needed for some practical purpose as with: "hang him on this tree" (*Titus Andronicus*, 5.1.47, Marlowe, *The Massacre at Paris*, 496–7); "take the shadow of this tree" (*King Lear*, 5.2.1); or "as I did sleep under this yew tree here" (*Romeo*, 5.3.137). Various figures end up tied to a "tree" (e.g., in *Common Conditions*, Fletcher's *The Beggar's Bush* and *The Coxcomb*, and Shirley's *The Imposture*) where a stage post seems the obvious solution. In the playhouse manuscript of Munday's *John a Kent*: "*Enter Shrimp leading Oswen and Amery about the tree*" (1393); the emphasis, however, is not upon the tree but upon the weariness of the two figures controlled by magic ("were ever men thus led about a Tree? / still circling it, and never getting thence?" – 1394–5). To introduce and then take off a property tree for such moments would add little that would justify interrupting the flow of the play (and no such property is signaled in the playhouse book of *John a Kent*).

In between these two extremes are those scenes where a property tree could contribute some added punch but theatrical efficiency would nonetheless warrant use of the stage posts. Relevant here is a cluster of scenes in which a figure is directed to climb a tree (so again the reader must decide if such a signal is theatrical or fictional). A property tree certainly would enhance the effect in Marston's *The Fawn*: "*Whilst the act is a-playing, Hercules and Tiberio enter; Tiberio climbs the tree, and is received above by Dulcimel*" (5.1.0.s.d.); this tree, moreover, is referred to in subsequent dialogue. Most of these climbings, however, strike me as fictional rather than theatrical, hence readily accomplished by means of a scaling of a stage post (as I have seen actors do regularly on the Elizabethan stage of the Oregon Shakespeare Festival). For example, in Jonson's *The Case is Altered* to avoid an angry Jaques "*Onion gets up into a tree*" (4.8.1.s.d.); in *The Honest Lawyer* to play a trick: "*Enter Benjamin, Robin, Thirsty; Thirsty climbing up into a tree. Robin into a bush*" (12r). More elaborate is the sequence in Dekker's *If this be not a good play the devil is in it* where Scumbroth, following the words of a prophecy, finds the grove of Naples and, according to the dialogue, climbs the black tree ("here's a black tree too, but art thou he?" – 4.2.19); Lucifer enters with various devils ("This is the tree" – 35) and "*sits under the tree, all about him*" (53.s.d.); after the meeting, Lucifer commands: "This Yew-tree blast with your hot-scorching breath" (123), then "*Fireworks: Scumbroth falls*" (125.s.d.).

From this excursion into Elizabethan onstage trees emerge no definitive conclusions, no neat dictionary entries. Rather, each "tree scene" must be examined on its own merits, with the question in mind: would a property tree have been necessary or efficient? Or would the narrative have been served as well, even better by an effect linked to the imagination of the spectator in concert with the dialogue and a gesture from the actor towards a stage post? Given the presence of fictional stage directions, signals such as *climbs the tree* and *gets up into a tree* do *not* establish the presence of a special stage property and *can* be fulfilled by means of a stage post. Clearly, onstage trees could be used for special effects, but my sense is that in most instances the flow of the play took precedence (so that an introduction of such a property for minimal gain would be counterproductive). Not to take such "fictional" options into account is to run the risk of undermining some of the imaginative play of Elizabethan staging.

In conclusion, if the evidence were more plentiful and the problems fewer, a series of dictionary entries *would* be an excellent way to set forth the theatrical vocabulary of Shakespeare and his contemporaries. Such, however, is not the case. Rather, the problems generated by the aside, "*enter to the Parliament*," and trees are representative of the varied difficulties. The purpose of this chapter has therefore not been to confess defeat before the battle has even begun but to explain why a less definitive approach is the only responsible course. The terms may be elliptical and the silences many, but various options and potential meanings can be teased out, especially if a wide enough net is cast so as to collect evidence from as many sources as possible. The danger of imposing yet another fiction (linked to my own tastes or sense of theatre) upon the evidence is a real one, but the opportunity to fill in some of the silences and expand some of the ellipses is worth the risk and the effort.

CHAPTER 4

Juxtapositions

"What trust is in these times?"

2 Henry IV, 1.3.100

To move beyond dictionary entries is to enter an area where theatrical effects can be generated not only by means of dialogue, costumes, and properties but also through the placement of various elements. From a playgoer's (as opposed to a reader's) perspective, when something happens onstage can make a big difference, especially if the timing of an entrance or action sets up a visible irony or strong image. Such effects, linked to the placement rather than the content of the extant stage directions, deserve consideration in any attempt to recover Shakespeare's theatrical vocabulary.

In this context, consider a phenomenon that turns up regularly in Shakespeare's plays but, to my knowledge, has not been seen as a category or family (in part because most family members have been screened out of our editions and often are not even cited in the textual apparatus). Let me characterize the larger category as juxtaposition (or overlap) in that elements that today's interpreter on the page or in the theatre would prefer to be kept discrete are apparently juxtaposed so as to co-exist onstage at the same time. Some of these moments are so fleeting as to be negligible; some may be errors. Enough examples survive in the Shakespeare quartos and the Folio, however, to make the category worthy of investigation. A few, moreover, are meaty enough to warrant close attention.

"EARLY" ENTRANCES

As a point of departure, let me play the role of defense attorney for the family of "early" stage directions whose members (as with Malvolio's famous entrance cited in chapter 2) regularly disappear from today's editions and productions. Because these signals do not appear in the original quartos or Folio at precisely the point where today's editor or actor expects them, they are often repositioned. Such adjustments have been justified on several grounds: authorial, scribal, or compositorial error; the exigencies of a crowded page or passage in the original text; the size of the original stage that necessitated one or more lines of dialogue to cover the movement of an entering figure from an upstage door to the actors already downstage.

Although I find the latter explanation highly suspect (given the large number of "normal" entrances with no such allowances made), some oddly placed stage directions undoubtedly do result from errors or printing shop exigencies.[1] Others clearly are part of a purposeful strategy and therefore, not being troublesome or intrusive, survive in modern editions. For example, in *As You Like It*, Rosalind (along with Celia and Corin) enters at 3.5.7 (at the end of Silvius' speech that begins the scene) but does not speak until line 35, so that the playgoer sees her observe at length Phebe's disdain for Silvius and then erupt into almost thirty lines of berating the shepherdess. Few would disagree that this early entrance is necessary to generate Rosalind's subsequent speech.[2]

Several other early entrances have made sense to at least some editors and directors and have therefore not been totally ignored or suppressed. Perhaps the best-known example is to be found in *Romeo and Juliet*, 2.3, where the Second Quarto (E1r) directs Romeo to enter not at the end of Friar Laurence's thirty-line speech but after line 22 (Q1 supplies no entry at all).[3] To have Romeo enter just in time to deliver his first line in the scene ("Good morrow, father") may be a tidier solution (so some editors *have* repositioned the entry),[4] but various possibilities emerge if Romeo is onstage for lines 23–30. For example, a Romeo who hears the friar talking about the presence of both poison and medicine within the same flower may be more likely to think of such poison (and the apothecary) in 5.1. Moreover, a playgoer who sees Romeo appear and meanwhile listens to the friar may be more likely to make a connection between "this weak flower" (in line 23, juxtaposed with Romeo's appearance) and Romeo, so that the friar's subsequent analysis, that builds to a postulation of "grace and rude will" (28) encamped in all of us, is not understood solely in highly abstract terms but is linked to the key chooser in the tragedy. Whatever the interpretation, the juxtaposition and timing here can be highly suggestive to both the actor and the playgoer and can form a significant part of the onstage vocabulary of this scene.

The juxtapositions occasioned by early entrances can therefore serve a variety of purposes in the theatre. For example, after the angry departure of his nobles in 4.2, King John reacts in confusion for three lines, then turns to the messenger from France who has just arrived ("A fearful eye thou hast" – 106). The Folio's stage direction ("*Enter Mes.*"), however, is placed in the margin after the first line of John's speech (next to "I repent" – TLN 1821) rather than two lines later at TLN 1823 (where there is also plenty of space in the margin – so no compositorial exigencies are evident here). The two-line gap is small but theatrically suggestive, for the same John who before 4.2 had been one step ahead of everyone else now is so rapt in his own problems he does not initially see what the playgoer sees but rather is a beat behind.

The same effect is repeated a second time in this scene at the entrance of the Bastard with Peter of Pomfret. The Pelican editor, who keeps the Folio's early placement of the messenger's entry, moves the Bastard's entry so that it immediately precedes John's question directed at the entering figure ("Now, what says the world / To your proceedings?" – 132–3). The Folio, however, has the Bastard and the prophet enter a line and a half earlier (TLN 1851) before John's final comment to the messenger about the news from France ("Thou hast made me giddy / With these ill tidings" – 131–2). Again, the difference is small but suggestive, for in the Folio version of the scene John again (in his giddiness or disorientation) is a step behind the playgoer.

To reposition either or both stage directions makes the scene smoother, especially for the first-time reader, but at the expense of a revealing clue for the actor or the audience about John's state of mind.[5]

To bring entering figures on early in this fashion (especially twice within thirty lines) is potentially to provide an insight, however brief, into the onstage character (in this instance, John) who does not see them. As an alternative, particularly appropriate to comedy, someone can arrive early and be deliberately ignored by an onstage figure. For example, in *As You Like It*, 4.1 the Folio directs Orlando to enter not before his first line (TLN 1945) but rather at TLN 1941, before Rosalind's previous speech directed at Jaques ("And your experience makes you sad ..." – 24). Jaques immediately reacts to Orlando's first line in the scene ("Nay then, God b' wi' you, an you talk in blank verse" – 29–30), but Rosalind continues to address Jaques as "Monsieur Traveller" for another five lines, only turning to Orlando at line 35 (TLN 1953) with "Why, how now, Orlando, where have you been all this while? You a lover? An you serve me such another trick, never come in my sight more." Clearly, Orlando is close at hand (Jaques hears and sees him), but Rosalind chooses to ignore him for roughly ten lines. The early entrance sets up some rich comic possibilities for a Rosalind–Ganymede who is both disposing of Jaques and calculating how best to chide her tardy lover.

To continue with some uncontroversial cases,[6] Ganymede–Rosalind's early entrance in 5.2 (TLN 2421) comes not at the point Orlando notices him–her ("for look you, here comes my Rosalind" – 15–16) but at the beginning of that speech (before "You have my consent" – 13), so that the entering figure overhears Orlando bless his brother's wedding to Aliena, set the wedding date for tomorrow, and announce that he will invite the duke and his followers to the ceremony. Before Orlando addresses her, she therefore has a moment to react, perhaps to consider new tactics. Figures who enter a beat early can size up a situation before the onstage figures are aware of their presence – as perhaps also with LeBeau in 1.2 whose Folio re-entry is positioned not before his speech to Orlando ("Good sir ..." –

242) but two lines earlier, mid way in Orlando's four-line speech (so at TLN 426, before "O poor Orlando" – 240). LeBeau can therefore overhear Orlando's lament and, if not already committed, may in this brief space make a visible decision to help, just as Rosalind can visibly react to the prospect of an Oliver–Aliena marriage the next day. Such overlapping is in keeping with the spirit of such comedies and can generate interesting options for the actors. In these instances from *As You Like It*, moreover, an abundance of white space on the page precludes any argument in favor of compositorial exigency.

With only one exception (the messenger's entrance in *King John*, 4.2) the examples cited so far have not proven especially troublesome or controversial. Other early entrances, however, have been deemed unacceptable by a majority of editors. For example, near the end of the first Kate–Petruchio scene the Folio directs Baptista, Gremio, and Tranio to enter not at "Here comes your father" (2.1.281, TLN 1159) but three lines earlier (TLN 1155), just before "For I am he am born to tame you, Kate" (2.1.278). In this play and throughout the canon, a "here comes ..." line is normally preceded or followed by the appropriate stage direction, but exceptions such as this one test the rule. The scene *can* be played effectively with the signal as repositioned in six of the eleven editions I consulted (including Riverside, Arden, Cambridge, and New Penguin), but the earlier entry, especially if Petruchio is immediately aware of the observers, provides some rich comic possibilities. For example, the actor can change his tone and posture, visibly adjusting his role for the benefit of such an onstage audience. Or, to gain a broader effect, the three entering figures, fearful of Kate's wrath, may tiptoe onto the stage, setting up a decided contrast to Petruchio's bold lines.

For another provocative example from the comedies, consider two comparable group entrances (on facing pages of the Quarto) in *Much Ado About Nothing*, 5.1. On H4r can be seen the kind of situation modern readers expect or take for granted. After Borachio reveals the truth to Claudio and Don Pedro and after Dogberry specifies that he is an ass, Verges says: "Here, here comes Master Signior Leonato, and the sexton too"

(244–5). Just below this line the Quarto provides a centered stage direction: "*Enter Leonato, his brother, and the Sexton*," with Leonato immediately launching into a three-line speech ("Which is the villain? ..."). In this instance, "here comes ..." indicates just that – the entrance of the designated figures.

The signal for the entrance of the previous group, however, is much less tidy. After the exit of Benedick (who has challenged Claudio and, in turn, been twitted by his two "friends"), Don Pedro and Claudio devote roughly ten lines to a discussion of what has just transpired. To start the next beat, the Quarto provides a centered stage direction: "*Enter Constables, Conrade, and Borachio*" (H3V). What strikes readers of the Quarto as irregular, however, is that this signal does not come at the end of the ten lines and just before Dogberry's first speech ("Come you, sir. If justice cannot tame you ..." – 198) but rather appears two speeches earlier (roughly two thirds of the way through the Prince-Claudio dialogue) at line 193. This placement could be an error in the Quarto (or the manuscript that stands behind it); it does not appear to be the result of printing-shop exigencies. Moreover, the entrance of Leonato's group on the facing page (and comparable entrances elsewhere in this Quarto) follow normative usage.

In singling out this and comparable moments my purpose is not to advance any revolutionary claims but rather to suggest that the editor, critic, teacher, director, or actor should confront such a signal and ask of it the same questions that would be asked when faced with an apparently anomalous word, image, property, or stage configuration. In whatever terms seem relevant, can such an early entrance be construed as part of a theatrical vocabulary or strategy available in the 1590s? What (if anything) do we gain by taking such a phenomenon seriously?

In this instance, to ask such questions is to come up with some interesting answers, questions and answers that are eliminated when an editor repositions the stage direction (as in the Arden, pp. 200–1, and four other editions of the ten I consulted). Here in *Much Ado*, the scene is building to the comeuppance of the two supposedly superior, witty figures who are about to be punched in the stomach by Borachio's revelations. In particular, Don Pedro's arch line referring back to Benedick ("What a pretty thing man is when he goes in his doublet and hose and leaves off his wit!" – 5.1.192–3) gets an immediate response in the entrance of the two constables and two villains, although the effect is for the playgoer (who sees the four entering figures, and perhaps makes the ironic connection) rather than for Don Pedro and Claudio, who "see" nothing (and would the two men under arrest be clad only in doublet and hose?).[7] Those entering figures would then be there but unseen until Dogberry actually speaks so as to break into the awareness of the two (supposed) wits.

Although such an interpretation is speculative (the early entrance *could* be an error), nonetheless it *is* based upon the evidence that survives in the Quarto (and is often filtered out of modern editions). In terms of dramatic technique, how better set up for the playgoer the comic hubris of these two "superior" figures before their balloon is punctured? The pay-off would then come with (1) the Dogberry–Don Pedro exchange (one final bit of witty superiority); (2) Borachio's big speech ("What your wisdoms could not discover, these shallow fools have brought to light" – 221–2); and (3) Leonato's entrance and his emphasis upon "seeing" ("Which is the villain? Let me see his eyes, / That, when I note another man like him, / I may avoid him" – 246–8). In this interpretation, the early entrance becomes a provocative signal (a form of theatrical *italics*) that highlights "what a pretty thing man is when he goes in his doublet and hose and leaves off his wit" so as to provide a summary example of the fashion–wit emphasis that reverberates throughout the comedy. To smooth out what appears to be an irregularity in the Quarto (as in the Arden edition) may be to translate the scene into our idiom and, in the process, to stifle an interesting and potentially meaningful effect geared to the theatrical vocabulary of the 1590s.[8]

A similar anomaly turns up in *All's Well* where all entries are normal until the last scene when two early appearances occur. The second, Parolles' entry at TLN 2960, two lines before the king notices him, has posed few problems. More provocative is

Bertram's re-entrance (TLN 2869) three lines before the king addresses him, an entrance, moreover, placed somewhat awkwardly in the middle of the king's speech (immediately after "Go speedily, and bring again the count" – 5.3.152) even though it could just as easily have preceded the king's "I wonder, sir ..." (155) directed at Bertram. In decided contrast to Parolles' early entry (retained in all the editions I consulted), all nine editors reposition Bertram's re-entry, with eight of them placing it before "I wonder, sir" and Wells–Taylor locating it one line earlier.

If a production, then or now, follows the Folio placement, Bertram is onstage for the exchange between the king and the countess in which the former states "I am afeard the life of Helen, lady, / Was foully snatched" and the countess responds: "Now justice on the doers!" (153–4) The Pelican editor inserts "*Enter Bertram [guarded]*" after the countess's line, a change that smoothes the Folio sequence so as to conform to our sense of timing. If Bertram, however, is already onstage, perhaps in her sight as well as the playgoer's, the actress (or boy actor) playing the countess (who has only one remaining speech in the play – 195–9) has some rich options for the delivery of "Now justice on the doers!" For example, here is an opportunity for her, with a look or gesture, to make a public and highly visible choice of justice and Helena over her own son (should the suspicions about Helena's demise prove true).[9]

Such apparent anomalies that provide theatrical options or suggestive onstage configurations are not limited to the comedies. Consider a small but representative example from *1 Henry IV* where (in a scene to which few interpreters pay attention) the two suspicious carriers depart, leaving onstage a Gadshill who calls out: "What, ho! chamberlain!" (2.1.45), at which point the chamberlain enters in all ten editions I consulted. But in both Q0 and Q1 the centered s.d. "*Enter Chamberlain*" (C2v) not only precedes Gadshill's call but also precedes the *Exeunt* of the two carriers (placed to the right on the same line).

The difference is small but telling. Is the playgoer to see a Gadshill (whose ploy with the carriers has just failed) as one who calls forth an accomplice who then appears upon command

("At hand, quoth pickpurse" – 46) as in modern editions or is that playgoer to see a Gadshill who is a plotter-conniver visibly one-upped or surprised by his accomplice? In the scene as scripted in the Quarto Gadshill could be looking at the two figures exiting through one stage door while the chamberlain (seen only by the spectator) appears through the other and sneaks up behind him (thereby giving more punch to the chamberlain's first line – "At hand, quoth pickpurse"). Without straining the bounds of this less than consequential scene, an alert playgoer may recognize a paradigm of a would-be deceiver momentarily upstaged or discomfited by a colleague, a paradigm that could prepare for the tricks to be played upon Falstaff in 2.2 and 2.4 and perhaps even upon Hotspur in 5.2 (the manipulation of Hotspur by Worcester and others starts in the previous scene, 1.3). To reposition such signals in a modern edition is, in effect, to risk eliminating some of the punch of a scene few have troubled with in the first place. And, here as with other examples cited, such transpositions of the original signals are not deemed important enough to warrant citing in the textual notes of the Pelican edition.

Troilus and Cressida provides four such early entrances. The most provocative of the four, however, is rarely encountered by the reader unfamiliar with facsimiles of the original texts. Thus, in both the Quarto (D2V) and the Folio (TLN 1082–3) Cassandra erupts into the Trojan council scene ("*raving*" in the Quarto, "*with her hair about her ears*" in the Folio) *before* her first speech. Of the editions I have consulted, only the Signet keeps this Quarto–Folio placement. Rather, most readers of this scene will find "*within*" inserted before her first two speeches ("Cry, Troyans, cry!"; "Cry, Troyans!" – 2.2.97, 99) and her entrance moved so as to follow Hector's "It is Cassandra" (100) and precede her third speech.

All four examples from *Troilus* involve onstage figures seemingly unaware of the presence of someone seen by the playgoer,[10] but the placement of Cassandra's entrance raises some provocative questions. Should she be onstage or *within* for her first two cries?[11] To keep her offstage until her third speech may increase the scene's verisimilitude, for to many readers

Troilus' "I do know her voice" (98) suggests that he hears but does not see her. But, in defense of the Quarto–Folio choice, this play offers repeated examples of figures who cannot or do not see or hear what should be apparent to them. This scene in particular, with its exploration of the Trojan code of honor and value, develops at length the distinctive myopia linked to Troilus and Hector. Again, to delay Cassandra's entrance is to offer a smoother, less jolting experience for the reader or playgoer, but what if the placement of her appearance (in this instance, found in both Quarto *and* Folio) is a calculated effect designed to ensure that the playgoer cannot miss the faulty seeing of the Trojan council that here is deciding the fate of their city ("Troy burns, or else let Helen go" – 112)? What if Priam and his sons, facing us, do not deem it worth the effort to turn and look at this intruder who bears what *we* know to be a true vision of the fate of Troy, particularly if these figures in this scene decide to keep Helen? Cassandra's early presence strikes me as richly suggestive, both for 2.2 and for the play as a whole, to the extent that any tinkering with the original strategy needs more justification than an additional dollop of verisimilitude for some readers.

Two provocative examples turn up in *Coriolanus*. First, according to the Folio the first citizens to be confronted by the protagonist in the gown of humility scene enter not at "So, here comes a brace" (2.3.59), as printed in the Pelican, but rather a sentence earlier (TLN 1452), immediately after Menenius' exit and just before Coriolanus' parting shot at the exiting patrician: "Bid them wash their faces / And keep their teeth clean" (58–9). The two subsequent entries of citizens (TLN 1475, 1516) *are* noted immediately by Coriolanus but, at least in the Folio, he does not react initially to this first group. Should the entering citizens hear this line? Does the patrician war hero deliver his contemptuous comment even though aware that the plebeians might hear it? Here the Folio placement of the entry (retained by seven of the nine editions I consulted), even though only a line early, can provide a strong signal about the protagonist's distinctive pride or contempt.

A comparable effect is to be found in the Folio version of 3.2

(this time repositioned not only in the Pelican but in seven of nine editions) where Coriolanus and various "nobles" (figures usually cut in modern productions) are joined by his mother (TLN 2090) after his first speech and before the lord's "You do the nobler" (6). The son does not notice or address his mother for six lines (not until "I talk of you" – 13), but rather devotes that interim to musing why she does not approve of his disdain for the mob. As with many of my examples, the sequence is smoother in our terms if Volumnia appears just before she is noticed and addressed by her son (the option chosen in the Pelican), but consider the advantages, for both the actress and the playgoer, if she is in sight, presumably listening carefully to what he is saying. The Arden editor, who (along with Wells–Taylor) keeps the Folio placement, notes that "Volumnia apparently approaches in the course of Coriolanus' speech" (p. 217). Does this juxtaposition help us to understand better what happens in the remainder of this scene or in Volumnia's successful appeal to her son in 5.3? The emendation found in most editions may enhance verisimilitude but, here as in 2.3, perhaps at the expense of some insights into Coriolanus' pride or myopia or distinctive vision.

Although the scholarly literature devoted to the two versions of *King Lear* is already extensive, a few relevant examples are worth pursuing in this context, especially since several entries that are normal in the Quarto become, for whatever reason, early in the Folio. I will here avoid entanglement with various items that have already been discussed at length (e.g., Goneril's entrance in 2.4, the bringing on of Goneril and Regan's bodies in 5.3).[12] However, the re-entrance of Lear and Gloucester in 2.4 is a small but interesting discrepancy. The Quarto (E4r) has them come in just before Lear's speech ("Deny to speak with me?" – 84), but the Folio brings them in two lines earlier at the conclusion of the Fool's song (TLN 1358) so as to have the two old men onstage for "Where learned you this, fool?... Not i'th'stocks, fool" – 82–3). At the risk of being overly ingenious, I sense some ironic counterpointing in the Folio placement (as with the situation in *Much Ado*, 5.1). Would Lear or especially Gloucester (two "fools" who have yet to learn through suffering) react to the Fool's punch line? Could such a juxtaposition (retained only in the Bantam of nine editions consulted) heighten, in however small a fashion, such key terms as "fool" and "learn"?

A second Gloucester entrance is also changed in the Folio. Thus, in 3.4 the Quarto (G2V) directs him to enter just after the Fool calls attention to the torch-bearing figure ("Look, here comes a walking fire" – 107), but the Folio places "*Enter Gloucester, with a Torch*" (TLN 1890) four lines earlier, before the Fool's "prithee, nuncle" speech and just after Lear's "come, unbutton here" (103–4). In the Folio version (retained only by Alexander and Wells–Taylor) the playgoer presumably sees the torch-bearing figure before he is seen by the Fool, with Gloucester as a result in view during the Fool's comment: "Now a little fire in a wild field were like an old lecher's heart – a small spark, all the rest on's body cold" (105–7). An onstage Gloucester would enrich this speech and add to the fire–lechery–adultery emphasis that feeds into Lear's powerful speeches in 4.6.

The most provocative example, however, is to be found in a third Gloucester entrance, this time in 3.6. In the Quarto (G4V) Gloucester re-enters just before his speech ("Come hither, friend" – 84), but the Folio (TLN 2039) directs him to enter after Lear's "You will say they are Persian; but let them be changed" (78–9) and before Kent's "Now, good my lord" (80). In this version, Gloucester is onstage for three speeches, one of them by Lear ("Make no noise, make no noise; draw the curtains. / So, so. We'll go to supper i'th'morning" – 81–2), and then he *still* can ask: "Where is the King my master?" (84).

For obvious reasons, all nine editors I consulted (including Wells–Taylor in their edition of the Folio text) chose the Quarto placement for Gloucester's arrival, for, one immediately asks, how can he ask "Where is the King?" if he is present during Lear's two-line speech? But could the change (revision?) be a calculated effect, especially taking into account the two previous early entries for this same figure unique to the Folio? If played as scripted in this version, the playgoer sees a Gloucester present but not really seeing or hearing what is going on around him (as perhaps also true with his wandering with the torch in 3.4). Indeed, such an effect would be hard to miss (much like *Romeo*, 2.3), so could function as another example of theatrical *italics*. Is not the playgoer who is made aware of such myopia or not-seeing here better prepared for the blinding of this same figure in the next scene and his subsequent admission: "I stumbled when I saw" (4.1.19)? For all three moments but particularly for this one, the Quarto placement is more logical and less troubling, but are the seemingly illogical Folio changes perhaps *designed* to trouble or provoke us? What price logic or consistency? Are not such changes found in the Folio worthy of the same respect as other much discussed differences?[13]

Two particularly provocative early entrances are to be found in *Macbeth*.[14] Consider, as an analogy to Romeo's entrance well before the end of the friar's speech, the two appearances of the ghost in the banquet scene (3.4) – the first ten, the second four lines before the ghost's presence is noted by Macbeth. For several reasons (see the note on p. 94), the Arden editor, Kenneth Muir, delays the first entrance until after Macbeth's lines 40–1 ("Here had we now our country's honor roofed / Were the graced person of our Banquo present"); directors often, by sleight-of-hand, have the ghost already on stage, seated at the table. But in the Folio (with lots of white space on the page, so that no crowding is evident), "*Enter the Ghost of Banquo, and sits in Macbeth's place*" (TLN 1299) is placed after Lady Macbeth's speech ("My royal lord, / You do not give the cheer ..." – 32–7) and before Macbeth's "Sweet remembrancer." The second appearance ("*Enter Ghost*" – TLN 1363) in the Folio comes in the middle of Macbeth's speech ("I do forget ..." – 84–92), after "Give me some wine, fill full" and before "I drink to th' general joy o'th'whole table" (88–9), though the Arden editor moves it two lines later (after "Would he were here!").

As Muir notes (p. 94), editors have chosen various moments for the ghost's first appearance (in my sampling, seven of nine retained the Folio placement), but "the favourite place" (at least in terms of the entire editorial tradition) is after lines 40–1. Given this emendation (and the second later entrance also chosen in the Arden), both times "the Ghost appears when summoned" by Macbeth, a timing that produces a forceful dramatic irony. The Folio placement does not cancel this effect but does change it somewhat; at the least, in the Folio no such clear, insistent link exists between Macbeth's hypocritical mention of Banquo (twice) and the ghost's appearance. Rather, the earlier Folio arrival changes the scene for the playgoer, who (especially if he or she has not read the play) sees a bloody ghost with "gory locks" (51) enter, sit at the table, and yet be unseen by everyone, *including* Macbeth, for ten lines. Instead of the obvious irony in the Arden version (with a Macbeth unwittingly invoking this apparition), the Folio provides a growing theatrical tension as the playgoer waits to see who if anyone will "see" this figure. Initially, no one on stage "sees"; eventually, the figure with guilty knowledge of this murder does "see" (and is ultimately shattered by that sight). The issues hinted at in other early entrances are thereby (in the scene as a whole, not just in the initial appearance of the ghost) explored at length.

"LATE" *EXIT*S

To move from early entrances to "late" *exit*s (in which figures remain onstage longer than a reader today would deem appropriate) is to move onto even murkier terrain. In the "early" category, even after allowing for errors or sloppiness, enough examples have survived in the quartos and the Folio to warrant discussion; for several reasons, however, the "late" category is more problematic. First, *exit*s and *exeunt*s often go unmarked in early printed editions (one explanation is that actors may have needed signals telling them when to enter but, as professionals, required less instruction when to depart). As a result, even if such an effect *were* scripted, it often will be invisible to a reader of the quartos or the Folio. In addition, ambiguity or confusion can result when the distinction between *exit* and *exeunt* (or *manet* and *manent*) is not observed (as is often the case); for example, at the end of *As You Like It* the Folio supplies *exit*s for Jaques, Duke Senior, and Rosalind but no *exeunt* for the rest of the ensemble. As noted in chapter 3, moreover, many scenes end with a clearly marked *exeunt* but no *exit–exeunt* for one or more figures who have previously departed. Such an omission, in turn, leaves open the possibility that some final *exeunts* are on-the-page scene-ending devices that do not accurately reflect the actual staging of the scene. In short, the extant evidence is spotty.

Despite the omission of many *exits*, normative examples (that spell out a practice that makes immediate sense to us today) are readily at hand, particularly at the ends of scenes. For example, at the end of *1 Henry IV*, 5.4, Q1 provides an *Exeunt* for Princes Hal and John, then Falstaff's speech, then an *Exit* for Sir John (K4r); the end of Folio *Henry V*, 5.1 provides a series of *exits* for Fluellen, then Gower, then Pistol (TLN 2963, 2974, 2983); and *Coriolanus*, 4.2 has separate exits for the tribunes, Volumnia and Virgilia, and Menenius (TLN 2557, 2568, 2569).[15]

The silences (and potential anomalies), however, equal or out-number such normative examples. One recurring problem is found when a scene ends with a speech that seemingly should not be heard by some of the figures included in the final *exeunt*. For example, should Sir Oliver Martext's speech that ends *As You Like It*, 3.3 be understood as an *aside* (with Jaques, Touchstone, and Audrey still onstage) or as a comic speech addressed to the audience after a group *exeunt* (as in many modern editions)? Similarly, at the end of *Macbeth*, 5.3 should the Doctor's couplet be an *aside* with Macbeth still onstage or a speech directed at the playgoer after Macbeth has gone? Both scenes in the Folio end with an *exeunt*.

Some of the speakers in question are more complex than Martext and the doctor. For example, at the end of *1 Henry IV*, 4.2 would Falstaff have been alone onstage for his final speech ("Well, to the latter end of a fray and the beginning of a feast fits a dull fighter and a keen guest") or, as in Q1 (H3v), would Westmoreland still be present so that the two *exeunt* together? The editor who inserts an earlier *exit* for Westmoreland (so as to leave Falstaff alone onstage for his final lines) provides a smoother effect, but a different Falstaff will emerge if Westmoreland is still in view (perhaps visibly signaling his impatience), particularly if Falstaff's speech is not played as an *aside* but rather as a devil-may-care statement with no concern as to who may hear it. Such final speeches before an *exeunt* (see Brutus in 2.2, Iago in 5.1, Winchester in *1 Henry VI*, 5.1) may indeed have been *asides* (or, in Shakespeare's terms, speeches "*to himself*"), but (as argued in chapter 3) to adjust the original signals may be to translate the effect into our idiom.

More provocative than such brief closing speeches are the various early or mid scene situations where no exit is signaled so that a figure, although given nothing more to say in the scene, may have lingered for a few lines or a beat so as to set up some meaningful effect. As with the early entrances, here an Elizabethan sense of juxtaposition or counterpoint may collide with a later theatrical logic, so that what seems the "obvious" editorial or onstage choice today could block the interpreter from a valid and potentially interesting theatrical option. In such cases, the absence of a specified *exit* in the original printed edition may conceivably be deliberate rather than inadvertent, an openness that leaves some flex to the actor onstage.

Many of these situations (and there are quite a few) can be summed up by the question: what would happen if...? What would happen if Prince Hal did not depart after his final line in *1 Henry IV*, 5.1 ("Why, thou owest God a death" – 126 – no *exit* is specified in Q1) but stayed onstage to hear some of Falstaff's catechism on Honor? What would happen if Edmund remained onstage in *Lear*, 1.1 for much if not all of the king's confrontation with his daughters, Kent, and the two suitors? What would happen in *2 Henry VI*, 5.1 if the recently knighted Alexander Iden (perhaps still carrying Jack Cade's head) remained onstage to witness the confrontation between the king and York? What would happen in *Measure for Measure*, 4.3 if Isabella did not exit at line 155 (as in the Pelican) after Lucio's second speech (no such *exit* is designated in the Folio) but rather stayed onstage to overhear the exchange between Lucio and friar Lodowick about the duke?[16]

Although rarely acknowledged in today's editions, some of these late or delayed departures *have* been incorporated into recent productions. In *Twelfth Night*, Olivia, anxious for a private interview with Cesario, orders Sir Toby, Sir Andrew, and Maria to "leave me to my hearing" (3.1.89–90), but the Folio provides no *exeunt*. Moments later, Aguecheek tells Toby that he saw Olivia "do more favors to the Count's servingman than ever she bestowed upon me. I saw't i' th'orchard" (3.2.4–6). Directors often have Sir Andrew linger a bit before exiting in 3.1 so as to witness some such interaction. Similarly, *Much Ado* Q1 provides no marked *exeunt* for Claudio, Don Pedro, and Don John after the breaking off of the marriage in 4.1. The Pelican editor is typical in inserting such an *exeunt* after John's last speech (109–10), but directors sometimes have Claudio linger so as to hear Beatrice's "dead, I think" (111) and then be pulled offstage by his two companions (a choice that can soften somewhat the image of a heartless Claudio).[17]

The most suggestive example involves Jaques as voyeur. In 3.2 in our editions, Jaques is directed to *exit* either after his final line ("I'll tarry no longer with you. Farewell, good Signior Love" – 278–9) or during Orlando's parting shot ("I am glad of your departure. Adieu, good Monsieur Melancholy" – 280–1), but, given the absence of a specific signal in the Folio, he could equally well stay on to overhear some of the Ganymede–Orlando exchange (and thereby set up the beginning of 4.1 where he seeks to be better acquainted with this youth). Again, in 4.1 Jaques is usually directed to depart after his final line directed at the entering Orlando ("Nay then, God b' wi' you, and you talk in blank verse" – 28–9) or after some or all of Rosalind's critique of "Monsieur Traveller" (30–4), but again, given the absence of any Folio signal, he could also linger to eavesdrop upon some of the Orlando–Ganymede exchange that follows.

The situation in 4.1, moreover, is complicated by several other factors. As noted at the outset of this chapter, Orlando's "early" entrance in the Folio (TLN 1941) sets up an onstage figure not acknowledged initially and not addressed by Rosalind for more than ten lines. Keeping Jaques onstage for another beat, also unacknowledged, would therefore be less of an anomaly and, indeed, could set up a parallel configuration with Orlando first observing Ganymede–Jaques and then Jaques, however briefly, observing Ganymede–Orlando. In 3.3, moreover, Jaques is directed to enter along with Touchstone and Audrey (3.3.0.s.d) and is therefore a voyeur for most of the scene until he steps forth (63) to "give" Audrey in marriage. If Jaques's exits in 3.2 and 4.1 are even slightly delayed, this voyeur status is acted out in three scenes, not one. That status as onstage audience–observer, moreover, is set up by the first account of Jaques (the description in 2.1 of how he moralized the spectacle of the wounded deer), furthered in his initial onstage appearance when he listens to the stanzos in 2.5, and reinforced at the end of that scene if the playgoer sees a detached Jaques watching Amiens deliver the *ducdame* verse (the singer or speaker of this last verse is not specified in the Folio). Such a sequence of observer–voyeur moments could then have an interesting pay-off in the final scene, particularly during the Hymen sequence (when Jaques is silent).

OVERLAPPING IMAGES

The resistance by both editors and theatrical professionals to what may be early entrances and late departures in the early printed texts acts out a desire to keep elements discrete that may have been designed to overlap in the original performances. As part of an Elizabethan theatrical vocabulary, such moments could have been highly visible and potentially meaningful (especially as part of a series – as perhaps with Jaques as voyeur). A few more distinctive moments remain to be cited – although, again, the evidence is anything but firm about the original staging.

In several instances, a potentially meaningful image may have been generated by leaving onstage a distinctive property. For example, what happens to the "*burden of wood*" (2.2.0.s.d.) that Caliban brings in before he meets Trinculo and Stephano? At the end of this scene, Caliban rebels against Prospero's authority so is unlikely to carry the wood off with him. Admittedly, he could throw his logs into an open trap or through a stage door, but in the next scene Miranda, referring to the log Ferdinand has brought in ("*Enter Ferdinand, bearing a log*" – 3.1.0.s.d.), says "Pray give me that: / I'll carry it to the pile" (24–5). Could "the pile" be onstage here and throughout the play? Or could Caliban's wood remain in view (as an act of defiance against Prospero) until the end of the final scene? What kind of "image" emerges when the interpreter today confronts rather than sidesteps this possible anomaly?

Similarly, in the climactic sequence of *Macbeth*, what happens to the boughs from Birnam Wood ("*Enter ... with boughs*" – 5.6.0.s.d.) that Malcolm orders to be discarded ("Your leavy screens throw down / And show like those you are" – 5.6.1–2)? Those boughs *could* have been thrown down eight lines later at the end of this brief scene or could have been thrown down at line 2, then subsequently picked up and carried off (a staging that seems to me awkward and redundant). Given, however, the possibility of overlapping images, the boughs could also have been deposited on the stage at the moment of the command (for me, the simplest interpretation) so as to remain in view for the rest of the action.

Would such a continuing presence then have been a meaningful signifier in that shared theatrical vocabulary? For example, what would be the impact upon a playgoer's sense of an ending if some kind of "greenery" is juxtaposed with Macbeth's encounters with young Siward and Macduff, then the awarding of the crown to Malcolm? Certainly, this climax is far removed from the "green world" of comedy-romance, but the emphasis upon barrenness and sterility is *very* strong throughout this script (especially in Macbeth's "My way of life / Is fall'n into the sear" – 5.3.22–3). Would onstage boughs juxtaposed with Macbeth's final moments underscore that gap between his Scotland and what has long been missing (see 3.6.32–6, much of 4.3, and 5.2.25–9)? Or would a playgoer see this greenery, now dead, as a discarded ploy, an *abuse* of nature by Malcolm (so his version of tumbling nature's germens)?

For a comparable overlapping property in a climactic sequence consider the possible presence of a scroll containing Hero's epitaph not only in the penultimate "monument" scene of *Much Ado* (5.3) but in the final scene as well. As noted in chapter 2, if the "monument" is a physical structure that is introduced for one scene and then removed, no such overlapping occurs. But if the "tomb" is instead represented by a stage post in conjunction with the imagination of the playgoer, the scroll could stay in view during the final moments placed in "Leonato's house" (a locale defined by the dialogue, the indoor clothing, and the figures present rather than by furniture or hangings). The presence of such a scroll (associated with Hero's "death") could then affect a playgoer's understanding of the climactic exchanges in 5.4, especially such lines as: "One Hero died defiled; but I do live"; "The former Hero! Hero that is dead!"; and "She died, my lord, but whiles her slander lived" (5.4.63, 65–6). Such a visible scroll would also provide added context for the papers written by Beatrice and Benedick that Hero and Claudio bring in as evidence.

Consider as well the practical theatrical problem of what to do with a corpse. In some instances, the early texts do provide specific signals for the disposition of bodies (e.g., with Hotspur, Polonius, Hamlet, and Enobarbus), but the usual situation is silence. The richest example arises from the choice of how or when to dispose of the onstage corpse of Sir Walter Blunt in *1 Henry IV*. With more fights to follow, today's director prefers to clear the stage so as to have more free space and to minimize the risk to combatants. Editors or readers can ignore the problem or, in response to the silence in the Quarto, can add their own signals after the last mention of the body. For example, editors since the eighteenth century have designated a scene division (signaled by a typographical break and other on-the-page conventions) after Falstaff's final lines on Blunt's "grinning honor" (5.3.57–60) and sometimes have inserted a stage direction such as "*Exit* [*with Blunt's body*]." But what happens if the interpreter follows the Quarto and keeps Blunt onstage, in full view, for the remainder of the play?

If Falstaff closes the visor on the dead figure's helmet, what the playgoer would see is a corpse "semblably furnished like the king himself" (5.3.21) and therefore indistinguishable from Henry IV (who soon appears to fight with Douglas). How then will that playgoer view the moments that follow, especially

Prince Hal's epitaphs over Hotspur and Falstaff, if such an "image" of a counterfeit king remains onstage? What would be the effect upon Falstaff's disquisition on Hotspur's body in which he uses the term *counterfeit* nine times? Since the Quarto provides neither evidence for Blunt's continued presence nor a signal for his removal, the editor or critic cannot be certain of the body's presence or absence, so what could be a highly visible and meaningful "image" is very much in doubt.

I cannot prove that Blunt's body remained onstage in full view after Falstaff's speech and presumed *exit*. Perhaps the point about counterfeit kings and "a borrowed title hast thou bought too dear" (5.3.23) has already been made. Perhaps the body *would* have been lugged off by Falstaff so as not to get in the way of the combats that involve first Henry IV, Douglas, and Prince Hal, then Hal, Hotspur, Douglas, and Falstaff. But if a counterfeit version of Henry IV indistinguishable from the real thing does remain in view, various lines and moments would have more resonance and impact. Indeed, the "image" could emerge as one of the most striking in the play.

A comparable situation is generated in the final sequence of *Macbeth* if young Siward's body remains in sight during much or all of the subsequent action, for, as Homer Swander argues, "through the presence of a corpse, the staged events are alive with new possibilities." For example, Swander would have Macduff recognize and even cradle the body in 5.7 and would have Macbeth sneer at his handiwork in 5.8.2–3. In this staging, the curious "*Exeunt fighting*" (5.8.34.s.d.) momentarily takes offstage Macbeth and Macduff but leaves "the body cruelly and imaginatively prominent" so that "the space will be filled with Macbeth's last inhuman act." Swander concludes: "The absence of an exit for the body is a defining richness; and editors who – whether in a note or a stage direction – provide an exit are using their editorial power to shut off areas that profit from being open to exploration."[18]

As with early entrances and late departures, my goal is not to defend any particular interpretation but rather to provide examples that can suggest the availability of an onstage signifier easily screened out today. Do we have room in our theatrical vocabulary or our sense of what "works" onstage for Caliban's wood, Hero's scroll, the Birnam boughs, or the bodies of Blunt and young Siward as a continuing presence or "image"?[19]

Some students of Elizabethan stage directions will balk at my defense of these apparent juxtapositions. For example, E. A. J. Honigmann argues that, since the Elizabethans were "careless about such matters," editors should be "free to standardise" early or late entries, especially those linked to "see where he comes" signals where the placement of the stage direction may vary before or after the spoken line. He notes that "editors usually prefer to leave well alone," but "by moving a stage direction a line or two we can quite often improve the sense or stage-effect, and so we must ask ourselves whether there is any real need to follow the first quarto or Folio."[20] Honigmann's preference for more rather than less intervention is therefore based upon his perception of Elizabethan carelessness and his sense, given today's greater editorial rigor, of an opportunity for improvement.

Honigmann is surely correct that in many respects the Elizabethans were far more casual than today's editor, so that, in all of my examples, authorial, scribal, or compositorial error cannot be ruled out. Moreover, as Honigmann and others will note, an obvious pitfall in my line of argument is that interpretative ingenuity may elevate authorial errors or printing shop exigencies into meaningful, significant signals. I have therefore spared the reader various suspect examples (e.g., a possible patterned sequence of early entrances linked to Henry IV) and have refrained from arguing that every juxtaposition once unearthed is a gem that has too long been ignored or suppressed.

But Honigmann's arguments and the working practice of many editors raise some troubling questions about the tangled links between editing and interpretation. In Honigmann's terms, at what point does appropriate intervention (to "improve the sense or stage-effect") end and translation or re-scripting begin? If (as I prefer to assume) Shakespeare and his colleagues knew what they were doing in theatrical terms, what is the price tag for "improvement" or standardization by a scholar who, although an expert on matters bibliographical and compositorial, may or may not be in tune with the logic of today's theatre, much less the onstage vocabulary of the 1590s or early 1600s? I agree that "we must ask ourselves whether there is any real need to follow the first quarto or Folio" (reason not the need?), but my own response can best be summed up in the vernacular: "If it ain't broke, don't fix it."

In the face of such editorial doubts and strictures, to pull together an array of early entrances, delayed departures, and juxtaposed images can serve various useful purposes. In particular, editors who focus solely upon one play (and therefore encounter at most one or two such anomalies) may dismiss such phenomena as a rarely seen aberration rather than as a possible recurring feature or meaningful technique. For example, despite Alfred Harbage's fine overall plan for the Pelican series, such repositioning of stage directions is *not* deemed worthy of inclusion in the textual notes (as opposed to David Bevington's Bantam Shakespeare where such transpositions *are* cited). To treat these moments as a family, a larger genus (in a fashion analogous to the comparative approach practiced by philologists and iconographers), is to take them seriously enough so as to view them as a potential part of that theatrical vocabulary shared by playwright, players, and playgoers in the age of Shakespeare. After all, how many times must a phenomenon recur before it ceases to be "accidental"?[21]

As I argue throughout this book, the scholar seeking to recover Elizabethan staging cannot afford to ignore the effects signaled by the stage directions in the early printed texts (our only plentiful evidence), especially (1) those effects that recur in a range of plays (my categories or families) and (2) those effects that strain our sense of verisimilitude or timing so as (perhaps) to open up a window into what was distinctively Elizabethan. Therefore, despite Honigmann's reasoned argument, wherein lies the logic for changing any feature found sporadically but nonetheless regularly in the quartos and the Folio if some, even most of these items *do* make theatrical and imagistic sense (at least in terms of the onstage logic in the age of Shakespeare)? To focus upon various juxtapositions is (perhaps) to find evidence for an onstage practice that, however, can easily be screened out by the editorial filter and by consistent relocation of some stage directions.

For me, at the root of this and related problems lies the issue of *trust*. Despite all the lip-service (Macbeth calls it "mouth honor") awarded Shakespeare's expertise, to what extent do editors, scholars, directors, and teachers *really* trust the surviving theatrical (as opposed to literary or poetic) signals *and* the dramaturgy that stands behind them? Given the many historicisms abroad in the land, which version of *Much Ado*, *Macbeth*, or *As You Like It* should serve as the basis for analysis and exploration? "What trust is in these times?" (*2 Henry IV*, 1.3.100).

CHAPTER 5

Theatrical *italics*

"*The Drawer stands amazed, not knowing which way to go*"
1 Henry IV, 2.4.76.s.d.

Evidence from the Shakespeare quartos and First Folio suggests the possibility of various forms of onstage juxtaposition, ranging from the early entrances of a Dogberry or Cassandra to the continued presence of a Jaques or Sir Walter Blunt. The resistance to such a practice today by editors, critics, and theatrical professionals acts out a dismissal of a phenomenon that seemingly defies "common sense" but a phenomenon that may equally well signal a gap between the theatrical vocabulary shared then and what is assumed today (or, in some instances, what has been assumed since the eighteenth century). By one set of yardsticks, such juxtapositions can be intrusive and therefore distracting, troubling. But what if such a technique is part of a theatrical strategy designed to highlight a figure or situation so as to make it unmissable? How would (or should) such a strategy predicated upon *italicized* signifiers in their theatrical vocabulary affect interpretation today?

Such questions are part of a larger set of problems (in the broad category of "validity in interpretation") that continue to bedevil literary theorists. To cite one recent formulation, Paul Armstrong posits: "Endless variety is possible in interpretation, but tests for validity can still judge some readings to be more plausible than others." As a pluralist who nonetheless believes in literary criticism as a rational enterprise, Armstrong proposes three such yardsticks for the validity of any interpretation: *inclusiveness*, *intersubjectivity*, and *efficacy*. For *inclusiveness*, he argues that "a hypothesis becomes more secure as it demonstrates its ability to account for parts without encountering anomaly and to undergo refinements and extensions without being abandoned." Although "as a normative ideal, or principle of correctness," this yardstick by itself may be useless, it can still be valuable "in that it can exclude bad guesses." As to *intersubjectivity* (linked to persuasiveness): "our reading becomes more credible if others assent to it or at least regard it as reasonable," while "the disagreement of others may be a signal that our interpretation is invalid because unshareable." By this criterion, "the ultimate indication" of correctness would be "universal agreement." To invoke *efficacy* is to see whether or not in pragmatic terms an interpretation "has the power to lead to new discoveries and continued comprehension," for "the presuppositions on which any hermeneutic takes its stand are not immune from practical testing" but "must continually justify themselves by their efficacy." If such presuppositions "repeatedly fail to lead to persuasive, inclusive readings, friends as well as foes may conclude that the problem lies not with the limited skills of the method's adherents but with its assumptions."[1]

To apply Armstrong's arguments and distinctions to the many warring approaches to Shakespeare's plays is a daunting task far beyond my province. In terms of recovering a lost or blurred theatrical vocabulary, however, is it possible to single out signifiers or techniques that would make it likely that a given interpretation does or could "work" – whether for a putative playgoer in the 1590s or a playgoer today? To respond to such a question, let me focus upon some onstage moments that not only stand out as noteworthy but actually cry out for interpretation – much like a trumpet or drum roll that in effect says "look at me!" As already noted, my term for such moments or images is *theatrical italics* in that they underscore some effect so as to ensure that a moderately attentive playgoer will recognize that *some*thing of importance is happening. Interpretations of such a moment may vary (in the spirit of Armstrong's pluralism), but, in keeping with his *inclusiveness*, a reading of that play should *some*how incorporate such an italicized moment – at least to be persuasive (or intersubjective) to me. My use of *should* invites a Coriolanus-like rebuke to a "Triton of the minnows" (I claim no moral or legal authority for such a stipulation), but in the search for yardsticks to judge or screen interpretations (or for solid building blocks to create interpretations) I have found few comparable tools that satisfy me.[2]

To apply my yardstick or tool, however, is by no means easy, for (as noted repeatedly in this book) many roadblocks prevent today's interpreter from seeing various theatrical effects that would have been obvious to Shakespeare's playgoers. First, given the paucity of stage directions in the original printed texts, the eye of a reader can readily slide over what may have been far more striking to a playgoer. Given various kinds of intervention, moreover, that reader who confronts today's editorial text rather than the original Quarto or Folio version may be spared exposure to such anomalies, just as today's playgoer watching a production may be screened from moments that a director deems unsuitable to our theatrical vocabulary. Since we lack a videotape of the Globe production (and are far removed from their culture and theatrical practice), to determine what was subtle versus what was obvious in *their* terms, in *their* productions, is no easy matter (and may at times be impossible).

Nonetheless (as seen with some of my juxtapositions), even on the page some images or moments do seem to stand out, to the extent that editors and directors regularly deem them "unrealistic" or offensive and therefore resist them, adapt them, or eliminate them. Here then is promising raw material for this category. What I am proposing, in part, is the converse of what I take to be one common interpretative procedure – to start with an agenda or interpretation and then find ways to realize it. Rather, I am suggesting that interpreters start with odd or extreme moments, assume they are especially noticeable *because* they seem so strident, and then build an interpretation upon them. Again, the apparent anomalies that do not fit "our" ways of thinking or problem-solving often can serve as windows into distinctive Elizabethan–Jacobean procedures. Not all such obvious moments or images are controversial or underinterpreted (e.g., few would disagree that the conjunction of the beautiful Titania and an ass-headed Bottom is both obvious and at the heart of that comedy), but what about equally visible moments that have received little attention or have been altered or suppressed? My goal is not to argue in favor of one obligatory reading based upon such italicized images but rather (in the spirit of Armstrong's *inclusiveness* and *intersubjectivity*) to question interpretations that do not in some way take into account what most would agree to be an unmissable, unforgettable moment in a given play.

As a point of departure, consider the practical joke played upon Francis the drawer by Prince Hal at the outset of the famous tavern scene in *1 Henry IV*. Whether owing to a sense of dramatic economy or a distaste for such pranks, this moment is often cut in performance (as in the television production for the BBC's "The Shakespeare Plays"). Nonetheless, the sequence has received its share of commentary, with the focus often upon Francis as an index to the prince's own uneasiness about his truancy or apprenticeship.[3] Indeed, once attended to, this sequence can generate a variety of questions, a situation reinforced when Poins himself asks: "But hark ye; what cunning match have you made with this jest of the drawer? Come, what's the issue?" (2.4.86–8)

What most concerns me here, however, is the stage direction at what I take to be the climax of the trick: "*Here they both call him. The Drawer stands amazed, not knowing which way to go*" (2.4.76.s.d.). Whatever the interpretation, should not the interpreter somehow build upon or take very seriously this highly visible onstage image? For example, what if the frenzied movement of Francis (as he responds alternatively to Poins's offstage calls and the prince's onstage questions) that climaxes in this amazed state would have strongly echoed onstage activity already seen (e.g., of Hotspur in the previous scene) or soon to be seen (e.g., of Falstaff confronted with the truth about his flight at Gadshill)? As I understand the scene, Shakespeare is here setting up for the playgoer a paradigm of the controller and the controlled, the puppetmaster and the puppet, so as to encourage us to recognize what makes Hal so distinctive. That interpretation may or may not satisfy other readers or viewers,[4] but the episode, especially the theatrical punch line signaled in the stage direction, cries out for *some* kind of explanation (as signaled also by Poins's question).

A similar effect is generated by Romeo's attempted suicide in 3.3 where the supposed "good" Quarto of 1599 provides no stage direction, but the "bad" Quarto of 1597 (perhaps based upon an actor's memory of some production) provides: "*He offers to stab himself, and Nurse snatches the dagger away*" (G1v). Some editors incorporate the Q1 signal into their texts, but New Arden editor Brian Gibbons rejects the Nurse's intervention as "neither necessary or defensible." Rather, for this editor "this piece of business looks like a gratuitous and distracting bid on the part of the actor in the unauthorized version to claim extra attention to himself when the audience should be concentrating on Romeo and the Friar" (p. 180). In the Arden edition the Nurse's intervention is therefore relegated to the textual notes and footnotes.

But, as with other possible examples of theatrical *italics*, what if the strategy behind Q1's stage direction is to call attention not to the actor but to the onstage configuration (as with the amazed paralysis of Francis the drawer), a configuration that in turn epitomizes images and motifs enunciated in the dialogue? After Mercutio's death, Romeo had cried out: "O sweet Juliet, / Thy beauty hath made me effeminate / And in my temper soft'ned valor's steel" (3.1.111–13). Then, after Romeo's aborted attempt at suicide, the Friar's long moralization starts:

Hold thy desperate hand.
Art thou a man? Thy form cries out thou art;
Thy tears are womanish, thy wild acts denote
The unreasonable fury of a beast.
Unseemly woman in a seeming man!
And ill-beseeming beast in seeming both! (3.3.108–13)

The playgoer who sees Romeo's self-destructive violence interrupted (surprisingly) by the Nurse and then hears the Friar's terms (e.g., "Art thou a man?"; "Thy tears are womanish"; "Unseemly woman in a seeming man") is therefore encouraged to consider: what kind of "man" *is* Romeo at this point in the play? What by one kind of interpretative logic may seem "gratuitous and distracting" or "out of character" or "unbelievable" may, in the terms of a different logic or vocabulary, prove imagistically or symbolically consistent or meaningful. Indeed, how better act out the ascendancy of the "womanish" or unmanly side of Romeo and call that ascendancy to the attention of a first-time playgoer?

For a third example, consider the context of one of the most famous moments in Shakespeare, Macbeth's "to-morrow, and to-morrow, and to-morrow." Seven lines into the scene a stage direction calls for "*a cry within of women*" (5.5.7), at which point Macbeth asks "What is that noise?" and Seyton responds: "It is the cry of women, my good lord." After a short speech ("I have supped full with horrors") Macbeth asks again: "Wherefore was that cry?" to which Seyton responds: "The Queen, my lord, is dead" (15–16), a revelation that elicits the famous speech. The Folio, however, provides no exit and re-entry for Seyton between his two lines, so the only authoritative text gives no indication how he finds out that the queen is dead. Editors therefore insert an exit for Seyton after his first line and an entrance before his second; a director may have Seyton *exit* or may have him send off a lesser functionary who then returns or may have Seyton walk to a stage door, confer with someone offstage, and return to Macbeth. If the playgoer is to understand that Lady Macbeth has died at the moment of the cry, the announcer of the news presumably must have some means of learning the news; our logic of interpretation or theatrical vocabulary therefore requires an exit or some comparable means of getting that news on stage.

But, again, can today's interpreter conceive of the scene as scripted in the Folio? Macbeth would ask his first question ("What is that noise?") and get the answer ("It is the cry of women"). No one then leaves the stage; Seyton remains by his side. After his ruminations about fears and horrors, Macbeth asks again: "Wherefore was that cry?" and Seyton responds: "The Queen, my lord, is dead." In this literal rendition of the Folio, the playgoer cannot help seeing that Seyton (to be pronounced *Satan*?) has no normal (earthly?) way of knowing what he knows. But he *does* know. Macbeth may be too preoccupied to notice the anomaly, but, if staged this way, the playgoer cannot help being jarred. Indeed, the anomaly then becomes a major part of the context for the nihilistic comments that follow. Such a staging (which adds nothing but rather takes the Folio at face value) strikes me as eerie, powerful, perhaps quite unnerving. A focus upon *how* Seyton knows of the death almost inevitably leads to the addition of stage business that can provide a practical explanation for that "how," but such literal-mindedness may lead to a masking of a truly distinctive Jacobean effect linked to a mystery behind that "how" and may erase today what would have been italicized then.

Such italicized moments can be especially visible in Shakespeare's earliest and least admired plays where such effects are less likely to be screened from view by the poetry or fully realized personae. Let me start with three of the many moments in *Titus Andronicus* that have troubled readers, editors, and playgoers and therefore have often been blurred or eliminated. First, consider the *exeunt* near the end of 3.1 that includes not only Titus, Marcus, and the armless, tongueless Lavinia but also the heads of Quintus and Martius and the severed hand of Titus. The Quarto provides no stage direction here, but the now one-handed Titus stipulates how each exiting figure is to handle an appropriate object:

Come, brother, take a head;
And in this hand the other will I bear.
And, Lavinia, thou shalt be employed in these arms:
Bear thou my hand, sweet wench, between thy teeth.
(3.1.279–82)

This passage has proved *very* troublesome for editors and directors. Although only one word changes in the Folio (*Armes* becomes *things* – TLN 1430), some editors (most recently Stanley Wells and Gary Taylor in their Oxford edition) have emended line 282 so as to eliminate the hand-in-mouth reference.[5] Readers of an unemended scene may ignore these lines, but directors, unwilling to risk an audience's reaction to the image of Lavinia exiting with the hand like a puppy carrying off its master's slippers, either cut the text or bring on young Lucius to help with the items to be carried.

But consider the *assets* of such an italicized moment. Given the heavy emphasis up to this point upon murder, rape, and dismemberment, how better act out the violation of the personal, family and political body than to have severed heads carried in the hands of the two old men and the warrior's severed hand carried off in the mouth of the violated woman? How better express the Andronici as prey to the wilderness of tigers or the chaotic disorder of the body politic or the failure of traditional norms? In Armstrong's terms, to build an interpretation upon such a strident, evocative onstage image is efficacious and intersubjective. Not to take this *exeunt* into account is to violate the yardstick of inclusiveness and, as with Francis, Romeo-Nurse, and Seyton-Macbeth, to sidestep what many would agree to be an especially noticeable, perhaps unforgettable moment.[6]

Consider next the appearance of Tamora, Chiron, and Demetrius in 5.2 disguised as Revenge, Rapine, and Murder. This lapse into allegory or near allegory poses particular problems in a modern production. The route taken by most actors and directors is to assume a mad or nearly mad Titus and a Tamora so confident in that madness that she is willing to take on a disguise that clearly would not "work" for a sane figure. To enhance the credibility of the moment, today's director will resort to a darkened stage (to heighten the possibility of concealment), heavy make-up, and some kind of outlandish disguise for the three figures so as to diminish Tamora's (and Shakespeare's) apparently anomalous choice of Revenge as a persona for this interview.

But much of the point of the moment as scripted lies not in Tamora's attitude to disguise or Titus' presumed madness (issues crucial to a twentieth-century theatrical vocabulary) but in the "image" of Revenge set up for the playgoer. What Shakespeare provides, at least in 1590s terms, is an individual (here Tamora) who for a moment "becomes" Revenge, a process certainly not irrelevant to Titus himself (whether mad or not) in the last two scenes of this revenge tragedy. Given the fact that in *The Spanish Tragedy* Revenge appears with Don Andrea at the outset and remains onstage throughout the remainder of the play, the presence of a figure of "Revenge" in the "real world" of Titus' Rome was at least possible in the theatre of the early 1590s. Our dominant mode of psychological realism (would such a "character" say or do X in this situation?) does not mesh comfortably with a figure posing as Revenge, even if that pose is to deceive a supposedly deranged figure with "miserable, mad, mistaking eyes" (5.2.66). But given the theatrical vocabulary available in the 1590s, Shakespeare may have had more rather than fewer options than a dramatist confined to "realism."[7]

What then are the assets of having this visible epitome of Revenge announce that she has been "sent from th' infernal kingdom / To ease the gnawing vulture of thy mind / By working wreakful vengeance on thy foes" (5.2.30–2)? Of particular interest here is her demand: "Come down and welcome me to this world's light" and, a few lines later, "come down and welcome me" (33, 43). Here, in a simple yet highly emphatic fashion, Titus' acquiescence to Tamora–Revenge's twice repeated "come down" clearly brings him from some removed position above to her level below. Such a movement downward is characteristic of many Revenge plays (whether that "below" is conceived of as Hell or as subterranean psychological forces) and, moreover, is set up forcefully in this play in the arrow-shooting scene where Publius brings word to Titus that Justice is not available (being employed "with Jove in heaven, or somewhere else") "but Pluto sends you word / If you will have Revenge from hell, you shall." Titus responds that Jove "doth me wrong to feed me with delays"; rather, "I'll dive into the burning lake below, / And pull her out of Acheron by the heels" (4.3.37–44).[8] Titus in 5.2 can therefore act out his literal and figurative descent to the level of Revenge, a descent that, by the end of the scene, yields the bloodiest moment in a bloody play and leads to the ultimate in revenge, the Thyestean banquet of 5.3.

To focus upon Tamora's overconfidence and Titus' madness (or upon darkness and a well crafted disguise), then, is to provide a workable scene in terms that make sense to playgoers today but to diminish the full range of the original effect. The acting out of Revenge as a force that can take over an individual, along with the descent of the title figure to the level of that Revenge, has a stark power and elegant simplicity that anticipates and feeds into the events of the final scene. Like the 3.1 *exeunt* with two heads and a hand, such an italicized effect generates fruitful questions and insights (in keeping with Armstrong's *efficacy*).

As a third example from this early tragedy, consider the signal for Titus to appear "*like a cook, placing the dishes*" (5.3.25.s.d.), an odd costume immediately called to our attention by Saturninus' question: "Why art thou thus attired, Andronicus?" Titus' answer ("Because I would be sure to have all well / To entertain your highness and your Empress") has not satisfied subsequent theatrical professionals, so that today's productions often do not present here a decidedly different image of the revenger. For the original audience, moreover, such a costume (along with "*placing the dishes*") would have served as part of a theatrical shorthand to denote the "place" (a banquet room) and would have suggested (wrongly) a subservient Titus debasing himself in degree in order best to serve his emperor and empress.

But to ignore this distinctive costume (or to play it for laughs – as in the 1987–88 Royal Shakespeare Company production) may be to blur a climactic image that brings into focus various motifs in the play linked to appetites, feeding, and revenge. Thus, the Folio stage direction for 3.2 indicates "*a banquet*" (TLN 1451), but Titus opens that scene with the order: "So, so, now sit; and look you eat no more / Than will preserve just so much strength in us / As will revenge these bitter woes of ours" (1–3). By the end of the play, however, revenge has become linked not to abstinence but to feeding and appetite, usually in dangerous or self-destructive terms. For example, in her overconfident claims to Saturninus, Tamora promises to "enchant the old Andronicus / With words more sweet, and yet more dangerous, / Than baits to fish or honeystalks to sheep"; the fish, she notes, "is wounded with the bait," and the sheep "rotted with delicious feed" (4.4.88–92). The most potent orchestration of "appetite" or feeding is found in Titus' long speech at the end of 5.2 where the revenger first torments the muted Chiron and

Demetrius with a detailed account of what he is going to do to or with them (e.g., "I will grind your bones to dust, / And with your blood and it I'll make a paste"), then promises to "make two pasties of your shameful heads," and finally announces that he will "bid that strumpet, your unhallowed dam, / Like to the earth, swallow her own increase" (186–91). After his command that Lavinia "receive the blood" and a second reference to paste and heads, Titus "*cuts their throats*" and announces "I'll play the cook" so as "to make this banquet, which I wish may prove / More stern and bloody than the Centaurs' feast."

When Titus enters to set up the banquet in 5.3 (with or without a cook's costume), the spectator is therefore well prepared. The savage ironies in his lines, moreover, are anything but subtle: starting with "although the cheer be poor, / 'Twill fill your stomachs; please you eat of it" (5.3.28–9); building to "Will't please you eat? will't please your highness feed?" (54); and climaxing, in response to the emperor's command to fetch Chiron and Demetrius: "Why, there they are, both baked in this pie, / Whereof their mother daintily hath fed, / Eating the flesh that she herself hath bred" (60–2). Indeed, these lines and the overall effect have seemed excessive to many directors and readers.

But what would have been the effect if Titus *does* appear "*like a cook*" (as predicted in the closing lines of 5.2) and, in this odd costume, does call emphatic attention to his culinary role as he hovers around the banqueters? In imagistic terms, what has so far been primarily verbal or aural (animals "rotted with delicious feed") now is being displayed visually, not only in the pasties being consumed by Tamora and others but also in the purveyor of such delicacies, Titus, who sets up the feeding of (and himself feeds upon) his enemies so as to become a visible part of the appetitive revenge process (just as Tamora had "become" Revenge in 5.2). The image of the revenger as cook builds upon what has gone before and, especially as *italicized* here by both the costume and Saturninus' question, brings to a climax the feed-and-be-fed-upon imagery earlier linked to the hunt and to the "wilderness of tigers" (3.1.54), a wilderness in which *both* families have now become prey. The same man who in 3.2 had urged his family to refrain from eating now sets up the meal for others and feeds upon his revenge. Moreover, if Aaron or Tamora's body is placed in the trap door, this cook–revenger has generated a feast that parallels and supersedes the "detested, dark, blood-drinking pit" and "fell devouring receptacle" (2.3.224, 235) that had claimed Bassianus, Quintus, and Martius. In short, at the climax of this revenge process, "*Titus like a cook*" makes very good sense indeed.

Much of the effect of such italicized moments (whether the *exeunt* with heads and hand, Tamora as Revenge, or Titus as cook) lies in their surprise value or initial illogic, a surprise that is designed to call attention to that moment and, ideally, to tease the playgoer into thought, into making connections. That effect, however, can be undermined, even eliminated entirely, if a subsequent interpreter on the stage or on the page resists such images or such logic of illogic, so that a provocative signpost (at least for the 1590s) is then lost. In such cases, to de-italicize is to diminish the range of possibilities, to weaken the signals, so as to preserve a post-1590s sense of decorum or verisimilitude, principles Shakespeare was aware of but was willing to strain, even violate, to gain his effects.

As a comparable example from another early Shakespeare play consider *1 Henry VI* where, at the nadir of her fortunes just before her capture by York, Joan la Pucelle appeals for help to a group of onstage "*Fiends*" (5.3.7.s.d.), but in response these fiends, according to the Folio stage directions, "*walk, and speak not,*" "*hang their heads,*" "*shake their heads,*" and finally "*depart*" (s.d.s at 12, 17, 19, 23). This exchange has not fared well on the page or on the stage, for to deal with this script is inevitably to run afoul of this scene and this appeal–rejection that in several ways tests the notions of today's interpreters. The Folio's call for fiends and for specific reactions is unusually clear (and presumably would have posed few problems in the 1590s for playgoers attuned to *Doctor Faustus*), but Elizabethan onstage presentation of the supernatural repeatedly strains "our" paradigms of credibility (and canons of taste), with this moment (along with the apparitions in the cauldron scene of *Macbeth*) a particular challenge.

Directors have therefore tinkered with the Folio signals. In Jane Howell's rendition for television, Joan speaks her lines while staring at the camera so that no supernatural entities are in sight to walk, refuse to speak, hang their heads, and eventually depart. In Adrian Noble's ninety-minute Royal Shakespeare Company rendition of Part 1 (1987–88), various onstage corpses from the previous battle rose as if animated to provide an onstage audience, but without the reactions to Joan's pleas specified in the Folio. In the Terry Hands 1977–78 Royal Shakespeare Company production, amid the onstage cannons that dominated the battlefield set Joan offered herself to the fiends who appeared suddenly "looking like gas-masked soldiers from the French trenches of the First World War."[9] In contrast, in his ninety-minute English Shakespeare Company production Michael Bogdanov cut the fiends and altered the text, so that, alone on stage and looking at the audience, Joan directed her appeal not to any diabolic entities but rather to the Virgin Mary, a change that eliminated any infernal climax for this sequence.

For generations idealizers of Shakespeare, who have been embarrassed by this play and especially offended by the chauvinistic depiction of St. Joan, have had great difficulty coming to grips with this moment.[10] Such reactions are revealing, for even to a casual reader the interaction between Joan and the fiends leaps off the page in vivid (and to many, offensive) fashion. What then are the advantages of singling out this moment as theatrical *italics*?

As one possible answer, consider Joan and her devils not as a one-shot effect but as the climactic example of a larger progression of images and moments that starts in Act 2. From her first appearance Joan has claimed supernatural powers (see 1.2.72–92), a claim tested in the first meeting between Joan and Talbot that results in a stand-off; still, Joan scorns his strength (1.5.15) and leads her troops to victory at Orleans. Moments later, Talbot, aided by Bedford and Burgundy, scales the walls and regains the town, so that a united English force wins back what had just been lost. The three leaders working together therefore accomplish what Talbot, facing Joan alone, could not.

Shakespeare then provides a gloss on both this victory and the larger problem of unity–disunity by means of Talbot's interview with the Countess of Auvergne. Her trap for Talbot fails, as he points out, because she has only caught "Talbot's shadow," not his substance. The set of terms is repeated throughout the remainder of the scene (e.g., "No, no, I am but shadow of myself. / You are deceived, my substance is not here") and is explained by the appearance of his soldiers, at which point he points out: "Are you now persuaded / That Talbot is but a shadow of himself? / These are his substance, sinews, arms, and strength, / With which he yoketh your rebellious necks..." (2.3.46–66). The individual standing alone, no matter how heroic (one thinks of Coriolanus), is but a shadow without the substance of his supporters, his army, his country.[11]

This play, however (as two generations of critics have reminded us), is about division, not unity, a division that has already been displayed in the split between Winchester and Gloucester and widens in the Temple Garden scene (that immediately follows Talbot's lecture to the countess), with its symbolic plucking of red and white roses. The figures who had joined Talbot in the victory at Orleans, moreover, soon disappear (Bedford dies, Burgundy changes sides). Factionalism thrives, to the extent that the division between York and Somerset (unhistorically) undoes Talbot himself who, in the terms of 2.3, is denied his substance and must face death (along with his son) as a shadow of his heroic self. Sir William Lucy's listing of Talbot's titles (4.7.60–71) can then be mocked by Joan as "a silly stately style indeed," for "Him that thou magnifi'st with these titles, / Stinking and flyblown lies here at our feet" (72, 75–6).

Joan's scene with her devils then follows less than a hundred lines after her exchange with Lucy. With the French forces fleeing the conquering York, all Joan can do is call upon her "speedy helpers" or "familiar spirits" to help with their "accustomed diligence," but neither the offer of her blood, with which she has fed them in the past, a member lopped off, her body, or even her soul will gain the needed support. She therefore concludes: "My ancient incantations are too weak, /

And hell too strong for me to buckle with. / Now, France, thy glory droopeth to the dust" (5.3.1–29).

No one makes grandiose claims for the imagery of this sprawling play. But a verbal patterning involving shadow and substance is clearly set forth in Act 2 (and echoed thereafter – as in Alencon's speech 5.4.133–7); moreover, Talbot eventually falls (and France ultimately is lost to England) because of divisions whereby "substance" is denied and the hero must stand alone as shadow of himself. In her scene with the fiends, Joan too is deserted, denied by those who formerly supported her. Like Talbot, her heroic status cannot exist alone, so she becomes a mere shepherd's daughter, not the figure who raised the siege at Orleans and was a match for Talbot in battle. The denial by the fiends is here equivalent to the squabble between York and Somerset that undoes Talbot, a link that (as with Francis the drawer and Hotspur or Falstaff) can be reinforced through the staging. For example, what if the fiends' scripted reactions to Joan's offer echo similar walking apart, hanging and shaking of heads, and departures by York and Somerset in 4.3–4.4 in response to Lucy's pleas in behalf of Talbot? If so, the playgoer would see two or three parallel failures by first Lucy and then Joan, rejections that visibly set up the deaths of the two previously unbeatable or "heroic" figures. Just as Lucy fails to get the necessary support, a failure that means Talbot must give way to the new factions, so Joan fails to get the support she too desperately needs and must give way to the third Frenchwoman, Margaret (who appears immediately upon Joan's exit with York). However interpreted in theological or political terms, these highly visible fiends can function as part of an ongoing pattern of images or configurations linked to the central themes of the play.

These italicized moments from two early Shakespeare plays (scripts not prized for their complexity or artistry) call attention to themselves and in the process call attention to major thematic or imagistic strands. All four therefore function not as ends in themselves but as indices to a larger network, a network whose presence is heightened by the theatrical italicizing of these images. Such a technique, needless to say, need not be limited to plays from the outset of Shakespeare's career. For some provocative examples, let me now turn to several juxtapositions not pursued in chapter 4.

Consider first the question (that turns out to be much trickier than it sounds): when should Macbeth appear on the stage after the murder of Duncan (that occurs between 2.1 and 2.2)? The Pelican editor, like most modern editors, places Macbeth's first line in the scene ("Who's there? What, ho?" – 2.2.8) "[*within*]" and then places the stage direction "*Enter Macbeth*" so as to break line 13, the end of Lady Macbeth's second speech (so after "... I had done't" and before "My husband!"). The Folio, however, provides a centered "*Enter Macbeth*" at line 8 (TLN 657) after Lady Macbeth's initial speech and before Macbeth's first line in the scene ("Who's there? what hoa?").

Although I have not done an exhaustive search, I have yet to find a modern edition that follows the Folio here. As with the placing of Cassandra *within* in the Trojan council scene (or the repositioning of Gloucester's entrance in 3.6 of the Folio *Lear*), note the logic of verisimilitude at work. How are we to imagine a Macbeth onstage but not noticed by his wife for five lines? In the frenzied dialogue that follows, moreover, she asks "Did you not speak?" and he queries in response "As I descended?" so that Macbeth's earlier half-line ("Who's there? ...") can, by this logic, be envisaged as part of an offstage sequence (or onstage in a production with a visible staircase) before his actual entrance signaled by "My husband!" (in the Folio, "My Husband?"). In modern productions, the playgoer often sees Lady Macbeth below and Macbeth above, backing out of Duncan's chamber, then either descending in our sight or reappearing below at the point marked in modern editions when she first sees him. Such an emendation or adjustment seems to fit with the dialogue ("As I descended?") and avoid any awkwardness with Lady Macbeth not seeing her husband for five lines. The Folio, in this instance, is deemed wrong – in a matter of relatively minor consequence.

But, as suggested in chapter 4, the theatrical vocabulary of the 1590s and early 1600s may have included signifiers linked to onstage figures limited in their ability to "see" important things around them. One possible way to signal or heighten such "not-seeing" (as with Claudio–Don Pedro and Dogberry, Gadshill and the chamberlain, the Trojan council and Cassandra, or Macbeth and the ghost) is to use an early stage direction so as to have entering figures onstage (and seen by the playgoer) before those already onstage are aware of their presence. To change the placement of Macbeth's entrance in 2.2 is to produce a much tidier scene, but what about the potential losses? What happens when we stage or imagine the scene as scripted in the Folio?

In practical theatrical terms, the Folio scene can be staged with the two figures facing in opposite directions and therefore backing into each other so as to produce a jolt that fits well with the tensions of the moment. But in terms of my emphasis upon "not-seeing," consider as well the related problem (rarely cited by editors and never, to my knowledge, linked to the early entrance): why does it take so long for Lady Macbeth to notice the bloody daggers (not until line 47), even though Macbeth says "This is a sorry sight" as early as line 20, presumably referring to his bloody hands holding the daggers, and also refers to "these hangman's hands" in line 27? Admittedly, the daggers can be covered (as in the 1988–89 Royal Shakespeare Company production) or somehow hidden – again to satisfy the logic of verisimilitude – but if the daggers were visible to the playgoer but, for some time, were not seen by Lady Macbeth that playgoer witnessed not one but two striking examples of "not-seeing" in the Folio version of this scene. Remember, in a famous speech at the end of the previous scene, Macbeth had seen and described a dagger that was not there: "There's no such thing. / It is the bloody business which informs / Thus to mine eyes" (2.1.47–9). In contrast, for a stretch of time in 2.2, Lady Macbeth does *not* see two bloody daggers that *are* there.

As already noted, an editor or a director can readily "solve" this problem, but what then is the price tag for such a "solution"? If twice in this short sequence Lady Macbeth does not see something that *is* there to be seen by the playgoer (first Macbeth, then the daggers), especially after the dagger speech of 2.1, what kind of "image" or effect is being set up or italicized? Given such a staging of the Folio signals, is not an audience better prepared for the sleep-walking (and her seeing or imagining there) or for the banquet scene when no one but Macbeth sees the ghost? Even here, playgoers may emerge from the Folio version with a different understanding of her "A little water clears us of this deed. / How easy is it then!" if, *twice*, she has *not* seen something they *have* seen. The scene and the tragedy as a whole are about darkness and blindness in various senses, so what happens if the editor, critic, or director trusts the Folio version that, in a curious but potentially telling fashion, italicizes (in symbolic or metaphoric terms) just such darkness and blindness? To filter out this effect is to produce a much tidier scene, especially in terms of verisimilitude, but, in doing so, an interpreter risks translating a rich moment into our (less metaphorical, less symbolic) theatrical language and losing something significant in the process.

An equally provocative juxtaposition is to be found in *As You Like It* where editors and critics continue to puzzle over Duke Senior's "banquet" that, according to the dialogue, is set up on stage in 2.5 (see lines 26–7, 55–6) and then enjoyed in 2.7 with no indication that it is removed for the brief 2.6 (the first appearance of Orlando and Adam in Arden). After reviewing various options (e.g., use of an "inner stage," transposition of scenes) the New Variorum editor (Richard Knowles) concludes: "the early setting of the table seems to me thoroughly puzzling; it is totally unnecessary, for the banquet could have been carried on, as banquets usually were, at the beginning of scene 7" (p. 109). Directors have therefore developed their own strategies for dealing with this anomaly: some transpose 2.5 and 2.6; some cut the offending lines in 2.5 so that the banquet first appears in 2.7; some play the Folio lines and sequence but darken the stage so that neither Orlando or the playgoer can "see" the banquet during 2.6.

As most editors and critics would agree, Shakespeare did not *have* to introduce a banquet into 2.5. Yet he *did*. The result, moreover, is a clear example of the kind of simultaneous staging often found in earlier English drama that yields for the playgoer a strong sense of overlapping images comparable to that produced by early entrances, by late departures, and by bodies, scrolls, or leavy screens not removed from the stage.[12] What then are the advantages of having such a banquet in full view during the speeches that constitute 2.6?

As one possible answer, consider how the presence of such food affects our reaction to Adam's "O, I die for food" and Orlando's subsequent "if" clauses: "If this uncouth forest yield anything savage, I will either be food for it or bring it for food to thee ... I will here be with thee presently, and if I bring thee not something to eat, I will give thee leave to die; but if thou diest before I come, thou art a mocker of my labor ... thou shalt not die for lack of a dinner if there live anything in this desert." What is the effect of such speeches if the food Orlando eventually finds in 2.7 is indeed visible to us while we are hearing these words? What seems anomalous or unrealistic to a reader nurtured upon our theatrical idiom could, in their vocabulary, be one of the striking moments or images in the show (as perhaps with Francis's amazed state, the *exeunt* of the Andronici, Joan and the fiends, or Macbeth's early appearance) if the playgoer somehow gains from the juxtaposition an understanding of the distinctive nature of Arden (to be discussed further in chapter 8). To what extent has our sense of "forest" or our resistance to simultaneous staging eclipsed a major signifier in Shakespeare's theatrical vocabulary?

Here, moreover, is where a modern sense of variable lighting and "design" becomes especially important. If interpreters can transcend their theatrical reflexes, they may be able to imagine a Forest of Arden in this instance defined not by onstage greenery but by the presence of food in the background while two figures are starving. Through such juxtapositional staging or signifying, that sense of an option available to be exercised or a potential there (under the right circumstances) to be fulfilled could emerge as the point of the sequence and a major building block for the final three acts. A director in a modern theatre who does introduce the banquet in 2.5 and does not remove it during 2.6 may still be tempted to darken part of the stage and highlight Orlando and Adam, but in a 1590s theatre where that option was *not* available (and where controlling the playgoer's sense of events by means of variable lighting was impossible), the rationale behind this moment and its potential richness – in their terms – could (perhaps) be realized.

The same is true in *King Lear* where, at the end of 2.2, Kent is left alone in the stocks, Edgar enters for a speech of twenty-one lines, and, after his departure, Lear and his group arrive to find Kent. As with my other examples, this sequence has puzzled modern critics, editors, and directors who worry about "where" Edgar is to be "placed." In our vocabulary, the presence of the stocks and the recently completed action involving Oswald, Edmund, Cornwall, and others imply one locale (the courtyard of a castle), but that "place" proves incompatible with a fleeing Edgar (especially given a lapse of time and the pursuit through open country implied in an escape by means of "the happy hollow of a tree" – 2.3.2). Editors therefore create a separate scene for Edgar's speech (2.3) and often provide a heading such as "the open country" or "a wood"; directors usually use a lighting change to black out Kent and highlight Edgar during his speech. Clearly, most interpreters would prefer not to have Kent and Edgar visible at the same time.

If Kent is eclipsed by modern lighting, neither Edgar nor the playgoer is conscious of the figure in the stocks (who also has lost his identity and been subjected to injustice). But what about the original production at the Globe where the King's Men had no way to black out Kent? Can the interpreter today at least entertain the possibility that Shakespeare, surveying the various options, *chose* to have these two figures visible simultaneously, not only making no effort to hide the juxtaposition but indeed encouraging a staging that would *italicize* it? On the unencumbered Globe stage with few distractions for the playgoer's eye, such a choice would yield a highly emphatic effect that would strongly enforce any interpretation based upon links between Kent and Edgar – again a form of theatrical *italics* that an attentive viewer would find hard to miss. The original audience would not have been troubled by the imaginary darkness in which Edgar failed to see Kent; indeed, Edgar's stage behavior in itself could have been a major signal for the existence of onstage night. The stocks would then signal not a courtyard or other specific public locale but rather a general sense of imprisonment or bondage (as in such moral plays as *The Interlude of Youth* and *Hickscorner*) or the perversion of an instrument of justice (as developed more fully, again with Cornwall and Regan, when Gloucester is bound to a chair in 3.7), just as Edgar would be assumed to be in flight, anywhere. The chameleon-like flexibility of the open stage here makes possible a juxtaposition rich with potential meanings, a juxtaposition that can easily be blurred or lost (as with *Macbeth*, 2.2 and *As You Like It*, 2.6) when an interpreter translates the scene into our theatrical vocabulary.

Such italicized juxtapositions and configurations that generate fruitful questions for the playgoer recur throughout the Shakespeare canon.[13] In keeping with Armstrong's yardsticks, my purpose in singling out such moments and patterns is to isolate various hit-the-playgoer-over-the-head stage effects that would have been difficult to miss in the original productions but can readily be blurred or lost today. Such a gulf between what was obvious then but can be invisible now raises some troubling questions. What if, as part of an overall strategy, Shakespeare and his fellow players chose to *italicize* X but editors, directors, or critics today ignore or filter out that choice? What is the effect of such filtering upon our interpretations? Given the language barrier that separates us from the 1590s and early 1600s, how are we to recognize when their emphases or theatrical vocabulary diverge significantly from ours (so that a drum-roll or look-at-me effect can be ignored or eclipsed)? Most troubling to me (as one sympathetic to various brands of historicism): are we inferring or creating our "meanings" from the same evidence that was available to the original playgoers? Again, how much is being lost in translation?

CHAPTER 6

Sick chairs and sick thrones

> "Thy deathbed is no lesser than thy land,
> Wherein thou liest in reputation sick"
>
> *Richard II*, 2.1.95–6

Implicit in the discussion of theatrical *italics* (for any period of drama) is the question: given the available resources, how can playwright and players present an image or concept onstage so as to make it evident, even obvious, to a first-time playgoer? Such a question, in turn, cannot be separated from the study of "imagery" in its various senses as applied to drama. In revisiting such well traveled terrain, I do not wish to denigrate the valuable work of several generations of close readers who have expanded and refined their formulations of Shakespeare's "image patterns" and other iterative devices. Few readers today, moreover, need to be reminded that imagery-in-the-theatre (which combines poetry, costumes, properties, gestures, and larger configurations for the eye) can yield effects and meanings not available to the reader attending only to imagery-on-the-page. Also of importance is the work of those scholars who have studied icons, emblems, and other manifestations of that larger language of the visual arts by no means irrelevant to Shakespeare's vocabulary.

Awareness of such distinctions and possibilities, however, does not necessarily aid in the process of "recovery." Rather, any discussion of Shakespeare's "theatrical," "dramatic," or "presentational" images, symbols, and metaphors inevitably involves considerable speculation about what a spectator, then or now, did or should "see." However, given the language barrier discussed in chapters 1 and 2 and the problems inherent in Taylor's para-text, what may have been an integral part of a play's "imagery" in the original production may no longer be visible to today's reader, editor, or director. As a result, close readers, students of icons and emblems, and even performance-oriented critics who work within the framework of today's assumptions about on-the-stage interpretation can sometimes miss or blur what may have been hit-the-playgoer-over-the-head stage effects in the original productions. Also relevant is the issue of theatrical exigency, for a particular "image" may be possible in a painting or in an emblem book (or on the pages of an interpretative essay) but not be realizable onstage. Theatrical imagery (like politics) is the art of the possible.

As one instructive example, consider a climactic moment in *1 Henry IV* where, after Falstaff wounds the dead Hotspur in the thigh, Q1 signals: "*He takes up Hotspur on his back*" (K3v, 5.4.127.s.d.). Falstaff may or may not sustain his burden throughout the subsequent interview with Princes Hal and John (e.g., he may put down the body at "There is Percy" – 137–8), but he does joke about being "a double man" (136), and Hal assumes that Sir John will carry off the body ("Come, bring your luggage nobly on your back" – 152). Owing, however, to the size of the actor playing Hotspur, the padding and other constraints involved in playing Falstaff, and end-of-the-show fatigue, playgoers today rarely get to see this image acted out. But apparently in the 1590s the final view of Falstaff in Part 1 involved his lugging off "*on his back*" the fallen epitome of chivalry.

Many rich ironies and potential meanings can be generated by such a theatrical moment. My purpose in citing this example, however, is not to advance my own interpretation but rather to note that this configuration builds upon a well-known and often cited image drawn not from Ripa, Alciatus, or proverbial lore but from the drama of the previous generation. If allusions from the 1580s through the 1600s are to be trusted, the best remembered figure from late Tudor and early Elizabethan drama was not Everyman, Mankind, or Wit but the Vice; and the most often cited event associated with that Vice (along with his flailing at others with his distinctive weapon, the dagger of lath) was his being carried off to Hell by Satan at the end of the play. That specific bit of business survives in only one play (Fulwell's *Like Will to Like*), but recognizable variations recur in two other moral plays (W. Wager's *Enough is as Good as a Feast* and *The Longer Thou Livest*) and in subsequent plays such as Greene's *Friar Bacon and Friar Bungay*, *Histriomastix*, and most notably *The Devil is an Ass* where Jonson calls attention to his inversion of the familiar formula in a couplet: "The *Devil* was wont to carry away the evil; / But, now, the Evil out-carries the *Devil*" (5.6.76–7).[1]

Today the image of Hotspur on Falstaff's back may be of interest to an occasional on-the-page interpreter but is easily ignored by most readers and is regularly sidestepped in performance. In contrast, such an *exeunt* was apparently both stageable and meaningful from the 1560s through 1616 – to the extent that Jonson not only noted his inversion of the formula in a couplet but also called the stage practice to Drummond's attention ("according to Comedia Vetus, in England the devil was brought in either with one Vice or other, the Play done the devil carried away the Vice").[2] What seems theatrically awkward or otherwise dismissible now was both feasible and familiar then and was clearly within the range of both the players' skills and the playgoers' interpretative vocabulary. To document the potential meanings in this moment, moreover, requires reference not to emblem books or iconographical dictionaries but rather to other plays and allusions to those plays.

This situation is not unique. Therefore, in this and subsequent chapters, I propose to focus upon potentially meaningful "images" and configurations generated in Shakespeare's theatrical vocabulary by means of Elizabethan staging practices, especially when those images and practices are sufficiently different from today's procedures that the original effects are concealed or blurred. The greater the gap between then and now, the more likely will some distinctive image or effect fall victim to the language barrier and be lost in translation.

To explore this gap, the remainder of this chapter will be devoted to images of onstage sickness. As a point of departure, consider the widely recurring situation wherein a playscript calls for a figure to enter "*sick*" – as with Edward IV (*Richard III*, 2.1.0.s.d.), John of Gaunt (*Richard II*, 2.1.0.s.d.), and Queen Katherine (*Henry VIII*, 4.2.0.s.d.). Sometimes an obviously sick figure (the king in *All's Well That Ends Well*) appears with no such signal; often additional details are provided. But such generic stage directions are widespread in the extant playscripts, because dramatists who were writing for theatrical professionals who knew their craft (and who therefore could take for granted Taylor's para-text) saw no need to spell out in detail each time how a figure should enter "*sick*," "*mad*," "*ravished*," or "*unready*" (to cite four such categories).[3]

To determine how such generic signals were implemented by Elizabethan theatrical professionals necessitates ranging over a large number of plays in search of clues. Some of the details that emerge are predictable. For example, a figure is obviously sick or wounded if he or she must be helped onto the stage. Queen Katherine enters "*sick; led between Griffith, her gentleman usher, and Patience, her woman*" (*Henry VIII*, 4.2.0.s.d.); Sir Walter Whorehound is "*led in hurt*" (*A Chaste Maid in Cheapside*, 5.1.6.s.d.); the sick Palsgrave enters and exits "*led in*" (W. Smith, *The Hector of Germany*, 162, 226); a figure recently on the rack enters "*led by two of the guard, as not yet fully recovered*" (Fletcher, *The Double Marriage*, VI, 364); Justina enters "*supporting Doron deadly wounded*" (*The Two Noble Ladies*, 221). Less commonly, a sick figure comes in alone – as with Davenant's Fredeline who enters "*creeping in, as he were sick*" (*The Platonic Lovers*, II, 100).

Another obvious way to signal "*enter sick*" is to have a figure accompanied by a doctor who is identified by a distinctive costume and properties. In *The Telltale*, "*Isabella sick*" is juxtaposed with "*Picentio as a doctor with her water*"; later Garullo is "*brought in a Chair with a doctor*" (1381–2, 2231–3). Similarly, doctors accompany Zenocrate in Marlowe's *2 Tamburlaine* (2.4.0.s.d.), Princess Elizabeth in *1 If you know not me* (I, 200), Paulinus in Massinger's *The Emperor of the East* (4.3.0.s.d.), and numerous other figures. As in *The Telltale*, moreover, a urinal with the patient's "water" is occasionally specified, as are vials and basins.[4]

A figure's sickness can also be signaled by means of costume, whether a gown or, more specifically, a kercher, coif, or nightcap. For the former category, the ailing Henry IV, unable to sleep, enters "*in his nightgown*" (*2 Henry IV*, 3.1.0.s.d.); the convalescent Dorothea enters "*in a nightgown*" (*James IV*, 1941); Falstaff tells Bullcalf (who claims to be sick): "thou shalt go to the wars in a gown" (*2 Henry IV*, 3.2.180). For the latter, in *Fair Em*, Trotter enters "*with a kerchief on his head and an Urinal in his hand*" (350–1); in *2 The Return from Parnassus*, a prospective patient is described as "a fellow with a night cap on his head, an urinal in his hand" (B4v); in *A Shoemaker, a Gentleman*, Barnaby enters "*with a Kercher on*" (3.2.10.s.d.); the sick Palsgrave in *The Hector of Germany* talks of casting "my Night-cap on the ground" (194). An early example is provided by the Marian moral play *Wealth and Health*, where Health enters "*with a kercher on his head*" and apologizes for appearing "thus diseased," for "I am infect both body and soul"; Remedy responds: "I perceive by your physnomy, that ye are very weak feeble and low" (781–8). In addition to gowns and kerchers, a crutch is sometimes specified – as with Northumberland in *2 Henry IV* (1.1.145) and old Capulet in *Romeo and Juliet* (1.1.74).

Shakespeare makes use of several of these techniques. In addition to Henry IV's nightgown, in the Dering manuscript of *Henry IV*, Northumberland enters "*alone in his garden and Night-Cap*" (p. 168, 4.9.0.s.d.); in the dialogue he renounces his "nice crutch" and his "sickly coif" (Part Two, 1.1. 145, 147). In *Julius Caesar*, Brutus complains that Ligarius ("a sick man that would speak with you" according to Lucius) has chosen a poor time "to wear a kerchief" (2.1.310, 315). In *King John*, Arthur tells Hubert: "when your head did but ache, / I knit my handkercher about your brows" (4.1.41–2). Clearly, the kercher or coif was one expedient way to signal a sick but mobile figure who did not need the help of others to lead or carry him onto the stage.

Along with doctors, costumes, and handheld objects, two substantial theatrical properties are regularly introduced to spell out "*enter sick.*" First, figures are often directed to enter in or on a bed: the dying Queen Elinor enters "*in child-bed*" (Peele,

Edward I, 2397.s.d.); "*Enter the Admiral in his bed*" (Marlowe, *The Massacre at Paris*, 256.s.d.); "*Enter Elizabeth in her bed*" (*1 If you know not me*, I, 200); "*A Bed thrust out, the Palsgrave lying sick in it*" (*The Hector of Germany*, 1.1.0.s.d.); "*Enter Genzerick King of the Vandals, sick on his bed*" (H. Shirley, *The Martyred Soldier*, 1.1.0.s.d.); "*Fowler, as if sick, upon a couch*" (J. Shirley, *The Witty Fair One*, 3.4.0.s.d.); "*Enter Lady Ample, carried in as sick on a couch*" (Davenant, *The Wits*, II, 183). For obvious reasons, beds are linked to dying figures (e.g., the Cardinal in *2 Henry VI*, 3.3) or to sickrooms (as in Jonson's *Volpone* or Middleton's *A Mad World My Masters*).

Thrusting a bed onto and then off the Elizabethan stage may not have been appropriate for all situations, however, so a more flexible solution was to use a portable chair in which the sick figure could be carried in and out expeditiously. Indeed, the evidence I have collected suggests that such a sick-chair was by far the most widely used signal for "*enter sick.*" To cite only a few of many examples, in *Westward Ho* Mistress Tenterhook, pretending to be sick, calls for "a chair, a chair"; a companion says "she's sick and taken with an Agony" (5.1.196, 201). In *Othello*, after "finding" the wounded Cassio, Iago cries "O for a chair / To bear him easily hence" (5.1.82–3) and mentions the chair twice more (95, 98); when the chair arrives, he adds: "Some good man bear him carefully from hence. / I'll fetch the general's surgeon" (99–100) and "O, bear him out o' th' air" (104); the 1622 Quarto (but not the Folio) then directs that Cassio in the next scene be brought in "*in a Chair*" (N1r). Elsewhere in Shakespeare's plays, chairs are specified for sick or dying figures in *1 Henry VI* (2.5.0.s.d., 3.2.40.s.d.), *2 Henry VI* (2.1.66.s.d.), *King Lear* (4.7.20.s.d.), *Henry VIII* (4.2.3), and *The Two Noble Kinsmen* (5.4.85.s.d.). Examples are also plentiful in the plays of Fletcher and Brome and can be found as well in Peele, Chapman, Dekker, Haughton, Heywood, Massinger, and Markham and in many anonymous plays.[5]

What then is to be gained from an exploration of the theatrical vocabulary linked to "*enter sick*"? So what? Consider first Shakespeare's presentation of the sickness of Caius Ligarius. Brutus' exclamation ("O, what a time have you chose out, brave Caius, / To wear a kerchief! Would you were not sick" – 2.1.314–15) initiates a revealing exchange:

CAIUS: I am not sick if Brutus have in hand
Any exploit worthy the name of honor.
BRUTUS: Such an exploit have I in hand, Ligarius,
Had you a healthful ear to hear of it.
CAIUS: By all the gods that Romans bow before,
I here discard my sickness. (316–21)

At this point the Pelican editor inserts the stage direction: "*Throws off his kerchief.*" In the subsequent lines the two conspirators play further with "sickness" (e.g., Brutus' "A piece of work that will make sick men whole" elicits "But are not some whole that we must make sick?" – 327–8). Ligarius (who earlier had compared Brutus to an exorcist who has conjured up his previously sickly spirit so as now to enable him to "strive with things impossible") ends with his statement: "And with a heart new-fired I follow you, / To do I know not what; but it sufficeth / That Brutus leads me on" (332–4).

The issues and images in this rich moment are generated not only by the sickness motif as iterated in the dialogue but also by the kerchief worn by Ligarius that presumably is discarded at line 321. The question follows: is the previously sick man (who initially answers Brutus "from a feeble tongue" – 313) actually cured by Brutus, or is his eventual determination to follow blindly "to do I know not what" so long as "Brutus leads me on" merely a reversion to a more insidious sickness associated with "the spirit of Caesar" or caesarism? Brutus' reference to the ear, moreover ("Had you a healthful ear to hear of it") links the kerchief specifically to the ear and to hearing, a link present throughout the play (most notably in Antony's famous "lend me your ears") and of particular importance in the preceding orchard scene and in 2.2 that follows in which Caesar is first swayed by Calphurnia, then by Decius. In the vignette involving Brutus and Ligarius, the discarding of the visible sign of sickness, the kerchief, exposes the ear to suasion and acts out a central paradigm for this tragedy.

Although not spelled out in the Folio, the role played by

Ligarius' kerchief and sickly ear can be pieced out without elaborate reference to a lost theatrical vocabulary. A more telling example arises from an awareness of the widespread use of the sick-chair as a property and shorthand device. Consider first a moment in *3 Henry VI* when Edward IV, having been surprised and captured by Warwick and Clarence, is carried onstage "*in his gown, sitting in a chair*" (4.3.27.s.d.). Given this juxtaposition of gown and chair, the initial signal for the original spectator would have been that this figure is entering "*sick*" or "*as sick*" (all the signs are there, although they are blurred in the television production for the BBC's "The Shakespeare Plays" where director Jane Howell has Edward *bound* to the chair and hence a prisoner). In this instance, the signals are wrong or misleading, for Edward is embarrassed and vulnerable but not sick.

But keep in mind that this play starts and ends with throne scenes, with that royal seat a symbol of the disorder in a kingdom in which three different figures are seen sitting upon the English throne. Indeed, in the opening scene the titular king, Henry VI, comes onstage to discover Richard of York seated upon his throne, an initial usurpation that typifies what is to follow. The presence of a king (or pseudo-king) brought onstage in what appears initially to be a sick-chair is therefore more than a momentary trick played upon the spectator. Rather, that initial confusion of throne-chair and sick-chair calls attention to an important set of associations that links disease to kings and power-brokers, associations reinforced by the unkinging, rekinging, and unkinging of Henry VI in the last three acts. Memories of both the opening confusion about the throne and the momentary sick-chair image of 4.3 should then inform the final moments, where the surface order assumed by Edward ("Now am I seated as my soul delights, / Having my country's peace and brothers' loves" – 5.7.35–6) is undercut by a continuing sense of the kingdom's diseases, as typified in Richard's asides (e.g., "I'll blast his harvest ..." – 21).

What is surprising (and, to my knowledge, has not been noted) is how often Shakespeare introduces one or more such sick-chair moments into plays that deal with some form of diseased authority, and, moreover, how often such plays also contain scenes with thrones or other chairs of state. Eight of the ten history plays provide clear or likely evidence for such combinations (all except *1 Henry IV* and *Henry V*), along with *Othello* and *King Lear* (and perhaps *All's Well That Ends Well* and *Antony and Cleopatra*). Here, then, is an available signifier in an onstage vocabulary that Shakespeare could adapt to heighten key political or moral meanings in a fashion highly visible, then or now.

In some plays the configuration is likely but not certain. For example, the last scene of *King John* provides no clear signal for a sick-chair, but the dying John is "*brought in*" ("*carried between two Lords*" in *2 The Troublesome Reign*, D2v), a situation that elsewhere usually calls for a sick-chair. Earlier in the play, moreover, the spectator had seen Arthur bound to a chair in 4.1 before Hubert relented. Thrones are not specified in this play (a common situation, even when the dialogue calls for them) but seem to me likely in the opening scene, 4.2, and perhaps 5.1. To have John brought onstage in a sick-chair in the final moments would then epitomize the crisis of authority critics have linked to his rule and, in addition, would recall Arthur's death sentence as part of that crisis. Given that set of associations, what seems subtle or murky in the telling could be clear and potent, especially if (as also in *3 Henry VI*, 4.3) that sick-chair resembled (or was clearly analogous to) the throne.

Similarly, in the diseased world of *Richard III*, the reigning monarch Edward IV enters "*sick*" in his only onstage appearance (2.1.0.s.d), a scene that clearly links sickness to the throne. Richard's machinations then bring him to the throne in 4.2, again a sitting that epitomizes the link between disease and kingship in England. Such associations are heightened in the dialogue when, in response to news of Richmond's impending invasion, Richard asks: "Is the chair empty?" (4.4.469). Whether with Edward or Richard (or Henry VI, seen only as a corpse on a bier), the absence of a "true" or healthy king is a major issue throughout the play, a vacuum made even clearer if in 2.1 a sick-chair is used to carry in Edward IV so as visually to anticipate (and elucidate) Richard's throne.

To see a sustained sequence of such moments consider *1 Henry VI* where squabbles in the presence of the king are a major symptom of the kingdom's diseases (so that in Howell's television production Exeter delivers his choric speech on "this base and envious discord" – 3.1.193 – while pointing to the empty throne). The scenes that precede and follow the chaotic activity around the boy-king seated on his throne in 3.1 are instructive. First, Shakespeare presents the plucking of red and white roses by Suffolk and York in the Temple Garden scene (2.4), a symbolic beginning to the divisions to come. Moments later, Mortimer, who is "*brought in a chair*" by his jailers (2.5.0.s.d.), provides a long disquisition to Richard about the Yorkist claim to the throne. This claim, passed from this dying figure to the up-and-coming Richard, is linked visually to a figure in a sick-chair. Mortimer's ominous laying on of hands (see lines 37–8) is immediately followed by our first view of the young Henry VI, presumably on his throne, who is unable to control the squabble between Gloucester and Winchester or the fight, offstage and then onstage, between their servingmen. The one action this vulnerable king does take, however, is to restore Richard to his dukedom, so the figure bequeathed a claim to the throne in the previous scene by a figure in a sick-chair now is given status and power by a demonstrably weak occupant of the royal seat. This sequence is then extended in the next scene where, during the loss and recapture of Rouen, the dying Bedford is "*brought in sick in a chair*" (3.2.40.s.d.) to witness Falstaff's cowardice and then the English victory. At the climax of this action, "*Bedford dies and is carried in by two in his chair*" (114.s.d.).

Throughout the play, Henry's "throne scenes" act out his inability to control internal divisions and, hence, England's diseases, but his first appearance in 3.1, sandwiched between scenes displaying figures dying in their sick-chairs, neatly sums up the problems to come, problems linked both to the Yorkist's claim to the throne (symbolized by Mortimer) and to the dying off of that loyal older generation devoted to the good of the country rather than factional interests (symbolized by Bedford). Indeed, much of the theatrical coherence of this episodic play arises from such linked images and configurations. If the final scene also has an onstage throne (as in *3 Henry VI*), Suffolk's convincing the king to take Margaret as his bride (made ominous by Suffolk's closing reference to Paris and the implicit analogy between Margaret–Helen and England–Troy) enacts a climactic link between the royal chair and potential diseases to come. Again, even in this early play, a set of associations made accessible by conventional theatrical practice (*enter sick*) can be used to italicize important meanings and effects.

In *2 Henry VI*, such chair–throne patterning is present but less emphatic, for Shakespeare uses violent deaths and the Cade rebellion to highlight the kingdom's diseases. The dead or dying Gloucester and Winchester are displayed onstage but (apparently) in sick-beds rather than sick-chairs. The impostor Simpcox, however, enters "*between two in a chair*" (2.1.66.s.d.) in front of a weak king who, early in the same scene, is unable to control the quarrel between Gloucester and Winchester. Humphrey's uncovering of Simpcox's fraud acts out his important role in keeping some semblance of order in England, but, owing to Elinor's disgrace and his own naivete, Humphrey's position is soon undermined. Simpcox in his chair therefore prepares us for a hapless Henry on his throne who is unable to protect Humphrey or Lord Say (the latter linked to the palsy and "full of sickness and diseases" – 4.7.81, 85); this king is therefore vulnerable to an obvious fraud (Cade) in Act 4 and defenseless against a formidable opponent (York) in Act 5 (so, as a result, Henry finds York seated in his throne in the first scene of Part 3). When the inevitable confrontation does come, York's critique pinpoints the vulnerability of Henry as possessor of the royal seat, for he begins "No! thou art not king," then cites the attributes of kingship ("That head of thine doth not become a crown; / Thy hand is made to grasp a palmer's staff / And not to grace an awful princely sceptre"), and concludes: "Give place. By heaven, thou shalt rule no more / O'er him whom heaven created for thy ruler" (5.1.93, 96–8, 104–5). Such powerful accusations are enhanced by even a subliminal memory of the purportedly lame Simpcox exposed as a fraud and forced by the beadle to "give place" from *his* chair (and leap over a stool).

The two most developed examples of such linking of sick-chair and sick-throne are found in *2 Henry IV* and *Richard II*. The former provides no stage direction calling for a sick-chair, but in his final sequence the dying Henry IV asks: "I pray you, take me up, and bear me hence / Into some other chamber" (4.4.131–2). As noted in chapter 2, this call brings about not an *exeunt* but a move to another part of the stage to set up the climactic interview between father and son initiated by a debate over the crown left upon the king's pillow (4.5.5, 20, 57), with Henry IV located either still in a chair or in a bed (as suggested by 4.5.181 – "Come hither, Harry, sit thou by my bed"). The disease imagery in this play has been orchestrated at length: Northumberland's sickness in 1.1; Falstaff's complaints in 1.2; the Archbishop's extended critiques of the kingdom's diseases in 1.3 and 4.1–2. At his first appearance "*in his nightgown*" Henry IV reveals his inability to sleep and concludes: "Uneasy lies the head that wears a crown" (3.1.0.s.d., 31). Indeed, the diseased kingdom is the primary focus for much of the first four acts, building to Falstaff's depredations in Gloucestershire (spreading his diseases into the countryside) and the sick events at Gaultree Forest.

To have Henry IV, then, in some or all of his final moments associated with a sick-chair that resembles a throne is to conflate two linked sets of images into one potent visual statement. Of equal importance is the appearance of the new king on a throne in 5.2 (presumably, the only time that throne is seen in this play). As opposed to the situation in many other historical or political plays, the movement here has been from the obvious (and perhaps incurable) disease associated with one king to a healthier situation under his son. As Henry IV tells Prince Hal: "all the soil of the achievement goes / With me into the earth"; in his terms, "all my reign hath been but as a scene / Acting that argument," but "now my death / Changes the mode" (4.5.189–99). If then in 5.2 Henry V ascends to a throne seen for the first time (with only one scene intervening since the sick-chair of 4.5), the changing of mode is visually italicized. This new mode is then acted out in the new king's choice of the Lord Chief Justice "as a father to my youth" (5.2.118), the arrest of the "pregnant" Doll, and, of course, the famous rejection of Falstaff. Associated with first the nightgown, then the sick-chair, Henry IV never achieves "Jerusalem" (in the sense he originally anticipated) or a healthy kingdom. An alternative chair, however, *is* available to a son who "the garland wear'st successively" (as opposed to his father's "honor snatched with boisterous hand" – 4.5.201, 191) and who chooses the Chief Justice, not Falstaff, as a new "father."

Equally rich are the associations generated in *Richard II*. Like *3 Henry VI*, this play begins and ends with throne scenes linked to two different monarchs. As in *2 Henry IV*, no sick-chair is specified, but in his famous prophetic scene Gaunt enters "*sick*" (2.1.0.s.d.) and later is helped off stage ("Convey me to my bed, then to my grave" – 137), a situation likely to have involved this property. Later in this scene, moreover, the associations between individual and political disease are as clear as anywhere in the canon, for, after Richard II says "I am in health, I breathe, and see thee ill" (2.1.92), Gaunt replies:

> Now, he that made me knows I see thee ill;
> Ill in myself to see, and in thee seeing ill.
> Thy deathbed is no lesser than thy land,
> Wherein thou liest in reputation sick;
> And thou, too careless patient as thou art,
> Committ'st thy anointed body to the cure
> Of those physicians that first wounded thee. (93–9)

Clearly and emphatically, Gaunt's "real" death-bed sickness is being played off against the metaphoric, political sickness at the heart of this play, a sickness first explored in the opening throne scene in the quarrel between Mowbray and Bolingbroke over the recently murdered Woodstock (so, at the outset, the royal seat is tainted by a political murder). Gaunt's death is quickly followed, moreover, by another sign of the prevailing sickness, Richard's confiscation of Gaunt's estate and, in effect, Bolingbroke's title, a choice questioned by the loyal but troubled York in terms linked closely to the monarch's own title and throne ("for how art thou a king / But by fair sequence and succession?" – 198–9).

In contrast to *2 Henry IV*, the alternative monarch in the final movement of this play, although a far more skillful ruler, cannot solve this problem either, for he too is infected with diseases linked to usurpation or denial of rightful succession. Henry's initial movement to his goal ("In God's name I'll ascend the regal throne" – 4.1.113) is first challenged by Carlisle's ominous speech ("My Lord of Hereford here, whom you call king, / Is a foul traitor to proud Hereford's king" – 134–5) and then momentarily upstaged by Richard's speeches and actions, especially "Here, cousin, seize the crown" (181). Henry may be seen resolving at least some of his difficulties if he delivers his verdict on Aumerle in 5.3 from a throne or chair of authority, but any gains or any distinctions between sick-chair and healthy-throne are eliminated in the final scene when, after messengers bring news of rebels captured or killed and after Carlisle is sequestered, Exton's appearance with the coffin recapitulates the situation of 1.1. Again, the king seated on his throne is responsible, directly or indirectly, for the murder of a royal relative. The imagery of the final speech stresses how blood has tainted the hand of the enthroned monarch (5.6.50) and, in effect, has become the manure for England's garden ("my soul is full of woe / That blood should sprinkle me to make me grow" – 45–6).

In the plays that follow the second tetralogy, this linking of sick-chair and throne is still to be found but is less frequent. Most obvious is the situation in *Henry VIII* where Queen Katherine is led in, "*sick,*" and says almost immediately: "Reach a chair"; later, before falling asleep, she asks Patience to "set me lower" and, near her death, announces at the end of the scene, "I must to bed" (4.2.0.s.d., 3, 76, 166). The chair here recalls the various chairs of 2.4, where, in a ceremony described at length in the opening stage direction, "*the King takes place under the cloth of state*; *the two Cardinals sit under him as Judges. The Queen takes place some distance from the King*," and the bishops, scribes and lords are seated accordingly. When called to "come into the court," Katherine "*makes no answer*, *rises out of her chair, goes about the court, comes to the King, and kneels at his feet*" (10.s.d.). The use (and perhaps abuse) of chairs in this scene, by both the king and the two cardinals, act out the murky political situation facing England, a situation reflected in the individual fates of Buckingham, Katherine, Wolsey, and Cranmer. That Cranmer, unlike Katherine, *is* awarded his proper chair by Henry ("good man, sit down" – 5.3.130) is then a manifestation of the romance ending of this play (equivalent to Act 5 of *2 Henry IV*), for Gardiner's attempt to block Cranmer from his place at the council table, unlike the plots against Buckingham and Wolsey, fails.

The image as presented in *Othello* is murkier and easily overshadowed. However, if the Duke of Venice delivers his judgments, first on the Turkish strategy and then on Brabantio's accusations, from a chair of state, the opening movement sets up an initial paradigm of decisions made on the basis of evidence, reason, and experience as opposed to rashness and the facts as tainted by Iago. As the Duke states to Brabantio: "To vouch this is no proof, / Without more certain and more overt test / Than these thin habits and poor likelihoods / Of modern seeming do prefer against him" (1.3.106–9). In contrast, Othello, as the equivalent Justice figure in Cyprus, has no analogous chair and delivers no such measured judgments, so the call for a sick-chair for Cassio in 5.1 can serve as a comment on what has happened to that removed seat in the second half of the tragedy owing to Othello's errors and Iago's poison. Cassio's arrival in the final moments "*in a chair*" (5.2.282.s.d.) then serves as a visual reminder of the results of giving in to one's particular weakness and underscores how, during the course of the final scene, the marriage bed has been turned by Othello into a deathbed ("Look on the tragic loading of this bed" – 5.2.363).

No single image or property can epitomize the complexity of *King Lear*. Still, if Lear divides his kingdom in 1.1 from his throne and thereby sets in motion the forces that will destroy him, it should come as no surprise that he delivers his judgments in the mock tribunal of 3.6 from some lesser chair or stool and then is carried off in a litter or sick-chair (Gloucester tells Kent:

"There is a litter ready"; "Take up thy master"; and "Take up, take up" – 88–93). In the next scene, Gloucester is tied to a chair ("To this chair bind him" – 3.7.33) for a brutal travesty of justice. Then, in his reunion with Cordelia, Lear, according to the Folio, enters "*in a chair carried by Servants*" (4.7.20.s.d.). Here the sick-chair is associated with curing and with Cordelia's "no cause, no cause" that transcends the errors of the opening scene, but the intervening chairs and litters[6] have conditioned this reunion, and the forces already set in motion have yet to wreak their havoc upon Lear and Cordelia.

To deal in these terms with *All's Well That Ends Well* is to venture far into the misty realm of conjecture, for no sick-chair is specified for the ailing king in 1.2 and 2.1 and no chairs of state are clearly signaled elsewhere. If Bertram judges Parolles in 4.3 from a chair of authority and if the king and perhaps the countess have such chairs to judge Bertram and others in the final scene, some suggestive links could be forged, but no such chairs are called for in the Folio. Similarly, in *Antony and Cleopatra* the number of actual throne scenes for Cleopatra or Octavius is not clear, but some such scenes could be linked to the image of the wounded and dying Antony who, at the end of 4.14, is carried off by his guards ("*Exit bearing Antony*" – TLN 2995), delivered to Cleopatra ("*They heave Antony aloft to Cleopatra*" – TLN 3045), and finally borne off again ("*Exeunt, bearing off Antony's body*" – TLN 3107). If Antony is seen during his final moments in a sick-chair, that image would set up some resonances with Cleopatra's final moments if, when being clothed in her royal robes and crown, she is seated in a chair that could be perceived either as a throne or a sick-chair. In this final vision of this enigmatic figure, should the playgoer "see" a marble constant queen seated in her throne or a still slippery quean (to be associated, in Roman terms, with disease) seated in a sick-chair?

In this abbreviated treatment of twelve plays I have made no attempt at extensive analyses, nor am I claiming startling "new" insights. Indeed, the richer the play, the less helpful such a built-in link may be for the modern interpreter already awash in significant images (as in *Othello*, *Lear* and *Antony*). Various problems remain, moreover. Thus, I can offer no evidence of what an onstage sick-chair looked like, so I cannot "prove" a close resemblance to the stage throne or chair-of-state. In addition, the latter property could be lowered from above (as with the heavenly throne in the B-text of *Doctor Faustus*) rather than carried or thrust onto the stage. The visual link between sick-chair and sick-throne seems to me likely, even highly probable, but hypotheses should not masquerade as facts.

But note the alternative problem epitomized by glosses in many modern editions. For example, the Pelican editor (in the text from which I have been quoting) glosses Iago's reference to "chair" ("O for a chair" – 5.1.82, p. 1052) as "litter"; for the reader of this edition, any link to the "throne" or chair-of-state is lost when the image of the sick-chair (something we would not normally supply) is translated into "litter" (a term for which we may have a mental picture – e.g., *stretcher*).[7] A similar problem may arise from our sense of "throne," for stage directions suggest that a "chair of state" was or could be no more than a chair placed under a canopy and therefore a piece of furniture not that different from a "normal" chair. In effect, our conceptions of both "litter" and "throne" may carry with them artificial distinctions that blur some revealing similarities or analogies basic to Shakespeare's onstage strategy.

To conclude, given his theatrical vocabulary, Shakespeare had available to him a built-in image or ready-at-hand technique to drive home the metaphor or concept that "the throne is a sick-bed" or "the kingdom is diseased." Today the crown as verbal and physical image may be more obvious, but the links between the sick-chair and the sick-throne would have been just as visible then and just as rich in possibilities to be developed or explored (hence the large number of Shakespeare plays that may have included this combination). What I am proposing is (1) a regular conjunction of highly visible images (sick-chair, sick-throne/kingdom) linked to (2) one of the dominant image patterns (disease) in Shakespeare's plays[8] that (3) is largely lost today because editors, critics, and directors see no obvious connection between "*enter sick*" or "*in a chair*" and "throne" scenes. Pulling together stage directions from a wide range of plays, then, can provide more than mere fodder for the stage historian. Rather, such a venture can be fruitful, even provocative, if it leads to insights and a range of possibilities that enhance the editor, critic, or director's awareness of Shakespeare's strategy and, in the process, recovers images or links woven into the original fabric but lost today.

CHAPTER 7
Much virtue in *as*

"Much virtue in If"
Touchstone, 5.4.97

To recover some of the signifiers in that onstage vocabulary shared by Elizabethan playwrights, players, and playgoers requires only a sampling of a sufficient number of plays. The modern reader (or editor) of *3 Henry VI* or *2 Henry IV* may not fully understand the theatrical use and potential significance of the sick-chair, but the evidence for the existence of such a visible (and practical) property is plentiful. As noted in chapters 2 and 3, comparable evidence from stage directions and dialogue can be found for other items widely used then but easily missed or misunderstood today (e.g., nightgowns, boots, disheveled hair, torches-tapers). In a few instances, recovering a lost theatrical vocabulary therefore requires little more than a determined look at the plays that have survived.

More often, however, invisible barriers created by an interpreter's unacknowledged assumptions and expectations block this process of recovery. The presence of such barriers should come as no surprise, for theorists and psychologists remind us that observers of phenomena regularly see what they are prepared to see or expect to see. Such predisposition is particularly strong when a reader confronting the drama of the past attempts to extrapolate a sense of staging from words on a page (even when those words come from a playscript actually used in a playhouse). As Bernard Beckerman notes, when such a reader confronts a book containing the printed words of a Shakespeare play he or she simultaneously puts on a pair of spectacles "compacted of preconceptions about what constitutes drama and how it produces its effects."[1] Viewing earlier drama through such spectacles inevitably blurs or distorts the original onstage procedures and vocabulary.

No magic wand is available to wave away these spectacles and put the would-be historicist in tune with the shared language of Shakespeare's theatre. The extant evidence, however, does generate several revealing phenomena that can serve as windows into what distinguishes our theatrical ways of thinking and staging from those of the 1590s and early 1600s. For example, in their theatres the players did not perform in a lighted space in front of playgoers seated in a darkened auditorium (today's deeply ingrained sense of "going to the theatre"); rather, players and playgoers shared the same illumination (a situation more akin to a modern outdoor afternoon sports event than today's theatre).

One such window (which I have discussed at length elsewhere)[2] is the absence in Elizabethan theatres of variable lighting. To convey "night" today, a director uses lighting to establish stage darkness and then has the actors enter carrying torches or groping in the dark or unable to see something of importance; we thereby *start* with a verisimilar stage night as a justification for confusion in the dark. But an Elizabethan dramatic company would have used dialogue, torches or tapers, nightgowns, groping in the dark, and failures in "seeing" – all presented in full light – to establish the illusion of darkness for a playgoer who, presumably, would infer night from such signals and onstage behavior. For us, the lighting technician supplies night and the actors perform accordingly; for them, the actors provided the signals and the playgoers cooperated in supplying the darkness. For us, one figure fails to see another *because* the stage is dark; for them, one figure failed to see another and *therefore* the stage was *assumed* to be dark. Our theatrical sense of cause-and-effect (the stage is dark, therefore a given action took place) may then at times be inappropriate. Rather, at the Globe a greater burden lay upon the playwright, the players, *and* the playgoers to sustain the illusion of night and darkness through imaginative participation.

My purpose in this chapter is to explore another comparable

but less visible distinction that emerges from a widely used yet easily misunderstood feature of Elizabethan stage directions – the recurrent use of the conjunction *as*. Stage directions containing *as* or some equivalent, as I shall demonstrate, are widespread in English drama from the middle ages through the Restoration. To attempt to recover an Elizabethan theatrical vocabulary is to pay close attention to such usages (and to consider as well the many comparable situations in which the *as* may be implied but not spelled out). As already noted, a reader's interpretation of dialogue or stage directions will inevitably be conditioned by a wide range of assumptions or reflexes (Beckerman's spectacles), some of them so deeply ingrained as to seem as natural as the air we breathe. Therefore, to confront a stage direction that calls for a figure to enter *in prison*, *in his study*, *in the forest*, or *a-shipboard* is almost inevitably to draw upon the experience gained from reading novels or watching cinema, television, and modern stage pictures linked to properties, sets, and lighting. But what if that same stage direction read (or clearly implied) *as in* or *as if in*? How would such an adjustment change our view of both individual signals and the larger problem?

The theatrical *as* has a long history. Indeed, it turns up in the most famous early example of English drama, the late tenth-century *Visitatio Sepulchri* included in the *Regularis Concordia* of St. Ethelwold. The *quem quaeritis* interchanges in this text drawn from the liturgy may be familiar to students of the drama, but the additional comments and instructions (a form of extended stage directions) are distinctive – and revealing. The author of this passage is well aware of the limitations of his medium, so he notes that these actions are to be done or performed (*aguntur*) in imitation (*ad imitationem*) of the angel seated in the tomb; similarly, the monks playing the three women are directed to move towards the sepulchre "in the manner of seeking something" (*ad similitudinem querentium quid*). Of particular interest here, moreover, is that in addition to these two passages the author of this account four times invokes the theatrical *if* or *as if*. One of the four monks is to enter initially "as if to take part" in the ceremony (*acsi ad aliud agendum*); the three women are to approach "as if wandering about and seeking something" (*velut erraneos, ac aliquid querentes*); the angel is to sing the antiphon "as if calling back the women" (*velut revocans illos*); and the women are to display the cloth "as if showing" (*veluti ostendentes*) that the Lord has risen.[3] Here, at the very beginning of recorded drama in England, to set up dramatic impersonations in a context far removed from any claims to verisimilitude is to invoke repeatedly such terms as *velut* or *acsi*. To add one word to Touchstone's dictum, "much virtue in *as if*."

This very early example calls attention to a consistent feature of the drama that follows. For example, in his analysis of medieval drama as play and game V. A. Kolve cites the *ad imitationem* passage from St. Ethelwold (but not the uses of *velut* and *acsi*). His larger concern is to document the widespread association of drama with play and game by drawing upon a wealth of evidence from both dramatic dialogue and non-dramatic contexts so as to substantiate his thesis that "never was a suspension of disbelief invited." Rather, he concludes: "The aim of the Corpus Christi drama was to celebrate and elucidate, never, not even temporarily, to deceive. It played action in 'game' – not in 'ernest' – within a world set apart, established by convention and obeying rules of its own." In Kolve's formulation, this form of drama is "a lie designed to tell the truth about reality" or, as he terms it, "significant play."[4]

Comparable insights have been generated by recent productions of the craft cycle plays. For example, in her suggestive account of the staging of a Resurrection play, Meg Twycross describes the flexibility of the contract between play and playgoer, ranging from "the extreme of distancing" (when a "framing effect" of a familiar iconic picture is set up within the posts on the wagon) to the very different effect of action very close to the spectator in the streets wherein that audience is made "very much an active factor in the performance." As Twycross sums up the contract she finds implicit in this form of theatre, the players are saying, "We know you're there, and we intend to use you"; and the audience responds, "We're willing to be used, and we'll answer to any role you like to cast us in, friend or enemy. But we are still both aware that we're playing a game."[5]

Although only a limited number of stage directions survives in the manuscripts of medieval English plays, enough *as* usages turn up to support Kolve's scholarly argument and Twycross's insights derived from modern performance. Often the specified details or actions are not especially distinctive or demanding, but, as with the St. Ethelwold text, the *as if* locution regularly calls attention to a way of thinking or a way of conceiving drama that heightens the pretense (the *if*) rather than the equation (in which the actor would *become* a figure mad, dying, or confused).[6] Even more revealing are those stage directions linked to locales or stage machinery. In the Chester *Judgment* (p. 450), Jesus is to descend "*quasi in nube, si fieri poterit* ..." (356.s.d.) or "as in a cloud, if it is possible." In *Ludus Coventriae*, for the meeting of the bishops and Pharisees "*a little oratory with stools and cushions*" is called for "*like as it were a council-house*" (p. 245); a bit later: "*the council-house before-said shall suddenly unclose showing the bishops, priests and judges sitting in their estate like as it were a convocation*" (p. 255). The reader nurtured on "realism" can readily translate "*quasi in nube*" or "*like as it were a council-house*" into a suitable stage picture, but both locutions leave open considerable latitude. Would the original playgoer have seen a "real" cloud or council-house? Or would the effect (in part or in whole) have been dependent upon that playgoer's imaginative participation (in the spirit of *as if* play or game – especially if a spectacular descent *non fieri poterit*)?

Equally revealing is a distinctive locution that turns up five times in the Chester plays: *faciet signum* or "let him make a sign." In *Noah* (p. 47), Noah and his family are to "*make a sign as though they wrought upon the ship with diverse instruments*" (112.s.d.); in *Abraham* (p. 76), after placing Isaac upon the altar, Abraham is to "*make a sign as though he would cut off his head with the sword*" (420.s.d.); in *Balaam* (p. 82), Moses is to make a sign "*quasi effoderet tabulas de monte*" ("as if he dug the tablets from the mountain" – 80.s.d.); in *Innocents* (p. 201), Herod is instructed to make a sign "*quasi morietur*" ("as if he is dying" – 433.s.d.); in *Purification* (p. 206), after Simeon erases the word *virgo* from the book, an angel takes the book "*faciens signum quasi scriberet*" ("making a sign as if he writes" – 40.s.d.), and then closes the book.

The directions to the actors playing Abraham, Herod, and the angel are unexceptional, but the actions involving Noah and Moses would strain the resources of any theatre (and, unfortunately, no such stage directions survive for some comparable moments – e.g., the parting of the Red Sea). As with the descent of Jesus "as in a cloud," the difference between "building" an Ark in view of the playgoer and "making a sign as though" a group is building that Ark is significant – and tells us something distinctive and important about pantomime, make-believe, and imaginative participation on the part of the playgoer. The *as if* or *as in* locution calls our attention to a revealing gap between theatrical effects linked to imaginative play and game (as described in very different terms by Kolve and Twycross) and theatrical effects geared to verisimilitude.

Stage directions are scarce (and often unrevealing) in the canon of Tudor and early Elizabethan plays before the 1580s (when professional companies with a base in the newly built London theatres begin to develop considerable expertise), but some of the signals that do survive are comparable to those found in the Chester and *Ludus Coventriae* manuscripts. Skelton, for one, provides an equivalent to *faciet signum* twice in one comic sequence in *Magnificence*;[7] without using the specific phrase, Thomas Preston calls for a comparable effect for the execution of Sisamnes in *Cambyses* ("*Smite him in the neck with a sword to signify his death*" – C3r). As in the craft cycles, moreover, *as* or related signals are scattered throughout these plays. In *Jacob and Esau* (p. 77): "*Ragan and the others must be supposed to be at the back of the stage, out of Esau's sight*"; in Skelton's *Magnificence* (324.s.d): "*Hic faciat tanquam legeret litteras tacite*" (which the Revels editor translates as "*Here let him make as if he were reading the letter silently*"); in George Wapull's *The Tide Tarrieth No Man*: "*Courage and Greediness enter as though they saw not Christianity*" (F3v); in Thomas Lupton's *All for Money*: "*Here money shall make as though he would vomit*" (B1r); in Ulpian Fulwell's *Like Will to Like*: "*Haunce sitteth in the chair, and snorteth as though he were fast a sleep*" (560–1); in Thomas Garter's *Susanna*: "*Note that from the entrance of Susanna, the Judges' eyes shall never be off her, till her departure, whispering between themselves, as though they talked of her*" (359–61); in R. B.'s *Apius and Virginia* (499.s.d.): "*Here let him make as though he went out.*" For an effect comparable to Jesus descending as in a cloud, the dumb show before Act 4 of *Gorboduc* calls for music, "*during which there came from under the stage, as though out of hell three furies*" (p. 38, 1–2). No one of these signals in itself is earthshaking, but collecting them (from a group of plays in which stage directions are sparse, sometimes limited to *enter* and *exit* or even less) suggests a continuing vocabulary that reflects a way of theatrical thinking in troupe plays (and even for the dumb show in *Gorboduc*) not far removed from the presentational logic implicit at Chester or *Ludus Coventriae*. Repeatedly, players are not asked to *be* X but rather to perform actions *as if* or *as though* they were X.

In the 1580s and especially by the 1590s, however, the rhetoric of the extant stage directions changes noticeably (sometimes into a shorthand or code difficult to decipher today). Still, the *as if* or *as though* or *as it were* constructions do persist, although not in great numbers. From the late 1580s and early 1590s one finds: "*as though they had been chiding*" (*The Three Lords and Three Ladies of London*, E4r); "*Make as if she swoons*" (*The Cobbler's Prophecy*, D4v); "*Make as if ye would fight*" (*Edward I*, 432.s.d.); and "*Let him make as though he would give him some*" (*Locrine*, 1669–70). Three examples turn up in the 1594 quarto version of *2 Henry VI*: "*Alarms within, and the chambers be discharged, like as it were a fight at sea*" (F1v); "*the Cardinal is discovered in his bed, raving and staring as if he were mad*" (F1v); and "*Enter the King and Queen with her Hawk on her fist... as if they came from hawking*" (C1v). Falstaff, after his bout with Douglas, "*falls down as if he were dead*" (*1 Henry IV*, K2v, 5.4.75.s.d.).

Such *as if* constructions, however, are not plentiful after the mid 1590s.[8] Rather, without significantly changing the theatrical rationale behind *as if*, playwrights and players adapted or adjusted their dramatic vocabulary to suit the needs of their onstage resources and narrative materials. In effect, the *if* or *though* drops out of the construction (and, in some instances, the *as* as well).

This change is easiest to see in those instances when *as* is followed by a participle or adjective without the intervening *if* or *though* characteristic of the theatrical vocabulary before the mid 1590s (although that *if-though* is still implicit) – what I term *as* [*if*]. Heywood provides figures "*as affrighted and amazed*" (*The Wise Woman of Hogsdon*, v, 309); "*as not being minded*" (*The English Traveller*, iv, 87); "*as being conducted by them into the City*" (1 *The Iron Age*, iii, 302); and "*as newly shipwrecked*" (*The Captives*, 653 – "*as shipwrecked*" also turns up in *The Thracian Wonder*, B4v). Jonson contributes "*as having a cold*" (*Epicoene*, 3.4.6.s.d.) and "*as come down*" (*The Devil is an Ass*, 2.7.28.s.d); Webster provides: "*Enter Flamineo as distracted*" (*The White Devil*, 3.3.0.s.d.). From *A Yorkshire Tragedy* comes: "*Enter Husband as being thrown off his horse, and falls*" (632); and enter "*as going by his house*" (715); similarly, in *Sir Thomas More* a group enters "*as walking*" (4.2.0.s.d.). In Marston's *Antonio's Revenge*, figures "*bear out Mellida, as being swooned*" (4.1.230.s.d.); in Middleton's *A Game at Chess*: "*Enter Black Queen's pawn as Conducting the White to a Chamber*" (1941–3); Fletcher provides "*as newly ravished*" (*The Queen of Corinth*, vi, 17) and "*as robbed*" (*Love's Pilgrimage*, vi, 262); Massinger offers "*with Sergeants, as arrested*" (*The City Madam*, 5.3.59.s.d.).[9]

Given a canon of over 600 plays, however, such a list is relatively small (as is also the case for *as to* and *as at*).[10] Rather, the most extensive categories are (1) *as from* or *as* [*if*] *from* and its many cognates and (2) *as in* or *as* [*if*] *in* (fewer in number than *as from* but of particular importance for today's reader or scholar).

Consider first the widespread use of *as from* – usually to denote a recently completed offstage action or event that (1) would have been difficult to stage or (2) can be staged but has been finessed to speed up the narrative. For example, to sidestep onstage torture (which *is* staged in some plays) figures are to enter "*in their shirts, as from Torments*" (W. Rowley, *A Shoemaker, a Gentleman*, 4.2.0.s.d.); "*as from the Rack*" (Denham, *The Sophy*,

p. 52); or "*led by two of the guard, as not yet fully recovered*" (Fletcher, *The Double Marriage*, VI, 364). Similarly, offstage battles can be bypassed (especially at the outset of a play) by having figures enter "*as from war*" (Goffe, *Orestes*, B1r) or "*on his head a wreath of Bays, as from Conquest*" (Sharpe, *The Noble Stranger*, B1r). For a completed journey, figures can enter "*as from horse*" (Davenport, *The City Night-cap*, 107) or "*as new come out of the Country*" (Heywood, *The Wise Woman of Hogsdon*, V, 340); for a forest or woods, "*as out of the woods, with Bow and Arrows, and a Cony at his girdle*" (Whetstone, *Promos and Cassandra*, K4r) or "*as out of a bush*" (*The Two Noble Kinsmen*, 3.1.30.s.d.). Comparable signals survive for: "*as from prison*" (Massinger, *The City Madam*, 5.3.59.s.d.); "*as out of the house*" (*How a Man may Choose a Good Wife from a Bad*, B4r); "*as out of his Study*" (Suckling, *The Goblins*, 4.1.32.s.d.); and "*as coming from a Tavern*" (Shirley, *The Example*, 4.1.0.s.d.). Shakespeare does not provide any *as from* directions (although one from *The Two Noble Kinsmen* is cited above), but does have figures enter: "*from dinner*" (*Merry Wives*, Q1, B1r); "*from the Courtesan's*" and "*from the Bay*" (*Errors*, TLN 995, 1073); "*from hunting*" (*Shrew*, TLN 18, *Titus*, E2r); "*from his Arraignment*" (*Henry VIII*, TLN 889); "*from the Murder of Duke Humphrey*" (*2 Henry VI*, Folio, TLN 1690–1); "*from the Pursuit*" (*Coriolanus*, TLN 759); "*from the Cave*" (*Cymbeline*, TLN 2245); "*from his Cave*" (*Timon*, TLN 2233); and "*out of his Cave*" (*Timon*, TLN 2360).

Often at stake in this category is theatrical economy. For example, banquet scenes are plentiful in this period, but so too are scenes that start just after such a meal. Typical are: "*as from dinner*" (Massinger, *A New Way to Pay Old Debts*, 3.3.0.s.d., Heywood, *The Wise Woman of Hogsdon*, V, 336) or "*as from supper*" (Dekker, *The Roaring Girl*, 3.2.0.s.d.; Ford, *Love's Sacrifice*, H1r). Other plays then provide the relevant details for fleshing out such a signal, for figures are directed to enter: "*with a napkin on his shoulder, and a trencher in his hand as from table*" (Dekker, *The Roaring Girl*, 1.1.0.s.d.); "*brushing off the crumbs*" (Dekker, *Satiromastix*, 3.1.98.s.d.); "*all with napkins on their shoulders*" (Dekker, *The Shoemakers' Holiday*, 5.4.0.s.d.); "*picking their teeth, and striking off crumbs from their skirts*" (Davenant, *The*

Fair Favourite, IV, 250); "*with Napkins on their arms and Knives in their hands*" (*Woodstock*, 2–3); "*with a Napkin on his sleeve, and a silver bowl in's hand*" (Chamberlain, *The Swaggering Damsell*, B1r); "*having his napkin on his shoulder, as if he were suddenly raised from dinner*" (Munday, *The Downfall of Robert Earl of Huntingdon*, 166–8); "*with a Trencher, with broken meat and a Napkin ... with a bowl of Beer and a Napkin ... with his Napkin as from Dinner*" (Heywood, *The Wise Woman of Hogsdon*, V, 335–6); and "*as it were brushing the Crumbs from his clothes with a Napkin, as newly risen from supper*" (Heywood, *A Woman Killed With Kindness*, II, 118). Such a technique leaves the impression of a rich, busy (and well fed) world just offstage.

Like dinners or banquets, beds can be brought on and off the stage in this period when needed, but equally common are situations where the emphasis falls upon one or more figures "*as from bed*" (Fletcher, *The Lover's Progress*, V, 128; Fletcher, *Thierry and Theodoret*, X, 30; Heywood, *2 The Iron Age*, III, 381), "*as out of her bed*" (Fletcher, *The Coxcomb*, VIII, 325), "*as out of his bed*" (Heywood, *The Royal King and the Loyal Subject*, VI, 77), "*as out of their beds*" (Suckling, *Aglaura*, 5.2.141.s.d.), "*as from his chamber*" (Massinger, *The Bashful Lover*, 5.1.71.s.d.), "*as from their chamber*" (Ford, *'Tis Pity She's a Whore*, 2.1.0.s.d.), and "*as newly come out of Bed*" (Heywood, *A Woman Killed With Kindness*, II, 141). As with "*as from dinner*," many supportive details are available: "*as from his bed, unbuttoned in slippers, a torch in his hand*" (Goffe, *Orestes*, B4r); "*Enter Dalavill in a Night-gown: Wife in a night-tire, as coming from Bed*" (Heywood, *The English Traveller*, IV, 70); "*half unready, as newly started from their Beds*" (Heywood, *2 The Iron Age*, III, 413). The most sustained account comes from a Caroline play where a figure enters "*unbutton'd as out of bed*," a second enters "*as newly awaked*," and then a third "*yawning and rubbing his eyes*" (Chamberlain, *The Swaggering Damsel*, H2v).

In contrast to dinners and beds (that *can* be introduced onto the stage), shipwrecks and immersions in water are far more difficult to display directly (the opening scene of *The Tempest* is highly unusual). Therefore, although specific *as from* signals are rare, dramatists find other ways to invoke actual water just offstage. Heywood does introduce Triton "*with his Trump, as from the sea*" (*The Silver Age*, III, 138) and Lodge and Greene offer "*wet from sea*" (*A Looking Glass for London and England*, 1369), but more typical are: "*as newly landed and half naked*" and "*to them Guy all wet*" (Heywood, *The Four Prentices of London*, II, 176–7); "*all wet as newly shipwrecked and escaped the fury of the Seas*" (Heywood, *The Captives*, 653–4); "*all wet*" (Marlowe, *Doctor Faustus*, A-text, 1175); or just "*wet*" (*Doctor Faustus*, B-text, 1553, Dekker, *The Witch of Edmonton*, 3.1.91.s.d., *The Tempest*, TLN 59). In Smith's *The Hector of Germany* the shipwrecked Floramell has no such stage direction, but in the subsequent dialogue he describes himself as "all wet and weary," says "I shall die with cold," and asks a bystander: "Sir, I am very cold, and wet, and ill, / Would you could help me to a little fire / To dry my self" (808, 815, 818–20). Note two unusually graphic accounts: "*Musidorus drawn in wet and half dead*" so that onstage figures "*take him by the heels while water runs out of his mouth*" (*Love's Changelings' Change*, 29.s.d., 38.s.d.); and: "*Enter old Antimon bringing in Ariadne shipwrecked, the Clown turning the child up and down, and wringing the Clouts ... Enter Radagon all wet, looking about for shelter as shipwrecked. Enter to him Titterus, seems to question him, puts off his Hat and Coat, and puts on him, so guides him off*" (*The Thracian Wonder*, B4v).

Also sidestepped by invoking *as from* are weddings or other church scenes, for figures are directed to enter: "*with rosemary as from church*" (Marston, *The Insatiate Countess*, 1.1.141.s.d); "*in black scurvy mourning coats, and Books at their Girdles, as coming from Church*" (*The Puritan*, B2v); "*with Rosemary, as from a wedding*" (Fletcher, *The Woman's Prize*, VIII, 2); "*from Church*" (*The Soddered Citizen*, 2327–8); "*from Church, and Music before her*" (Peele, *Edward I*, 746.s.d.); "*in Magnificent state, to the sound of loud music, the King and Queen as from Church*" and later "*with Rosemary in their hats*" (*The Noble Spanish Soldier*, 265, 322); and, for a related effect, "*all in mourning apparel, Edmond in a Cypress Hat. The Widow wringing her hands, and bursting out into passion, as newly come from the Burial of her husband*" (*The Puritan*, A3r).

Also kept just offstage are various sports or contests, with racket sports especially popular. Figures are directed to enter:

"*from Tennis*" (*Blurt, Master Constable*, 2.1.43.s.d.) but more commonly: "*with their Rackets*" (S. Rowley, *When You See Me*, 1819–20); "*with Rackets*" (Cooke, *Greene's Tu Quoque*, D4r); "*with a Racket and Tennis-ball in his hand*" (*Claudius Tiberius Nero*, 1306–7); "*in their waist-coats with rackets*" (Barnes, *The Devil's Charter*, I2v); or "*one with a Shuttlecock, the other a battledore*" (Middleton, *Women Beware Women*, 2.2.79.s.d.). For comparable activities, figures enter: "*as from Walking*" (Heywood, *The English Traveller*, IV, 44); "*as newly come from play*" (Heywood, *The Wise Woman of Hogsdon*, V, 279); "*from tilting*" (*Pericles*, D1r); "*with a spear in his Rest as from the tilt*" (*Tom a Lincoln*, 798–9); "*her head and face bleeding, and many women, as from a Prize*" (Brome, *The Antipodes*, III, 300); "*with her Hawk on her fist ... as if they came from hawking*" (*2 Henry VI*, Q1, C1v); "*as from Hawking*" (Brome, *The Queen's Exchange*, III, 506); "*as from hunting*" (Heywood, *The Late Lancashire Witches*, IV, 171); "*from bowling*" (Porter, *The Two Angry Women of Abington*, 271); and "*throwing down his Bowls*" (Field, *A Woman is a Weathercock*, 3.3.0.s.d.).

Such signals are not unique to theatre between the 1580s and 1642 but will be found in any onstage presentation wherein narrative economy takes precedence over the impulse to display all the facets of a story. A good example (without a specified *as from*) can be seen in *The Woman Taken in Adultery* of *Ludus Coventriae*, for when the officers knock upon the woman's door: "*Hic juvenis quidam extra currit in deploido calligis non legatis et braccas in manu tenens*" (p. 215 – "Here a certain young man runs out in his doublet with his shoes unlaced and holding his trousers in his hand"); the audience therefore sees a rendition of "*enter as* [*if*] *from adultery*." As a device basic to most forms of drama (even the director who brings on an elephant in *Aida* must omit *some*thing), the *as from* effect is also to be found in the Restoration (despite the emergence of scenery and therefore the ability to shift scenes).[11] Nonetheless, this technique is omnipresent in Elizabethan, Jacobean, and Caroline plays where, even given the flexibility of the chameleon open stage, the emphasis upon narrative pacing and the exigencies of telling a story expeditiously often demand that the players provide a sense of actions, places, or a "world" just offstage that must then be imagined by the playgoer.

The most suggestive group of *as* signals constitute the category of *as in* or *as [if] in*. Some of these are unrevealing; some call attention to a specific locale.[12] A few set up an activity: "*as in the Army*" (Carlell, 1 *Arviragus and Philicia*, D3v); "*Two soldiers meet as in the watch*" (Heywood, *Rape of Lucrece*, V, 204); "*enter the Satyrs as in the chase*" (Heywood, *The Golden Age*, III, 32). One repeated signal directs one or more figures awaiting a duel to appear "*as in the field*" (Fletcher, *The Little French Lawyer*, III, 391; Brewer, *The Country Girl*, H1r), "*as in a Grove*" (*The Knave in Grain*, 905), or "*as to a Duel*" (Suckling, *The Goblins*, 1.1.o.s.d.).

Many of the items in this category, however, can be highly provocative in that they pose a challenge to deeply ingrained assumptions about verisimilitude (an essential part of Beckerman's spectacles for reading drama) still in evidence today. For example, readers, playgoers, scholars, and theatrical professionals who take variable lighting for granted can readily pass over "in the dark" scenes and signals, but a direction such as "*as in the dark*" (Brome, *A Mad Couple Well Matched*, I, 76), "*as if groping in the dark*" (Heywood, 2 *The Iron Age*, III, 380), or "*softly as by night*" (*Captain Thomas Stukeley*, 924–5) forces such an interpreter to confront something distinctive about Elizabethan staging. As noted earlier, to "create" night or darkness on a stage in which the actual illumination does not vary throughout the performance is to defy verisimilitude. Rather, such onstage darkness must be generated by a combination of suitable acting (e.g., groping in the dark, tiptoeing), a shared theatrical vocabulary (e.g., the use of lighting implements and appropriate costumes such as nightgowns), and the imaginative participation (and acquiescence) of the playgoer – all in the spirit of *as if*.

Similarly, prison scenes are very common in this period (as are "*in prison*" or "*enter in prison*" signals), but four Caroline playwrights provide "*as in prison*" (Suckling, *Brennoralt*, 1.4.o.s.d.; Brome, *The Queen and Concubine*, II, 35; Davenport, *The City Night-cap*, 176; Carlell, 2 *Arviragus and Philicia*, F4v). As

I have argued elsewhere,[13] the "prison" effect could have been realized onstage in a variety of ways (the simplest and most efficient option would have been fetters on the prisoner and the presence of a distinctively costumed gaoler), but the *as* [*if*] *in* construction highlights the non-verisimilar foundation of this locale and also of the larger theatrical rationale behind it. "*In prison*" (like "*in the dark*") may conjure up a familiar image to today's reader whose eye and imagination have been conditioned by cinema, television, and recent plays, but "*as in prison*" provides a window into pre-1642 notions of staging wherein (in the spirit of *as if* that goes back as far as St. Ethelwold) such a distinctive locale is generated by means of the signals provided by the entering actor in conjunction with the playgoer's imagination. When reconstituting or recovering an Elizabethan theatrical vocabulary, should not the many "*in prison*" or "*enter in prison*" stage directions then be understood as "*as* [*if*] *in prison*" – a signal that *is* provided by Suckling, Brome, Davenport, and Carlell?

Indeed, the particular value of isolating and then focussing upon *as in* signals is that such a process forces today's reader to revaluate assumptions about what is or is not "necessary" to stage a given scene or effect. The presence of onstage "rooms" in eighteenth, nineteenth, and twentieth-century productions has conditioned generations of scholars to "place" Shakespeare's scenes accordingly, but what happens to such post-1700 assumptions when that same reader confronts: "*as in his house at Chelsea*" (Munday, *Sir Thomas More*, 4.4.0.s.d.); "*as in his chamber in the Tower*" (*Sir Thomas More*, 5.3.0.s.d.); or "*as in her chamber*" (Rider, *The Twins*, p. 41). In *Amends for Ladies*, Field provides "*Enter Scudmore, as in his Chamber in a morning, half ready*"; "*Enter Seldome and Grace working as in their shop*" (2.1.0.s.d.); and "*Enter Welltried and Bould putting on his doublet, Fee-Simple on a bed, as in Bould's chamber*" (4.1.0.s.d.). Twice in *The Conspiracy* Henry Killigrew directs figures to enter "*as in their Tent*" (H3r, I3r); twice in *The Amorous War* Jasper Mayne calls for entrances "*as in a Wood*" (pp. 18, 20). Elsewhere one finds: "*as in sessions*" (*Sir Thomas More*, 1.2.0.s.d.); "*as in a Tavern*" (Glapthorne, *Wit in a Constable*, I, 231); "*as in the Duke's garden*" (Shirley, *The Gentleman of Venice*, 2.1.0.s.d.); "*as in his Study*" (Fletcher, *The Fair Maid of the Inn*, IX, 193); and "*as in his study reading*" (Cooke, *Greene's Tu Quoque*, B4v). When viewed as a category (or as signifiers in a lost theatrical vocabulary), such evidence encourages the question: if the *if*, although still implicit, has dropped out of most *as from*, *as in*, and *as* participle-adjective stage directions, has an implicit *as* similarly dropped out of the many "*in ...*" and "*from ...*" signals? What would happen to our reconstruction of pre-1642 staging and theatrical vocabulary if an implicit *as* were regularly factored into the equation?

My goal in chapters 8 and 9 (in the spirit of my *so what?* question) is to pursue some of the implications of such a suggestion. For now let me provide some representative problems and tentative solutions.

First, numerous Shakespeare stage directions warrant scrutiny in terms of *as in* or *as from* thinking. As will be shown in chapter 8, one interpretative issue that often emerges is the possible presence onstage of distinctive, even italicized images. For example, in *Titus Andronicus* Marcus is directed to enter "*from hunting*" (E2r, 2.4.10.s.d.), a signal that can readily be read as part of the narrative fiction rather than as a theatrical signal. But what if this stage direction is construed as "[*as if*] *from hunting*" and is then linked to Whetstone's 1578 spelling out of "*as out of the woods*" cited earlier in which a comparable figure had "*Bow and Arrows, and a Cony at his girdle*"? If "[*as if*] *from hunting*" can include a small animal "at his girdle" (especially a bloodied animal without its limbs), consider the effect upon the "imagery" of the remainder of *Titus*, 2.4, Marcus' painful confrontation with Lavinia ("*her hands cut off, and her tongue cut out, and ravished*" – o.s.d.), an encounter that includes such lines as: "what stern ungentle hand / Hath lopped and hewed and made thy body bare / Of her two branches ..." (16–18).

Other distinctive *as* stage directions also have their uses. Admittedly, odd or unique examples may be unreliable as a basis for extrapolation (as with Jonson's couple in *The Devil is an Ass* who play a scene "*at two windows, as out of two contiguous buildings*" – 2.6.37.s.d.). As the only one of its kind, Killigrew's "*as in their Tent*" (cited above) may also be suspect, but at the least this usage should encourage the historian to consider carefully the options for staging "tent" scenes. To invoke again Richard Hosley's distinction, is such an effect *theatrical* (so that a playgoer would have seen a verisimilar property) or *fictional* (so that the "tent" would instead be a to-be-imagined space just offstage)?

Without doubt, Elizabethan players did at times introduce onstage tents, particularly for effects of some importance or duration. The clearest example is to be found in the theatrical "plot" of *2 The Seven Deadly Sins* which begins: "*A tent being placed on the stage for Henry the sixth . he in it asleep*" (1–2). Not as clear, however, is an entry from the *Troilus and Cressida* "plot" fragment: "*Enter Diomede to Achilles' Tent to them Menelaus, to them Ulysses to them Achilles in his Tent to them . Ajax with Patroclus on his back. exeunt*" (34–8).[14] At the other extreme is the obviously fictional stage direction from Quarto *2 Henry VI*: "*Alarms again, and then enter three or four, bearing the Duke of Buckingham wounded to his Tent*" (H3v); also likely to be fictional is "*Enter three Watchmen to guard the King's Tent*" (*3 Henry VI*, TLN 2220, 4.3.0.s.d.). In neither Shakespeare scene does the tent play a significant role in the staging (and Buckingham's fate in battle is not even included in Folio *2 Henry VI*).

Most of the other tent scenes fall between such extremes (so that Killigrew's "*as in their Tent*" may be instructive). Of the extant plays, Peele's *Edward I* provides the most examples: "*the Queen's Tent opens, she is discovered in her bed*"; "*They close the Tent*"; "*The Queen's Tent opens*"; "*The Nurse closeth the Tent*"; "*Enter the Novice and his company to give the Queen Music at her Tent*"; "*Then all pass in their order to the king's pavilion, the king sits in his Tent with his pages about him*" (s.d.s at 1453, 1517, 1587, 1686, 1715, 1932). The number of scenes involved, along with the reference to "*the king's pavilion,*" makes likely the presence of some onstage property (that may have remained in place throughout the performance), although many, perhaps all of these moments *could* have been represented by means of a curtain and a discovery space.

Other comparable scenes involve discoveries or entrances from a tent and therefore would fit well with an *as* [*if*] *in* or *as from* approach. Marlowe has Tamburlaine's two sons enter "*from the tent where Caliphas sits asleep*" (*2 Tamburlaine*, 4.1.0.s.d.); Heywood provides "*Achilles discovered in his Tent, about him his bleeding Myrmidons, himself wounded, and with him Ulysses,*" and later "*Enter Achilles from his Tent*" (*1 The Iron Age*, III, 324, 328). In a play without other emphasis upon tents, Caesar Borgia threatens Countess Katherine by having her two sons brought forth "*from Caesar's Tent*"; later, in a moment reminiscent of Alonso being shown Ferdinand and Miranda playing chess, Borgia surprises Katherine (who thinks her sons are dead): "*He discovereth his Tent where her two sons were at Cards*" (Barnes, *The Devil's Charter*, H4r, I1v). Seen in isolation, such scenes may conjure up for a reader images of property tents, but what if that reader has been conditioned by the many *as from* and *as in* signals, including Killigrew's "*as in their Tent*"?

The two major Shakespeare examples are found in *Richard III* and *Troilus*. In the former, Richard starts this long scene by twice referring to his tent: "Here pitch our tent, even here in Bosworth field"; "Up with my tent! Here will I lie to-night" (5.3.1, 7). Richmond then invites his followers "in to my tent; the dew is raw and cold" so "*They withdraw into the tent*" (5.3.46, TLN 3483–4). Two subsequent stage directions cite Richmond's tent (although curiously none of the stage directions refers to Richard's): "*Enter Derby to Richmond in his Tent*" (TLN 3520; Q1, L3r); "*Enter the Lords to Richmond sitting in his Tent*" (TLN 3685–6). To clarify matters, the Pelican editor inserts "*Soldiers begin to set up the King's tent*" after Richard's "Up with my tent!"; "*Some of the Soldiers pitch Richmond's tent*" at his entrance at line 18; and "*King Richard withdraws into his tent, and sleeps*" at line 79. Such specific signals for the pitching of tents onstage, however, are exactly what is missing in the extant playscripts – with the notable exception of the opening of *2 The Seven Deadly Sins* (where presumably Henry VI was to remain onstage for the entire performance).

A long demanding scene such as *Richard III*, 5.3 (that builds to a display of two sleeping figures who are visited by eleven ghosts) certainly would justify the pitching of two tents onstage (as opposed to several of the other scenes cited where the theatrical pay-off would be negligible). Considerably murkier, however, is the situation in *Troilus* where Achilles and Patroclus are to "*stand in their tent*" (Q1, F4v) or "*Enter ... in their Tent*" (Folio, TLN 1888). In both the Quarto and the Folio Ulysses comments that "Achilles stands i'th' entrance of his tent" (3.3.38), but awareness of an implicit *as* (made explicit by Killigrew) can enable today's reader more readily to envisage this particular "tent" as keyed not to an object introduced for this scene (and irrelevant to the Troy scenes that precede and follow it) but rather to a stage hanging or a stage door, Ulysses' line, and the playgoer's imagination. Again, is such a "tent" (or forest or study or cave or tomb) a product of the property master or is it generated by the dialogue, the actor, and the imaginative participation of the playgoer? Is Killigrew's "*as in their Tent*" a Caroline anomaly or (as with Glapthorne's "*as in a Tavern*," Shirley's "*as in the Duke's garden*," and the four examples of "*as in prison*") does it spell out late in the period a way of thinking or staging taken for granted then but easily eclipsed today?[15]

For another instructive example from Shakespeare consider a stage direction from *Coriolanus* (TLN 1203–4, 2.2.0.s.d.): "*Enter two Officers, to lay Cushions, as it were, in the Capitol.*" The locale for this scene is clearly "the Capitol," but that "place" is created by the dialogue, by the costumes of first the officers, then the senators, and by the laying down of cushions, an action that defines the theatrical space. Such "*as it were, in ...*" thinking makes possible a quick (and efficient) switch in 2.3 to "the street" for Coriolanus's confrontation (in his gown of humility) with the plebeians and then a switch back to a more formal setting with Coriolanus, senators, and tribunes in 3.1. Here and elsewhere, both *as in* and *as from* thinking are essential elements in the rationale behind Shakespeare's chameleon stage and narrative flexibility.

To invoke an implicit *as* or *as if* is then to open up various possibilities but also to raise some perplexing questions. In particular (as noted in chapter 3), Hosley's useful and apparently clear distinction between fictional and theatrical stage directions can become murky. At first glance, Middleton's "*Enter a Groom before Phoenix and Fidelio, alighting into an Inn*" (*The Phoenix*, B2v) may seem to tell the story rather than provide a signal to an actor, but "[*as if*] *alighting into an Inn*" *can* be staged (the two actors could enter while handing over their crops and riding cloaks to the groom). Similarly, several of the *as in* stage directions cited earlier can be read as theatrical signals, as with Heywood's "*Two soldiers meet as in the watch*" (*Rape of Lucrece*, V, 204) and "*enter the Satyrs as in the chase*" (*The Golden Age*, III, 32) wherein the actors are to supply accoutrements and behavior appropriate to the watch or the hunt in the spirit of *as if*. Elsewhere, an opening stage direction that directs two figures to "*Enter as upon the Exchange*" (*How a Man may Choose a Good Wife from a Bad*, A2r) may, in the spirit of *as if*, call for some distinctive costumes, properties, or activity.

Various signals in Shakespeare's plays that at first seem "fictional" may similarly be read theatrically in terms of *as if*. For example, several stage directions appear to correspond to the designations of locale in modern editions: "*Enter ... within the forest of Gaultree*" (*2 Henry IV*, F3v, 4.1.0.s.d.); "*Enter before Angiers*" (*King John*, TLN 292, 2.1.0.s.d.). But what happens when these two signals are placed beside "*as before the City Corioles*" (*Coriolanus*, TLN 479–80, 1.4.0.s.d.)? To what extent are "[*as if*] *within the forest of Gaultree*" and "[*as if*] *before Angiers*" implicit theatrical signals – at least for a playwright, his player-colleagues, and his playgoers who share a vocabulary that includes signifiers for "creating" an onstage forest or city?

In this context, consider another instance of the "*enter to ...*" construction (as with "*to Council*" or "*to the Parliament*" discussed in chapter 3) – in this case, "*enter to execution*." In the many plays that end with one or more executions, the condemned figures usually enter, give a farewell speech, and then depart to die offstage; however, some are hanged (or, in several instances, beheaded)[16] onstage. The locution "*enter to his execution*" is to be found in both situations. Is this phrase then a "fictional" telling of the story or is it a coded signal to be understood as "[*as if*] *to his execution*"?

Explicit uses of *as* linked to executions are rare,[17] but the "*to execution*" locution is fairly common. Some of these usages can be construed as a "fictional" part of the narrative, as perhaps in *Titus Andronicus*: "*Enter the Judges and Senators, with Titus' two Sons bound, passing on the stage to the place of execution, and Titus going before, pleading*" (3.1.0.s.d.); or in Folio *Richard III*: "*Enter Sir Richard Ratcliffe, with Halberds, carrying the Nobles to death at Pomfret*" (TLN 1933–4, 3.3.0.s.d.). Others, however, cannot be neatly characterized: "*Enter Buckingham to execution*" (Quarto *Richard III*, L1v); "*Enter Buckingham with Halberds, led to Execution*" (Folio *Richard III*, TLN 3371–2, 5.1.0.s.d.); "*Then is young Aire brought forth to execution by the Sheriff and Officers*..." (Heywood, *2 Edward IV*, I, 180). The final sequence of *The Witch of Edmonton* provides two representative examples: "*Enter Sawyer to Execution, Officers with Halberds, country-people*"; "*Enter Frank to Execution, Officers, Justice, Sir Arthur, Warbeck, Somerton*" (5.3.20.s.d., 53.s.d.).

Other stage directions provide relevant details with or, more often, without the "*to execution*" locution. At least one play calls for a figure to be brought in "*on a hurdle*" (Peele, *Edward I*, 2361.s.d.), a common fate for condemned figures in the "real world." As in the examples already cited, many of the signals call for either a distinctive figure (sheriff, justice, executioner, hangman), a distinctive weapon (ax, halberd), or both: "*Enter Buckingham from his Arraignment, Tipstaves before him, the Axe with the edge towards him,*[18] *Halberds on each side*..." (*Henry VIII*, TLN 889–91, 2.1.53.s.d.); "*Enter master Browne to execution with the Sheriff and Officers*" (*A Warning for Fair Women*, I2v); "*Enter Bonavida with Officers, and executioner*" (Heywood, *A Challenge for Beauty*, V, 66); "*Enter Vice-Admiral, and the Captain of the Isle of Wight, with Falconbridge bound, the Headsman bearing the axe before him*" (Heywood, *1 Edward IV*, I, 53); "*Enter one bearing a silver oar before Stranguidge, Shore, and two or three more pinioned, and two or three with bills and a hangman*" (Heywood, *2 Edward IV*, I, 136); "*Enter Petruchi, after the hangman bearing the axe before Alphonso, with Officers*" (Ford, *The Queen*, 230–2). Also possible is a change in coiffure for a woman: "*Enter Isabella, with her hair hanging down, a chaplet of flowers on her head, a nosegay in her hand, Executioner before her, and with her a Cardinal*" (Marston, *The Insatiate Countess*, 5.1.66.s.d.); "*Enter executioner before Salassa, her Hair loose, after her, Almada, Collumello and officers*" (Ford, *The Queen*, 3115–17). If the execution is to be onstage, the dramatist may call for a scaffold, ladder, or block: "*A scaffold thrust forth ... Enter a guard bringing in Dorothea, a headsman before her ...*" (Dekker, *The Virgin Martyr* 4.3.4.s.d., 32.s.d.); "*Enter Merry and Rachel to execution with Officers with Halberds, the Hangman with a ladder, etc.*" (Yarington, *Two Lamentable Tragedies*, K1v). The plot of *The Dead Man's Fortune* (49–59) provides details for an interrupted execution: "*Enter King Egereon Allgerius Tesephon with lords the executioner with his sword and block and officers with halberds ...*"

At first glance, "*enter to execution*" does read as fictional rather than theatrical (as do some comparable locutions, such as "*Enters ... to sanctuary*" – *The True Tragedy of Richard III*, 586–7), but the wealth of detail found in a wide range of comparable scenes offsets that initial impression. Awareness of the explicit use of *as* [*if*] elsewhere, including two related *as to* constructions in Shakespeare's plays,[19] then makes it even more likely that "*to execution*" could be a meaningful signifier in that original shared theatrical vocabulary.

Merely invoking the theatrical magic of *as if* cannot resolve every problem. For example, I remain puzzled by the theatrical shorthand invoked in the signal for the entrance of Posthumus' family: "*Solemn Music. Enter* (*as in an Apparition*) ..." (*Cymbeline*, TLN 3065, 5.4.29.s.d.). In their shared theatrical vocabulary, "*as in an Apparition*" made theatrical sense, but today's reader can only conjecture as to the properties, costumes, make-up, or sound effects used to implement such an effect. Elsewhere, when a group is directed to enter "*in ambush*" (*All's Well That Ends Well*, TLN 1912, 4.1.0.s.d.), is the signal to be understood as fictional (a telling of the story for the reader) or is "[*as if*] *in ambush*" a meaningful theatrical signal? Similarly, when Mark Antony is directed to enter "*for the Course*" (*Julius Caesar*, TLN 84, 1.2.0.s.d.), the effect need not be fictional if Antony is attired not in a toga but in a costume appropriate for a race – hence "[*as if*] *for the course.*" That kind of thinking is clearer in *Henry*

VIII where "*The Bishops place themselves on each side the Court in manner of a Consistory*" (TLN 1346–7, 2.4.0.s.d.).[20]

To focus upon *as in* entrances and related effects is then to confront a variety of situations that bring into focus distinctive features of the drama before 1642. Starting in the Restoration but especially in the 1700s, movable scenery became an integral part of both staging and theatrical thinking, so that, from the beginning of the editorial tradition until very recently, scholars, drawing upon their sense of playgoing or imagined performances, have attached specific locales to Shakespeare's scenes, even when such specificity clashed with the original effects. What is assumed in such post-1660 or post-1700 thinking is that an actor arriving onstage enters to a pre-existing, already established "place." But as indicated by the plentiful *as from* and *as in* signals, before the emergence of scenes and sets the pre-1642 actor entered to a neutral, unlocalized space. If the locale was for some reason important, that actor then, whether through dialogue, properties, costume, or distinctive actions, brought that "place" with him or somehow signaled the place-activity he had left behind him offstage. In short, the locale did not precede the actor; rather, the actor created or signaled the locale.[21] To specify "place" in our editions (a practice still to be found in editions of Shakespeare) is then to impose a later theatrical–editorial logic upon the received texts so as to eclipse features basic to the original theatrical vocabulary.

Such eclipsing, moreover, is not limited to the editorial tradition but can also be seen in Shakespeare productions, including many recent ones. Indeed, at the opposite pole from *as if* thinking in the theatre stands not only the Arden editions (with their designations of locale) but also many productions linked to what has been termed Designer's Theatre. During the last decade, for example, one of the most visible directors for the Royal Shakespeare Company has been Bill Alexander who, along with his designers, regularly crafted imposing sets that, although adjustable in some details, nonetheless stayed in place for the duration of the performance. In his 1990–91 *Much Ado About Nothing*, for example, that set included greenery and other outdoor "arbor" features that worked very effectively for many scenes (most notably the conning of Benedick in 2.3) but had to be ignored as an intrusive element when the playgoer watched other moments (e.g., an obvious "indoor" scene such as 3.4 in which Hero and her women dressed for the wedding while the outdoor arbor, although dimmed, was still visibly in place). The same situation pertained to the sun-whitened buildings of the street scene that constituted the set for his *Twelfth Night* and the bridge and other Venetian city features that stayed in view during the Belmont scenes and the indoor trial scene in *The Merchant of Venice*. Here a sense of "place" is not only something for an actor to enter to but even something to fight against – as opposed to the original theatrical vocabulary that was predicated upon a neutral space and an entrance *as if in* or *as if from*.

In the search for a lost theatrical vocabulary, to collect *as* stage directions from two hundred years of drama cannot offset the absence of eyewitness accounts or other contemporary records. Nonetheless (as when invoking the Elizabethan approach to night and darkness), to isolate and analyze such materials is to force today's reader to attend to the presence in pre-1700 playscripts of an idiom often out of phase with widely held assumptions in both the academic and theatrical communities today. To focus upon the *as if* approach to staging and representation, especially the *as* [*if*] *in* variety, is therefore to make a dent in that language barrier that stands between us and the conversation carried on between Shakespeare and his colleagues.

CHAPTER 8

The vocabulary of "place"

"*Enter Seldome and Grace working as in their shop*"
Field, *Amends for Ladies*, 2.1.o.s.d.

"*Enter Geraldine as in his study reading*"
Cooke, *Greene's Tu Quoque*, B4v

To concentrate upon the many stage directions that invoke a theatrical *as* [*if*] is to bring into focus some fruitful questions and problems. Among the most challenging is how "place" or locale was signaled in the original productions. For centuries, readers of Shakespeare's plays have conjured up images in the theatres of their minds of famous moments linked to specific places (so who knows not "the Balcony Scene" or "the Forum Scene"?). Few of those readers, however, are aware of how little evidence has survived about the presentation of such places at the Globe. Admittedly, Elizabethan dramatists and players often *did* call attention to distinctive locales as significant parts of their narratives, so that the extant manuscripts and printed texts regularly direct figures to enter *in prison*, *in the shop*, or *in his study*. To determine how such effects were actually implemented, however, is no easy matter. The varying formulations, moreover, can have significant implications for the interpretation of Shakespeare's plays.

Why is "place" such a problem for the historian or interpreter? One reason (as noted in chapter 7) is a product of the limited resources available in a "minimalist" theatre that lacked variable lighting, elaborate sets, and a fourth wall convention. Readers accustomed to the wealth of details found in productions for television, cinema, and many modern theatres can easily forget that a forum, orchard, or battlefield at the Globe was largely a product of the spectator's imagination – as opposed to the visual treats for the eye supplied by a 1990s stage designer or property master. Admittedly, some modern interpreters *have* become sensitive to the assets and liabilities of the open stage. Today's director or stage historian therefore will usually link this sense of prison, forest, tavern, or ship to some visible property that defines the space (a grate, a tree, a bush for an inn, ropes thrown down for a ship) – a solution that makes excellent sense in today's terms and can work effectively in today's productions.

My survey of roughly 600 plays and manuscripts, however, has yielded limited evidence for such a practice. What seems self-evident or logical to a reader today (e.g., onstage trees or other greenery to convey a sense of "the forest" in *A Midsummer Night's Dream* and *As You Like It*) apparently was not standard stage practice in the age of Shakespeare. Rather, as I have argued elsewhere,[1] the scattered evidence suggests that, at the Globe or Fortune or Blackfriars, place was signaled primarily by means of costume. For example, a prison would be signaled not by a grate or by onstage objects comparable to our sense of a "set" but rather by the presence of a gaoler along with manacled prisoners. Similarly, a forester or woodsman would signal a forest; a host or vintner, an inn; figures in nautical costume, a ship. In such an onstage vocabulary, distinctive properties or costumes serve as visual clues: the gaoler's keys; the forester's green garments or weapons; the vintner's apron or handheld glasses.

Such inferences, however, are anything but definitive, for when dealing with "place" the student of theatrical vocabulary is especially hampered by the dearth of external evidence (e.g., comments from contemporary playgoers) and hence is cut off from information that would have been taken for granted by the original spectators. Rather, the investigator is left with the stage directions and with the dialogue with its many references to trees, castles, walls, bushes, gardens, and caves that most likely were to be imagined by the playgoer rather than introduced onstage. As so often happens in attempts at recovery, interpreting the extant stage directions can be highly problematic, for discussions of place and locale can quickly go astray if the editor or historian (1) ignores an implicit *as* [*if*] and (2) fails to factor in a distinction between theatrical and fictional signals. As to the latter, matters can get very sticky when the reader of a playscript cannot be sure whether an entrance *in his study*, *in the shop*, or *in the forest* is indeed theatrical (so that properties or a discovery is called for) or fictional (so that a dramatist, a theatrical annotator,[2] or an actor drawing upon his memory is thinking not in terms of what an audience would see but rather in terms of what is happening in the narrative). As I will argue in chapter 9, a different set of primary onstage images can emerge if "*Romeo opens the tomb*" (1597 quarto, K1r) is read as fictional rather than theatrical.

As with the sick-chair, moreover, to be aware of the use of costume and portable properties to convey a sense of place is to make available to the interpreter visible onstage items that, in turn, may form part of iterative patterns or strategies or may reinforce effects and meanings already noted by careful readers. In contrast, to impose upon these scripts a sense of place linked to modern stage pictures or techniques (as with the dying Henry IV as noted in chapter 2) is often to blur or block out completely what may have been integral (even italicized) parts of the original theatrical language or imagery. For those committed to historical or historicist agendas, what kind of interpretations will emerge if scholars supply details and onstage structures not seen by the original playgoers (a classic example is a bed introduced into the closet scene of *Hamlet*) and, in turn, omit from their formulations the few distinctive properties and costumes that playgoers then *did* see?

THE FOREST OF ARDEN

Certainly, the most discussed locale in Shakespeare's plays is the forest or country that often serves as a "green world" contrast to a court or city. In plays ranging from *Two Gentlemen of Verona* to *The Winter's Tale*, Shakespeare makes adept use of such symbolic landscapes that in turn have been explored at length by generations of critics and directors. Sometimes the emphasis falls upon the failure or perversion of this alternative (as in *3 Henry VI*, *Titus Andronicus*, and *King Lear*), but more often in the plays of Shakespeare and his contemporaries scenes in the forest or countryside form the stuff of comedy and romance.

The most famous of such "green world" settings is the Forest of Arden in *As You Like It*. Although generations of critics and editors have rhapsodized over the joys of Arden (for Oscar J. Campbell "an English woodland, where one might catch faint echoes of Robin Hood's horn and the shouts of his Merry Men"), A. Stuart Daley has argued forcefully against the misleading use of "forest" in such discussions. As Daley notes, the scenes associated with Duke Senior and his followers (2.1, 2.5, 2.7, 4.2) are indeed woodland scenes, but the remaining twelve "Forest of Arden" scenes are "placed" in a pastoral or pastureland setting associated with sheep-grazing and with figures such as Silvius and Corin. Much of the confusion, notes Daley, arises from "the distinctive and changing meanings of the word *forest*" which, in the age of Shakespeare, "denoted a largely untilled district composed of pastures, wastes, and usually but not necessarily woods." Daley demonstrates that, here and elsewhere, Shakespeare uses the term "forest" both ways and, after a close reading of various passages, identifies two Arden settings: "One features dark, perilous woods, hunters, native deer (and other still more emblematic beasts), a brawling brook, and a cave of self-knowing. The other is characterized by sunny fields, shepherds, sheep (and goats), a murmuring stream, and a cottage fenced with olives."[3]

Daley's critique of undifferentiated "Forest of Arden" thinking serves as a useful corrective, but his treatment of a playscript as a pastoral novel to be pored over for clues about settings and distinctions sometimes blurs important effects and meanings. On the whole, the Folio stage directions support his distinctions as applied to the experience of a spectator in the 1590s. Thus, the first Arden scene starts with the signal: "*Enter Duke Senior, Amiens, and two or three Lords, like Foresters*" (2.1.0.s.d.); later the Folio provides: "*Enter Duke Senior, and Lords, like Outlaws*" (2.7.0.s.d.) and "*Enter Jaques; and Lords,* [*as*] *Foresters*" (4.2.0.s.d.). Three of Daley's four "woodland" scenes therefore call specifically for figures dressed as "foresters" or "outlaws," presumably carrying hunting weapons, horns, and dressed in green.[4] Similarly, about fifteen lines into their first Arden scene Rosalind, Celia, and Touchstone are joined by Corin and Silvius, two shepherds, who in subsequent scenes (along with Audrey, William, and the re-costumed outsiders) help to signal the pastureland or sheep-grazing setting.

If pushed too far, however, Daley's distinctions (like any firm insistence upon "place") can mask some distinctive effects. Rather, Shakespeare's way of presenting woodland or pastureland in *his* theatre, a method that requires not a single tree, bush, or blade of grass, frees the imagination of the spectator from the trammels of verisimilar sets and provides instead distinctive images easily blurred or lost in woodsy productions. Ironically, the Elizabethan approach to onstage forests is especially conducive to interpretations of Arden as a state of mind, a potential for growth, or an interior landscape, an approach that has become commonplace in recent years among critics but does not always mesh comfortably with today's editions or productions.

What images, then, *do* emerge if an interpreter thinks in terms of an Elizabethan production of this comedy? First, if costume is to serve as a major signal, the firm distinction between woodland and pastureland does not hold up for every scene, for Orlando (addressed as a forester by Rosalind) and Jaques (presumably dressed as one of Duke Senior's men) co-exist onstage with Rosalind–Ganymede and her group in a "neutral" area. Both "places" co-exist and interact – the forester–outlaw–hunters (whose activities culminate in the song over the slain deer in 4.2) and the shepherd–grazers–nurturers. Both Rosalind's group and Orlando–Adam arrive in Arden tired and hungry only to find sustenance and support from shepherds or foresters. The full union of these two groups does not take place until the final scene, but the Orlando–Ganymede scenes, thanks to the links between "place" and costume, provide some crossover throughout.

Relevant as well in this context is the italicized moment (noted in chapter 5) when Adam and Orlando complain of starving but a banquet stands onstage in the sight of the playgoer. The previous three Arden scenes (as noted by Daley) were keyed to foresters (2.1), shepherds (2.4), and, presumably, foresters again in the setting up of this banquet for the duke (2.5). Orlando and Adam "find" the group of foresters in 2.7 and join the banquet, but in 2.6 their first entry into Arden (here described as a "desert") is associated with no visible figures but rather with a banquet table they do not or cannot "see."

What then happens if this italicized moment is treated not as an embarrassing lapse but as a defining moment? Arden would then be characterized as an apparently barren place where nonetheless sustenance is or can be available (or *if*s can come true), but first one must "see" or "find" that sustenance (or perhaps earn it). Similarly (in terms of the proxy wooing to come), Arden is a place where one's dreams can be realized, but first one must "see" them, whether the food just out of reach or Rosalind beneath the Ganymede surface. That the spectator in both instances knows that Orlando is "near" food or in the presence of his cherished Rosalind is important for the romance effect, an effect missed or blurred (along with the "seeing" motif) if the banquet is *not* visible to the playgoer in 2.6. Indeed, by means of this juxtaposition of a banquet and two starving figures, Shakespeare's Arden (first characterized by Duke Senior's famous speech in 2.1) is as well defined or orchestrated as at any point in the comedy. That definition or orchestration, however, is presented by means of an onstage vocabulary easily lost in translation.

"*ENTER IN THE SHOP*"

The Elizabethan vocabulary of "place" has many signifiers – far too many to be covered in one or more chapters. Consider as one paradigm the available ways to stage a "shop scene" in an Elizabethan theatre. Clearly, one workable option was to draw a curtain and "discover" one or more figures in such a shop. For example, "*Enter discovered in a Shop, a Shoemaker, his Wife Spinning, Barnaby, two Journeymen*" (W. Rowley, *A Shoemaker, a*

Gentleman, 1.2.0.s.d.); "*A Mercer's Shop discovered, Gartred working in it, Spendall walking by the Shop*" (Cooke, *Greene's Tu Quoque*, B1r); "*At the middle door, Enter Golding discovering a Goldsmith's shop, and walking short turns before it*" (*Eastward Ho*, A2r).[5] Occasionally such discoveries can be elaborate: "*The three shops open in a rank: the first a Pothecary's shop, the next a Feather shop: the third a Seamster's shop: Mistress Gallipot in the first, Mistress Tiltyard in the next, Master Openwork and his wife in the third*" (Dekker, *The Roaring Girl*, 2.1.0.s.d.).

Many comparable signals, however, do not specify a discovery (wherein "the shop" would be revealed by opening a curtain) but rather direct the players to enter "*in the shop*" – a locution that could be read as "*enter* [*as if*] *in the shop.*" Some of these situations could be discoveries, but most are unclear: "*Enter Signior Alunio the Apothecary in his shop with wares about him*" (Sharpham, *The Fleer*, 4.2.0.s.d.); "*Enter in the shop two of Hobson's folks, and opening the shop*" (Heywood, *2 If you know not me*, I, 283); "*Enter Luce in a Seamster's shop, at work upon a laced Handkercher, and Joseph a Prentice*" (Heywood, *The Wise Woman of Hogsdon*, V, 284); "*Enter Ralph, like a Grocer in's shop, with two Prentices, reading Palmerin of England*" (*The Knight of the Burning Pestle*, VI, 172); "*Candido and his wife appear in the shop*" (Dekker, *2 Honest Whore*, 3.3.0.s.d.). Two plays provide a series of such signals. In Heywood's *The Fair Maid of the Exchange*: "*Enter Boy in a Shop, cutting up square parchments*"; he and Phyllis "*Sit and work in the shop*"; after they *exeunt*, "*Enter Frank. The Cripple at work*"; later "*Enter Cripple in his shop, and to him enters Frank*" (II, 40–1, 44, 64). Similarly, in Dekker's *1 Honest Whore*, "*Enter Candido's Wife, George, and two prentices in the shop*" (1.5.0.s.d.); figures subsequently enter "*in the shop*" (3.1.0.s.d.) and "*in her shop*" (4.3.0.s.d.).

To call for one or more figures to "*enter in the shop*" may or may not then be equivalent to calling for a discovery. But in at least some scenes, the actors were not suddenly revealed "in" this place (a theatrical option that jibes with a post-Elizabethan fourth wall convention) but rather brought "the shop" with them onto the main stage, an option supported by Field's signal: "*Enter Seldome and Grace working as in their shop*" (*Amends for Ladies*, 2.1.0.s.d.). Thus, some tradesmen enter with their work rather than being discovered: "*Enter a Shoemaker sitting upon the stage at work Jenkin to him*" (*George a Greene*, 971–2); "*Enter Strumbo, Dorothy, Trompart cobbling shoes and singing*" (*Locrine*, 569–70). Several scenes call for a setting forth of furniture on the stage. Dekker directs: "*A Table is set out by young fellows like Merchant's men, Books of Accounts upon it, small Desks to write upon, they sit down to write Tickets*" (*If this be not a good play*, 2.2.0.s.d.). Similarly, in Heywood's *1 Edward IV* two prentices enter "*preparing the Goldsmith's Shop with plate*"; after some relevant dialogue (e.g., "come set out"; "Is here all the plate?"; "Where is the weights and balance?"; "All ready"), "*Enter Mistress Shore, with her work in her hand*," after which "*The boy departs, and she sits sewing in her shop*" (1, 63–4). At the outset of Brome's *The City Wit* (1, 279–80) a series of stage directions in the right margin reads: "*A Table set forth with empty Money-bags, Bills, Bonds, and Books of accounts, etc.*"; "*He takes up the bags*"; "*He takes up the bills and papers*"; "*He puts the Bills and Bonds into a Bag.*"

As with tent scenes, tree scenes, or "*enter sick*," Elizabethan players therefore had various options: (1) to draw a curtain so as to discover figures in a shop (and set up an initial tableau); (2) by means of furniture, costume, and properties to have figures set forth "the shop" (so that Heywood's "*opening the shop*" may have entailed the carrying onto the stage of a stall and merchandise, perhaps even an awning); or (3) have figures enter working or with the tools of their trade (one way of realizing "*as in the shop*"). The options are comparable to (1) a banquet revealed behind a curtain (from which figures come forth) versus (2) a table and food set up upon the stage versus (3) figures entering "*as from dinner.*" Given the demands of a particular narrative and the investment in shop, banquet, or other place-event, the players could present considerable detail or could opt for a more economical approach *as in* or *as from*. The latter option both increases the narrative pace and, if done deftly, sets up "images" that (perhaps) link scenes together.

For the reader primarily interested in Shakespeare's plays, shop scenes would not seem a fruitful example with which to work. Indeed, the only major "shop" in the canon is evoked by Romeo's description of the apothecary's "needy shop" in which

> a tortoise hung,
> An alligator stuffed, and other skins
> Of ill-shaped fishes; and about his shelves
> A beggarly account of empty boxes,
> Green earthen pots, bladders, and musty seeds,
> Remnants of packthread, and old cakes of roses
> Were thinly scattered, to make up a show. (5.1.42–8)

The playgoer, however, sees no such interior, for when Romeo seeks out the apothecary ("As I remember, this should be the house"), he notes "Being holiday, the beggar's shop is shut" (55–6). As with Claudio's "Is this the monument of Leonato?" (*Much Ado*, 5.3.1), whatever the actor gestures to at "this should be the house" "becomes" the shop. The apothecary then enters to Romeo's call ("Who calls so loud?" – 57) and soon after provides the vial of poison requested ("Put this in any liquid thing you will ..." – 77).

To discover a shop here would go against the dialogue and interfere with the thrust of the scene. After all, the focus is upon Romeo, not the supplier of the poison, so an elaborate display of a shop would be counterproductive. But what if the apothecary enters "[*as*] *in his shop*"? In addition to some distinctive costume, such a staging would involve some handheld property or properties, so that the vial would be brought forth not from a pocket but from a larger supply of wares (as with several figures cited above who enter bearing their "work").

Such an entrance is conjectural (although it does conform to practice elsewhere). Nonetheless, the particular asset of such an *as* [*if*] *in* approach to this moment is that the image presented would then echo comparable images presented earlier so as to set up a potentially meaningful progression. Thus, at the outset of his first scene, Friar Laurence enters "*with a basket*," talks of filling up "this osier cage of ours / With baleful weeds and precious-juiced flowers," and, in his moralization, refers specifically to "the infant rind of this weak flower" (2.3.0.s.d., 7–8, 23). To some readers and editors 2.3 may be a "garden" scene (i.e., located in a "place" where a friar can gather weeds and flowers), but the original playgoer probably saw only an actor carrying a basket from which he produced one object, a flower.

A comparable onstage image is accessible when a desperate Juliet seeks out the friar in his cell. A reader wedded to geographical "realism" may see no connection between the "place" (garden? field?) where the friar gathers weeds–flowers and "the cell" (and such "placing" is reinforced by the locale headings in many editions), but what would the original playgoer actually have seen? Previewing the apothecary ("Put this in any liquid thing you will ..."), the friar produces an object: "Take thou this vial, being then in bed, / And this distilling liquor drink thou off" (4.1.93–4). Here as in 5.1, the actor could pull forth the vial from a pocket, but he equally well could be carrying the same basket as in 2.3, a handheld property that could then reappear in 5.1 (as a version of "*enter* [*as*] *in the shop*"). Back in 2.3 the friar had noted that within the same flower (taken from his basket) "Poison hath residence, and medicine power" and had linked these two opposites or options to "grace and rude will" within humankind (2.3.24–30). If the apothecary pulls *his* vial out of a basket, the links among the three moments need not be subtle (something to be teased out after many readings) but could instead be italicized.

To postulate such a staging (which cannot be established with any degree of certainty) is to move beyond the many scripted "shop" and related signals cited earlier. Yet given the Elizabethan theatrical vocabulary such links and images are possible, perhaps even likely. A post-1660 sense of place-locale (that distinguishes firmly among garden-field, cell, and a street in Mantua outside a shop) blocks today's interpreter from even minimal awareness of a staging of the apothecary's entrance and brief appearance that would establish some meaningful connections and enhance a playgoer's sense of the choices made by the two title figures, choices visibly linked to two contrasting basket-bearing suppliers of vials. Once again, something significant may be lost in translation.

"*ENTER IN HIS STUDY*"

"Study" scenes (far more numerous than "shop" scenes) exhibit comparable staging options and, as a result, offer comparable insights into the the difficulties of interpreting the original theatrical vocabulary. Thus, one standard procedure is for a figure to be discovered behind a curtain "*in his study*": "*Horace sitting in a study behind a Curtain, a candle by him burning, books lying confusedly*" (Dekker, *Satiromastix*, 1.2.0.s.d.); "*A curtain drawn by Dash* (*his clerk*) *Trifle discovered in his study. Papers, taper, seal and wax before him, bell*" (Davenant, *News From Plymouth*, IV, 167).[6] Occasionally, an actor is directed to start a scene in a study behind a curtain and then move (or be moved) onto the main stage. For example, in the final sequence of *The Devil's Charter*, Alexander is first seen "*unbraced betwixt two Cardinals in his study looking upon a book, whilst a groom draweth the Curtain*"; then, after one speech; "*They place him in a chair upon the stage, a groom setteth a Table before him*" (L3r). Other scenes suggest comparable movement into and out of a study: "*Bacon and Edward goes into the study*" (Greene, *Friar Bacon and Friar Bungay*, 633); "*Enter Throte the Lawyer from his study. books and bags of money on a Table, a chair and cushion*" (Barry, *Ram Alley*, 426–7).[7]

Equally common, however, are scenes where no discovery is specified, but a figure is directed to "*enter in his study*," so that (as with "*enter in the shop*") the intended staging is not clear.[8] When the actor is to be surrounded by books and other objects, a discovery seems likely: "*Enter Theophilus in his study, Books about him*" (Dekker, *The Virgin Martyr*, 5.1.0.s.d.); "*Enter Bernard in his Study, Candle and Books about him*" (*The Two Merry Milkmaids*, B1r); "*Enter Guadagni in his Study. A Taper, Bags, Books, etc.*" (Brome, *The Novella*, I, 110). Relatively few of the "*enter in his study*" signals, however, include such details.

Rather, most of the relevant scenes present only the simple formula,[9] even though most of the figures involved are in the process of reading – as is spelled out in Ford's *'Tis Pity She's a Whore*: "*Enter Soranzo in his study, reading a book*" (2.2.0.s.d.). For example, in one of the playhouse manuscripts the title figure enters "*in his Study*" reading letters (Fletcher and Massinger, *Sir*

John van Olden Barnavelt, 1883), but no marginal annotations call for a discovery or additional properties. When reading "*enter in his study*" signals today, the two examples cited in the previous chapter may therefore be instructive: "*as in his Study*" (Fletcher, *The Fair Maid of the Inn*, IX, 193); "*as in his study reading*" (Cooke, *Greene's Tu Quoque*, B4v). As with "the shop," in some, perhaps many instances the actor may have brought "his study" with him onto the stage so as to enter "[*as if*] *in his study*."

Also of significance is that a large number of scenes do not specify a "study" (or do so only later in the scene) but instead direct an actor to enter reading or carrying a book.[10] If no discovery of table, books, and candle is specified, the playgoer observing a solitary figure "*enter in his study*" may have seen no more than an actor with a book. If then the theatrical emphasis was upon an entering actor in the act of reading rather than upon a discovery, "*enter in his study*," "*in his study*," or (several times) "*in a study*" in the original theatrical vocabulary may have been understood as "in his study of a book" (as opposed to "in a designated space within his house"). For example, Heywood's Frankford expresses his satisfaction with his education ("How happy am I ... I am studied in all Arts") after he enters "*in a study*" (*A Woman Killed With Kindness*, II, 102). A similar sense of "study" may be present in Heywood's *The Royal King and the Loyal Subject*: "*Enter Clinton to the Earl Chester in his study*" (VI, 74). Clinton asks: "What not at rest my Lord?"; Chester, who is hatching (studying?) new plots against his enemies, responds: "Why who can sleep / That hath a labouring brain ..."

If then a "study" (at least in some instances) can be keyed to an actor *as* [*if*] *in* such a place, an activity (reading), and a property (a book), such moments can be linked visually to other scenes in the same play in which the presence of books or reading is more obvious. The most revealing example is to be found in *'Tis Pity She's a Whore* where Ford provides an elaborate stage direction for the friar's lecture to Annabella on Hell, a theatrical signal that begins: "*Enter the Friar in his study, sitting in a chair*" (3.6.0.s.d.). Earlier editors, much concerned with "placing" such scenes, added their own headings for this action, such as "The Friar's Cell" or "Florio's House" or "Annabella's Chamber." In his Regents edition, N. W. Bawcutt provides "*Enter the Friar sitting in a chair*" and notes (p. 57): "Q's *in his study* clearly seems an error, as the scene takes place in Annabella's bedroom," an inference drawn from Florio's earlier line: "Come, father, I'll conduct you to her chamber" (3.4.33). In his Revels edition, Derek Roper does include the full stage direction from the Quarto but then provides a long note that begins: "It is uncertain where Ford meant this impressive scene to be located." Roper suggests that the dramatist initially may have been thinking of the friar's cell, yet line 44, with its reference to "below," "suggests that we are still in Annabella's chamber, with Soranzo waiting downstairs" (p. 69).

Such "place"-oriented thinking by an editor or critic, however, can blur or eclipse Ford's adept use of his shared theatrical vocabulary. Rather, when seen as part of a larger family, this "*in his study*" stage direction would call for an entrance by the friar carrying a chair (assuming such a chair was not already onstage) and, most important, carrying one or more books – in my imagined reconstruction, impressive religious tomes to support the lecture on Hell. For the playgoer conscious of imagery or iterative patterns, such an interpretation of "*in his study*" (keyed not to a distinctive "room" but rather to books and a figure reading) would then set up a clear visual analogy to two other significant moments in the play. Most obvious is Soranzo's first appearance ("*in his study, reading a book*" – 2.2.0.s.d.) where Annabella's chief suitor first reads aloud and then rejects Sannazaro's negative comments on love and indeed goes so far as to rewrite the lines to suit his own romantic optimism. Here the act of reading ("*in his study*") clearly is associated with the imposition of the reader's values and worldview upon evidence that would seem to deny or contradict them. Even more revealing, in a later climactic moment (5.3) Giovanni (in some undefined place) receives from the friar Annabella's warning letter, notes that it indeed is in her hand, reads it, but then ends up rejecting both its truths and its authenticity, thus acting out in extreme form the kind of blindness or willful misreading demonstrated earlier in Soranzo's treatment of Sannazaro.

If, however, the friar's lecture to Annabella is linked to the presence of religious books, the second of these three moments provides a decided contrast to the first and third. Instead of rejecting what is in his hand, the friar as reader accepts the efficacy of such words and indeed (here and later) stresses the danger of not paying heed. In contrast, in their handling of texts Soranzo and Giovanni act out their unwillingness or inability to face concepts that do not or cannot fit with their ruling passions, a rejection that in Giovanni's case translates into a dismissal of Hell, Heaven and God as dreams or superstitious fictions. Whether one thinks of the specific warning of danger in Annabella's letter or the larger religious truths also being rejected, matters of considerable significance are not being factored into Giovanni's equations, so that the friar's books (if present in 3.6) and the larger framework they symbolize call attention to that missing element and help to clarify the tragic protagonist's distinctive blindness as reader and chooser. To worry about where to "place" the friar's study (or Giovanni's reading of Annabella's letter) is therefore to ask a question that blurs an important part of a potentially meaningful series of scenes or configurations.

Other plays (e.g., *The Two Noble Ladies*)[11] also combine one or more "study" stage directions with a significant use of books elsewhere in the action. The best-known example can be seen in *Doctor Faustus* where books are repeatedly carried and read. For example, in the B-text Faustus enters "*in his study*" three times (29, 389, 569); later "*Thunder and lightning: Enter devils with covered dishes; Mephostophilis leads them into Faustus' Study*" (1775–6). Five books play a prominent role in the first of these scenes, Faustus' rejection of logic, medicine, law, and divinity in favor of necromancy; books provided by the devil or stolen by the clowns ("*Enter Robin the Ostler with a book in his hand*" – A-948) play a significant role later. An *as [if] in* approach to the staging of the three early study scenes that heightens the role of books would then enhance understanding of Faustus' last line: "I'll burn my books; oh Mephostophilis" (B-2092).

Both books and a verbal emphasis upon "study" are evident in several Shakespeare plays (most notably *Love's Labor's Lost* and *The Tempest*) that do not explicitly call for entrances *in his study*. Indeed, the former contains more than a third of Shakespeare's dialogue usages of study and its varying forms[12] (with most examples coming in 1.1 and 4.3, both of which scenes are centered upon books and writings). The only actual "study" stage direction in Shakespeare's plays is found in *Titus Andronicus* when Tamora and her sons (disguised as Revenge, Rapine, and Murder) "*knock and Titus opens his study door*" (13r, 5.2.8.s.d.). In a play in which books and letters have played such a major role (most notably in 4.1 where Lavinia uses Ovid's *Metamorphoses* to reveal the rape), the onstage image of a Titus who appears "[*as if*] *out of his study*" with a book in his one remaining hand could provide the climax to a sequence of linked moments, a climax easily missed when the original vocabulary is translated into today's idiom.

INSIDE THE HOUSE

Stage directions citing "the study" outnumber any comparable category linked to a specified room within an Elizabethan house (the only competitor is "the chamber" and by extension "bed scenes"). Given the requirements of the narratives, however, a significant number of scenes in Elizabethan plays are located less specifically inside homes, prisons, palaces, churches, or other buildings. As opposed to more (apparently) demanding locales (e.g., forests, tombs, or ships), such moments would not seem to pose severe staging problems, even without any equivalent to a modern set. Nonetheless, to focus upon such scenes is to confront the practical problem of how to present at the Globe something akin to what a playgoer today would expect from a scene "inside" a house.

To convey a sense of an exterior or a threshold poses few problems, for a stage door can readily represent a house door as seen from the outside, a practice familiar from both Roman comedy and Renaissance continental practice where the action takes place in the street in front of a facade representing two or three houses.[13] But to convey a sense of the interior of a house requires further adjustments that in turn may have implications for interpretation, especially for onstage imagery. How then would such an interior have been presented at the Globe or other theatres?

In such cases the primary signals are provided by the dialogue, for the action is "placed" wherever the characters tell us it is placed. To cite an extreme example (that, given Jonson's revision of his playscripts into reading texts, may not reflect actual theatrical practice), Cordatus (the choric spokesman in *Every Man Out of His Humour*) tells Mitis and the reader: "we must desire you to presuppose the stage, the middle aisle in Paul's; and that, the west end of it" (2.6.183–4). To rely upon spoken signals in this fashion is quick, flexible, and efficient. Occasionally, by means of dialogue and appropriate gestures, a playwright can even convey a sense of moving from room to room within a house. For example, in Fletcher's *The Maid in the Mill* (VII, 65) the king keeps asking "what rooms are these? ... and those?" and finally "this little Room?" until the hidden Florimel is discovered. In Heywood's *The English Traveller*, young Geraldine describes going from one room to another in Wincot's house: "The house is known to me, the stairs and rooms; / The way unto her chamber frequently / Trodden by me at midnight, and all hours" (IV, 69). After he delivers "And this the path that leads to my delight," the stage direction reads: "*He goes in at one door, and comes out at another*"; at his re-entrance he concludes: "And this the gate unto't" (only to discover Mrs. Wincot in bed with Dalavill).

The vocabulary of "place" as applied to the interiors of buildings was not, however, limited to gestures, signals in the dialogue, and re-entrances. Rather, even though playwrights and players could not present a verisimilar "room" in the terms familiar to today's viewer nurtured on cinema and television, various practical and efficient means were available to characterize an "inside" scene. As with forests, ships, and prisons, a primary tool was the use of costume – in this instance, indoor as distinguished from outdoor dress. A playgoer would therefore infer "inside" when an actor entered wearing a nightgown but "outside" if that actor was wearing a cloak. The technique can be seen at work in various *as in* signals. Thus, in general terms figures are directed to enter "*as in his house at Chelsea*" (Munday, *Sir Thomas More*, 4.4.0.s.d.); "*as in his chamber in the Tower*" (*Sir Thomas More*, 5.3.0.s.d.); or "*as in her chamber*" (Rider, *The Twins*, p. 41). To spell out "*as in his chamber*," however, Field calls for "unready" clothing (and a bed): "*Enter Scudmore, as in his Chamber in a morning, half ready, reading a Letter*" (*A Woman is a Weathercock*, 1.1.0.s.d); "*Enter Well-tried and Bould putting on his doublet, Fee-Simple on a bed, as in Bould's chamber*" (*Amends for Ladies*, 4.2.0.s.d.).

Similarly, interiors could be signaled by means of distinctively indoor properties such as chairs, stools, tables,[14] and candles-tapers (as opposed to outdoor lanterns-torches) – as in *Othello*, 5.1 (where Iago bears a torch) versus 5.2 (where Othello carries a candle). "Inside" can also be keyed to distinctively indoor personae (women, children, household servants) and to characteristic domestic activities – as in *Coriolanus* where Volumnia and Virgilia enter and "*set them down on two low stools and sew*" (1.3.0.s.d.).[15] A strong sense of "inside" is provided in Heywood's *A Woman Killed With Kindness* when a group enters "*with Cards, Carpet, stools, and other necessaries*"; then "*They spread a Carpet, set down lights and Cards*" (II, 121). The sense of a meal being served is best seen in Rowley's *A Match at Midnight* which first calls for "*A Table set out. Enter two servants, Jarvis and John, as to cover it for dinner*" and then "*Enter Jarvis with a Rabbit in one hand, and a dish of eggs in another*" (2.1.0.s.d., 34.s.d.).

As with the shop and the study, of interest here are not only the staging practices in their own right but also the implications for interpretation. To cite some representative examples, the last scene of *Arden of Feversham* is centered around Arden's chair (his domestic equivalent to a throne), an object that functions not only as a "place" signal but also (as a highly visible property on an otherwise uncluttered open stage) as a symbolic focus for the climax of the action (as opposed to being merely a piece of "furniture"). The locale for the final scene of *Othello* could be described "*as in a bed-chamber*," but a playgoer then would not have seen many items necessary for a modern director's sense of a "bedroom set." Rather, the original effect would have been keyed to: (1) Desdemona's nightly wearing (and hence her added vulnerability); (2) the candle Othello brings into the scene and subsequently addresses in symbolic-metaphoric terms ("Put out the light, and then put out the light" – 5.2.7); and (3) a bed that has been thrust onto the stage (presumably with curtains that can be drawn, first to hide Desdemona's body from Emilia, later to hide three bodies from public view – "The object poisons sight; / Let it be hid" – 364–5). In both scenes, the objects necessary to signal the place also convey potentially rich meanings. To signal a house or other interior for an Elizabethan spectator is then to introduce some distinctive costumes or properties that can in turn lead to complex meanings and effects, as with Arden's chair, Othello's candle, and Desdemona's bed.

Elizabethan staging of interior scenes was therefore flexible and economical. Shakespeare's colleagues could not provide the wealth of detail we associate with cinema or naturalistic plays, for, in practical theatrical terms, everything that was carried or thrust onto the stage for a "house" scene in turn had to be carried or pulled off moments later. Except for the rare spectacular or special effect, a premium was therefore placed upon portability and flexibility, so that scenes regularly move from street to interior or vice versa without a clearing of the stage. For example, *The Jew of Malta*, 2.3 starts with a public slave market, keyed to the presence of officers, slaves, and customers, but at the departure of those associated with the market (around line 927), the "place" becomes momentarily neutral (anywhere in Malta) until the growing controversy over Abigail becomes explicitly typed as a domestic action when Barabas forbids any sword-fighting "in my house" (around line 1036). Similarly, in Day's *Law Tricks*, the long final scene begins with the duke and others returning to his house to find his son supposedly conjuring "in his study." Without any clearing of the stage, the various unravelings of the complex plot take place, climaxing with the supposedly dead countess being discovered "*in the Tomb*" (2277) just before her husband and Horatio, her would-be poisoner, were about to be thrust "into that grave, that dead man's Inn" (2271). The stage, however, has never been cleared, so that for Day's playgoer a "house" that includes a "study" in which a figure can be discovered can co-exist with or bleed into a "tomb" (a locale already established as a major focus in the previous scene).

AN ASSORTMENT OF KEYS

To glimpse some of the interpretative potential in "house" scenes, let me focus upon one distinctive theatrical signal that, like the sick-chair, has not been sufficiently explored: the stage key or set of keys. The key is a ubiquitous onstage property throughout the period that is regularly linked (verbally and visually) to prisons, wealth (e.g., chests with money or treasure), and households[16] (and a high percentage of the likely usages are not spelled out and hence may go unnoticed by readers today). One reason for such wide usage is that a sense of locking or enclosure is basic to many narratives; indeed, so many figures in Elizabethan drama are locked into closets, studies, or other rooms that providing a list would be pointless.[17] Typical is the stage business spelled out in Tailor's *The Hog Hath Lost His Pearl*: "*Enter Hog in his chamber with Rebecca laying down his bed, and seeming to put the keys under his bolster conveyeth them into her pocket*" (1567–9).

In this wide range of scenes, the giving or taking of keys is often linked to the giving or taking of responsibility or control, whether of a prisoner (as in *Richard III*, 1.4), money, a house, some valued object, even an entire city.[18] Consider Massinger's *The City Madam* where Luke Frugal gets "the key of his counting house" (3.2.90) and hence control of Sir John Frugal's fortune after the latter's supposed death ("*Enter Luke with a key*" – 3.3.0.s.d.); in the final moments, Sir John takes back the key ("This key too / I must make bold with" – 5.3.141–2). Although the money itself is never actually shown, the control of that money central to the plot is dramatized by means of the key. Shakespeare calls attention to civic keys in *3 Henry VI* when Edward appeals to the Mayor to relinquish the title and hence the control of the city of York and concludes: "What, fear not, man, but yield me up the keys" (4.7.37). The Folio stage direction reads "*Takes his Keys*" (TLN 2538); the stage business is even more prominent in the 1595 octavo edition (D7r) where "*The Mayor opens the door, and brings the keys in his hand.*"

Interesting interpretative possibilities can then emerge when a play with a rich verbal-poetic texture includes several scenes with visible keys that serve one or more of these functions. Today's reader or playgoer may miss the connotations (and, indeed, may miss the presence of keys altogether), especially if a verisimilar sense of "prison," "house" or "closet" takes precedence over what the original spectator actually saw. Often such networks of keys or related images cannot be firmly established today, but rich signals that cry out for interpretation are apparent in such challenging scripts as *A Woman Killed With Kindness*, *The Duchess of Malfi*, *The Changeling*, and *Cymbeline*. As with the three disparate scenes in *Romeo* (i.e., "garden" versus "cell" versus "a street in Mantua"), today's reader may infer two or more distinctively different "places" in some of these plays (a prison, a madhouse, a bedchamber, a house, a closet), but, given the original staging and shared vocabulary, links among such moments may in fact have been readily grasped and hence highly suggestive. Today's reader may have lost to the passage of time a useful and potentially meaningful interpretative "key."

Typical is *Measure for Measure* which offers several clear references to keys, albeit in widely varying contexts. First, in the "convent scene" a nun tells Isabella "turn you the key" so as to let Lucio enter (1.4.8). This key need not have been visible (the phrase could be a way of saying "open the door"), but, along with the two women's costume, a key that does or does not allow a man to enter is a useful signal for setting up "a convent" on the Elizabethan stage. The presence of keys is clearest in 4.1 when Isabella displays two keys given her by Angelo to facilitate their assignation. His garden, she reveals, has a vineyard with "a planched gate, / That makes his opening with this bigger key. / This other doth command a little door / Which from the vineyard to the garden leads" (4.1.29–32). As opposed to the convent key in 1.4, these two keys are associated with lust and stealth. Finally, the duke, pretending to rebuke the Provost for beheading Claudio, states: "For which I do discharge you of your office; / Give up your keys" (5.1.457–8), a comment that suggests that the Provost, like other stage gaolers, was identified throughout the play (not merely in the final moments) by a visible set of keys.

Many passages scattered throughout this play can be cited as possible context for such iterated keys, whether discussions of liberty-restraint (e.g., 1.2.121–30), Angelo's "devilish mercy" that Isabella describes to Claudio "that will free your life, / But fetter you till death" (3.1.65–7), and even the "strange picklock" (3.2.15) found by Elbow on Pompey. In prison Pompey is told that if he helps Abhorson, "it shall redeem you from your gyves" (4.2.8–9), a line that suggests that Claudio and the other prisoners are wearing fetters throughout (as does Posthumus in *Cymbeline*, 5.4).

To note the presence of keys in three different contexts is not necessarily to offer a major re-interpretation of this complex play. Nonetheless, a network of visible (and hence readily linked) images may have been available to the original playgoers, a network easily missed (and nearly invisible) today. Should the one "nunnery" scene (1.4) somehow be linked to the series of "prison" scenes in terms of liberty versus restraint or some other set of associations? Why italicize Angelo's keys in 4.1 if not to heighten some kind of linkage? Since "place" often is generated by costume signals, relevant too is the question: how is Isabella costumed after 1.4? Does she continue to wear a wimple or some equivalent so as to carry with her a sense of the convent or has she shed any such visible link? Are such questions tangential in an already highly problematic play or do they call attention to signposts that have dropped out of sight?

For another good example of the potential significance of visible keys in terms of the original theatrical vocabulary consider *The Merchant of Venice*. Although not cited in any stage directions, keys are mentioned in the dialogue (and presumably used as props) three times in the play. (1) When Shylock goes forth to dine with Bassanio and the Christians, he tells Jessica "there are my keys" and cautions her to "lock up my doors" and "shut doors after you" (2.5.12, 28, 51). Jessica may be holding or wearing these keys when she throws down the casket to Lorenzo and announces: "I will make fast the doors, and gild myself / With some moe ducats, and be with you straight" (2.6.49–50). (2) At the end of the next scene, Morocco makes his golden choice by saying "deliver me the key. / Here do I choose, and thrive I as I may!" and Portia responds: "There, take it, Prince; and if my form lie there, / Then I am yours" (2.7.59–62). (3) Two scenes later, Arragon makes his silver choice: "I will assume desert. Give me a key for this, / And instantly unlock my fortunes here" (2.9.50–1). Not specified but to be inferred is (4) a key for the leaden casket in 3.2. (5) Another possibility (comparable to no. 1) comes when Portia, about to leave Belmont with Nerissa, states: "Lorenzo, I commit into your hands / The husbandry and manage of my house / Until my lord's return" (3.4.24–6), a speech that (like Shylock's to Jessica in 2.5) would presumably have been accompanied by the handing over of the keys that epitomize "the husbandry and manage" of a household (as in *Romeo*, 4.4.1). (6) The previous scene includes another figure likely to be bearing keys, for the profession of the non-speaking gaoler who accompanies Antonio in 3.3 presumably was signaled for the Elizabethan playgoer by a large set of keys.

Note that these moments involving keys fall into three categories. Most obviously, keys are linked to the three caskets and thereby to three different interpretations of the riddling text (and to the values behind those choices). In addition, once and perhaps twice keys are linked to the control of a house or household. Finally (as in *Measure*), keys are associated with jail and bondage, especially if Antonio is manacled in 3.3 (and today's productions often have him manacled in the trial scene as well, sometimes accompanied by a gaoler, but the Quarto is silent on both details).

In effect, in 2.5 Shylock gives to Jessica not only the keys to his house but also a theatrical property that metaphorically signals the house itself, so that any further use of those (or similar) keys carries added meaning (as would any further appearances of the keys to the three caskets). For example, in the 1590s Shylock's comment at the end of the trial scene that "you take my house when you do take the prop / That doth sustain my house" (4.1.373–4) may have been accompanied by a brandishing of his keys (Falstaff refers to wealthy city merchants who "do now wear nothing but high shoes, and bunches of keys at their girdles" – *2 Henry IV*, 1.2.37–8).

Given such staging practices, note the potential links between house keys and casket keys. As emphasized repeatedly in the dialogue, the choosers who unlock the caskets hope to find within a portrait of Portia ("if my form lie there, / Then I am yours"), but the false choosers find instead "a carrion Death" (2.7.63) and "the portrait of a blinking idiot" (2.9.53). Shylock, like Portia's father, locks up his daughter and leaves her the keys, but, unlike Portia, Jessica writes her own rules (Lorenzo announces that "she hath directed / How I shall take her from her father's house" – 2.4.29–30), so Lorenzo gets both a valuable casket and "moe ducats" in 2.6 without solving the riddle posed for Morocco, Arragon, and Bassanio. The analogy between Jessica in the house (2.5, 2.6) and Portia in the casket (2.7, 2.9, 3.2) need not be abstruse given the close proximity of the scenes, the limited number of female figures, and the prominence of the keys, especially if, for both practical and symbolic reasons, the same set of large, very noticeable keys was used in all five scenes. Such an economical use of one visible property would enhance a network of links in this part of the play. For example, a viewer would be encouraged to compare Bassanio's "freeing" of Portia from her casket-restraint through his leaden choice ("I am locked in one of them; / If you do love me, you will find me out" – 3.2.40–1) to Lorenzo's "freeing" of Jessica from her house-hell, especially if the Venetian casket thrown down in 2.6 to the lover below resembled one or all of the three Belmont caskets first seen in 2.7 and prominent thereafter.

Various other interpretative possibilities are generated by onstage keys. Critics regularly link the casket choices in Belmont to the Antonio–Shylock plot or, in general, to the play after 3.2. What if a gold and a silver key remain as visible properties after the caskets themselves have disappeared? For example, Shylock could wear or brandish a silver key during the trial when his "what judgment shall I dread, doing no wrong?" (4.1.89) or "my deeds upon my head!" (204) echoes Arragon's "I will assume desert." Here or elsewhere, the continuing presence of such a property would underscore the persistence of gold and silver choices, especially by figures not linked to the Belmont caskets.[19]

Consider another conjectural possibility. In her big speech after Bassanio's leaden choice, Portia notes that until now she "was the lord / Of this fair mansion, master of my servants, / Queen o'er myself" (so she controlled the keys), "but now, / This house, these servants, and this same myself / Are yours, my lord's." Portia does not transfer her mansion, servants, and self by handing over her keys; rather, she states: "I give them with this ring, / Which when you part from, lose, or give away, / Let it presage the ruin of your love / And be my vantage to exclaim on you" (3.2.167–74). If the casket keys (or the household keys of 2.5) are on a ring (as in Elizabethan illustrations), for these two lovers one ring has superseded another (with the second and more prominent ring crucial to the final movement of the comedy). Unlike Morocco and Arragon (and perhaps Lorenzo), Bassanio has passed one test involving a ring (of keys) and so will face a second challenge linked to the bond symbolized by this newly won ring of betrothal. Again, what may sound overly ingenious in the telling could be (then or now) obvious to a spectator who may have seen a ring of keys as many as seven times between 2.5 and 3.4.

Relevant too are the potential links between keys and interpretation. Thus, the Geneva Bible glosses Matthew 16:19 ("And I will give unto thee the keys of the kingdom of heaven"): "The preachers of the Gospel open the gates of heaven with the word of God, which is the right key: so that where this word is not purely taught, there is neither key, nor authority."[20] Whether in scriptural terms or in Bassanio's leaden choice, "the right key" is therefore linked to correct interpretation and true authority. Conversely, false or "lewd" interpreters (see 3.4.80) such as Morocco, Arragon, and Shylock misuse or fail to use their keys and, as a result, suffer deprivation, whether financial, familial (Shylock's loss of Jessica), or marital (Morocco and Arragon have sworn "never to speak to lady afterward / In way of marriage" – 2.1.41–2). Relevant too may be the subjection of the Antonio of 3.3 (as opposed to the Antonio at the end of 4.1) to a key-bearing gaoler. If Shylock during the trial does indeed brandish a large ring of gold and silver keys, various subtle points and links advanced by literary critics would be clearly visible to any playgoer.

Readers looking for a tidy interpretation of this comedy (or *Measure for Measure*) will be frustrated by my questions, conjectures, and open-ended approach. To the skeptic, moreover, I can offer no evidence from the Quarto that the Lord Chamberlain's Men in the 1590s brought onstage a ring of keys as posited here (or gold and silver keys in 4.1). My goal in presenting such conjectures is neither to provide a "definitive" reading nor to display my ingenuity but rather, here and elsewhere in this book, to demonstrate a significant but easily overlooked feature of all theatrical scripts but especially those that survive in the quartos and the Folio. Not only are many meaningful signals missing, but Shakespeare, at the stage in the creative process represented by this quarto, may have taken for granted a subsequent stage when he and his actor–colleagues would have a further opportunity to deal with such matters as they bodied forth his script. As a result, the combination of missing signals and post-1660 assumptions about "place" and imagery may block off today's reader from both the presence and the potential meaning of keys and similar properties. Again, we are eavesdropping on the early stages of a conversation conducted in a language we only partly understand. What and how much is therefore being lost in translation?

As argued throughout this chapter, such problems are particularly acute when dealing with the Elizabethan vocabulary of "place." Whether with Henry IV's "Jerusalem" (see chapter 2), the Forest of Arden, the apothecary's shop, the friar's study in '*Tis Pity*, or the keys in *Merchant*, to explore the original staging of various distinctive "places" is to witness a collision between their theatrical vocabulary and ours. Awareness of this collision, in turn, occasions some hard questions. In particular, in setting up various interpretative edifices, to what degree are editors, directors, and historicists in tune with the original blueprint? What are the implications when an italicized moment (e.g., the unseen banquet in *As You Like It*, 2.6) is eclipsed but an unhistorical image (e.g., an onstage bed in *Hamlet*, 3.4) is prized? Whose images are being developed, today's interpreter's or Shakespeare's?

CHAPTER 9

"*Romeo opens the tomb*"

"*a Tomb, placed conveniently on the Stage*"
James IV

Regardless of the original staging or theatrical vocabulary, various "places" in Shakespeare's plays have captured the imaginations of generations of readers: the Forest of Arden; the castle at Elsinore; the Forum. Included in any such list, especially for those with a romantic bent, is the final sequence of *Romeo and Juliet*, for who knows not this scene of murder, suicide, and thwarted love – first in a graveyard, then in the Capulet tomb or monument? Here, moreover, the onstage configuration for the playgoer is (apparently) not in doubt, for the unusually explicit stage directions in the 1597 ("bad") Quarto spell out what readers for centuries have taken for granted: "*Paris strews the Tomb with flowers*" (I4v); "*Romeo opens the tomb*" (K1r).

My goal in this chapter, however, is to explore in detail these stage directions, the scene from which they come, and the larger category of tomb–monument scenes, for, unlike most readers today (including editors of *Romeo*), I find these and comparable signals highly problematic. Indeed, in the case of "*Romeo opens the tomb*," I may understand *Romeo*, but, after much effort, I still have considerable difficulty with both *opens* and *the tomb*.

The reasons for those difficulties should by now be evident, for to tackle "*Romeo opens the tomb*" is to run head-on into the problem generated by Hosley's distinction between *theatrical* and *fictional* stage directions. If such a signal is *theatrical* and hence directed at an actor, Romeo would have opened and Paris would have strewn his flowers upon an onstage tomb property of some kind (as assumed by the Arden editor and most readers). In contrast, if such signals are *fictional* and hence a telling of the story, the two actors would have strewn flowers and performed some kind of opening, but the playgoer would not necessarily have seen an elaborate, verisimilar structure that served as "The Tomb." In the latter option, the narrative fiction of a graveyard or tomb could have been sustained by means of dialogue, appropriate gestures and actions, and the imaginative participation of the playgoer, but that playgoer may, in fact, have witnessed only Juliet in a coffin thrust onto the stage.

To pursue such a fictional versus theatrical distinction is to return to my question number 2: what constitutes evidence? Where can the historian turn to determine the staging of tomb scenes in this period? Since the external evidence is limited to three entries in Philip Henslowe's papers (to be discussed below),[1] what (if anything) can that historian learn about "*Romeo opens the tomb*" from other plays and playwrights?

As with many of my categories, examples are plentiful, but clear indications about staging are rare. Tomb or monument scenes (and graveyard scenes with strong similarities) turn up in roughly thirty plays, a few of them antedating *Romeo* but most following. The signals about staging provided in the extant texts vary widely. A few plays keep open the possibility that a tomb–monument–vault may be linked to a trap door and hence be located below, but that option is hard to document. Several tombs are discovered, presumably by means of a curtain or a stage door, but most scenes do not specify a discovery; at least twice, moreover, stage directions call for tombs to be carried or placed upon the stage (and hence not discovered).

These thirty scenes vary widely in placement and complexity. There are several last scene tombs, as in *Romeo*, 5.3, and several first scene tombs. Some scenes are very brief, almost in shorthand (e.g., the dumb show in *Pericles*, 4.4), but two plays from the early 1600s involve elaborate sequences of more than one scene, an investment in time that *may* suggest the presence of a verisimilar tomb property. Most common, however, is a one-scene effect (comparable to many of the "tree" scenes noted in chapter 3) wherein the action at a tomb is clearly part of the flow of the play, with no indication of (or apparent time for) the introduction of some special onstage structure. A few of the scenes therefore suggest that onstage structures *could* (perhaps) be introduced to display a tomb, but the largest group of scenes provides no such evidence and, as I read the relevant signals, *could* have been staged by means of a coffin in conjunction with a stage door, a stage post, or a trap door. In what follows I will therefore focus upon this evidence and upon the question: what are the possible theatrical meanings of *tomb* in the extant stage directions or dialogue? In their theatrical vocabulary (or system of differences) what are the options or possible meanings for "*Romeo opens the tomb*"?

To start with an early example from the 1560s, in the final moments of *Apius and Virginia* "*Doctrina and Memory and Virginius bring a tomb*" (1185–6). In this play or venue, "a tomb" is something that can be carried by three actors (at least two of whom are boys). According to the dialogue, moreover: "We Ladies three have brought the Corse in earth that must be placed" (1184), so that a corpse to be placed in the earth is implicitly or explicitly included in this portable "tomb." A subsequent stage direction reads: "*Here let Memory write on the tomb*" (1192–3); and Fame adds: "Then sing we round about the Tomb in honour of her name" (1201). In this pre-public theatre example the tomb cited in two stage directions and the dialogue appears to be a coffin or hearse that can be brought onstage by three actors.[2]

Consider, at the other end of the chronological spectrum, one of several Caroline tomb scenes – in Ford's *Love's Sacrifice* (pr. 1633) – where, as in *Apius* (and *Romeo*), the final scene is centered upon a tomb. First, "*A sad sound of soft music. The Tomb is discovered*" (L1v); then enter four with torches, two friars, "*after the Duke in mourning manner*"; "*Coming near the Tomb they all kneel, making show of Ceremony. The Duke goes to the Tomb, lays his hand on it. Music cease.*" After a long speech, in which he refers to "the bosom of this sacred Tomb," the duke says: "set ope the Tomb, that I may take / My last farewell, and bury griefs with her"; "*One goes to open the Tomb, out of which ariseth Fernando in his winding sheet, only his face discovered*" (L1v).

This climactic "tomb" is therefore something that can be discovered, knelt before, touched, then opened so that a figure can arise in a winding sheet. An elaborate verisimilar structure is possible, but equally possible (and very efficient) would be a closed coffin discovered behind a curtain or door that either remains in this upstage "within" position or is thrust forward to become a more visible focus for the action (eventually to be opened). In this latter interpretation of the theatrical vocabulary, the *fiction* of a tomb would be set up and sustained, but the playgoer would actually *see* a single coffin.

I cite these two examples that span over sixty years of theatre in part as context for "reading" the relevant entries in Henslowe's inventory. In his papers Henslowe lists three tombs, two of them linked to specific plays ("1 tomb of Guido, 1 tomb of Dido"), one of them not (so the previous line reads: "1 rock, 1 cage, 1 tomb, 1 Hell mouth").[3] The tombs linked to Guido and Dido are associated with lost plays and hence can only be speculated about (e.g., would Dido in this instance have been burned on her funeral pyre?). The apparent all-purpose tomb listed separately, however, suggests the availability of a theatrical property that may have corresponded to our sense of "tomb."

Before coming to such a conclusion, however, the reader should be aware of the presence in this inventory (p. 320, line 83) of "2 coffins" – a relevant and widely used portable property essential for many scenes. Should Henslowe's reference to a generic tomb (as opposed to the two items specifically linked to Dido and Guido) be construed as the kind of tomb-property the Arden editors would associate with *Romeo*, 5.3 and *Much Ado*, 5.3? Thus, for the latter the Arden editor deems that "an impressive tomb (a stage-property, as in *Romeo and Juliet*) is essential to symbolize the gravity of death and the purgatorial nature of Claudio's reverence" (p. 210). Or should this tomb be read as a portable and practical stage device that, to us, would look more like a coffin than a monument, perhaps a sarcophagus that, with or without an occupant, could be brought or thrust onstage by several actors (as in *Apius and Virginia*)? That possible tomb–coffin equation is supported by a passage in

Marston's *Antonio and Mellida* where "the breathless trunk of young Antonio" (5.2.211) is brought onstage in "*a coffin*" (according to the stage direction at 208) or a "mournful hearse" (according to the dialogue – 210), but the still living Antonio rises from the coffin-hearse to announce: "There stands my tomb" (251). In short, the reader of Henslowe's inventory may be facing the same vocabulary problem that bedevils the reader of stage directions.

To introduce more plays and stage directions does not resolve this problem. Consider a play that antedates *Romeo*, Greene's *James IV*, where the opening stage direction reads: "*Enter after Oberon, King of Fairies, an Antique, who dance about a Tomb, placed conveniently on the Stage, out of the which, suddenly starts up as they dance, Bohan a Scot, attired like a ridstall man, from whom the Antique flies*" (2–5). Oberon asks "why thou dwellest in a Tomb...?" (41); and Bohan talks of "shutting my self into this Tomb" (71). As with a comparable Jacobean example (*The Valiant Welshman*),[4] an opening-scene call for "*a Tomb, placed conveniently on the Stage,*" out of which a figure "*suddenly starts up*" *could* signal a special onstage structure (as many scholars envisage in *Romeo*, 5.3) set up before the play starts, but (here and in a later dumb show) it could just as likely signal a coffin or sarcophagus that, like a bed, could be carried or thrust on and off the stage as needed. What is essential at the outset of *James IV* is the *fiction* of Bohan's tomb and the effect of having that figure suddenly start up from it so as to frighten away all save Oberon.[5] What the playgoer actually saw is open to question, although "*placed conveniently on the Stage*" would rule out something behind the stage facade available to be discovered.

A few plays keep open the possibility that a tomb–monument–vault may be linked to the trap door and hence be located below. Such an effect would be comparable to burial scenes (e.g., *Hamlet*, 5.1, *The Two Maids of More-Clacke*) where a body is interred; similarly, a Globe play, *A Larum for London*, uses a "vault" below for a murder. A tomb sequence in *Fidele and Fortunio*, a play from the 1580s, locates the tomb either in the trap or in a coffin,[6] but, as a translation from the Italian that may never have been staged, this text is suspect as evidence about English theatrical procedures. The original staging of the opening scene of *Titus Andronicus* is by no means clear, but the interment of first the sons brought back from the wars and then of Mutius may have been done by means of a trap door, a choice that, in turn, would set up a visual analogy to the clear use of the trap in Act 2 for the bloody pit in the forest (and perhaps as well for the disposition of Aaron in the final moments).[7]

Plays with more than one tomb scene can place greater demands upon the staging (and hence involve more investment of time and energy in this distinctive "place"). In *The Second Maiden's Tragedy*, the Tyrant calls for "the keys of the Cathedral" (1702) and "close lanterns and a pickax" (1705); after an *exeunt*, "*Enter the Tyrant again at a farther door, which opened, brings him to the Tomb where the Lady lies buried; The Tomb here discovered richly set forth*" (1725–7). His speeches then provide the appropriate details and atmosphere: "Softly, softly" for "the vaults e'en chide our steps" (1728–30); "the monument woos me, I must run and kiss it" (1736); "All thy still strength / thou grey-eyed Monument shall not keep her from us" (1749–50). After the soldiers refuse, the Tyrant himself uses an axe to "strike" and "pierce the Jaws / of this cold, ponderous creature" (1751–3); once the monument is open, he orders the soldiers to "remove the stone that I may see my mistress" (1786). After referring again to the monument (1822) and "this sanctified building" (1821), he takes away the body and orders: "place you the stone again where first we found it" (1870). Comparable to yet still different from *Romeo*, 5.3, this violation of a tomb is therefore a two-step process that starts with a penetration of the tomb-monument (by means of an axe) and builds to a removal of a stone to get access to the actual body. That the tomb is "*here discovered richly set forth*," moreover, could be read as a signal that, after the opening of a door or arras, an ornate object is thrust or set forth onto the stage (although the more obvious meaning would be that the discovered tomb-coffin is richly decorated).

A very different picture is painted in the next scene of the contrasting lover. First, "*Enter Govianus in black, a book in his hand, his page carrying a Torch before him*" (1877–8); after a dialogue reference to the "monument" (1879), "*Govianus kneels at the Tomb wondrous passionately, His Page sings*" (1891–4); then: "*On a sudden in a kind of Noise like a Wind, the doors clattering, the Tombstone flies open, and a great light appears in the midst of the Tomb; His Lady as went out, standing just before him all in white, Stuck with Jewels and a great crucifix on her breast*" (1926–31). The stage directions for both scenes are unusually elaborate, but the designated effects *could* be managed by means of a stage door, a coffin "*richly set forth,*" and a stone to be removed. Although highly suggestive to the reader today, such phrases as "*the Tomb where the Lady lies buried*"; "*The Tomb here discovered richly set forth*"; "*Govianus kneels at the Tomb*"; and "*the Tombstone flies open, and a great light appears in the midst of the Tomb*" are *not* self-evident clues to what happened at a Jacobean performance. Complex onstage activity is needed to sustain the required narrative fiction, but the actual images witnessed by the original playgoers need not have been all that elaborate, for what is "necessary" in addition to a stage door, an ornate coffin, and a stone is unclear.

The most demanding tomb sequence (and hence the best evidence for some separate structure) is to be found in Chapman's *The Widow's Tears*, although, again, the signals can be puzzling, even contradictory. The long sequence starts when Lysander in disguise "*discovers the Tomb, looks in and wonders*" (4.2.0.s.d.). He describes Cynthia (not yet seen by the playgoer) "tearing her hair, and drowned in her tears" (8); after calling "Ho! who's in the Tomb there?" (14), he talks first to Ero, the servant, then to Cynthia (no *enter* stage directions are provided for either woman). At the end of the scene, Ero "*shuts up the Tomb*" (179); after Lysander's speech and exit, the next scene begins: "*Cynthia, Ero, the Tomb opening*" (4.3.0.s.d.); after Lysander successfully woos Cynthia, the scene ends with Ero hearing a noise, so "*She shuts the tomb*" (77). New figures arrive in 5.1, so Tharsalio "*looks into the tomb*" (22) and sees Lysander and Cynthia; after an *exeunt*, "*The Tomb opens, Lysander, Cynthia, Ero*" (5.2.0.s.d.); the women exit (although no stage direction is provided) and Lysander, after overhearing that he is being sought, "*slinks away.*" The next scene begins: "*Tomb opens, and*

Lysander within lies along, Cynthia and Ero" (5.3.0.s.d.); after Lysander leaves to get implements to open the coffin, the women "*Shut the Tomb*" (60); Tharsalio "*knocks*," says he has food and drink, so "*Ero opens, and he sees her head laid on the coffin, etc.*" (137); again, the scene ends: "*Shut the Tomb*" (177).

To begin the final sequence, Lysander returns with tools to open the coffin ("*a crow of iron, and a halter which he lays down*" – 5.5.0.s.d); he knocks (16.s.d.) and Ero "*opens and he enters*" (18). The scene that follows is centered on the debate over whether or not to open the coffin (clearly distinguished, in this instance, from the tomb). Finally (and most curiously), Lysander is captured, so that "*Soldiers thrust up Lysander from the Tomb*" (126). This latter "*thrust up*" is the only such evidence that "the tomb" is below, for the other opening and closings (although possible with a trap) sound more like a door or opening to some standing structure (in which a coffin can be housed). Nonetheless, this one "*up*" stands out as opposed to the emphasis upon "*within*" earlier.

Certainly, this long sequence of "tomb" scenes (central to the final third of this comedy) *could* be done effectively with an onstage "pavilion" or other temporary structure (and some of the stage directions would make good sense in such a context). As with the comings and goings in other plays in various "house" or "room" scenes, however, the reader should never underestimate the flexibility of the chameleon open stage. Something is opened and closed with regularity (more so than in any comparable play), whether an arras, a stage door, or a trap door; the latter option seems limited, given the dialogue and extended business, but *is* reinforced by the appearance of *up* in the final relevant stage direction. Here, in conjunction with Henslowe's inventory, is the best evidence for an elaborate and distinctive onstage "tomb."

In contrast to these two sustained tomb sequences, a much larger group of plays present their tomb scenes as part of the flow of the play (and not necessarily as the final scene), so that a "tomb" is introduced as necessary for the fiction or narrative but with no break in the sequence of scenes, no indication of anything especially elaborate. Closest perhaps to *Romeo*, 5.3

(and less than a decade later) is the tomb scene in *How a Man may Choose a Good Wife from a Bad.* Like Juliet, the good wife (Mistress Arthur) has (in this instance, unknowingly) drunk a sleeping potion (although her husband intended to poison her). Anselmo, who (like Paris) has wooed Mistress Arthur but been rejected, visits the tomb to mourn (H2r): "This is the Church, this hollow is the Vault, / Where the dead body of my Saint remains, / And this the Coffin that enshrines her body" (he also provides a lot of verbal atmospherics, as in "This place of dead men's bones is terrible"). Echoing Romeo, he gives his last farewell and kisses her, only to discover: "Her lips are warm, and I am much deceiv'd / If that she stir not." A centered stage direction then reads: "*Mistress Arthur in the Tomb*"; according to Anselmo, "she sits upright" and asks: "How come I then in this Coffin buried?" (H2v). Anselmo replies that he "Was hither sent by some strange providence, / To bring you from these hollow vaults below." After a comic interlude in which a schoolmaster and several boys are frightened away ("what's that in the white sheet?"), Anselmo takes her away.

How would this scene have been staged in the early 1600s? An elaborate tomb property *could* have been introduced but would seem superfluous for a relatively short scene two-thirds of the way through the play (followed by a quick shift to another locale with no noticeable break in the sequence). Note too that the body is visible, approachable, even kissable in its vault-tomb (with nothing, whether tomb or coffin, for Anselmo to pry open). Obviously, a coffin is needed, but that coffin–tomb could be either thrust out from the stage facade (as with a bed scene) or (perhaps) thrust up from the trap (a choice that would enhance the dialogue emphasis upon a vault).

A comparable effect is to be found in Day's *Law Tricks*, where the virtuous Countess is poisoned by her husband, old Count Lurdo, and Horatio, a would-be lover, but, unknown to all three, Horatio's page has given her a sleeping potion instead. In 5.1 the page enters "*with a Thieves' Lantern*" (1740–1) fearful "thus late to tread the cloister vaults" (1749); he announces: "But here's the tomb" (1759) and apparently can see the Countess ("her cheeks now are chilly, as is the pale lily, / But when her eye uncloses, they'll look like two fair Roses" – 1761–2). When Horatio enters "*with a light*" (1763), the page hides behind the tomb ("For once this tomb shall be my screen"; "*He hides himself*" – 1767–8); Horatio then laments and repents: "Soft, stay, this same's the chilly monument, / That hugs her body in his marble arms" (1784–5). After some extended business (Horatio departs, returns, the page provides an echo), the Countess awakes to ask: "how came I in this tomb?" (1874). As in *How a Man May Choose*, much is made of the tomb or vault in the dialogue, but apparently the body is visible from the outset (though here a tomb cloth is mentioned several times). Again, the limited evidence does not rule out an elaborate tomb structure or property, but the required fiction of a tomb *could* be sustained with only an open coffin.[8]

A more elaborate mid play tomb sequence is to be found in Fletcher's *The Knight of Malta*, 4.2, where Miranda and Norandine, visiting a churchyard to pray at night, hear the groans of the buried, supposedly dead Oriana. In the dark, the two seek the source of the noise ("Here, 'tis here Sir, 'tis here Sir; / A devil in the wall") and discover "a new tomb, new trickments too" and eventually "a Tablet / With rhymes upon't" (VII, 139). After more groans ("Sure from the monument, the very stone groans for her" – 140), the stage direction reads "*She rises up*"; Oriana speaks, then "sinks again" (141), then provides more groans, so Miranda exhorts: "Help with the stone first, oh she stirs again" and "Come help the Coffin out softly, and suddenly" (141). After their departure, a second group enters (including Mountferrat, the person responsible for Oriana's fake death), "*with a dark Lantern*" (142) to discover that the body is gone: "how is this, the stone off?"; "I, and nothing / Within the monument, that's worse; no body / I am sure of that, nor sign of any here, / But an empty Coffin" (143). Then Gomera (Oriana's husband) arrives "*with Torch*" only to discover: "The Tomb wide open / The Stone off too? the body gone" (145).

The theatrical signals here are plentiful but highly ambiguous. Clearly, Oriana is within a coffin (from which she can rise, so it is presumably uncovered) within a monument either blocked or covered by a stone. The stone sounds theatrical or verisimilar, not fictional – hence an object to be removed (as in *The Second Maiden's Tragedy*), but is the "monument" a verisimilar structure introduced solely for this scene? Or is it a to-be-imagined space behind a stage door (as may be suggested by references to the noise in the wall) with a stone placed in front of that door or a to-be-imagined space beneath a trap door that is covered with a stone? A tablet with the epitaph could then be discovered hanging on the stage door or a stage post (an epitaph-scroll is also present in *Much Ado*, 5.3). As with most of my examples, what is essential is (1) a coffin and (2) the fiction of a monument or tomb. In this instance, the presence of a stone leads to added business but does not in itself necessitate a verisimilar onstage monument. Indeed, the presence of such a stone (perhaps placed adjacent to the coffin in the space left open by the stage door) could have served as a theatrical signal to the playgoer for the fiction of "a monument."[9]

The lengthy sequence in Marston's *Antonio's Revenge* could be staged efficiently with relatively few demands. To be sure, the initial signal for Andrugio's funeral (2.1.0.s.d.) calls for an elaborate procession that includes cornets and a sennet, mourners with torches and streamers, and a herald with the dead man's helm and sword: "*the coffin set down, helm, sword and streamers hung up, placed by the Herald, whilst Antonio and Maria wet their handkerchiefs with their tears, kiss them, and lay them on the hearse, kneeling.*" This bedecked coffin or hearse then may stay onstage for some time (there is no signal for its removal). In a dumb show that begins Act 3, Piero woos Maria, but "*she seemeth to reject his suit, flies to the tomb, kneels and kisseth it*" (3.1.0.s.d.); given Marston's apparent equation of tomb and coffin–hearse in *Antonio and Mellida* (as noted above), here Maria presumably kisses the coffin (or bedecked hearse). What follows clearly takes place "in the church"; so at his entrance Antonio asks "Is this Saint Mark's Church?" and "Where stands my father's hearse?"; the page responds: "Those streamers bear his arms" (3–5). After ordering "Set tapers to the tomb, and lamp the church" (6), Antonio defines the "place" further by addressing "Graves, vaults, and tombs," "Most honoured sepulchre," and "Tomb" (9–13); Andrugio's ghost then "Forsakes his coffin" (34) and "that sepulchre" (83); and Antonio tells Julio: "This is Andrugio's hearse" (170). Finally, after killing Julio, Antonio sprinkles the blood on the coffin–hearse–tomb: "I sprinkle round his gore, / And dew thy hearse with these fresh-reeking drops" (210–11). Again, the original staging cannot be recovered without doubt, but all this action could be done with a bedecked coffin–hearse (the same object that is brought in in 2.1) that is then referred to (along with the theatrical space around it) as "the tomb" or "sepulchre."[10]

In *The Atheist's Tragedy* Tourneur provides a distinctive "monument scene." Initially, two hearses are brought in for two funerals (though Charlemont is not dead), so that the bodies–hearses are "set down" (3.1.1): "There place their arms, and here their epitaphs, / And may these lines survive the last of graves" (13–14). A ceremony follows that involves the reading of the two epitaphs, three volleys, and such references as "These two Herculean pillars where their arms / Are plac'd there may be writ *Non ultra*" (44–5); and "I've bury'd under these two marble stones / Thy living hopes and thy dead father's bones" (51–2). When the public mourning is over, "*Enter Castabella mourning, to the monument of Charlemont*" (52.s.d.); she reads the epitaph and sheds tears "on / The altar of his tomb" (57–8). At this point, Charlemont arrives to visit "the fatal monument" of his father (65), only to find Castabella "mourning o'er my hearse" (71); a bit later (126.s.d.): "*Charlemont finds his father's monument.*" Clearly two hearses–coffins are brought in and deposited and then arms and epitaphs are hung up so that Castabella and Charlemont can see and read them, but the dialogue references to "Herculean pillars," "marble stones," and "the altar of his tomb," and the two stage directions that call for a "*monument*" do not distinguish for today's reader what was seen from what was "fictional."[11]

In the Shakespeare canon, if one sets aside the burial of Ophelia and the laying out of the bodies of Cloten and Imogen–Fidele, four relevant scenes are to be found in addition to *Romeo*, 5.3. As noted above, the placing of bodies in the tomb of the Andronici in 1.1 could have been done by means of a trap door or stage door. The penultimate scene of *Much Ado About Nothing*, the appearance of Claudio, Don Pedro, and mourners at the monument of the supposedly dead Hero, requires at a minimum not even a coffin but only a place for a scroll-epitaph to be hung (e.g., a stage door or stage post). Here, moreover, the locale is established efficiently by Claudio's opening line ("Is this the monument of Leonato?" – 5.3.1), for whatever he points to "becomes" that monument for the playgoer.

The "tomb scenes" in two later Shakespeare plays are greatly abbreviated. The scene in *Pericles* is encompassed by one stage direction (4.4.22.s.d.): "*Enter Pericles at one door, with all his Train; Cleon and Dionyza at the other. Cleon shows Pericles the tomb, whereat Pericles makes lamentation, puts on sackcloth, and in a mighty passion departs.*" Gower frames this dumb show with his speeches and provides the epitaph; earlier, Dionyza had noted that "her monument / Is almost finished, and her epitaphs / In glitt'ring golden characters express / A general praise to her" (4.3.42–5). I find it hard to imagine that an elaborate tomb structure would have been brought onstage just for this dumb show; indeed (as in *Much Ado*, 5.3), an epitaph ("in glitt'ring golden characters"?) somehow prominently displayed, even without a visible coffin, could suffice.

A similar theatrical shorthand appears to be invoked in *Timon of Athens* where, sandwiched between two Senator scenes, we find: "*Enter a Soldier in the woods, seeking Timon*" (5.3.0.s.d.). Finding a grave or tomb ("What is this?" – 2), the soldier concludes: "Dead, sure, and this his grave. What's on this tomb / I cannot read; the character I'll take with wax" (5–6). In the next scene he reports that Timon is dead "And on his gravestone this insculpture, which / With wax I brought away" (5.4.65–8). Again, the fiction is of a tomb or grave, but the object that must, in fact, be visible or available is the epitaph, here linked to a gravestone (that could be verisimilar or fictional). "This tomb" as identified by the actor–soldier could be a coffin, a stage pillar, a trap door, or a stage door.[12]

As suggested by these (and other) examples, *tomb* is a slippery term that (in the original theatrical vocabulary as revealed in stage directions) can refer to something verisimilar or, even more likely, to something to be partly or wholly imagined. None of the examples cited disproves the proposition that in such situations Elizabethan, Jacobean, or Caroline companies brought onstage (or discovered) a verisimilar tomb–monument property. Nonetheless, a sifting through the evidence suggests that in some, many, perhaps even most supposed "tomb scenes" the original playgoer may have actually seen little more than a single coffin (however bedecked) and in a few instances (as in *Much Ado*, *Pericles*, and *Timon*) perhaps even less. Henslowe's "1 tomb" must be played off against Marston's Antonio's equation of "*a coffin*" or a "mournful hearse" as "my tomb."

To emphasize what may *not* have been onstage in this canon of scenes, however, is to neglect one distinctive feature of *Romeo*, 5.3 that rarely turns up elsewhere. Thus, a large number of figures other than Paris and Romeo seek out loved ones in a tomb or graveyard; Juliet is the first of a series of heroines who wake up to find themselves in coffins or tombs. But if one puts aside the digging implements used for putting bodies into the ground (as in *Hamlet*, 5.1), only four plays I have found actually call for tools to pry open a tomb (with *Romeo* the earliest). In *The Widow's Tears* a disguised Lysander enters "*with a crow of iron, and a halter*" (5.5.0.s.d.) to open his own (empty) coffin; this final testing of his wife backfires, however, for he is hesitant ("my very arm relents / To strike a stroke so inhumane, / To wound a hallow'd hearse?" – 64–6), but "*She snatches up the crow*" (68.s.d.) and offers to do it herself. This prying tool, however, is invoked to open a coffin, not the tomb (in which this coffin is housed). In Davenant's *The Wits* a "*crow of iron*" (II, 211) is brought onstage (supposedly to dig up treasure buried in a coffin) and, after being discarded, leads to the arrest of a hapless figure for sacrilege ("Look; a dark lantern, and an iron crow; / Fine evidence for a jury" – 215). Only in *Romeo* and *The Second Maiden's Tragedy*, however, does a lover use such tools to pry open the tomb of his beloved.

Consideration of the latter scene, even though a decade or more later, may be useful as a window into *Romeo*, 5.3. To be true to Govianus and resist the Tyrant, the Lady has killed herself, but the Tyrant persists in his pursuit even after her death. After the tomb is discovered, the Tyrant tells a soldier to "strike" (24) and "Pierce the jaws / Of this cold, ponderous creature" (25–6), but the soldier is afraid: "I shall not hold the axe fast, I'm afraid, sir" (27). The Tyrant orders: "Take thou the axe from him" (32) and, when the soldiers subsequently hesitate to remove the stone: "Set to your hands, you villains, and that nimbly, / Or the same axe shall make you all fly open!" (53–4). As in *Romeo*, this scene provides a strong sense of the penetration of the tomb (by means of an axe) and (as in *The Knight of Malta*) the subsequent removal of a stone (so a two-step process); that axe, moreover, is used first as a prying-opening tool by an intemperate lover, then as a threat of violence against those who would interfere (so as to provide a distant equivalent to Romeo's fight with Paris). The Tyrant's axe therefore emerges here as a major image in its own right, not merely a tool for a practical purpose.

With all this context in mind, let me return to the final scene of *Romeo and Juliet* and to my questions (1) and (3): what would an audience in the mid 1590s actually have seen; and, equally important, so what? That some special structure or large property was introduced to serve as a tomb cannot be ruled out, but no such unequivocal signals survive here or in the twenty to thirty comparable scenes. Moreover, although Brian Gibbons concludes that "the scene requires that the bodies [of Tybalt and Juliet] are visible once the tomb is open" (New Arden edition, p. 225), the evidence in the quartos supports no such requirement, for Romeo's reference to Tybalt ("liest thou there in thy bloody sheet" – 97) need not "require" that a playgoer see the actual body. Rather (as often happens in today's productions), Romeo can "create" the corpse by conjuring it up in our imaginations – as Juliet had conjured it up before she took the potion (and, to my knowledge, no other play of the period calls for such additional bodies to be visible). In simplest terms, the tomb may have been represented by a stage door (or, less likely, a trap door), and Juliet's body (in its coffin–bier) would then have been thrust forth at the appropriate time (just as Desdemona would have been thrust forth upon her bed to start the final scene of *Othello*). In this interpretation of the original theatrical vocabulary, a coffin (however ornamented or enhanced) would therefore be to a tomb as a bed is to a bedroom – a form of onstage synecdoche wherein the part generates the whole.

If one takes such a minimalist approach, note what follows, starting with the entrance of Paris. The Q1 stage directions spell out what is implicit in the Q2 dialogue: "*Enter County Paris and his Page with flowers and sweet Water*"; "*Paris strews the Tomb with flowers*" (I4v). The Q2 speech that accompanies the latter action begins: "Sweet flower, with flowers thy bridal bed I strew / (O woe! thy canopy is dust and stones)" (5.3.12–13). If the Q1 stage direction is *theatrical*, then Paris here strews his flowers on or around some verisimilar structure. On the other hand, if the stage direction is *fictional*, by strewing flowers and talking about a "canopy" Paris defines an otherwise unlocalized stage space, perhaps linked to a stage door (or trap door), as "the tomb" (so, in this "minimalist" interpretation, the spectator would *not* see a special onstage structure that represents "*the Tomb*"). As with Claudio at the outset of *Much Ado*, 5.3, Paris (in this reconstruction of the staging) in effect "creates" the tomb for the playgoer. Meanwhile, this figure shows himself to be a particular kind of lover, one obsessed "with tears distilled by moans" and "obsequies and true love's rite" (15, 20).

Next, according to Q1, Romeo and Balthasar enter "*with a torch, a mattock, and a crow of iron,*" with those implements cited in both quartos' dialogue ("Give me that mattock and the wrenching iron"). In a major speech, Romeo then lies about "why I descend into this bed of death," threatens Balthasar if he returns ("I will tear thee joint by joint / And strew this hungry churchyard with thy limbs"), and characterizes "the time and my intents" as "savage-wild, / More fierce and more inexorable far / Than empty tigers or the roaring sea" (22–39). Romeo, like Paris, helps to create a sense of the churchyard and "this bed of death" by his lines and behavior. In addition, the contrast between the two lovers of Juliet, one with flowers and sweet water, the other "savage-wild" with mattock and crow of iron, could hardly be more striking.

At this point (before Paris intervenes) comes the Q1 stage

direction: "*Romeo opens the tomb*" (K1r); the Q2 speech reads: "Thou detestable maw, thou womb of death, / Gorged with the dearest morsel of the earth, / Thus I enforce thy rotten jaws to open, / And in despite I'll cram thee with more food" (45–8). What follows is familiar to everyone: the fight and the death of Paris (not in the source), the finding of Juliet in "this vault" (86), and the deaths of the two lovers. What is often glossed over, however, is the twin problem of (1) what does Romeo "open" ("Thus I enforce thy rotten jaws to open" – later to be closed: "Seal up the mouth of outrage for a while" – 216) and (2) what is the function of the two tools? The answers seem self-evident to the reader with a naturalistic bent who imagines a verisimilar tomb that must be pried open by "real" tools. But, for a variety of practical and imagistic reasons, these implements are invariably omitted from modern productions (so of roughly a dozen renditions I have seen, the only one to include an actual mattock and crow of iron was the wildly hilarious version presented in the Royal Shakespeare Company's *Nicholas Nickleby*).

To return to the many virtues of *as* [*if*], what then happens if we conceive of the entrances of both Paris and Romeo (on a bare apron stage) *as* [*if*] *in a graveyard*? In this staging, a sense of "the tomb" would be conveyed not by a physical structure thrust onto the stage but by dialogue references ("thy canopy," "this vault," "the stony entrance of this sepulchre" – 141) accompanied by gestures to a stage door or trap door. Paris's flowers and sweet water (as objects that would be carried by a conventional mourner) further establish a sense of place (as in *Much Ado*, 5.3), as do the digging or prying implements brought in by the inexorable, savage-wild Romeo. The latter's highly visible properties would therefore function not as tools to be used for "real" prying but rather as signals or theatrical shorthand to convey a sense of a tomb. Just as a playgoer knows it is "dark" when figures on a fully lit stage cannot see each other or infers "in prison" when manacled figures are accompanied by gaolers wearing keys, so that playgoer recognizes a tomb when figures enter with accoutrements appropriate to a graveyard.

How then are we today to "read" or understand "*Romeo opens the tomb*"? If this tomb was a distinctive property (in keeping with the item in Henslowe's inventory), some structure would either have been discovered behind a curtain or stage door (as signaled in several comparable scenes) or "*richly set forth*" downstage (a possible reading of the stage direction in *The Second Maiden's Tragedy*) or "*placed conveniently on the Stage*" (as in *James IV*). In this interpretation of the vocabulary, Romeo would use verisimilar tools to pry open a verisimilar tomb. Here, moreover, is the scene most familiar to today's reader (although, as I have noted, not to today's playgoer, who rarely gets to see the tools).

On the other hand, if the tomb is "fictional," Romeo would use his verisimilar (and, given roughly thirty comparable scenes, very distinctive) tools to attack and open some otherwise neutral part of the open stage – most likely a stage door (although a trap door cannot be fully ruled out). In this interpretation of the vocabulary, the Romeo-actor would go through the motions of using a mattock and crow of iron to open a tomb but, in fact, would actually attack some permanent feature of the stage. Indeed, by such actions the actor would establish for the playgoer that the stage door (or trap door) is, in fact, to be understood as the opening to that tomb. Once the actor "*opens the tomb*," Juliet, in an open coffin, would then be "*richly set forth*" downstage or "*placed conveniently on the Stage.*" The possibility does exist, in either reading of the Q1 stage direction, that the action around the coffin takes place within the discovery space and not on the thrust stage, for neither here nor with Juliet's bed earlier (4.3–5) is there a specific signal to thrust forth a large property. Such "*bed thrust forth*" stage directions, however, do turn up regularly in later plays, so that I am assuming that for both scenes Juliet is positioned downstage of the tiring house facade rather than within it (so that a strong visual analogy between the two moments is encouraged).

What are the advantages in teasing out such options? So what? First, note the added metaphoric or symbolic potential of a minimalist staging. On an obvious level, when watching the conflict between Paris and Romeo the playgoer is presented with two contrasted lovers or sets of values, with one of them literally and symbolically destroying the other. Indeed, one reason for a director's cutting the mattock and crow of iron today is to sustain a "romantic" view of Romeo undercut or qualified by Shakespeare's signals. Equally important, if Romeo uses verisimilar tools to pantomime an opening of an imagined tomb, his speech addressed to "thou detestable maw, thou womb of death," can take on added meaning, especially: "Thus I enforce thy rotten jaws to open, / And in despite I'll cram thee with more food." The metaphoric emphasis here is upon a forcing open, a violation, associated with Death and Appetite, for Romeo is forcing open the "jaws" and cramming himself into the "maw" that will devour him (and Juliet). If that violation, moreover, is of an imagined, not a verisimilar tomb, Romeo (like the Tyrant with his axe) is not merely performing an action necessary to the story (opening the tomb to reach Juliet) but, more important, is acting out his tragic error by breaking open what should be inviolate and thrusting both himself and, unknowingly, Juliet into the maw of death (with overtones perhaps of violated virginity), a choice presented in terms of savage-wild appetites out of control (a maw gorged with morsels, "cram thee with more food," "hungry churchyard"). Such associations could be further enforced if Juliet thrust forth in her coffin occupies the same stage space as had Juliet in her bed when taking the potion.

The minimalist approach to this scene best suits my own interpretative tastes and reflexes, for, as noted above, various images and ideas are brought into sharp focus by a staging that combines verisimilar tools and an imagined tomb. Nonetheless, what a playgoer in the 1590s actually saw when watching 5.3 must remain in doubt, for none of the evidence cited here can firmly establish how Shakespeare and his colleagues staged this scene. In a curious fashion, however, post-1590s scholarly and theatrical emphasis upon a verisimilar tomb has pulled attention away from what does emerge as the most distinctive (and unusual) "image" in this particular tomb scene – the savage-wild lover using a mattock and crow of iron to rip open whatever separates him from his beloved (while also dispatching his more conventional rival wooer, whether by means of a sword or, more savagely, by means of his prying tools). Examples of lovers at the tombs of their beloveds may be plentiful, but only the Tyrant with his axe and Romeo with his two prying tools provide such a strident (and, for me, highly disturbing) image.

As often happens in this book, the evidence from my canon of relevant plays turns out to be opaque rather than transparent so as to generate questions rather than answers. Have scholars, editors, and readers seriously confronted the implications of "fictional" stage directions? To what extent do scenes such as *Romeo*, 5.3, actually *need* a verisimilar tomb? What are the possible functions of verisimilar tools on the open stage, especially if there is no verisimilar structure to pry open? To what extent does the straitjacket of scenic naturalism or the conditioned reflexes drawn from cinema and television (all of which lead inexorably to the postulation of an elaborate verisimilar tomb) stand as a barrier between today's reader and the full range of possibilities available in the original production? Here and with the "place" examples cited in chapter 8, upon whose images are historicists building their interpretations?

CHAPTER 10

Vanish and vanishing

"*they heavily vanish*"

The Tempest, 4.1.138.s.d.

As is evident in the preceding chapters, a recurring problem in any attempt to recover a lost theatrical vocabulary of the 1590s and early 1600s is our inability today to distinguish between (1) onstage effects that would have been accepted as verisimilar by the original playgoers and (2) comparable effects that would have been accepted as "real" by figures onstage but, in turn, realized fully only by means of the imaginative participation of those playgoers. With access only to stage directions, dialogue, and the rare eyewitness account, the interpreter today often cannot determine whether a tomb, a forest, a tent, or a prison was represented by verisimilar properties brought onto the stage or, in contrast, was represented by means of dialogue, appropriate actions, costume, and portable properties in conjunction with the imaginary forces of the spectator. Interpretations today, whether on the page or on the stage, can therefore be skewed if the interpreter invokes an elaborate object or effect that was not there in the original (a tree, a tomb, a bed) and at the same time buries some object or effect that would have been obvious, even *italicized* for the original playgoer (e.g., Romeo's mattock and crow of iron).

As a particularly revealing (and often puzzling) demonstration of the dimensions of the problem, let me turn for a final example to a word – *vanish* – that recurs in stage directions and related dialogue throughout the period and is to be found in eight stage directions in Shakespeare. Again, my purpose in singling out such scenes is to pose the questions basic to my work: (1) what would the original playgoers have seen at such moments? (2) how can we tell? and (3) so what?

Consider first the instances of *vanish* in the Shakespeare canon. Two of the relevant stage directions deal with objects rather than with people. In *The Two Noble Kinsmen*, when Emilia enters to make her plea to Diana, she is preceded by an attendant "*carrying a silver hind, in which is conveyed incense and sweet odors*" (5.2.136.s.d.). The hind is set upon an altar which is set on fire. After Emilia's long speech, the stage direction at line 162 reads: "*Here the hind vanishes under the altar and in the place ascends a rose-tree, having one rose upon it*"; six lines later, "*Here is heard a sudden twang of instruments and the rose falls from the tree.*" In a better known moment in *The Tempest*, just as Alonso and his courtiers are about to partake of the banquet that had been brought in by "*several strange Shapes*" (3.3.17.s.d.), Ariel "*like a harpy*" appears (accompanied by thunder and lightning), "*claps his wings upon the table; and with a quaint device the banquet vanishes*" (52.s.d.). Clearly, in both instances the "vanishings" are linked to "*a quaint device,*" some form of stage trickery (facilitated in *The Tempest* by the harpy's wings which, when clapped upon the table, conceal the mechanism).[1]

The other instances, however (involving actors rather than a silver hind or a banquet), may or may not have involved a theatrical trick or special effect (such as a sudden disappearance through a trap door). All of these vanishings, moreover, involve magic or the supernatural. Later in the same scene in *The Tempest*, after Ariel's thirty-line speech to the "three men of sin," "*He vanishes in thunder*" (82.s.d.). In the next scene, the masque builds to its climax in the dance of Nymphs and Reapers "*towards the end whereof Prospero starts suddenly and speaks; after which, to a strange, hollow, and confused noise, they heavily vanish*" (4.1.138.s.d.). In *Macbeth* stage directions twice call for the witches to vanish: after their encounter with Macbeth and Banquo (1.3.78.s.d) and, in a moment that editors deem an interpolation from another play, at the end of the cauldron scene (4.1.132.s.d.). In *Cymbeline*, shortly after Jupiter has ascended upon his eagle, the father, mother, and two brothers of

Posthumus (who are directed to enter "*as in an apparition*" and who "*circle Posthumus round as he lies sleeping*" – 5.4.29.s.d.) also "*vanish*" (122.s.d.). Similarly, shortly before her death both a sleeping Queen Katherine and the playgoer see six "personages" who dance and take turns holding a garland over her head. Just before she wakes up and speaks "*(as it were by inspiration) she makes (in her sleep) signs of rejoicing and holdeth up her hands to heaven. And so in their dancing vanish, carrying the garland with them*" (4.2.82.s.d.).

How then would such moments have been staged at the Globe or Blackfriars? The sudden disappearance of one figure (Ariel, the ghost of Julius Caesar or Hamlet's father) *may* be accounted for by means of theatrical technology or trickery. At the other extreme, I find it hard to imagine the four family members in *Cymbeline* or the graceful dancing figures in *Henry VIII* being whisked off instantaneously through a trap door. And what exactly does "heavily vanish" mean in *The Tempest*, 4.1? The most obvious gloss of *heavily* would be "with sorrow, grief, displeasure" (*OED* no. 3) so as to describe the dejected mood of the departing figures, but the term could equally well refer to the manner in which the disappearance is to be handled ("with heavy, laborious, or dragging movement; laboriously, sluggishly; without elasticity or animation" – *OED* no. 2).[2] In such cases, what would the original playgoers have seen? What are the options?

To answer such questions, the performance historian or would-be detective must consider more than the few stage directions already cited. Here the end of *Julius Caesar*, 4.3 can prove useful, for that moment sets up a paradigm relevant to the two scenes in *Macbeth*, at least one *exit* in *Hamlet*, and comparable moments in non-Shakespeare plays.[3] Thus, shortly after his quarrel with Cassius and his decision to fight at Philippi, Brutus is seen reading while three other figures (Lucius, Claudius, Varro) are asleep onstage, at which point "*Enter the Ghost of Caesar*" (4.3.274.s.d.). The Folio, however, not only signals no *vanish* for this figure but provides no *exit* at all (as noted in chapter 4, not an uncommon omission in printed playscripts of the period).

Rather, after the ghost's third and final line ("Ay, at Philippi"), Brutus responds: "Why, I will see thee at Philippi then" and then adds: "Now I have taken heart thou vanishest" (285–7).

From the vantage point of this onstage observer, "this monstrous apparition" (277) has vanished, a reaction that, as already noted, cannot establish firmly what a playgoer at the Globe would have seen. Shakespeare, moreover, then has Brutus cross-examine Lucius and the other two figures who had slept through this manifestation ("Didst thou see anything? ... Saw you anything?") so as to stress that Brutus alone was witness to the ghost (that identifies itself not as Julius Caesar but rather as "Thy evil spirit, Brutus" – 282). Does the presence of Brutus' "thou vanishest" and his quizzing of the three sleepers suggest the use of a "vanish" trick (so that the dialogue reinforces what the playgoer has witnessed) or does such verbal underscoring after the fact indicate that the playgoers are being encouraged to *imagine* a "vanish" they have not actually seen? How are we to read this evidence?

The interpreter faces the same problem twice in *Macbeth*. When the witches vanish at the end of the cauldron scene, Macbeth reacts: "Where are they? Gone?" (4.1.133) and then asks Lennox: "Saw you the weird sisters?" (136) and "Came they not by you?" (137). Earlier, after the first encounter with the witches and their *vanish*, the two figures react:

BANQUO: The earth hath bubbles as the water has,
  And these are of them. Whither are they vanished?
MACBETH: Into the air, and what seemed corporal melted
  As breath into the wind. Would they had stayed!
BANQUO: Were such things here as we do speak about?
(1.3.79–83)

As in *Julius Caesar* 4.3, what is the function of this kind of exchange? To enhance a stage trick, a verisimilar vanishing? Or to establish a sense of vanishing by means of signals in the dialogue in conjunction with the playgoer's imagination (as with Oberon's "I am invisible" – 2.1.186)? What kind of *exeunt* by the three witches would have preceded this exchange at the Globe? A "real" disappearance? Or a "normal" departure witnessed by the playgoer but somehow not seen by Macbeth and Banquo?

Consider also some comparable business in *Hamlet* where the ghost at its second appearance is "about to speak" but then "started, like a guilty thing / Upon a fearful summons" and "faded on the crowing of the cock" (1.1.147–9, 157). None of the three early printed editions specifies an *exit* or *vanish*, but, according to one onstage observer, the ghost "faded," and, according to Horatio in the next scene, the ghost, at the sound of the cock, "shrunk in haste away / And vanished from our sight" (1.2.219–20). The problem of how the ghost should exit is further complicated by the business signaled in the dialogue where the three figures note "'tis here," "'tis here," "'tis gone" as two of them seek to forestall the ghost's departure with their partisans. Curiously, only this one of the ghost's five exits is signaled in a special way or given unusual emphasis (presumably owing to the cock-crowing).[4] Again, is the dialogue emphasis enough (with a normal *exit*) to gain the effect? Or does this moment require something trickier, more illusionistic?

Given the dearth of stage directions in the printed texts of the period, the would-be reconstructer of Elizabethan–Jacobean onstage procedures often must build upon the evidence in the dialogue, a seemingly logical avenue to pursue but one fraught with difficulties. In these instances (the disappearances of the witches and the two ghosts), does the presence of dialogue that calls our attention to vanishing or fading indicate that X *was* seen by the original playgoer (so that the spoken words reinforce a verisimilar effect) or, conversely, does such dialogue indicate that X was *not* seen (so that the sense of vanishing sought by playwright and players must therefore be spelled out in the spoken words, with the total effect then completed by the imaginative participation of that playgoer)?[5] The latter option is in tune with various often-cited passages in *Henry V* – such as the choric plea for the playgoers to use their "imaginary forces" to "piece out our imperfections with your thoughts" or "eke out our performance with your mind" – and is essential for at least some Elizabethan stage effects (battle scenes, onstage darkness).

My own tastes lead me to prefer the imaginative rather than the verisimilar approach to this problem. Nonetheless, whether the *vanish* pertains to a single figure (Ariel as harpy, the ghost in *Hamlet*, the spirit of Caesar), three witches, four members of Posthumus' family, six dancing figures bearing a garland, or a group of nymphs and reapers, the interpreter today cannot be certain whether in the original productions such figures disappeared (or "faded") by means of a quaint device that sustained an illusion of vanishing (as is clearly the case with the disappearing banquet and silver hind) or disappeared by means of a "normal" *exit* visible to the playgoers but (for whatever reason) unseen by the onstage observers. Is the playgoer to accept the *vanish* because of a verisimilar stage effect or because of some theatrical convention or because of some oral–aural signal (as with "I am invisible")? Wherein is the source of *vanish*? Given our distance (in various senses) from the original productions and culture, how are we to tell?

The obvious way to answer such questions is to pursue evidence outside the Shakespeare canon. After an extensive search I have found widespread use of the term in stage directions and dialogue, but I am still left with questions rather than answers. Let me summarize.

First, the verb *vanish* turns up in two of the very few eyewitness accounts of actual productions.[6] First, in his 1623 letter to Robert Carr recounting a viewing of *A Game at Chess*, John Holles starts with Ignatius Loyola who (in the prologue or induction) rages at how slowly his plots are being carried out but is comforted by a disciple. According to Holles, "the plot is revealed him [Ignatius], prosperously advanced by their design upon England: with this he vanisheth, leaving his benediction over the work."[7] Of the many extant manuscripts of the play, however, none has a *vanish* stage direction here; rather, the manuscripts in Middleton's hand designate no *exit* or *exeunt* at all; in his transcripts Ralph Crane adds an *Exeunt*. Holles's *vanisheth* may therefore be only an equivalent for *depart* or *exit*, although it *could* refer to some special stage effect.

Similarly, writing in 1637 R. Willis describes a lost late moral play, *The Cradle of Security*, seen in his youth in Gloucester. After the three ladies corrupt the prince-hero, "they got him to lie down in a cradle upon the stage" and put "a vizard like a swine's snout upon his face, with three wire chains fastened thereunto, the other end whereof being holden severally by those three Ladies." At this point, two old men appeared who "went along in a soft pace round about by the skirt of the Stage, till at last they came to the Cradle, when all the Court was in greatest jollity, and then the foremost old man with his Mace struck a fearful blow upon the Cradle; whereat all the Courtiers with the three Ladies and the vizard all vanished; and the desolate Prince starting up bare faced, and finding himself thus sent for to judgment, made a lamentable complaint of his miserable case, and so was carried away by wicked spirits."[8]

Given some misdirection, to make a vizard *vanish*, especially one held on wire chains by three ladies, *is* theatrically feasible. However, to have the courtiers and the three ladies "vanish" in some verisimilar fashion is another matter indeed, especially for a company on the road offering a moral play in the 1570s or 1580s. As in many later plays, a sense of sudden vanishing *is* important to the narrative fiction – here to highlight the gap between what is transitory and what is permanent. The experience of watching this play and particularly this ending, moreover, had a major impact upon Willis who writes some sixty years later: "This sight took such impression in me, that when I came towards man's estate, it was as fresh in my memory, as if I had seen it newly acted." But here (as for different reasons with Holles's "vanisheth") "all vanished" is highly suspect as a literal or factual description of an onstage action, for, even on a London stage, much less on the road in front of the Mayor of Gloucester, to make a minimum of five actors *vanish* is a formidable undertaking. Rather, taken together these two accounts suggest the usefulness of *vanish* as a narrative tool to summarize the *fiction* conveyed by the staging rather than a term to provide an accurate account of the onstage *event* – in Hosley's terms, a *fictional* as opposed to a practical *theatrical* description.

Similarly, other evidence does not support a verisimilar

vanish. As indicated by the stage directions in *The Tempest* and *The Two Noble Kinsmen*, objects (a banquet, a silver hind) could be made to vanish before a playgoer's eyes by onstage trickery, but, after much looking in a large canon of plays, I have found little firm evidence that points to a comparable effect with an actor.[9] Given no variable lighting, the obvious way to stage such a verisimilar *vanish* would be by means of either a trap door or some cloaking effect (such as fireworks or a mist), so I have looked at every play I could find in which figures depart through a trap or in which a mist or fireworks are invoked. I *have* found one clearly marked *vanish* linked to a mist, but most of the "mist" scenes do not involve vanishings, and no other vanish situations call for mists.[10]

Trap-door scenes are equally unhelpful. Examples are plentiful from the 1580s through 1640 of figures that, according to the stage directions or dialogue, descend or sink into the ground, whether spirits associated with magic wells, sinners, or especially devils, but sinking or descending is rarely linked to *vanishing*. The best case for a verisimilar *vanish* by means of a trap door is found in *The Two Noble Ladies*, where the devils driven off by an angel "*sink roaring*; *a flame of fire riseth after them*"; and the angel points out: "at my sight with fear / the fiends are vanish'd" (1860–3). Here a verisimilar *vanish* is possible but uncertain given the emphasis upon sinking, roaring, and fire and the departure of two or more devils. Overall, there are many clearly marked *vanish* effects and many departures through trap-doors, but the two groups rarely overlap.[11]

In dialogue as opposed to stage directions, the verb *vanish* is widely used to describe departures, often in contexts that have nothing to do with either the supernatural or stage trickery. Rather, in Shakespeare and elsewhere (including perhaps the eyewitness accounts of Holles and Willis), *vanish* regularly serves as an equivalent to *go* or *depart*, often as an imperative that means "get out of here!" – as when an angry Antony tells Cleopatra: "vanish, or I shall give thee thy deserving" (4.12.32).[12] Indeed, dramatists such as Jonson, Fletcher, Massinger, and Davenport have characters say "I vanish" and mean no more than "I'm out of here!".[13] Some usages are tantalizing, as when a figure is described as "vanish'd as suddenly as a dumb show" (Robert Tailor, *The Hog Hath Lost His Pearl*, 992), but most instances in the dialogue cover "normal" situations. For example, in *1 Hieronimo* at Don Andrea's departure, Bel-Imperia remarks: "Yet he is in sight, and yet – but now he's vanish'd" (2.67), wherein a disappearance from her view, presumably by means of a normal exit through a stage door, can be described as "he's vanish'd."

Some straightforward uses of *vanish* in the dialogue may shed light on the more problematic situations. Thus, in several instances a normal if fast *exit* (e.g., to avoid recognition) can be described as a *vanish*. For example, in Brome's *The English Moor*, Arthur brings in Millicent, "*unveils her, and slips away*" (II, 77); in response to the question "how went he?", the page responds: "I know not, Sir, he vanish'd suddenly."[14] Moreover, as with several of the Shakespeare scenes (e.g., *Cymbeline*, *Henry VIII*, *The Tempest* 4.1) some uses of *vanish* in the dialogue refer to groups, even large groups, rather than individuals. For example, at the end of Shirley's *Chances* four masked couples "*march over the stage, and Exeunt*" (K2v); an onstage observer reacts: "What are they vanished?" so clearly to him an *exeunt* of eight figures can be described as a *vanish*. Similarly, in Brome's *The English Moor*, "How now! all vanish'd!" (II, 16) is a reaction to the *exeunt* of a group of masquers.

When a dialogue use of *vanish* is linked to the supernatural, the results can be puzzling. For example, in a clumsy imitation of *Richard III*, eleven ghosts appear to Messalina in Nathaniel Richards' tragedy of that name; after their *Exeunt* (2553), she reacts: "Close eyes and never open, all's vanish'd now. / 'Twas but the perturbation of my mind / So let it pass – " (2554–6). For this villain–protagonist, a *vanish* is to close her eyes upon such horrors, then open them to find all eleven ghosts gone. Even closer to *Richard III*, 5.3 is a final dream experienced by a sleeping Bajazet in Thomas Goffe's *The Raging Turk* where Nemesis leads in seven ghosts who "*One after another strike at Bajazet with their swords, Nemesis puts by their blows. Exeunt in a solemn dance*" (3398–9). After a short speech and exit by Nemesis, an angry Bajazet awakes and says: "You meager devils, and infernal hags, / Where are you? Ha? what vanish'd?" (3406–7). As with the non-supernatural instances cited earlier, here "what vanish'd" can describe seven figures who "*Exeunt in a solemn dance.*"[15]

If trap door scenes and dialogue usage are less than conclusive, the obvious place to turn is the widespread use of *vanish* in stage directions, but, as in Shakespeare, these signals can be singularly unrevealing about the actual staging. Typical is the situation in *A Looking Glass for London and England* when the first of a series of angels appears to Jonas, gives its message, and "*This said, the Angel vanisheth*" (985). No such signal, however, is to be found in the three other comparable scenes (where an angel exits or departs). A verisimilar disappearance is indeed possible here (in a play with several spectacular effects that require the use of the trap), but unlike figures in other plays Jonas himself does not remark upon this vanishing. Equally uninformative is the situation in one of the playhouse manuscripts, *The Two Noble Ladies*, after Cyprian the conjuror brings forth a spirit bearing a shield upon which Lysander reads the truth about his parentage. Once the message has been conveyed: "*Recorders play. The Spirit vanishes*" and Lysander adds: "It vanishes, and I can read no more" (1099–1100). The "*Angel shaped like a patriarch*" (1101), however, who then appears with a comparable message on his breast for Cyprian, is given an *exit*, not a *vanish* (1122), as are the other supernatural figures in this magic-laden romance.

The most puzzling single stage direction occurs in Dekker, Ford, and Rowley's *The Witch of Edmonton*. Here, with Frank Thorney lying on his bed, the stage direction reads: "*He lies on one side: the Spirit of Susan his second Wife comes to the Bed's-side. He stares at it; and turning to the other side, it's there too. In the mean time, Winnifride as a Page comes in, stands at his Bed's-feet sadly: he frighted, sits upright. The Spirit vanishes*" (4.2.69.s.d.). Should the movements from one side of the bed to the other and then the *vanish* be portrayed from Frank's point of view or the playgoer's (two very different effects)? In his 1981–82 Royal Shakespeare Company production director Barry Kyle sidestepped any verisimilar trick or stage illusion; rather, he had his Susan enter to a drowsy Frank, then move to the other side (with him turning to see her there), then exit, so that he followed her with his eyes but slowly, after the fact. Are we to imagine a verisimilar approach to this moment in the seventeenth century? If so, how would the effect have been achieved?

Vanishing is especially important in Dekker and Massinger's *The Virgin Martyr* where an angelic figure brings heavenly fruit to Theophilus and then "*Angelo vanisheth*" (5.1.56.s.d.). After the devil–tempter Harpax "*sinks a little*" (152.s.d.) when threatened with the fruit, Angelo appears and departs a second time and Theophilus reacts: "It is, it is some Angel, vanish'd again!" (165). Editor Fredson Bowers inserts "[*Harpax vanishes.*]" at line 156 immediately after "*Enter Angelo,*" but, in the original printed text, angels vanish and devils sink. Thus, after a Theophilus tormented on the rack has a vision of Angelo and the martyred Christians: "*Exit Angelo, the devil sinks with lightning*" (5.2.238.s.d.). In the original edition, a devil therefore sinks twice, but only the angel vanishes (however it was done).

Of special interest for those interested in the closet scene in *Hamlet* is Heywood's *2 The Iron Age* where Orestes kills Egistus, then calls upon "you powers of Heaven" to "Give me some sign from either fiends or angel" of what to do to his mother, at which point: "*Enter the Ghost of Agamemnon, pointing unto his wounds: and then to Egistus and the Queen, who were his murderers, which done, he vanisheth*" (III, 422–3). Like Gertrude, Clytemnestra does not see a ghost visible to both Orestes and the playgoer, but her son takes the ghost's appearance and pointing as "that sacred testimony, / To crown my approbation." Orestes does not mention a *vanishing* effect (or even remark about the ghost's departure), but initially he says "Lady see," then "Rest Ghost in peace, I now am satisfied, / And need no further witness," followed by a change to the past tense: "saw you nothing?" Clearly, to Orestes the ghost is present up to a point, then gone.

The clearest example of a *vanish* that is *not* verisimilar is to be found in Barnes's *The Devil's Charter* when Pope Alexander calls forth a devil to reveal how two figures had been murdered. For the first, the devil "*goeth to one door of the stage, from whence he bringeth the Ghost of Candy ghastly haunted by Caesar pursuing and stabbing it, these vanish in at another door*"; for the second: "*He bringeth from the same door Gismond Viselli, his wounds gaping and after him Lucrece undressed, holding a dagger fixed in his bleeding bosom: they vanish*" (G2r). If only the second of these instant replays had survived, "*they vanish*" would be as unrevealing as most of my other stage directions, but, unlike any other evidence I have found, the first set of figures "*vanish in at another door*" (i.e., at a door other than the "*one door of the stage*" from which the devil originally brought them). If one can trust Barnes,[16] these two vanishings were therefore effected not by means of a verisimilar trick but by means of a movement across the stage and an *exeunt* through a stage door.[17]

Dekker's *Old Fortunatus* poses an interesting problem, for although one imperative *vanish*–depart does occur in the dialogue (5.2.9), the term is *not* used in any of the three instances in which, according to the narrative fiction, figures suddenly disappear by means of a magical wishing hat. Fortunatus, the first user of the hat, says: "Would I were now in Cyprus with my sons" (2.1.108) and has an immediate *Exit*; the Soldan reacts appropriately ("get me wings, I'll fly / After this damn'd Traitor through the air" – 110–11) but has no *vanish* lines. Later, after gaining the hat, Agripyne says: "O England, would I were again in thee," a line again followed by *Exit* (4.1.90); like the Soldan, Andelocia reacts as might be expected ("She flies like lightning" – 94), but again no *vanish* is mentioned in stage directions or dialogue. Finally, a disguised Andelocia retrieves the hat, takes Agripyne by the hand, and says: "Would I were with my brother Ampedo" (5.1.159); in the original text, "*Exit with her*" then precedes Agripyne's line: "Help, Father, help, I am hurried hence perforce" (160). In response to the king's order ("Draw weapons ... / Stay the French Doctor" – 161–2), his men can do nothing, for "so flies this hell-hound / In th'air with Agripyna in his arms" (166–7). Since Agripyne "flies like lightning" on her own and is "hurried hence" by Andelocia, these three departures by means of a wishing hat sound rapid but not instantaneous (as opposed to a verisimilar *vanish*).

Let me conclude my account of the diverse Elizabethan,

Jacobean, and Caroline evidence with two instances where X sees but then ceases to see Y (who therefore *vanishes* to *him*), but the playgoer *continues* to see Y, so that unquestionably the *vanish* effect is from the point of view of an onstage observer rather than from the point of view of the playgoer. In *1 Hieronimo* the penultimate scene starts with Horatio and others at "*the funeral of Andrea*" (xii.o.s.d.), to which group enter the ghost of Andrea and Revenge. Of the mourners onstage only Horatio can see Andrea (although he cannot hear him), so Horatio says: "See, see, he points to have us go forward on. / I prithee, rest; it shall be done, sweet Don. / Oh, now he's vanish'd" (17–19). Horatio and his group may depart here or may stay onstage, but clearly Andrea does not exit, despite "now he's vanish'd," for he has the next speech ("I am a happy ghost" – 19). Clearly, from *Horatio*'s point of view Andrea has vanished, but the spectator sees the ghost stay to deliver another speech and then exeunt with Revenge (23.s.d.). The effect is a *vanish* witnessed and described by Horatio but seen in *very* different terms by the playgoer.

Similarly, in Henry Shirley's *The Martyred Soldier*, Bellizarius, about to convert to Christianity, calls upon "some Divine power" to "open my blind judgment / That I may see a way to happiness"; the stage direction reads: "*Thunder*: *Enter an Angel*" (188). Initially, Bellizarius cannot see the angel, so when the angel finally does speak the man replies: "What heavenly voice is this? shall my ears only / Be blest with raptures, not mine eyes enjoy / The sight of that Celestial presence / From whence these sweet sounds come?" The angel responds: "Yes, thou shalt see; nay, then, 'tis lost again" (189) – somehow revealing itself, then becoming invisible once more.[18] Here the angel is unseen, seen, and vanished not only without leaving the stage but within a single line.

As a final gloss, note that *vanish* or some equivalent term turns up in both medieval and Restoration drama. After 1660, a verisimilar effect is not only possible but likely, for a *vanish* effect can be keyed to changes in scenery – as in Davenant's *The Play-House to be Let* where "*a beautiful lady tied to a tree*" is discovered, but "*The Scene is suddenly changed again, where the lady is vanished, and nothing appears but that prospect which was in the beginning of the Entry*" (IV, 68–9).[19] To confront the relevant scenes in the cycle and saint's plays, however, is to run afoul of the same problems found in Shakespeare and his contemporaries. Thus, a verisimilar *vanish* is possible in *The Conversion of St. Paul* where a set of devils is directed to "*vanish away with a fiery flame and a tempest*" (501.s.d). Most of the medieval *vanish* effects, however, are linked to Jesus' sudden departures from Mary Magdalen or the disciples (moments I find hard to imagine as verisimilar in the original productions). Thus, three times in the Chester plays Jesus is directed to vanish (*evanescit*) with no other details available (*Lazarus*, 284.s.d.; *Emmaus*, 123.s.d.; *Thomas*, 215.s.d.). In the Digby *Mary Magdalen* "*Here avoideth Jesus suddenly*" (1095.s.d.) – a phrasing that suggests a rapid exit, not a verisimilar vanishing.

Of particular interest for the subsequent drama are the stage directions from *Ludus Coventriae* and the Towneley *Peregrini* where, as in Chester and Digby, the Jesus actor is directed to disappear suddenly from Cleophas and Luke. In both instances, however, a potentially revealing phrase is provided. Thus, in *Ludus Coventriae*: "*Hic subito discedat Christus ab oculis eorum*" (p. 353 – here let Christ suddenly disappear from their eyes). In Towneley, Jesus, sitting in the midst of the disciples, blesses and breaks the bread "& *postea evanebit ab oculis eorum*" (290.s.d. – and afterwards he shall vanish from their eyes) so that Luke can ask: "Where is this man become, / Right here that sat betwixt us two?" (291–2). To disappear or vanish "from their eyes" ("*ab oculis eorum*"), a locution not to be found in later stage directions, *may* be a signifier in a fifteenth-century theatrical vocabulary that distinguishes a verisimilar disappearance (a vanishing from the point of view of the playgoer) from a fictional–imaginative disappearance (a vanishing from the point of view of the onstage disciples but seen as a sudden yet "normal" exit by the playgoer – as in "*Here avoideth Jesus suddenly*").

To sum up my plentiful but ultimately inconclusive evidence: in plays from the 1580s to the early 1640s, the term *vanish* as used in dialogue often means *go*, *depart*, or "I'm out of here!", a usage that *may* gloss the verb as invoked in two eyewitness accounts of actual performances. Although few if any clues about the actual staging survive, some of the *vanish* stage directions and a few of the trap door descents *could* be verisimilar *vanishes*, but some are definitely not (as when two ghosts cross the stage and "*vanish in at another door*"). Rather, onstage observers describe situations as a *vanish* when the playgoer actually sees (1) a normal but rapid or surreptitious exit; (2) a large group departing in a procession or a dance; (3) a figure close her eyes and open them to find eleven ghosts gone; or, in two instances, (4) the supposedly vanishing figure not leaving the stage at all. As a signifier in a shared theatrical vocabulary, *vanish* therefore *may*, in some instances, have carried the primary meaning it has today, but elsewhere it could signal an effect wherein playgoers were encouraged to use their imaginary forces to sustain a narrative fiction that was *not* backed up by verisimilar staging.

To pursue *vanish* situations in sixteenth and seventeenth-century English drama is therefore to open up some options easily eclipsed or blurred for a reader today. By now, however, the reader less than enthusiastic about theatrical curiosities and anomalies is ready for my question (3). So what?

To respond to what I consider a legitimate question, let me turn to *The Tempest* and to a much-discussed question: what is the nature and function of Prospero's magic? Much has been written and debated by several generations of scholars about whether this "art" is to be understood as positive–heavenly–"white," negative–diabolic–"black," or ambiguous–ambivalent. Is Prospero a magus, a witch, or a wizard?[20] A traditional scholarly method has been to read widely in occult lore and other magician plays and then link Prospero's speeches, actions, and properties to this pre-existing body of material so as to build a case. Meanwhile, today's director or actor must find some means to convey a sense of the nature of that magic to an untutored playgoer.

What has not been explored in the learned debates on this subject, however (and has received only limited exploration on the stage), is the *playgoer*'s potential role in establishing the nature of Prospero's (and Ariel's) magic. The viewer who at various points witnesses an Ariel wink out of sight in John Gorrie's television production for the BBC's "The Shakespeare Plays" is playing a different role from the playgoer who is asked to *imagine* the invisibility of a figure clearly in view, for, if the latter effect is to "work," that playgoer must be a more active participant in the process than the television viewer. Similarly, the nineteenth or twentieth-century production that includes a flying Ariel and other elaborate effects provides a different sense of "magic" from a "minimalist" production that relies more heavily (or solely) upon the poetry, the skills of the actors, and the playgoer's imagination.

Various theatrical choices, then or now, can therefore strongly affect our sense of the "magic" in a production of this script. For example, directors of *The Tempest* telegraph their working assumptions by how they choose to present the storm of 1.1. In the Folio, that storm is keyed to (1) some noise ("*A tempestuous noise of thunder and lightning heard*"); (2) the information conveyed in the dialogue; (3) the agitation of the actors who convey to us a sense of storm and urgency; and (4) mariners who enter "*wet*" (47.s.d). Shakespeare and his players thereby provide various theatrical signals, but the playgoer is a major participant in "creating" the storm. Given the theatrical resources of the last century and a half, however, few directors have been satisfied with the Folio signals alone, so today's playgoer usually will encounter elaborate sound and lighting effects, some sense of a ship in the set design, and a diminished emphasis upon the spoken words which are often drowned out by storm noise.[21]

How the playgoer experiences (and perhaps participates in creating) the initial tempest can then have a significant effect upon what follows. A "realistic" storm sets up for an audience comparable expectations about the "magic" and special effects to follow; in contrast, a "minimalist" storm more in tune with the Folio signals encourages a playgoer to participate more actively in subsequent scenes. In particular, after the initial reaction to the storm (and the subsequent revelation that that storm is a product of art, not of meteorology), how is that playgoer to see or imagine the magic of the isle, first in Prospero's relationship to Ariel and then most tellingly in Ariel's entrance with Ferdinand (the first of a series of moments that rely upon a spectator seeing a figure invisible to one or more onstage observers)? Thus, in recent productions I have seen Ariel enter riding upon Ferdinand's back or, more commonly, leading Ferdinand onto the stage, sometimes dancing around him, almost touching him, but never seen by the dazed, mourning prince. Here or later, is the technical capability to make Ariel instantly invisible (as on television) necessarily an advantage? Rather (as with the humans oblivious to Oberon and Puck), the inability of onstage figures to see what to a playgoer is clearly present can yield a distinctive sense of "magic" (or, as a corollary, a sense of myopia or mental–spiritual blindness). If the playgoer is a more than passive participant, a different sense of Prospero's magic and the special qualities of the island can therefore emerge (so that the "quaint device" by which the banquet disappears is the exception, not the norm).

The relationship between magic and playgoing assumptions is especially interesting in *The Tempest*, not only because the term *vanish* turns up in three separate stage directions but because a sense of vanishing–evanescence is central to this romance. The two scenes that contain the relevant theatrical signals, moreover, are crucial to this sense of evanescence. In the first, the sudden disappearance of the seemingly eatable banquet is a striking theatrical event with strong symbolic overtones (so that what the courtiers, especially the three power-hungry figures, take to be "real" or substantial is suddenly gone). The same is true of Ariel's disappearance as harpy, a departure that underscores the helplessness of the three men of sin in the face of the (to them) inexplicable events and forces set in motion by Prospero's art. In the subsequent scene, the vanishing of nymphs, reapers, and goddesses occasions the best-known speech in the play in which Prospero (using such terms as *melted*, *dissolve*, and *faded*) links the evanescence of this vanity of his art to the insubstantiality of the towers, palaces, and temples that many in his culture (and ours) would deem permanent.

Exactly how these vanishing *exits* are carried out in the theatre can then have a major impact upon a playgoer's understanding of such moments or speeches. Presumably, the banquet vanishes suddenly, both for the courtiers and the playgoer. But a different point is being made about Ariel as harpy and especially about the departure of the nymphs and reapers if, on the one hand, such vanishings are "real" for both onstage and in-the-theatre observers and if, on the other, the evanescence is striking for the courtiers, Ferdinand, and Miranda but "imagined" by an audience. Is the "magic" of Prospero and Ariel equally impressive to the onstage figures and to the spectators (so that the latter are dazzled along with the former)? Or are the playgoers conscious of the theatrical tricks being performed and therefore, to gain the full effect, being asked to piece out the imperfections of Prospero and his fellow actors in their wooden O so as to be sharers in the creation of that magic? The former option makes possible a more impressive Prospero and Ariel, at least in 3.3; in contrast, the latter option makes the magic contingent upon the playgoer's implicit consent and may therefore open the door to various reservations about Prospero's art (as with Stephen Orgel's question: "is the magic a strength or a weakness?").[22] Such "imaginative" (as opposed to verisimilar) vanishing could produce a poignant effect if the spirits slowly and laboriously ("heavily") or sadly ("heavily") leave the stage (so that the playgoer is conscious of their labored, unwilling departure), but Ferdinand and Miranda lose sight of them immediately – at the point that the dance is broken (just as Ferdinand had not "seen" Ariel in 1.2 or the clowns had heard but not seen Ariel in 3.2). In short, when do the nymphs and reapers "vanish" for the young couple? When do they disappear from the playgoer's sight? Are the moments the same (hence a verisimilar effect) or discrete?

Nor are such questions limited to 4.1, for two moments at the climax of this romance are an integral part of this problem. First, the final exit of Ariel is not labeled as a *vanish* (indeed, as with the spirit of Caesar, the Folio provides no stage direction at all), but, given what has gone before, this departure *could* be seen or understood in these terms. How indeed did or should the Ariel actor leave the stage for the final time? To cite some recent directorial choices, in Ron Daniels' 1984–85 Royal Shakespeare Company production Derek Jacobi's Prospero addressed empty space in his final address to Ariel, for no actor was onstage to play the already departed spirit. In the 1989–90 Shakespeare Theatre at the Folger production, the director chose to have his Ariel actor physically collapse when freed but then had his Prospero continue to address not the fallen body but rather the spirit that now was no longer bound by fleshly constraints. In this rendition, the actor did not leave the stage, but Ariel did "vanish" (as indicated by Prospero's delivery of the lines to an entity not visible to the playgoer).[23]

Consider then a possible *exit* for Ariel in keeping with "heavily vanish" and with the effects in such plays as *1 Hieronimo* and *The Martyred Soldier*. As with my hypothetical slow departure of nymphs and reapers (seen by the playgoer but not by Ferdinand and Miranda), what if Prospero in his final moments also can no longer "see" an Ariel that an audience *does* see depart? After promising the royal party "calm seas" and "auspicious gales" for their return trip, Prospero says: "My Ariel, chick, / That is thy charge. Then to the elements / Be free, and fare thou well!" (5.1.314–18) If Ariel starts to move after the words "be free" but the erstwhile magician directs his farewell (perhaps with some visible confusion) at the space just vacated by the spirit, the playgoer would be alerted to the loss of magical powers in powerful, even poignant, terms and, perhaps as in 4.1, would witness a spirit "heavily" (sadly? slowly?) vanish (e.g., if a departing Ariel lightly touched a puzzled, unseeing Prospero).

Exactly how Ariel departs (or vanishes) can, in turn, affect our understanding of Prospero's Epilogue in which the actor who has been playing the part starts by noting his new weakness ("Now my charms are all o'erthrown, / And what strength I have's mine own, / Which is most faint" – 1–3) and then posits the controlling role of the audience if "my project" is not to fail.

> Now I want
> Spirits to enforce, art to enchant;
> And my ending is despair
> Unless I be relieved by prayer,
> Which pierces so that it assaults
> Mercy itself and frees all faults.
> As you from crimes would pardoned be,
> Let your indulgence set me free. (13–20)

Often this speech amounts to no more than a conventional appeal for applause, especially if Prospero has consistently shown us his potent control by means of verisimilar stage magic (why should we help such a figure?). But what if the playgoer has just witnessed a magician who visibly (and perhaps movingly) has lost control over (and even the ability to see) his Ariel? Which Prospero – the potent magus or the lapsed magician who clearly has lost his powers – speaks the Epilogue?

The speaker of this Epilogue asks the playgoer to make a choice with significant implications for Prospero and for the actor playing Prospero. The speech therefore provides the final and most significant index to that complex contract between playgoer and players in this unusual play, a contract that has been signaled in a variety of ways starting with the opening storm, however presented. Then or now, the way that the players stage and the audience understands the various vanishings is one significant part of that contract. To choose between the verisimilar and imaginative–conventional options is therefore not merely to indulge in scholarly–historical games but rather (especially if Ariel's final departure is included among the vanishings) to focus upon a choice or problem at the heart of this romance. What do the onstage figures see? What do the playgoers see? What emerges from the conjunction or disparity between the two?

CONCLUSION

So what?

"No more; the text is foolish"

Goneril, 4.2.37

"So much for that"

Richard II, 2.1.155

The problems generated by the *vanish* stage directions epitomize the difficulties inherent in any attempt to recover Shakespeare's theatrical vocabulary. With a few categories or problems, to survey the extant signals is to clarify matters if not to provide solutions. With the *vanish* scenes, however, to amass a considerable amount of evidence from an unusually wide range of plays does not resolve some basic questions. Rather, from the point of view of today's interpreter, onstage practices that were obvious and meaningful then have vanished.

For both scholars and theatrical professionals, such indeterminacy can be disconcerting. Admittedly, those in both camps hostile to (or uncomfortable with) historicism in its varying forms will merely have their skepticism about such projects reinforced. Thus, scholarly formulations about both theatrical and cultural matters have been very visible in recent years, formulations often based upon subtle readings of both a wide range of previously ignored Elizabethan texts and selected passages from Shakespeare's plays. In such arguments much has been assumed about the play-as-event as it interacts with its audience. But the skeptic may ask: what if significant parts of those onstage events, moments that are integral to *any* interpretation, remain puzzles, to the extent that today's editor, critic, or scholar cannot be certain what the original playgoer would have witnessed? What if not only Ariel and Prospero's masquers have vanished but essential evidence as well, evidence that would have been obvious to the spectators then but is murky now? To what extent should Prospero's famous speech on evanescence and fading pertain to historicist interpretations of *The Tempest*?

Whether in theatrical or cultural terms, such questions warrant our attention. As demonstrated throughout this book, significant items or bits of evidence *have* (in one sense or another) vanished, especially in terms of performance-oriented analysis of plays not of our age. Owing to both the editorial tradition that started in the eighteenth century and the wide gap of time between Shakespeare and us, various signifiers in the Elizabethan–Jacobean theatrical vocabulary have vanished (or been blurred) – again, often without our realizing it (whether because we use modern editions or because our interpretative reflexes supersede or blot out the original signals). Periodically, the non-historicist is made conscious of such changes (as when dealing with the soliloquy, invisibility, and boy actors playing female roles), but other components of that original theatrical language can easily be missed or eclipsed. The reader may or may not accept my various hypotheses about *The Tempest*, but the fact that such effects are possible within the original theatrical vocabulary but can so easily be screened from our eyes should be chastening to any historicist.

The past is always vanishing. But the theatre of the past, particularly that theatrical past that antedates various forms of audio or visual recording, is especially vulnerable to this process (and in his often quoted lines Prospero calls our attention to this essential feature of theatre – and life). My purpose in making such observations, however, is not to conclude with a despairing lament about the irrecoverability of the past. Many racks *have* been left behind. Performance-oriented approaches to plays not of our age *can* be rewarding and exciting (at least for those who care about performance, plays, and history). To be conscious of the problems, small and large, is to take a major step toward some solution of those problems. As an historian seeking to understand more about our theatrical past, I therefore consider a healthy skepticism to be an essential part of any such study, a skepticism reinforced by the various perplexing questions generated by the *vanish* stage directions.

Such skepticism underlies the *recovering* in my title, a participle that signals an ongoing process that does not lend itself to precise dictionary definitions or a clearly mapped terrain. As noted in chapter 3, many readers of this book would have preferred a study of vocabulary that would have produced lists, definitions, and glosses in the fashion of the *OED* or an iconographical handbook. I too would have preferred to solve the problems and answer the questions regularly posed by editors, historicists, and directors. Firm conclusions, neat distinctions, and confident truth claims, however, do not emerge from the extant evidence. Rather, the history of scholarship in this area is a narrative replete with Solutions and Answers that have not stood the test of time and have fallen by the wayside (the postulation of an "inner stage" provides one chastening example).

Given such an ongoing (participial) process, a formal conclusion is inappropriate. Rather, to bring my arguments and evidence into focus, let me return to the three linked questions that serve as my rationale for building edifices upon thousands of stage directions in roughly 700 plays from the 1400s to the 1680s: (1) for any given moment or effect, what was the original staging, onstage business, or shared theatrical vocabulary? (2) what evidence and procedures are available to answer question number (1)? and (3) what difference does our knowledge (or, more often, our lack of knowledge) make to interpretation and general understanding today? Again, in simplest terms: (1) what did a playgoer at the original production actually see? (2) how can we tell? and (3) so what?

As I have argued at length, to set up what we know and, equally important, what is in doubt about the original staging and theatrical vocabulary demands care and precision with both external evidence (eyewitness accounts, Henslowe's papers) and internal evidence (stage directions, dialogue). Here the recurring *vanish* situations provide a particularly good paradigm, but equally provocative are the many *as* [*if*] stage directions, various juxtapositions, distinctive onstage images (as with the sick-chair or various italicized moments), and the many problems linked to "place." In formulating answers to question number (1), interpretative battle lines often can be drawn between a verisimilar approach (that assumes or invokes "real" vanishings, "real" forests–studies–tents, and "real" tombs and avoids jarring juxtapositions) and a minimalist–fictional approach linked to *as [if]* or *[as if] in* (that places greater emphasis upon the imaginative participation of the playgoer and assumes fewer onstage details and more overlapping).

At issue in such a debate (in Bernard Beckerman's terms) are the spectacles we don when we read a play not of our age. Much has been made in cultural studies (and in Tillyard-bashing) of the spurious distinction between what is *opaque* (privileged "literary" texts) and what is *transparent* (other non-"literary" works that supposedly can be used freely as context). Those who challenge this distinction when reading cultures as texts, however, regularly assume that the evidence found in stage directions is transparent and unproblematic. In contrast, the previous chapters offer repeated instances (as with Marston's apparent equation of a *coffin* with a *tomb*) that serve as warnings that the collapsing of this distinction must be applied as well to stage directions, eyewitness accounts (as with the use of *vanish* by Holles and Willis), and even Henslowe's inventory (as with the references to tombs), all of which are encoded in a vocabulary readers today may or may not understand.

Evidence and questions elicited when pursuing questions (1) and (2) are (or should be) of interest to theatre historians, editors, and historicists in general (although some of these practitioners may be impatient with the indeterminacy of my findings). The *so what?* question also generates issues that will vary widely among interpreters of Shakespeare (including teachers dealing with first-time readers of the plays). My evidence and arguments (e.g., about early entrances) have obvious implications for editors and editorial practice (although much depends upon the nature of the edition and its implied audience), but let me turn first to the *so what?* challenge as posed by today's actors or directors.

In any age, success (commercial, artistic, or both) in the theatre depends to a large extent upon the finding, creating, or maintaining a shared theatrical vocabulary among playwright, players, and playgoers. To invoke on today's stages the theatrical signifiers of another age (e.g., to have the actors presenting a Sophocles tragedy wear masks) may provide excitement for some playgoers but may also run the risk of diminishing the accessibility of a script in the pursuit of novelty or authenticity. Therefore, with few exceptions, when "classical" plays are performed in today's highly competitive commercial theatres, "translation" of Elizabethan signals into our idiom is taken for granted, even seen as mandatory, so that the paying playgoer will not be mystified. In an age when doublet-and-hose Shakespeare productions have nearly become extinct, the original vocabulary (although never totally irrelevant) has ceased to be a central concern. Rather, those Shakespeare directors who assume (perhaps correctly) that their playgoers, uncomfortable with blank verse and early modern English, would rather look than listen regularly choose to pare down their acting scripts (e.g., by cutting opaque passages and mythological allusions), streamline their narratives, and use their resources to provide treats for the eye. A strong imperative therefore exists to eliminate juxtapositions and other seemingly awkward moments (e.g., the unseen banquet in *As You Like It*, 2.6). For many actors and directors faced with severe limits in budget and rehearsal time, wrestling with the original theatrical vocabulary is a luxury reserved for professors removed from the hurlyburly of the commercial arena.

Having spent much time over the last two decades talking to such theatrical professionals in many different venues, I am both aware of and sympathetic to the problems of staging Shakespeare's plays today. In the preceding chapters I have therefore offered critiques of current editorial practice, but I have not preached sermons directed at actors and directors. For example, I do not advocate an equivalent in the commercial theatre to the performance of baroque and early classical music upon the original instruments (although such an analogy might be appropriate for performances at a reconstituted Globe Theatre in London or North Carolina).

A surprising number of today's theatrical professionals, however (as I have discovered in my many conversations), have a strong interest in "how they did it" (or even "how they may have done it"). Directors who do trust the original scripts (e.g., Deborah Warner, who cut no lines from her superb productions of *Titus Andronicus* and *King John* and cut only one brief speech from *King Lear*) do not need lectures about their craft from theatrical amateurs but are open to information that will enable them to make more informed choices. As readers know, the best translations may not be word-for-word, but the best translators are the most knowledgeable about the original texts and the larger language. Most directors do not attack a Shakespeare script with the *OED* at their side, but many *are* concerned with what the words mean and hence with the larger issue of how those words and actions "mean" in the theatre.

What is most pernicious in this script-to-stage process is the longstanding canard that Shakespeare's theatrical craft is primitive (and hence to be superseded by today's "superior" technology, realism, and knowhow). Admittedly, that craft was geared to playhouses, players, and playgoers that no longer exist, but, as argued throughout this book, it has many distinctive assets that are difficult to match today. In some instances insights into how the King's Men did or may have done X will have little impact upon today's productions. Nonetheless, the knowhow exhibited at the Globe and other contemporary playhouses need not be of solely academic interest (e.g., exploration of the vocabulary of "place" can have suggestive implications, as I have been told by one artistic director of a Shakespeare festival, for today's theatrical design). In working with my many categories and examples, my purpose therefore has *not* been to imply to today's theatrical professional: "Here is how you must do it," but rather: "Here is how I believe *they* did it. Can you find a comparable device or idiom that would accomplish the same thing for *your* playgoer?"

The implications of the recovery process (or the responses to *so what*?) for editors, critics, and historicists can be highlighted by an almost endless series of questions. What is to be staged versus what is to be imagined by the playgoer (and how is today's interpreter to tell)? What happens to interpretative options when a critic or editor assumes a verisimilar *vanish* for moments when the original playgoer may have seen a Brutus, Macbeth, or Prospero react to such a sudden disappearance but also have seen the departing figure or figures exit slowly ("*heavily*") or (as in two documented instances) not exit at all? What happens when interpreters today invoke verisimilar notions about staging that bring onstage (or into their readerly imaginations) images and properties that were not visible in the original production (a bed in the closet scene of *Hamlet*) and, conversely, blur or eclipse Elizabethan hit-the-playgoer-over-the-head effects (Romeo's prying tools, the banquet juxtaposed with a starving Orlando and Adam)? What are the implications when fictional and theatrical signals are confused (as perhaps with "*Romeo opens the tomb*") so as to impose a later sense of theatre upon that of Shakespeare's company? Conversely, do we understand their shared theatrical vocabulary well enough to dismiss apparently fictional signals that could indeed be theatrical or other seemingly anomalous signals (early entrances, "*It spreads his arms*")? Can our post-Ibsen theatrical vocabulary mesh with an implicit *as* or *as if*?

As emphasized throughout this book (in which I have repeatedly slipped into the interrogative mode), my purpose in raising such questions is to be suggestive rather than prescriptive, with an emphasis upon opening up rather than closing down options for the interpreter of Shakespeare's plays. What I find most troubling about the practices of editors (whose texts form the basis for interpretations in the study, in the classroom, and on the stage) is not that they are wrong-headed, unlearned, or imprecise (some of my best friends are editors) but that they (often unwittingly) close down options that might seem negligible to them but could be of considerable interest to another interpreter, whether in the theatre or on the page. Again, my primary goal has not been to offer my readings of Shakespeare's meaning or meanings but rather to tease out from the limited evidence signifiers, images, and juxtapositions that were the basis for the original playgoers' interpretation but, for a variety of reasons, are often filtered out of today's editions. Is such filtering indeed an inevitable part of the process of editing (or translation)?

For a final paradigm consider Heywood's presentation in *The Brazen Age* (III, 175–6) of the confrontation between Hercules and the shapeshifter Achelous by which the hero wins Dejanira. The narrative fiction requires that Achelous start in his own shape, shift three times, and reappear in his own guise to confess defeat. The actual stage directions read: "*Achelous is beaten in, and immediately enters in the shape of a Dragon*"; "*Alarm. He beats away the dragon. Enter a Fury all fire-works*"; "*When the Fury sinks, a Bull's head appears*"; "*He tugs with the Bull, and plucks off one of his horns. Enter from the same place Achelous with his forehead all bloody.*" The now bloodied figure spells out the results of the confrontation: "No more, I am thy Captive, thou my Conqueror."

Although not all the details can be pieced out, Heywood's solution in his theatre to what might seem an insurmountable staging problem is clear. To re-enter "*in the shape of a Dragon*" is to establish the shape-shifting not by means of onstage trickery but by means of a rapid transition ("*immediately*") that draws upon the playgoer's imaginary forces. The "dragon" may be thrust forth from a trap or stage door; clearly the "fury" sinks through the trap (and may arise "*all fire-works*" in the same fashion); the bull's head could appear from a door or the trap (anywhere within Hercules' reach), but a door would be practical if the Achelous–actor is immediately to "*Enter from the same place*" with his bloody forehead. The in-the-theatre timing is crucial here: the players provide the rapid actions; the playgoer (in the spirit of *as if*) supplies the continuity that underlies such signals so as to make the connections between Achelous and the three shapes. This combination of strong onstage signals with the imaginary forces of the spectators epitomizes the unspoken contract essential to this (or any) theatre.

To win his Dejanira Heywood's Hercules must control and defeat an elusive antagonist; in this world of heroic romance, the hero accomplishes his goal against formidable odds. If scholars carried on their struggles in such an idealized world, they too would win through to their version of Dejanira by using the tools of their trade to control elusive evidence and overcome their version of Achelous. In the real world of historical scholarship, however, such victories are rare. Rather, the target keeps changing shape, blurring into something related but discrete. Meanings get lost in translation; anomalies go unexplained; what was obvious in the 1590s and early 1600s is impenetrable today. Meanwhile, the nagging *so what*? question will not go away.

Nonetheless, even if clear-cut Herculean victories are few, there are advances. If the conversation between Shakespeare and his colleagues is worth attending to (as many interpreters today believe), then exploration of the language in which that conversation took place remains a worthwhile pursuit as does reduction of mystification or language barriers. Although Herculean triumphs are rare (and the bloodied head may more often be linked to the scholar than the antagonist), to wrestle with the plays and problems is to open up areas that otherwise would remain closed. To explore Shakespeare's theatrical vocabulary is not to pluck out the heart of Hamlet's mystery or to answer Lear's "who is it that can tell me who I am?" but such an ongoing process *can* provide today's interpreter with a better grasp of the larger onstage language in which such mysteries or questions are couched. For the scholar, the answer to "so what?" is therefore: why not?

Notes

1 THE PROBLEM, THE EVIDENCE AND THE LANGUAGE BARRIER

1 John Shearman, *Mannerism* (Middlesex: Penguin, 1967), p. 136.

2 See chapter 1 of *Shakespearean Negotiations* (Berkeley and Los Angeles: University of California Press, 1988).

3 Richard L. Levin, "The Problem of 'Context' in Interpretation," in *Shakespeare and Dramatic Tradition: Essays in Honor of S. F. Johnson*, ed. W. R. Elton and William B. Long (Newark: University of Delaware Press, 1989), p. 91.

4 For a recent sampling of performance-oriented criticism of Shakespeare's plays see the essays collected in *Shakespeare and the Sense of Performance*, ed. Marvin and Ruth Thompson (Newark: University of Delaware Press, 1989). For astute critiques of the rhetoric, claims, and assumptions of such critics see Richard Levin, "Performance-Critics *vs* Close Readers in the Study of English Renaissance Drama," *Modern Language Review* 81 (1986): 545–59; W. B. Worthen, "Deeper Meanings and Theatrical Technique: The Rhetoric of Performance Criticism," *Shakespeare Quarterly* 40 (1989): 441–55; and Harry Berger, Jr., *Imaginary Audition: Shakespeare on Stage and Page* (Berkeley, Los Angeles, and London: University of California Press, 1989).

5 See Ann Jennalie Cook, *The Privileged Playgoers of Shakespeare's London, 1576–1642* (Princeton University Press, 1981); and Andrew Gurr, *Playgoing in Shakespeare's London* (Cambridge University Press, 1987). For an excellent overview on Spanish and London playhouses, see John J. Allen, "The Spanish *Corrales de Comedias* and the London Playhouses and Stages," in *New Issues in the Reconstruction of Shakespeare's Theatre*, ed. Frank J. Hildy (New York: Peter Lang, 1990), pp. 207–35. Other essays in this volume deal with the Wanamaker Globe project and the findings at the Rose Theatre excavation.

6 I use theatrical *language* and *vocabulary* – rather than *signifying practices* or some comparable term – deliberately and self-consciously. Again, I am not unaware of Saussurian and post-Saussurian terms and distinctions, but my intended readership includes many for whom post-structuralist terminology might prove mystifying and hence counter-productive.

7 For thoughtful essays on what can and cannot be learned from both Henslowe's papers and the "plots" see Bernard Beckerman, "The Use and Management of the Elizabethan Stage," *The Third Globe: Symposium for the Reconstruction of the Globe Playhouse*, ed. C. Walter Hodges, S. Schoenbaum, and Leonard Leone (Detroit: Wayne State University Press, 1981), 151–63; and "Theatrical Plots and Elizabethan Stage Practice," *Shakespeare and Dramatic Tradition*, ed. Elton and Long, pp. 109–24. For a recent book-length re-investigation of plots and plotters (with an emphasis upon Peele's *The Battle of Alcazar*) see David Bradley, *From Text to Performance in the Elizabethan Theatre: Preparing the Play for the Stage* (Cambridge University Press, 1992).

8 *From Writer to Reader: Studies in Editorial Method* (Oxford: Clarendon Press, 1978), p. 245. After illustrating his distinctions with material from *Travesties*, Gaskell concludes (pp. 260–2) with some shrewd observations targeted at would-be editors of plays. For example, he notes that "the performance texts of most plays are lost beyond recall, but when a text survives that appears to incorporate any elements of an early performance text we should be ready to recognize and appreciate the performance features." For Gaskell, "a reading text prepared by the author may have artistic value; but it is not the whole play." His closing advice is that "the editor should be very clear about what the evidence represents" and "should be prepared, when it includes what may be performance features, to raise his eyes from the play text and to have another look at the play."

9 For critiques of some long-standing editorial terms and practices, see William B. Long, "Stage Directions: A Misinterpreted Factor in Determining Textual Provenance," *Text* 2 (1985): 121–37; Paul Werstine, "McKerrow's 'Suggestion' and Twentieth-Century Shakespeare Textual Criticism," *Renaissance Drama* 19 (1988): 149–73; and Paul Werstine, "Narratives About Printed Shakespearean Texts: 'Foul Papers' and 'Bad' Quartos," *Shakespeare Quarterly* 41 (1990): 65–86.

10 For example, Stephen Orgel notes "how much the creation of a play was a collaborative process, with the author by no means at the center of the collaboration"; therefore, "if it is a performing

text we are dealing with, it is a mistake to think that in our editorial work what we are doing is getting back to an author's original manuscript: the very notion of 'the author's original manuscript' is in such case a figment." According to Orgel, as an attached or in-house dramatist, Shakespeare was not an exception but "was simply in on more parts of the collaboration." See "What is a Text?" *Research Opportunities in Renaissance Drama* 24 (1981): 3–4, and, for a further elaboration of his argument, "The Authentic Shakespeare," *Representations* 21 (1988): 7–10. See also T. H. Howard-Hill, "Playwrights' Intentions and the Editing of Plays," *Text* 4 (1988): 269–78.

11 "General Introduction," *William Shakespeare: A Textual Companion*, ed. Stanley Wells and Gary Taylor (Oxford: Clarendon Press, 1987), pp. 2–3.

12 See, in particular, Leslie Thomson, "Broken Brackets and 'Mended Texts: Stage Directions in the Oxford Shakespeare," *Renaissance Drama* 19 (1988): 175–93.

13 "The Monks and the Giants: Textual and Bibliographical Studies and the Interpretation of Literary Works," in *Textual Criticism and Literary Interpretation*, ed. Jerome J. McGann (Chicago and London: University of Chicago Press, 1985), p. 187.

14 Jonathan Goldberg, review of Leah Marcus, *Puzzling Shakespeare* in *JEGP* 89 (1990): 548; and "Textual Properties," *Shakespeare Quarterly* 37 (1986): 215. An alternative is Randall McLeod's concept of "the *infinitive* text," which he defines as "a polymorphous set of all versions, some part of each of which has a claim to substantive status, and possibly presents, by whatever independent means of transmission, an element of Shakespearean dramaturgy" ("The Marriage of Good and Bad Quartos," *Shakespeare Quarterly* 33 [1982]: 422). In pragmatic terms, I also take comfort in Fredson Bowers' summary comment about the original punctuation: "No one is so foolish any more as to argue that the punctuation ... is Shakespeare's own or that it represents in any way the authority of the playhouse. But such as it is, it is the most authentic that we have ..." (*On Editing Shakespeare* [Charlottesville: University Press of Virginia, 1966], pp. 177–8).

15 William B. Long has demonstrated in a series of essays that the actual adjustments to or insertions in authorial scripts in the extant playhouse manuscripts are far fewer than scholars today (especially editors) expect (e.g., only seven in all of *John a Kent*), a situation likely to pertain as well to an attached dramatist such as Shakespeare already in tune with his company and his medium. Indeed, authorial scripts often provide more performance-oriented

information than playhouse manuscripts – in the form of what Long terms "playwright's advisory directions." He rightly cautions that such signals may not have been followed strictly by the actors, but they do provide revealing information about the concept in the author's mind at the moment of writing – again, at the beginning of the conversation with the players. See William B. Long, "Stage Directions: A Misinterpreted Factor in Determining Textual Provenance," *Text* 2 (1985): 121–37; "'A bed / for woodstock': A Warning for the Unwary," *Medieval and Renaissance Drama in England* 2 (1985): 91–118; and "*John a Kent and John a Cumber*: An Elizabethan Playbook and Its Implications," *Shakespeare and Dramatic Tradition*, ed. Elton and Long, pp. 125–43. For a recent shrewd reassessment of stage directions, see Antony Hammond, "Encounters of the Third Kind in Stage-Directions in Elizabethan and Jacobean Drama," *Studies in Philology* 89 (1992): 71–99.

16 The distinction between repeatability (and practicality) in repertory theatre and one-shot extravagant effects in the masque is no small matter. For example, in one of his masques Campion calls for nine trees to be "*suddenly conveyed away,*" but a note in the printed text informs the reader: "Either by the simplicity, negligence, or conspiracy of the painter, the passing away of the trees was somewhat hazarded; the pattern of them the same day having been shown with much admiration, and the nine trees being left unset together even to the same night." As the editor notes: "Apparently a stagehand had forgotten to reattach the trees to the engine after displaying them to the nobility during the day." See *The Works of Thomas Campion*, ed. Walter R. Davis (Garden City, NY: Doubleday, 1967), p. 222.

2 LOST IN TRANSLATION

1 Harley Granville-Barker, *Associating With Shakespeare* (London: Oxford University Press, 1932), p. 7.

2 Bernard Beckerman, "Theatrical Plots and Elizabethan Stage Practice," *Shakespeare and Dramatic Tradition: Essays in Honor of S. F. Johnson*, ed. W. R. Elton and William B. Long (Newark: University of Delaware Press, 1989), pp. 115–16.

3 The pioneering essay on this subject is William J. Lawrence, "The Practise of Doubling and Its Influence on Early Dramaturgy," *Pre-Restoration Stage Studies* (Cambridge, Mass.: Harvard University Press, 1927), pp. 43–78. Of the many speculative essays, see particularly Stephen Booth, "Speculations on Doubling in Shake-

speare's Plays," *Shakespeare: The Theatrical Dimension*, ed. Philip C. McGuire and David A. Samuelson (New York: AMS Press, 1979), pp. 103–31; and John C. Meagher, "Economy and Recognition: Thirteen Shakespearean Puzzles," *Shakespeare Quarterly* 34 (1984): 7–21. For the number of actors in Shakespeare's company (he estimates twelve to sixteen) see William A. Ringler, "The Number of Actors in Shakespeare's Early Plays," in *The Seventeenth-Century Stage*, ed. Gerald Eades Bentley (Chicago, 1968), pp. 110–34. For a thorough reassessment of the allocation of parts by Shakespeare's company see T. J. King, *Casting Shakespeare's Plays: London Actors and their Roles, 1590–1642* (Cambridge University Press, 1992).

4 A comparable effect *may* be present in the other play with a cast list – *The Fair Maid of the Exchange* (usually attributed to Thomas Heywood). This cast list as printed, however, does not work, for, in several instances, an actor would have to play two figures who are on stage at the same time, but with some tinkering, a pattern similar to *Mucedorus* emerges. Instead of Envy–Tremelio–Bremo–Envy, here two actors (call them, by their placement on the list, A and C) first play Bobbington and Scarlet, two villains who in the first scene try to rob and rape Phyllis (the fair maid) and Ursula. The same two actors reappear in scene 8 as Gardiner and Bennett, two gentlemen who quarrel with Phyllis and are exposed as lacking in true gentility. Elsewhere in the play, A and C take on the parts of the two fathers, Mr. Berry and Mr. Flower, each of whom is a typical comic *senex* figure who oppresses Youth (Phyllis, Barnard) and stands in the way of comic fruition and marriage. In this romance plot, Phyllis and Mall Berry must overcome the opposition of their fathers, just as Phyllis and Ursula had escaped Bobbington and Scarlet, just as Phyllis had emerged triumphant over Gardiner and Bennett, with all three sets of antagonists played by A and C. As in *Mucedorus*, to gain the romance closure the enemies of Comedy (ruffians, false gentlemen, misguided fathers) must be transcended, with (perhaps) the blocking figures or forces given some added punch or continuity by being played by the same two actors, A and C. Again, the play can "work" without such reinforcement in the casting-tripling, but, as in *Mucedorus*, something extra is added (call it the X-factor) if a playgoer does recognize the patterning. For a fuller discussion, see Alan C. Dessen, "Conceptual Casting in the Age of Shakespeare: Evidence from *Mucedorus*," *Shakespeare Quarterly* 43 (1992): 67–70.

5 See Alan C. Dessen, *Elizabethan Stage Conventions and Modern Interpreters* (Cambridge University Press, 1984), pp. 40–3.

6 For a discussion of today's intervals–intermissions as reflecting

Shakespeare's two-part structure see chapter 3 (pp. 66–88) of Emrys Jones, *Scenic Form in Shakespeare* (Oxford: Clarendon Press, 1971). For further comments on the implications of such breaks see Alan C. Dessen, "'The Interim is Mine': Placing the Intermission–Interval in Today's Shakespeare Productions," *Shakespeare Bulletin* 7 (September–October 1989), 5–7.

7 The most familiar example is *Macbeth*, 3.3 where such putting out of a light allows Fleance to escape. In Tailor's *The Hog Hath Lost His Pearl*, Albert climbs to Maria's window "*and being on the top of the ladder, puts out the candle*" (265–6); with the only light on stage extinguished, Maria then mistakes Albert for her lover, Carracus. For other examples, see Fletcher, *The Maid in the Mill*, VII, 59; Fletcher, *The Queen of Corinth*, VI, 17; Cooke, *Greene's Tu Quoque*, L2v; and Tourneur, *The Atheist's Tragedy*, 2.4.

3 INTERPRETING WITHOUT A DICTIONARY

1 Ann Jennalie Cook, *The Privileged Playgoers of Shakespeare's London, 1576–1642* (Princeton University Press, 1981); and Andrew Gurr, *Playgoing in Shakespeare's London* (Cambridge University Press, 1987).

2 For recent essays by such leading scholars as Andrew Gurr, John Orrell, and Walter Hodges see *New Issues in the Reconstruction of Shakespeare's Theatre*, ed. Frank J. Hildy (New York: Peter Lang, 1990). The best overview on such matters is Andrew Gurr, *The Shakespearean Stage, 1574–1642*, 3rd ed. (Cambridge University Press, 1991).

3 For example, in a series of books William J. Lawrence presented a wealth of valuable material about staging problems in the plays of the period even though some of his reasoning is suspect or untenable today. See *Pre-Restoration Stage Studies* (Cambridge, Mass.: Harvard University Press, 1927); and *Those Nut-Cracking Elizabethans: Studies of the Early Theatre and Drama* (London: Argonaut Press, 1935). The most valuable of such books from the first half of this century is G. F. Reynolds, *The Staging of Elizabethan Plays at the Red Bull Theater, 1605–25* (New York: Modern Language Association of America, 1940).

4 Muriel Bradbrook, *Themes and Conventions of Elizabethan Tragedy* (Cambridge University Press, 1935); Bernard Beckerman, *Shakespeare at the Globe, 1599–1609* (New York: Macmillan, 1962). See also Nevill Coghill, *Shakespeare's Professional Skills* (Cambridge University Press, 1964); J. L. Styan, *Shakespeare's Stagecraft* (Cambridge University Press, 1967); T. J. King, *Shakespearean Staging*,

1599–1642 (Cambridge, Mass.: Harvard University Press, 1971); and Alan C. Dessen, *Elizabethan Stage Conventions and Modern Interpreters* (Cambridge University Press, 1984).

5 See, for example, David Bevington, *Action is Eloquence: Shakespeare's Language of Gesture* (Cambridge, Mass.: Harvard University Press, 1984); Jean E. Howard, *Shakespeare's Art of Orchestration: Stage Technique and Audience Response* (Urbana: University of Illinois Press, 1984); Ann Pasternak Slater, *Shakespeare the Director* (Brighton: Harvester Press, 1982); Frances Teague, *Shakespeare's Speaking Properties* (Lewisburg: Bucknell University Press, 1991).

6 Several recent scholars dealing with comparable problems have sought to break with prevailing narratives by taking a fresh and rigorous look at the evidence. See, for example, Leeds Barroll, *Politics, Plague, and Shakespeare's Theater* (Ithaca and London: Cornell University Press, 1991); and William Ingram, *The Business of Playing: The Beginnings of the Adult Professional Theater in Elizabethan London* (Ithaca and London: Cornell University Press, 1992).

7 For fuller discussion and documentation of some of these signals see Dessen, *Elizabethan Stage Conventions*, pp. 36–8 (disheveled hair), pp. 38–40 (boots), and pp. 40–3 (nightgowns). For an interpreter's misreading of *muffled*, note the final moments of *Measure for Measure* where the duke (referring to Claudio) asks the provost "What muffled fellow's that?" (5.1.482). The New Arden editor (p. 147), drawing upon the *OED*, glosses *muffled* as *blindfold* and explains that "Claudio, led in with his eyes covered, does not see Isabella until line 487" and hence may act out an "emblem of 'blind love.'" If contemporary stage directions (as opposed to the *OED*) are invoked, however, the theatrical meaning of *muffled* is clear, as in: "*The King enters again, muffled in his cloak*" (Heywood, *1 Edward IV*, I, 67); "*Enter Bellarius muffled in his cloak*" (*The Second Maiden's Tragedy*, 589–91); "*Enter soldiers muffled up in their cloaks*" (Suckling, *The Goblins*, 4.3.35.s.d.); enter two figures "*muffled up in their cloaks, and walk over the Stage*" (*The Faithful Friends*, 2837–9). For figures directed to enter *muffled* with no further details, see *The Puritan*, F1r; Heywood, *The Brazen Age*, III, 220; Massinger, *The Guardian*, 1.1.80.s.d.; *The Knave in Grain*, 2542; Suckling, *Aglaura*, 1.4.1.s.d.

8 Lawrence, *Pre-Restoration Stage Studies*, pp. 204–5.

9 For a discussion of some possible thematic implications of an astringer bearing a hooded falcon see Dessen, *Elizabethan Stage Conventions*, pp. 132–5.

10 One early Shakespeare text with unusually detailed stage directions does not use this shorthand; in Quarto *2 Henry VI* the penitent

Elinor enters "*accompanied with the Sheriffs of London, and Sir John Standly, and Officers, with bills and halberds*" (D2r). More representative, however, is the situation in *Henry VIII* where the bearers of various weapons are implied: "*Enter Buckingham from his Arraignment, Tipstaves before him, the Axe with the edge towards him, Halberds on each side*" (TLN 889–91). The Pelican editor provides "[*Officer bearing*] *the* [*executioner's*] *axe with the edge towards him*" (2.1.53.s.d.) but leaves the tipstaves and halberds as in the Folio. For some non-Shakespeare examples: "*Enter with Welsh hooks, Rice ap Howell, a Mower, and the Earl of Leicester*" (Marlowe, *Edward II*, 1912.s.d.); "*Enter Sheriff bringing in Trusty Roger with halberds*" (*A Warning for Fair Women*, K3r); "*Enter Young Thorney and Halberds ... Enter Sawyer to Execution, Officers with Halberds, country-people*" (Dekker et al., *The Witch of Edmonton*, 5.3.0.s.d., 20.s.d.). In his *Two Lamentable Tragedies*, Robert Yarington seems not to use the shorthand form: "*Enter Constable, three watchmen with Halberds*"; "*Enter Merry and Rachel to execution with Officers with Halberds ...*" (I1v, K1v); similarly, Marston calls for a group to enter accompanied by "*three with halberds*" (*The Dutch Courtesan*, 4.5.0.s.d.). "Officers with halberds" also turn up in one of the plots (*The Dead Man's Fortune*, 51) and are visible in the Peacham drawing of *Titus Andronicus*. The unusual sequence of three such "halberd" scenes in Folio *Richard III* may indicate a patterned series involving these three moments.

11 Occasionally the implicit verb is spelled out. Thus, the only marked *aside* in Armin's *The Two Maids of More-Clacke* comes when the wife asks "Sir, what is your will?" and her husband replies "To murder thee"; the marginal signal reads: "*he speaks aside*" (G3r).

12 For boxed asides see lines 150, 166, 173, 336, 427, 428, 952, 953, 960, 1026, 1176, 1361, 1461, 1467, 1472, 1494, 1497; for unboxed see 175, 208, 211, 453–4, 455–8, 459–62, 463–5, 853–4, 2085–6. A much earlier playhouse manuscript from the 1580s or 1590s, *John a Kent*, has several *asides* marked in the right margin (177, 179) along with "*to her aside*" (1118).

13 For stand aside: *Two Gentlemen*, 4.2.78; *Ado*, 4.2.28; *Love's Labor's*, 4.1.56, 5.2.580; *Dream*, 3.2.116; *As You*, 3.2.118; *Shrew*, 2.1.24, 5.1.53; *All's Well*, 5.3.266; *2 Henry IV*, 3.2.116, 3.2.215, 3.2.220; *3 Henry VI*, 3.3.110; *Caesar*, 2.1.312; for "walk aside": *Measure*, 4.1.58, *Ado*, 3.2.63, *Love's Labor's*, 4.3.208; for "take him aside": *Twelfth Night*, 5.1.94; for "step aside": *1 Henry IV*, 2.4.30, *Romeo*, 1.1.154; for "turn aside": *Antony*, 1.3.76; and for "aside, aside": *Winter's Tale*, 4.4.671, *Timon*, 2.2.116. The only stage direction

linked to any of these moments is in *3 Henry VI* where, after the French king asks Margaret, her son, and Oxford "to stand aside," the Folio directs: "*They stand aloof*" (TLN 1847). The latter term also is to be found in *The Two Noble Kinsmen* when Emilia sets fire to the silver hind upon the altar "*her maids standing aloof*" (5.1.136.s.d.) and elsewhere in the dialogue (e.g., *Dream*, 2.2.26, *Merchant*, 3.2.42).

14 Roughly half of the asides marked in the Oxford edition of the plays of Philip Massinger are provided by Massinger himself and the other half by editors Philip Edwards and Colin Gibson. With other dramatists, the percentage of asides marked by the editor is higher. As noted above, almost all the marked asides in Shakespeare's plays are provided by editors.

15 In contrast, another speaker whom many would classify as a master of the aside, Marlowe's Barabas, does have a large number of marked asides in the 1633 Quarto of *The Jew of Malta* (including five on D1r, seven on D4v–E1r, and six on H4r). In his introduction to his Revels edition (Manchester University Press, 1978, p. 32), N. W. Bawcutt argues that Barabas's distinctive posture is keyed to the *aside*, an effect that *is* spelled out in the Quarto, but comparable Shakespearean figures such as Richard III, Iago, and Aaron are given no such signals.

16 For example, early in *King Leir* the servants of first Cornwall, then Cambria have speeches "*to himself*" not heard by their masters (404–5, 414–15); later, Gonorill has lines marked "*to herself*" (1393) and "*Speaks to her self*" (1425–6). In *The Death of Robert Earl of Huntingdon* Munday designates no *asides* but does signal two speeches "*To himself*" (1034, 1134). Similarly, to reveal his secret hatred for Corineus the title figure of *Locrine* has a five-line speech designated not *aside* but rather "*Locrine to himself*" (1565). In an exchange between two lovers in *The Four Prentices of London*, Heywood has Guy direct part of his long speech "*private to himself*" and then designates two of the lady's subsequent reactions "*private*" (II, 179–80). In *Two Lamentable Tragedies* Yarington signals thirteen asides which are marked as "*To the people*" (B2v, D2r, G4v, H1r, three on B1v, three on D4v) or merely "*People*" (B4R, H3r, I3r). From another early play with no marked asides, *Fair Em*, comes a more elaborate locution: "*Blanch speaketh this secretly at one end of the stage*" (235). Clearly, in the 1590s and early 1600s some dramatists, when they did choose to be prescriptive, preferred *to himself* or other locutions to *aside*.

17 Typical situations (without any dialogue) include: "*Juno and Ceres whisper, and send Iris on employment*" (*Tempest*, 4.1.124.s.d., TLN

1792); the Dauphin "*Whispers with Blanch*" (*John*, 2.1.503.s.d., TLN 820); Talbot and his allies "*whisper together in counsel*" (*1 Henry VI*, 3.2.59.s.d., TLN 1495); Brutus and Cassius "*whisper*" while the other conspirators debate where the sun is to rise (*Caesar*, 2.1.100.s.d., TLN 730); and to give instructions to Tyrrel Richard III (4.2.78.s.d.) either "*Whispers*" (Folio, TLN 2676) or "*whispers in his ear*" (Q1, I1v). See also Q1 *2 Henry VI*, 2.1.0.s.d., B3r; O1 *3 Henry VI*, 5.1.80.s.d., E2r; Q1 *Richard III*, 3.2.111.s.d., F4v; Q1 *Merry Wives*, 3.4.75.s.d., E4v; Q1 *Romeo*, 1.5.122.s.d., C4r; *Antony*, 2.7.39.s.d., TLN 1378; and *Henry VIII*, 1.4.81.s.d., TLN 780; 2.2.120.s.d., TLN 1171; 3.2.137.s.d., TLN 2000; 3.2.203.s.d., TLN 2081. For some comparable examples from roughly the same period see *Edmond Ironside*, 96, 1416–18; Greene, *Friar Bacon and Friar Bungay*, 391 ("*All this while Lacy whispers Margaret in the ear*"); *Histriomastix*, F4v; Tourneur, *The Atheist's Tragedy*, 4.5.13.s.d.; Day, *Law Tricks*, 993. For an exception to this practice, see *The Spanish Tragedy* where Kyd's signal "*He whispereth in her ear*" (3.10.77.s.d.) precedes Lorenzo's speech aside to Bel-Imperia that is not to be overheard by Balthasar.

18 For a particularly good example, see the first meeting of Margaret and Suffolk in *1 Henry VI* where each comments upon the other's inattention (5.3.83–109). See also *The Changeling*, where Alsemero tells Beatrice–Joanna (who has been formulating her plans to herself): "Lady, you hear not me" (2.2.48); and *The Revenger's Tragedy* where, when Vindice reacts privately to Lussurioso's proposition, the latter reacts: "why dost walk aside?" (1.3.127). In Heywood's *The Four Prentices of London* after Guy delivers a long passage "*private to himself*," the lady reacts: "Fie niggard, can you spend such precious breath, / Speak to your self so many words apart; / And keep their sound from my attentive ear, / Which save your words no music loves to hear?" (II, 179)

19 The practices of other dramatists vary widely and cannot be easily summarized, but some do use *aside* to denote movement rather than a form of speech. A play such as *The Weakest Goeth to the Wall* provides a mixture that includes several *whispers* (the first reads "*He takes him aside and whispers*" – 470), two normative asides (2040, 2281), and Lodowick's speech: "Be silent Bunch, till we be rid of these" that is followed by a centered stage direction: "*Close aside to Bunch*" (1260–1). In *The Widow's Tears* Chapman provides no designated asides (even though many such situations exist – as with Tharsalio's comments on the Governor in the final scene), but early in the play Lysander "*takes Tharsalio aside*" and says: "Will you not resolve me brother?" (1.3.117). Similarly, in Day's *Law*

Tricks, when a figure enters unseen by those already onstage, the signal is: "*Enter Horatio a side*" (695); in Barry's *Ram Alley* "*The Drawer stands aside*" (1737–8). Such variations persist into the 1630s. Thus, Richard Brome provides some normative asides but also uses the term for physical movement. For example, in *A Mad Couple Well Matched* a figure says "Stand off a while" and the marginal stage direction reads "*Goes aside*" (I, 91); in *The Damoiselle* "*They go aside*" and "*They aside*" (I, 424–5); and in *The City Wit* "*Ticket talks aside with Toby,*" "*They two go aside,*" "*He pulls her aside,*" and "*Tryman takes Pyannet and Toby aside*" (I, 307, 315, 356).

20 Beckerman, *Shakespeare at the Globe*, p. 162.

21 Ernest Rhodes, *Henslowe's Rose: The Stage and Staging* (University Press of Kentucky, 1976), p. 164.

22 E. A. J. Honigmann, "Re-Enter the Stage Direction: Shakespeare and Some Contemporaries," *Shakespeare Survey* 29 (1976): 119–20.

23 "The Gallery over the Stage in the Public Playhouse of Shakespeare's Time," *Shakespeare Quarterly* 8 (1957): 16–17. Such alternative ways of describing the same action can co-exist in the same passage. For example, in his discussion of *Jocasta* Bruce R. Smith notes that the title figure "is said to enter first 'out of her house' and in the next sentence 'out of her Palace'," a sequence that "probably reflects two different ways of looking at that action, first in theatrical terms" (because "'House' is the technical name for a stage-mansion") "and then in fictional terms" (because " 'palace' is how the house figures in the story"). See *Ancient Scripts and Modern Experience on the English Stage 1500–1700* (Princeton University Press, 1988), p. 82.

24 For a sampling of such evidence, see Dessen, *Elizabethan Stage Conventions*, pp. 32–4.

25 "Tree Properties and Tree Scenes in Elizabethan Theater," *Renaissance Drama* 4 (1971): 69–92.

26 *The Plays of John Lyly*, ed. Carter A. Daniel (Lewisburg: Bucknell University Press, 1988), p. 145.

27 Rhodes, *Henslowe's Rose*, p. 132.

28 Beckerman, *Shakespeare at the Globe*, p. 81.

29 See *Philip Henslowe's Diary*, ed. R. A. Foakes and R. T. Rickert (Cambridge University Press, 1961), pp. 319–20, lines 63, 75–6. For "2 moss banks" see line 74.

30 See also the allegorical dumb show in *A Warning for Fair Women* where "*the great tree*" that "*suddenly riseth up*" is subsequently cut down (E3v); *The Spanish Tragedy* where stage directions direct the murderers to hang Horatio "*in the arbour*" (2.4.53.s.d.) and where

Isabella later "*cuts down the arbour*" (4.2.5.s.d.); and Heywood's 1 *The Iron Age* where "*Hector takes up a great piece of a Rock, and casts at Ajax; who tears a young Tree up by the roots, and assails Hector*" (III, 300).

4 JUXTAPOSITIONS

1 For an example of an error, in *2 Henry IV*, 2.1, after Falstaff makes his peace with the Hostess, she asks: "Will you have Doll Tearsheet meet you at supper?" (156–7). But the Quarto stage direction for her departure ("*exit hostess and sergeant*" – C3r) is placed *above* both this question and Falstaff's response ("No more words. Let's have her"). Perhaps this stage direction could be reinterpreted as "*starts to exit*" or "*offers to go*" (a common signal in such playscripts), but the layout of the page in the Quarto suggests that the expanse of white space above the Hostess's line (an expanse broken only by the word *on* that concludes Falstaff's previous speech) proved irresistible to the compositor. For an example of an on-the-page exigency, the Second Quarto of *Hamlet* (but not the Folio, TLN 2619) brings in Guildenstern a line before Claudius calls for him (4.1.32), because "*Enter Ros. & Guild.*" fits in the margin beside "We must with all our Majesty and skill" but not beside "Both countenance and excuse. Ho Guildenstern" (K1v). The one example I have found of an early entrance clearly linked to theatrical exigency is to be found in *The Tempest* where the Folio's direction, "*Juno descends*" (TLN 1731, 4.1.72), is placed some thirty lines before Ceres actually addresses Juno (TLN 1762, 101). Clearly, this descent was slow, not free-fall. I have found no evidence, however, that dramatists or playhouse annotators allowed extra time for "normal" entrances.

2 Similarly, Lucius appears four lines before he actually speaks (*Titus Andronicus*, 3.1.22), for he must overhear at least some of his father's speech in order to tell Titus "you lament in vain" (27); and Henry V enters three lines before he speaks (4.3.16) so that he can overhear Westmoreland's wish for more men at Agincourt, a speech that generates the king's rejoinder: "What's he that wishes so?" (18)

3 The absence of a designated entrance for Romeo in Q1 is certainly not unusual in either a "good" or (in this instance) a "bad" quarto. This particular silence, however, may be linked to the comparable absence of an *exit* for Romeo in 2.2, so that, if a reader takes the signals literally, Q1's Romeo remains onstage at the end of the balcony scene so as eventually to address the friar. The reader who finds this juxtaposition unlikely should remember that

in both quartos at the end of 1.4 the masquers do not *exeunt* but remain onstage to be joined by the Capulets, their servants, and their guests. If both quartos call for the ball to come to the masquers (rather than calling for the masquers to exit and re-enter to a new place), Q1's friar conceivably could also join a Romeo already onstage.

4 Here and with subsequent examples I have surveyed the choices in a representative sampling of editions: two older complete works (edited by G. L. Kittredge and by Peter Alexander); four more recent complete works (the Pelican, the Riverside, the Signet, and Wells–Taylor); and five series of single volume editions (Arden, New Penguin, Bantam, Oxford, and Cambridge). Since the latter two series are not yet complete, my total number on a given play may vary between nine and eleven. For the three instances above from *As You Like It* 3.5, *Titus*, and *Henry V*, no editor changes the original placement; in my sampling of *Romeo*, 2.3, seven of ten retain Q2's placement.

5 Of eleven editions consulted, only three (Alexander, Pelican, Oxford) move the entrance of the Bastard; in contrast, six of eleven move the messenger's entrance. Only four (Kittredge, Riverside, Signet, Arden) retain both early entries.

6 Of nine editions consulted, all retain Orlando's early entrance in 4.1; seven retain Rosalind's early entrance in 5.2 (the dissenters are Alexander and the Arden); and eight retain LeBeau's entrance in 1.2 (with Alexander again a dissenter).

7 An even more strident violation of our sense of "realism" would occur if the two already onstage do not have their backs turned but rather are actually facing the entering figures but not seeing or "noting" them.

8 In a workshop at Goucher College on October 15, 1988 (built around the five ACTER actors who were performing *Much Ado*), this early entrance was instinctively resisted by the actors playing Claudio and Don Pedro (Allan Hendrick, Dudley Sutton) who immediately moved as far downstage as they could with their backs to the entering figures so as to justify their not seeing them. The only one who liked the effect was Dogberry (Richard Cordery), for it gave him a moment to strut or call attention to himself while waiting to be noticed by his superiors. An ironic juxtaposition from the point of view of the playgoer may be of considerable interest to a critic or a director but will often be eclipsed by the (necessary) tunnel vision of an actor wedded to psychological realism (who understandably "sees" the play through the eyes of his or her "character").

9 One possible objection to the Folio's placement of Malvolio's entrance and Bertram's re-entry is that an immediate appearance of the figure after Olivia's "call him hither" (3.4.13) or the king's "Go speedily, and bring again the count" (5.3.152), as printed in the Folio, does not allow enough time for the order to be carried out. Examples from comparable scenes, however, demonstrate that such a hiatus was not essential for the Lord Chamberlain's Men. For example, in *Julius Caesar*, 4.3 Lucius, at Brutus' request, calls for Varro and Claudius (244) who then enter immediately. Even more telling is Bolingbroke's "Call forth Bagot" to open the deposition scene (*Richard II*, 4.1.1), with Bagot entering immediately so as to be addressed in line 2 ("Now, Bagot, freely speak thy mind"). See also *Pericles*, 3.2.1 and *Hamlet*, 3.2.49 (following Q2, G4r but not the Folio, TLN 1902). Today's editor may feel the need to allow two or more lines to accommodate "call him hither," but Shakespeare and his colleagues apparently *could* manage without such a hiatus.

10 For example, in both the Quarto (E2r) and the Folio (TLN 1364) Ulysses in 2.3 re-enters from Achilles' tent two speeches before he speaks, just before Ajax's "I do hate a proud man..." (153). In contrast, in the Quarto (G3v) Thersites enters just before his first speech at 3.3.242 ("A wonder!"), but in the Folio he enters two lines earlier (TLN 2096) so that he is onstage for the final lines of Achilles' speech. Of greatest interest is the situation in 4.4 where the Quarto provides no entry for Diomedes and the others but the Folio (TLN 2499) provides "*Enter the Greeks*" not at Troilus' "Welcome, Sir Diomed" (108) but two lines earlier. To follow the Folio here so as to have Diomedes onstage during Troilus' closing lines to Cressida ("Fear not my truth; the moral of my wit / Is 'plain and true'; there's all the reach of it" – 4.4.106–7) could yield an ironic or ominous effect well worth preserving. These early entrances have been treated variously by editors (most keep the first and reject the second, with opinion divided evenly on the third).

11 A large number of *within*s are indeed signaled in the quartos and the Folio. Many are linked to offstage sound effects (e.g., see *Tempest*, TLN 45, 70; *Dream*, F4v; *All's Well*, TLN 1977, 2007; *Love's Labors*, D4r; *Coriolanus*, TLN 47; *Troilus*, TLN 1477, M1r; *Caesar*, TLN 2688; *Macbeth*, TLN 2328, and, most elaborately, *Kinsmen*, M1v, M3v). By far the largest number of *within*s call for a voice or shout offstage followed by an entrance of that figure or figures; for representative examples of a sizable group see *Tempest*, TLN 451, 458; *Measure*, TLN 2101, 2114 and 2191, 2198; *Errors*, TLN 1657,

1665; *Troilus*, TLN 2279, 2280 and 2435, 2488, 2490, 2499 (also H3v–H4r); *Coriolanus*, TLN 1988, 1993 and 3366, 3369; and *Macbeth*, TLN 127, 136 and 1229, 1237. Admittedly, a figure clearly *within* is sometimes not designated as such. E.g., in both Quarto and Folio *Richard III*, Hastings in 3.2 first answers the messenger ("Who knocks?" – 3.2.2 – the Pelican editor adds "[*within*]") and then is directed to enter (F3r, TLN 1800); the Folio stage direction that starts the scene, moreover, reads: "*Enter a Messenger to the Door of Hastings*" (TLN 1794). Although the procedures are not consistent, the early printed editions often do designate *within* when such is the case and usually specify an entrance for the heretofore offstage figure. In contrast, both Cassandra and Macbeth (in 2.2) clearly are directed to *enter* at the point that most editors would have them *within* (so that to emend *Troilus* 2.2 and *Macbeth* 2.2 is to transform an apparent anomaly into normative usage). Both *Troilus* and *Macbeth*, it should also be noted, already specify a number of *withins* (several more than those cited above).

12 See in particular Steven Urkowitz, *Shakespeare's Revision of* "*King Lear*," (Princeton University Press, 1980), pp. 36–7, 117–20.

13 For the same reason that I find a provocation in a normal Quarto entrance that becomes early in the Folio (when the Folio is deemed the chronologically later text), I have chosen not to pursue various instances that move in the opposite direction. Thus, a large number of both early and late entrances are to be found in the Quartos of the two parts of *Henry IV* but most of them are normalized in the Folio. Someone (author, bookkeeper, scribe, compositor) apparently saw them as anomalous or intrusive. I confess to a strong interest in Puck's presence in the Quarto at the outset of 3.2 (D4r), even though Oberon does not address him until line 4, but this early presence is eliminated in the Folio (TLN 1025), so I have not included that scene. Two early entrances in Quarto *Othello* (for Iago and Cassio in 3.4, I1v, and for Othello, Lodovico, and others in 4.2–4.3, L2r) are also normalized in the Folio (TLN 2259, 2966–7).

14 Macbeth's early entrance in 2.2 will be discussed in chapter 5. The indefatigable reader who wants more material should look at *1 Henry VI*, TLN 2732 and *Timon*, TLN 787. As that reader may have noted, I have for the most part sidestepped the problems occasioned by the three early printed texts of *Hamlet*. Of the many questions generated by the discrepancies, consider the following sampling. When should Hamlet and Horatio enter in 5.1: just before the clown's song (Q1, H4r); just before Hamlet's first line (Q2, M2v); or considerably earlier (before the clown's "Cudgel thy

brains no more about it" – 53) where the Folio has the two entering figures "*a far off*" (TLN 3245)? In 3.2, should Rosencrantz and Guildenstern re-enter just before Guildenstern's first line (285 – as in Q2, H3v) or four lines earlier (Folio, TLN 2163) so as to give added point to Hamlet's "Aha! Come, some music!" (281) as he notices their arrival and shifts his tone? Should the first entry of the mad Ophelia in 4.5 be just before her first line (21 – as in Folio TLN 2766) or four lines earlier before Gertrude's "To my sick soul ..." (as in Q2, K4r)? A few lines later, should Claudius enter just before Gertrude's "Alas, look here, my lord" (37, as in Q2) or a beat earlier, before the queen's "Nay, but Ophelia – " (34, as in TLN 2775)? In Q1's closet scene the Ghost enters so as to be noticed immediately by Hamlet (G2v), but in both Q2 (I3v) and F (TLN 2482) that entrance is placed one line early (before "A king of shreds and patches" – 3.4.103). Of the editions consulted, seven keep this early entrance, and four (New Penguin, Arden, Oxford, Wells–Taylor) move it one line later so as to have it precede Hamlet's first awareness of the Ghost ("save me ..." – 104).

15 See also *1 Henry VI*, 5.5, TLN 2923, 2925, 2931; Folio *2 Henry VI*, 4.8, TLN 2845, 2847; *Shrew*, 4.5, TLN 2375, 2378; Folio *Richard III*, 1.4, TLN 1113, 1118; and Folio *Hamlet*, 3.3, TLN 2371, 2373. The highest concentration of such normative examples is to be found in *Cymbeline* (see the ends of 2.1, 2.3, 2.4, and 3.5), but even here exceptions turn up in 1.5 and 5.4.

16 Some of these options *have* been discussed by scholars. For example, Michael Warren notes that after Lear in 1.1 commands that Gloucester attend France and Burgundy the Folio provides an *Exit* (TLN 40) but the Quarto (B1v) is silent. For Warren, "to indicate an exit for Edmund here is an act of editorial presumption that shapes the reader's perception," for "Edmund's experience of Lear's mistreatment of the daughters – something that Gloucester does not witness – can be an important aspect of an actor's performance of Edmund and, particularly, can color for an interpreter the perception of Edmund's behavior in the second scene." See "Textual Problems, Editorial Assertions in Editions of Shakespeare," in *Textual Criticism and Literary Interpretation*, ed. Jerome J. McGann (Chicago and London: University of Chicago Press, 1985), p. 29. Various critics have commented upon the theatrical possibilities if the gravedigger in *Hamlet*, 5.1 stays on to observe the remainder of the scene.

17 Elsewhere in *Twelfth Night*, the Folio provides no marked *exeunt* for Sir Toby and Sir Andrew in 5.1; even though Olivia says of the wounded Toby "get him to bed, and let his hurt be looked to"

(200), in some recent productions the two bloodied figures have lingered to add to the amazement at Sebastian's entrance. The disposition of Feste in 2.3 (he has no lines after Malvolio's *exit*) also poses a puzzle. In Terry Hands' 1977–78 production of *Henry VI*, in Part 1, 4.1 Talbot (who has no marked *exit* in the Folio) lingered briefly onstage so as to observe in amazement the behavior of a "new" breed of courtiers that he could not fathom.

18 Homer Swander, "No Exit for a Dead Body: What to do with a Scripted Corpse?" *Journal of Dramatic Theory and Criticism* (Spring, 1991): 141, 147, 151.

19 The two richest examples of juxtaposition–continuity will be discussed in chapter 5: Kent's presence onstage in the stocks during Edgar's speech in the modern 2.3; and the onstage banquet in view during Orlando and Adam's lines in 2.6. Another (perhaps fanciful) possibility arises if the dying Richard II's comment to Exton ("thy fierce hand / Hath with the king's blood stained the king's own land" – 5.5.109–10) is translated into ample stage blood (Exton too refers to the blood he has "spilled" – 114). If such blood remained visible on the stage floor, Henry IV's closing speech moments later would have been enhanced, especially "Lords, I protest my soul is full of woe / That blood should sprinkle me to make me grow" and "I'll make a voyage to the Holy Land / To wash this blood off from my guilty hand" (5.6.45–6, 49–50).

20 E. A. J. Honigmann, "Re-Enter the Stage Direction: Shakespeare and Some Contemporaries," *Shakespeare Survey 29* (1976): 118.

21 I cannot offer a wide array of early entrances and late exits from other dramatists. In his analysis of the playhouse manuscript of Munday's *John a Kent*, William B. Long notes that the bookkeeper's additions or insertions consist of only seven brief annotations, two of which create situations in which either John a Kent or John a Cumber is brought onstage one or two lines early. See "*John a Kent and John a Cumber*: An Elizabethan Playbook and Its Implications," in *Shakespeare and Dramatic Tradition: Essays in Honor of S. F. Johnson*, ed. W. R. Elton and William B. Long (Newark: University of Delaware Press, 1989), pp. 134–5. George Walton Williams has noted comparable examples to me from the Fletcher canon.

5 THEATRICAL ITALICS

1 Paul Armstrong, *Conflicting Readings: Variety and Validity in Interpretation* (Chapel Hill: University of North Carolina Press, 1990), pp. ix, 13–16.

2 In his recent book, Robert Hapgood also raises this issue in the context of a performance-oriented approach to Shakespeare. Citing Stephen Booth's rejection of "either/or" interpretive choices in reading the sonnets, Hapgood suggests that "at an extreme, critical tolerance can mask a failure of nerve, an unwillingness to say: 'this is more likely than that', 'this is given greater emphasis than that', 'this is more central or better balanced than that'." Rather, for him even though Shakespeare's texts "do not provide hard and fast directions for their own interpretation," nonetheless they "do permit such discriminations," for "they do provide guidelines, do set limits to the latitudes they allow." Hapgood concludes that, "although no single reading is definitive, some are downright wrong and among the rest some are in certain respects to be preferred to others." See *Shakespeare the Theatre-Poet* (Oxford University Press, 1988), p. 13.

3 For example, see S. P. Zitner, "Anon, Anon: or, a Mirror for a Magistrate," *Shakespeare Quarterly* 19 (1968): 63–70. In his *Shakespearean Negotiations* (Berkeley and Los Angeles: University of California Press, 1988, p. 43), Stephen Greenblatt treats the moment as one of "the play's acts of *recording*, that is, the moments in which we hear voices that seem to dwell outside the realms ruled by the potentates of the land."

4 So Greenblatt (p. 45) concludes his section: "The prince must sound the base-string of humility if he is to play all of the chords and hence be the master of the instrument, and his ability to conceal his motives and render opaque his language offers assurance that he himself will not be played on by another." For my own reading see *Shakespeare and the Late Moral Plays* (Lincoln: University of Nebraska Press, 1986), pp. 69–70.

5 The Wells–Taylor old-spelling version reads: "And *Lauinia* thou shalt be imployde, / Beare thou my hand sweet wench betweene thine Armes" (*The Complete Works: Original Spelling Edition* [Oxford: Clarendon Press, 1986], lines 1296–7). In their textual note Wells and Taylor build upon an earlier editor's conjecture that someone made the correction "to soften what must have been ludicrous in representation," a correction that in turn led to an error in Q1; according to this reconstruction, a scribe then "made sense of the passage by substituting 'things' for 'Armes'" (*William Shakespeare: A Textual Companion* [Oxford: Clarendon Press, 1987], p. 212). "To soften" a "ludicrous" moment, a series of editors have therefore closed down a meaningful option present in the quartos and the Folio. One of these emended editions, moreover (volume 34 in the New Temple Shakespeare, ed. M. R. Ridley

[London and New York, 1934]), served as the basis for two landmark productions of this script (Peter Brook's in Stratford-upon-Avon 1955, Gerald Freedman's for the New York Shakespeare Festival in 1967), so that both of these directors could sidestep the problem completely.

6 For my own treatment of parts of the body in this tragedy, see *Titus Andronicus* (Manchester University Press, 1989), pp. 86–9.

7 For example, in a dramatic romance published at about the same time as *Titus* (*A Knack to Know an Honest Man*) a banished figure in disguise as a hermit announces his name to be Penitential Experience. In the early 1590s such mixing of allegorical nomenclature and "literal" action, if not widespread, was at least possible. See also the allegorical dumb shows used to make explicit the forces at work behind a contemporary murder in *A Warning for Fair Women* (printed 1599).

8 Most editors gloss "her" in line 45 as "Justice," but equally likely is a confusion between Justice–heaven and Revenge–Acheron–hell, a confusion that feeds into Tamora's appearance in disguise with her request for Titus to "come down." The link, moreover, can be enforced in the theatre. For example, in the 1988 Shakespeare Santa Cruz production Tamora–Revenge entered bearing an arrow with the message still attached, thereby suggesting that her appearance was in response to his quest in 4.3.

9 David Daniell, "Opening up the text: Shakespeare's *Henry VI* plays in performance," *Themes in Drama* 1 (1979): 257.

10 For some recent revisionist interpretations of Joan, however, see Leah Marcus, *Puzzling Shakespeare* (Berkeley and Los Angeles: University of California Press, 1988), pp. 51–96; Gabriele Bernhard Jackson, "Topical Ideology: Witches, Amazons, and Shakespeare's Joan of Arc," *English Literary Renaissance* 18 (1988): 40–65; and Nancy A. Gutierrez, "Gender and Value in *1 Henry VI*: The Role of Joan de Pucelle," *Theatre Journal* 42 (1990): 183–93.

11 For treatments of 2.3, see especially Edward I. Berry, *Patterns of Decay: Shakespeare's Early Histories* (Charlottesville: University Press of Virginia, 1975), pp. 1–28; James A. Riddell, "Talbot and the Countess of Auvergne," *Shakespeare Quarterly* 28 (1977): 51–7; and Alexander Leggatt, *Shakespeare's Political Drama* (London and New York: Routledge, 1988), pp. 1–8.

12 For the reader skeptical about the juxtaposition of onstage food with starving figures I can offer two comparable examples from plays that antedate *As You Like It* in the 1590s. First, in *Locrine*, with a starving Humber onstage, Strumbo the clown enters saying "it is now breakfast time, you shall see what meat I have here for my

breakfast" (1626–8); the stage direction reads: "*Let him sit down and pull out his vittles*" (1629–30). Humber (like Orlando) then has a speech on the fruitless land but does not see the clown or his food; rather, "*Strumbo hearing his voice shall start up and put meat in his pocket, seeking to hide himself*" (1648–9). Eventually, a Humber near death sees Strumbo, asks for meat, and threatens the clown: "*Let him make as though he would give him some, and as he putteth out his hand, enter the ghost of Albanact, and strike him on the hand, and so Strumbo runs out, Humber following him*" (1669–73). Similarly, in *King Leir* "*Enter the Gallian King and Queen, and Mumford, with a basket, disguised like Country folk*" (2091–2); then "*Enter Leir and Perillus very faintly*" (2109–11) to talk of starving (Perillus goes so far as to offer his own blood to his master, Leir – 2128–9). After a long sequence, Perillus calls on God for help (2166–7) and at last sees the food ("Oh comfort, comfort! yonder is a banquet" – 2168). Both Humber and Perillus (unlike Adam and Orlando during their brief scene) eventually do see the onstage food, but not until after they have spoken at length about their plight.

13 Such thought-provoking italicized moments are common in the romances, most notably in *Cymbeline*, 4.2 where Fidele–Imogen awakens next to the headless Cloten whom she mistakes for Posthumus.

6 SICK CHAIRS AND SICK THRONES

1 For a full account of the evidence (including the allusions) see Alan C. Dessen, *Shakespeare and the Late Moral Plays* (Lincoln: University of Nebraska Press, 1986), pp. 20–1. For my reading of Falstaff's carrying off Hotspur in this context, see pp. 87–9.

2 Herford and Simpson, I, 143–4, lines 410–12. As late as 1626 Jonson has one of his foolish choric figures in *The Staple of News* praise the Devil who "would carry away the Vice on his back, quick to Hell, in every Play where he came, and reform abuses" (First Intermean, 64–6).

3 For fuller discussion of such generic signals and of stage directions as evidence, see chapter 2 of Alan C. Dessen, *Elizabethan Stage Conventions and Modern Interpreters* (Cambridge University Press, 1984).

4 For more doctors who accompany their patients, see Fletcher, *Valentinian*, IV, 76; Fletcher, *Monsieur Thomas*, IV, 120; Fletcher, *Thierry and Theodoret*, X, 64; H. Shirley, *The Martyred Soldier*, 3.4.0.s.d.; Brome, *The Court Beggar*, I, 257; *The Soddered Citizen*, 2216–17; J. Shirley, *The Witty Fair One*, 3.4.0.s.d.; J. Shirley, *The*

Politician, 4.3.0.s.d. For onstage urinals, see *Fair Em*, 350–3; Fletcher, *Monsieur Thomas*, IV, 116; *The Wit of a Woman*, 581; and Brome, *The City Wit*, I, 309.

5 For a sampling of the evidence, see Fletcher, I, 374, 378; IV, 76; VI, 254; Chapman, *The Gentleman Usher*, 4.3.0.s.d.; 5.4.39.s.d.; Dekker, *Satiromastix*, 5.2.37.s.d.; Heywood, *2 Edward IV*, I, 155; Massinger, *The Emperor of the East*, 4.3.0.s.d.; Peele, *Edward I*, 40.s.d. and *The Battle of Alcazar*, 1193.s.d.; Markham and Sampson, *Herod and Antipater*, H3r, I2v; Haughton, *Englishmen for My Money*, 2434; Brome, I, 218, 257; II, 127 (*The Queen and Concubine*); III, 180, 263, 546; *Locrine*, 33; *A Yorkshire Tragedy*, 720; *A Warning for Fair Women*, G4r. Sick-chairs are also to be found in plays as diverse as Marston's *Sophonisba*, Middleton's *Hengist, King of Kent*, Jonson's *The Magnetic Lady*, Ford's *The Broken Heart*, May's *The Old Couple*, Drue's *The Duchess of Suffolk*, *The Second Maiden's Tragedy*, *The Soddered Citizen*, and *The Telltale*.

6 The dialogue references in *Lear* to *litter* and *chair* (along with the stage direction in 4.7) are presumably to the same portable property (what I envisage as a chair that can readily be carried either on poles or by the arms). The many stage directions in Shakespeare and elsewhere that call for chairs along with the few signals that call for litters are then the basis for my hypothesis that this property would more resemble a chair of state than a stretcher. For one specific (and elaborate) call for a litter rather than a chair consider: "*The trumpets sound, Queen Elinor in her litter borne by four Negro Moors, Joan of Acon with her, attended on by the Earl of Gloucester, and her four footmen, one having set a ladder to the side of the litter, she descendeth, and her daughter followeth*" (Peele, *Edward I*, 1015.s.d.). Here the emphasis is upon Elinor's pride ("I tell thee the ground is all too base, / For Elinor to honor with her steps" – 1031–2), not upon any physical sickness.

7 A comparable problem is found during the first trial scene in *Volpone* when Volpone, supposedly diseased, "*is brought, as impotent*" (4.6.21.s.d.). The sense of diseases (associated with the sick-bed of Acts I and III) penetrating the halls of justice is strong whether a playgoer sees a litter or a sick-chair, but the latter image sets up a clear (and potentially disturbing) visual link with the seats of judgment held by the four avocatori in a sequence in which the innocent (Celia and Bonario) are convicted and the guilty exonerated. As with sick-chair and throne, a juxtaposition of sick-chair and judge's seat could be richly suggestive.

8 For just a few of the many treatments of "disease" in the history plays, see J. P. Brockbank, "The Frame of Disorder: *Henry VI*," in

Early Shakespeare, ed. J. R. Brown and Bernard Harris, Stratford-upon-Avon Studies 3 (1961): 72–99; Edward I. Berry, *Patterns of Decay: Shakespeare's Early Histories* (Charlottesville: University Press of Virginia, 1975); and L. C. Knights, *Some Shakespearean Themes* (London: Chatto and Windus, 1959).

7 MUCH VIRTUE IN *AS*

1 Bernard Beckerman, *Dynamics of Drama* (New York: Knopf, 1970), p. 3.

2 See chapter 4 of Alan C. Dessen, *Elizabethan Stage Conventions and Modern Interpreters* (Cambridge University Press, 1984).

3 For the full text see Karl Young, *The Drama of the Medieval Church*, 2 vols. (Oxford: Clarendon Press, 1933), I, 249–50. I am indebted to June Schlueter for calling my attention to the *as if*s in this passage. Note that in describing the approaching "women" "as if wandering about," the author of this passage uses the masculine rather than the feminine plural (*erraneos*), as is also true for calling them (*illos*) back. The action may be *ad imitationem* or *as if*, but, for this author, the gender of the monks who are the actors takes precedence over the gender of the performed roles. How would we react if a contemporary, writing in Latin, referred to Rosalind or Lady Macbeth (played by boy actors) in such masculine terms?

4 *The Play Called Corpus Christi* (Stanford, 1966), pp. 27, 32.

5 Meg Twycross, "Playing 'The Resurrection'," *Medieval Studies for J. A. W. Bennett Aetatis Suae LXX*, ed. P. L. Heyworth (Oxford: Clarendon Press, 1981), pp. 274–7.

6 For example, in *Ludus Coventriae*, the accusers of the woman taken in adultery go off "*quasi confusi*" or "as if confused" (p. 218); the Jews lay hands on Jesus "*as they were wood*" (p. 275); Mary is to lie on the ground "*quasi semi mortua*" (p. 314) or "as if half-dead."

7 "*Here Folly maketh semblant to take a louse from Crafty Conveyance shoulder*" (1199.s.d.); and "*Here Folly maketh semblant to take money of Crafty Conveyance*" (1208.s.d.).

8 Among the most interesting are Heywood's direction for the figures emerging from the Trojan horse who are to meet "*as if groping in the dark*" (*2 The Iron Age*, III, 380); and two comparable signals: "*having his napkin on his shoulder, as if he were suddenly raised from dinner*" (Munday, *The Downfall of Robert Earl of Huntingdon*, 166–8); and "*as it were brushing the Crumbs from his clothes with a Napkin, as newly risen from supper*" (Heywood, *A Woman Killed With Kindness*, II, 118). Elsewhere can be found a Caroline sound effect (Henry Killigrew, *The Conspiracy*: "*A noise is heard as if the gates were*

broken" – K2V), and an occasional action. Massinger directs: "*This spoke as if she studied an evasion*" (*The Great Duke of Florence*, 4.1.106.s.d.); a foolish figure "*tolls the bell, as if he pulled the rope*" (Armin, *The Two Maids of More-Clacke*, B4V); "*Clown tears off his doublet, making strange faces as if compelled to it*" (Fletcher, *The Fair Maid of the Inn*, IX, 201); "*Fowler, as if sick, upon a couch*" (Shirley, *The Witty Fair One*, III.4.0.s.d.); and "*Enter Ventidius as it were in triumph*" (*Antony and Cleopatra*, TLN 1494).

9 The Caroline dramatists are particularly fond of this usage. Davenant provides "*as he were sick*" (*The Platonic Lovers*, II, 100) and "*as sick on a couch*" (*The Wits*, II, 183); Jasper Mayne, "*as taken prisoners by them*" (*The Amorous War*, p. 79); Richard Brome gives us lawyers "*as conferring by two and two*" (*The Damoiselle*, I, 407); *The Bloody Banquet* offers "*as being hard pursued*" (229). Thomas Nabbes provides four examples in one play: "*as travelling together before day*"; "*with lights, as pursuing them*"; "*as going to milking*"; and "*as walking to Tottenham-Court*" (*Tottenham Court*, I, 101, 103, 106, 116). Shirley provides "*as peeping*" (*The Example*, 4.2.92.s.d.); "*as desirous to speak with him*" (*The Cardinal*, 3.2.85.s.d.); and "*as taking opportunity to go to her chamber*" (*The Example*, 2.2.207.s.d.). Suckling provides "*as going to prison*" (*The Sad One*, 1.2.0.s.d.); "*as talking earnestly*" (*Brennoralt*, 4.7.0.s.d.); and "*as seeking the horses*" (*The Goblins*, 3.4.9.s.d.).

10 *As to* situations often are the reverse of *as from*: "*as though to bed*" (Brome, *The Queen's Exchange*, III, 507); "*in her night-clothes, as going to bed*" (Rowley, *A Match at Midnight*, 4.5.0.s.d.); "*pass over the Stage with Pillows, Night clothes, and such things*" (Fletcher, *The Little French Lawyer*, III, 416). In two dumb shows in *The White Devil*, Isabella enters "*in her nightgown as to bed-ward ... she kneels down as to prayers*"; and, after the arrest of Flamineo and Marcello, officers "*go as 'twere to apprehend Vittoria*" (2.2.23.s.d., 37.s.d.). Most *as to* usages are linked to specific places or events: "*as to the Ordinary*" (Cartwright, *The Ordinary*, 3.4.0.s.d.); "*as to Council*" (Denham, *The Sophy*, p. 18); "*as to see the Execution*" (*The Witch of Edmonton*, 5.3.0.s.d.); "*A Table set out. Enter two servants, Jarvis and John, as to cover it for dinner*" (Rowley, *A Match at Midnight*, 2.1.0.s.d.); "*in solemnity as to marriage*" (Fletcher, *Four Plays in One*, X, 338); "*as to the Wedding with Rosemary*" (Brome, *The City Wit*, i, 358); "*going to be Married*" (Fletcher, *The Scornful Lady*, I, 281); "*as to Combat*" (*Clyomon and Clamydes*, G3V); "*Hermione (as to her Trial)*" (*The Winter's Tale*, TLN 1174–5); "*as to the Parliament*" (*Richard II*, Folio, TLN 1921). The relatively few *as at* signals are usually linked to sound effects ("*Alarum afar off, as at a Sea-fight*" – *Antony and Cleopatra*, TLN 2752),

to specific places ("*marching as being at Mile end*" – Heywood, *1 Edward IV*, I, 25), or to an ongoing activity ("*Enter Queen and her Women as at work*" – *Henry VIII*, TLN 1615; "*as at Dice*" – Fletcher, *Valentinian*, IV, 17).

11 For some examples, Dryden provides: "*Enter as from Dinner*" and "*as new rising from sleep*" (*The Wild Gallant*, 2.1.0.s.d., 3.2.0.s.d.); "*as returning from the Sally*" (1 *The Conquest of Granada*, 2.1.0.s.d.); Davenant: "*as from victory*" and "*as from a bush*" (*The Rivals*, V, 223, 273); Wycherley: "*as newly from a journey*" (*Love in a Wood*, 2.4.0.s.d.) and "*as from a journey*" (*The Plain Dealer*, 4.2.132.s.d.); Behn: "*as from out of the Garden*" (*The Dutch Lover*, I, 283); "*as from Church*" (*The City Heiress*, II, 210, 213); and "*as just risen in Disorder from the Bed, buttoning himself, and setting himself in order*" (*Sir Patient Fancy*, IV, 53). Also to be found in the Restoration are *as* [*if*] usages. From Dryden, "*as with Child*" (*The Wild Gallant*, 4.2.72.s.d.); "*his sword drawn; as pursued*" and "*as affrighted*" (2 *The Conquest of Granada*, 2.1.10.s.d., 2.2.8.s.d.); "*Charmion stands behind her Chair, as dressing her head*" (*All for Love*, 5.1.501.s.d.); and "*as at their Devotion*" (*An Evening's Love*, 1.2.0.s.d.). From Etherege: "*as having just ended the dance*" (*The Man of Mode*, 4.1.0.s.d.); from Davenant "*as at liberty*" (*The Rivals*, V, 248); from Vanbrugh: "*Rasor struggles with her, as if he would throw her down*" (*The Provok'd Wife*, I, 173). Behn provides the most examples: "*in her Night-Gown, at a Table, as undressing*" (*The Dutch Lover*, I, 254); "*as disturbed and out of Humour*" (*The City Heiress*, II, 259); "*as aboard the ship*" (*The False Count*, III, 145); "*as going to dance*" (*Sir Patient Fancy*, IV, 44); "*in their Cloaks muffled as in the dark*" (*The Forc'd Marriage*, III, 347); "*in her Night-gown, in a Chamber as by the dark*" (*Sir Patient Fancy*, IV, 49); "*groping as in the dark*" (*Sir Patient Fancy*, IV, 53); "*creeping as in the dark*" (*The Widow Ranter*, IV, 293); "*as to the Bed-chamber*" (*The City Heiress*, II, 269). Vanbrugh uses a distinctive *as just* construction: "*Enter Amanda, in a Scarf, etc. as just returned*" (*The Relapse*, I, 89); "*Enter Lady Arabella, as just up, walking pensively to her Toilet*" (*A Journey to London*, III, 162); "*The Scene opens to a Dressing room. Lady Townly, as just up, walks to her Toilet*" (*The Provok'd Husband*, III, 246). Given the presence of scenery and scenic locales, examples of *as in* are rare from 1660 on. I can offer from Etherege: "*Mrs Trinket sitting in a shop, people passing by as in the Exchange*" (*She Would If She Could*, 3.1.0.s.d.); from Sedley: "*Enter Photinus as within the Town*" (*Antony and Cleopatra*, 4.4.0.s.d.); and from Behn: "*as in a Bed-chamber*" (*The Forc'd Marriage*, III, 312).

12 I find unrevealing "*as in haste*" (Denham, *The Sophy*, p. 24); "*Francisco speaks this as in scorn*" (*The White Devil*, 3.2.46.s.d.);

"*falls down as in a swoon*" (Jonson, *The Alchemist*, 4.5.62.s.d.). For locales consider: "*as in Baynard's Castle*" (Davenport, *King John and Matilda*, p. 11); "*Two Devonshire Merchants, as being in Sherris*" (*Dick of Devonshire*, 93). I have found no *as if in* stage directions, but in other contexts *as* clearly includes the implication of *as if* – as when Macbeth describes Duncan's two grooms who cried out "as they had seen me with these hangman's hands" (2.2.27).

13 See Dessen, *Elizabethan Stage Conventions*, pp. 97–100. For some suggestive prison details consider: "*Enter Sir Charles in prison, with Irons, his feet bare, his garments all ragged and torn*" (Heywood, *A Woman Killed With Kindness*, II, 127); and Dick Pike "*in shackles, nightcap, plasters on his face*" and later "*an Iron about his neck, two Chains manacling his wrists; a great Chain at his heels*" (*Dick of Devonshire*, 941, 1624–5).

14 Although the "plots" are usually deemed the most theatrical of documents, the *Troilus* signals could still be fictional rather than theatrical in Hosley's terms (and hence not specify a verisimilar tent). The same plot later offers two fictional entries: "*on the walls*" and "*they on the wall descend to them*" (47, 50), a usage that turns up also in another plot ("*upon the walls . come down*" in *Frederick and Basilea* – 36). If a plot can designate an actor standing *above* or *aloft* as "*on the walls*" or "*upon the walls,*" then a plot could also designate an actor standing in or near a stage door as "*in his Tent.*"

15 These seven Caroline instances of *as* [*if*] *in* demonstrate one of many vagaries in the surviving evidence. Such variations have been or can be attributed to: (1) chronology (e.g., Peele's often ample signals versus subsequent dramatists' succinctness versus the spelling out of some details in the 1630s); (2) the auspices of the manuscript ("foul papers" versus playhouse manuscript versus scribal transcript); (3) the status of the playwright (writing for known colleagues versus freelance versus amateur or neophyte); or (4) authorial idiosyncrasy. After looking at thousands of stage directions, I have found that many of these distinctions do not hold up (e.g., the attached Heywood spells out more detail for his colleagues than the independent Middleton) or have limited value. Rather, I find a remarkable consistency in theatrical language, at least between the mid 1590s and the plays of Brome and Shirley, with authorial idiosyncrasy apparently the most telling factor. For example, as noted in chapter 3 Shakespeare in his stage directions rarely uses *aside*, a term that *is* regularly used by others.

16 For onstage beheadings see R. B.'s *Apius and Virginia*: "*Here tie a handkercher about her eyes, and then strike off her head*" (971–2);

Dekker's *The Virgin Martyr*: "*Her head struck off*" (4.3.179.s.d.); and Fletcher and Massinger's *Sir John van Olden Barnavelt* where, according to the dialogue (2996–8), the executioner strikes off not only Barnavelt's head but also some of his fingers ("you have struck his fingers too / but we forgive your haste"). Such onstage beheadings are also likely in other plays (e.g., Marston's *The Insatiate Countess*).

17 In the second dumb show of Middleton's *Hengist, King of Kent* two figures "*are Commanded to be hurried away as to execution*" (p. 24, 14–15). In addition to two examples of "*to Execution*" *The Witch of Edmonton* also directs a group to: "*Enter as to see the Execution*" (5.3.0.s.d.).

18 As specified for Buckingham in *Henry VIII* ("*the Axe with the edge towards him*"), an ax or other weapon may have been held so that its cutting edge was pointed at the condemned figure. Such a practice may also pertain to the halberds regularly found in these scenes, but I have found no specific evidence for such an onstage practice (and such is not the case for the halberds in the Peacham drawing of *Titus Andronicus*, 1.1, although Aaron's sword *is* pointed in the direction of two kneeling prisoners, one of whom may be Alarbus).

19 "*Enter as to the Parliament ...*" (Folio *Richard II*, TLN 1921, 4.1.0.s.d); "*Hermione* (*as to her Trial*)" (*The Winter's Tale*, TLN 1174–5, 3.2.10.s.d.).

20 Related to the *as* [*if*] usage but far less common is the presence in some stage directions of *seems*. Such a locution makes immediate sense to us in a dumb show, as in *Hamlet* where "*the poisoner with some three or four come in again, seem to condole with her, the dead body is carried away, the poisoner woos the Queen with gifts, she seems harsh awhile, but in the end accepts love*" (Q2, H1v; 3.2.129.s.d.). For other examples of *seems* or some equivalent (e.g., "*makes show of...*") in dumb shows see *Captain Thomas Stukeley*, K1r; *A Warning for Fair Women*, C3v, G3r; Marston, *Antonio's Revenge*, 3.1.0.s.d.; Day, *The Travels of the Three English Brothers*, 404; and Middleton, *Hengist, King of Kent*, second dumb show, 11–12. More puzzling is the situation in *Henry VIII*, 5.1.86 where the king (who wants to be alone with Cranmer) says "Avoid the Gallery" to the right of which phrase the Folio prints "*Lovel seems to stay*" (TLN 2877). Most revealing are the many scenes involving keys and locks (to be discussed further in chapter 8). The most common signals are straightforward: "*locks the door*" (Fletcher, *The Island Princess*, VIII, 137); "*Montsurry turns a key*" (Chapman, *Bussy* D'Ambois, 5.1.40.s.d.); "*Lock the door*" and "*Locks the door*" (Massinger, *The Fatal Dowry*, 3.1.401.s.d.,

4.1.154.s.d.); "*locks him into a closet*" (Webster, *The Devil's Law-Case*, 5.4.167.s.d.). However, in Munday's *The Death of Robert Earl of Huntingdon* Brand "*seems to lock a door*" (1921); in Shirley's *Love's Cruelty* "*Hippolito seems to open a chamber door and brings forth Eubel*" (4.2.15); in Davenant's *The Platonic Lovers* Ariola exits, "*Theander seems to lock her in*" (II, 47). Upon reflection, such a distinction does make sense, for an actor never "really" locks a door (although a key may be turned) but only "seems" to do so (a distinction retained by the neo-classical Chapman whose actor-figure "*turns a key*" as opposed to Fletcher or Massinger's "*locks the door*"). "*Turns a key*" is then "theatrical" (a signal directed at an actor), and "*locks the door*" is "fictional" (what the narrative fiction requires), although, in the spirit of *as [if]*, the latter could equally well be shorthand for "*makes as if to lock the door*" or, in short, an elliptical version of Munday's "*seems to lock a door.*"

21 Bernard Beckerman comes to similar conclusions (albeit in somewhat different terms) in his shrewd analysis of Henslowe's inventory. Today's actors and directors, he argues, "expect to turn the stage area into an idiosyncratic world that can house the events of the play in question," so that "somehow the stage is to be altered to suit the play at hand and *only* the play at hand," a practice he links to "our prevailing belief in environment as a crucial force affecting human behavior." For the Elizabethans, however, "whatever sense of locale a play or scene showed was derived from what the actors brought on stage," so that "doors, posts, and walls did not convey information about locale independently." Rather, "the players projected an identity upon the individual part of the stage by calling, for instance, the upper level the walls of Corioli or one of the doors Brabantio's house," so that "the environment that the players projected onto the facade or about the platform needed to be only as detailed as the narrative required for the moment." As a result, "the behavioral space was not naturalistic in our sense of the term, but idealistic in the sense that the players located themselves in an idea of a place." See "The Use and Management of the Elizabethan Stage," in *The Third Globe*, ed. C. Walter Hodges, S. Schoenbaum, and Leonard Leone (Detroit: Wayne State University Press, 1981), pp. 152, 158.

8 THE VOCABULARY OF "PLACE"

1 Alan C. Dessen, *Elizabethan Stage Conventions and Modern Interpreters* (Cambridge University Press, 1984), pp. 96–101. See also chapter 3 above for a discussion of the evidence for onstage trees.

2 The insertions made by playhouse annotators in the surviving manuscripts (far fewer than the modern reader would expect) are primarily "theatrical" in nature (e.g., clarifications of entrances, exits, properties, casting), but, despite the assumptions of several generations of editors, such annotators did not as a rule adjust "fictional," "permissive," or other seemingly less-than-fully-theatrical stage directions so as to create a regular, consistent "prompt-book" (our term rather than theirs). Apparently, fictional signals were a part of that shared onstage vocabulary so as to make good sense to Elizabethan and Jacobean theatrical professionals. For a fuller discussion of such matters, see the essays by William B. Long cited in chapter 1, especially "Stage Directions: A Misinterpreted Factor in Determining Textual Provenance," *Text* 2 (1985): 121–37.

3 A. Stuart Daley, "Where are the Woods in *As You Like It*," *Shakespeare Quarterly* 34 (1983): 174, 180. The citation from Campbell (along with several others with a similar emphasis) is from Daley, p. 172 and is taken from *The Reader's Encyclopedia of Shakespeare*, ed. Oscar James Campbell and Edward G. Quinn (New York: Thomas Y. Crowell, 1966), p. 42.

4 For the evidence for staging the forest or hunt (e.g., weapons, green costumes, horns, sound effects), see Dessen, *Elizabethan Stage Conventions*, pp. 32–3.

5 For shops discovered, see also Jonson, *The Case is Altered*, 1.1.o.s.d., 4.5.o.s.d.; Middleton, *A Chaste Maid in Cheapside*, 1.1.o.s.d.; Dekker (?), *Match Me in London*, 2.1.o.s.d.; Massinger, *The Renegado*, 1.3.o.s.d.; Brome, *A Mad Couple Well Matched*, I, 55. Sometimes "the shop" is advertised: "*a Banner of Cures and Diseases hung out*" (Middleton, *The Widow*, G1v).

6 For other figures discovered in their studies, see *Thomas Lord Cromwell*, D1r; Fletcher, *The Woman Hater*, X, 128; *The Two Noble Ladies*, 82–3; Jonson, *Catiline*, 1, 15.s.d.; Jonson, *The Staple of News*, 2.5.o.s.d, 44.s.d.; and perhaps Day, *Law Tricks*, 1974. In Marston's *The Insatiate Countess* the countess is "*discovered sitting at a table covered with black, on which stands two black tapers lighted, she in mourning*" (1.1.o.s.d.). Another possible discovery is: "*Cromwell in his study with bags of money before him casting of account*" (*Thomas Lord Cromwell*, B1v). For sustained and therefore more demanding study scenes, see *Captain Thomas Stukeley*, 226–61, and *Thomas Lord Cromwell*, C4v–D1r. An occasional stage direction will provide the kind of detail associated with Romeo's description of the apothecary's shop: "*Sharkino's Study, furnished with glasses, phials, pictures of wax characters, wands, conjuring habit, powders and paintings*" (Shirley, *The Maid's Revenge*, I, 139).

7 By far the most extensive use of "the study" (and discovery scenes in general) is to be found in Barnes's *The Devil's Charter*. In addition to the final sequence noted above, Alexander starts an earlier scene "*in his study beholding a Magical glass with other observations*" (F4v); then "*Alexander cometh upon the Stage out of his study with a book in his hand*" (G1r). At end of the same scene: "*Exit Alexander into the study*" (G2v); later "*Enter Alexander out of his study*" (I2r). Once such a "study" has been designated, moreover, many related effects are possible. as with: "*Enter Harpax in a fearful shape, fire flashing out of the study*" (Dekker, *The Virgin Martyr*, 5.1.122.s.d.). Directions to move *into* a study (*Friar Bacon*) or *from* a study could also be read as *as* [*if*] *into* or *as* [*if*] *from*, as with the situation in *Ram Alley* or with "*Enter in his chamber out of his study, Master Penitent Brothel, a book in his hand reading*" (Middleton, *A Mad World My Masters*, 4.1.0.s.d).

8 Perhaps the most unusual stage direction is to be found in *Histriomastix*: "*Enter Lyon-rash to Fourchier sitting in his study: at one end of the stage: At the other end enter Vourcher to Velure in his shop*"; the two sets of figures then speak separately ("*They sit and whisper whilst the other two speak*" – F4r–F4v). The effect could be linked to the two stage doors, but, even for this anomalous play, to have a shop and study visible simultaneously is to provide a particularly strong challenge to verisimilar thinking. In an earlier "study" scene in the same play ("*Enter Fourchier, Vourcher, Velure, Lyon-rash and Chrisoganus in his Study*"), the first four decide "Why then let's to the Academy to hear Chrisoganus"; "*So all go to Chrisoganus' Study, where they find him reading*" (B1v).

9 For typical examples of "*enter in his study,*" see Marlowe, *The Massacre at Paris*, 364.s.d.; Peele, *The Old Wives Tale*, 334.s.d; *Thomas Lord Cromwell*, E4v; and *The Two Merry Milkmaids*, I1v. Several dramatists seem to bring the study onto the stage. In Arthur Wilson's *The Swisser*: "*Two Servants bring in a table with books. Arioldus follows*" (1.2.0.s.d.); in Fletcher's *The Humourous Lieutenant*: "*Enter Leucippe* (*reading*) *and two Maids at a Table writing*" (II, 300). In *The Welsh Embassador* (a manuscript with playhouse annotations), an anticipatory stage direction in the left margin reads "*be ready Carintha at a Table*" (1156–7), then "*Enter Carintha at a Table reading*" (1183); later "*be ready Clown and Eldred*" (1925–6) and "*set out a Table*" (1934–5), then "*Enter Clown in his study writing*" (1962).

10 For figures who enter carrying one or more books (sometimes a prayerbook), see Kyd, *The Spanish Tragedy*, 3.13.0.s.d.; Heywood, *2 Edward IV*, I, 162; Chapman, *Caesar and Pompey*, 4.6.15.s.d., 5.2.0.s.d.; *The Wit of a Woman*, 1531; Massinger, *The Bashful Lover*, 3.1.0.s.d.; Massinger, *The Renegado*, 4.1.48.s.d.; Ford, *The Lover's*

Melancholy, 2.1.47.s.d; Ford, *'Tis Pity She's A Whore*, 2.2.0.s.d.; Davenport, *The City Night-cap*, p. 95; *The Bloody Banquet*, 388, 1013–14; Rider, *The Twins*, 5.1.0.s.d. At least one scene reverses the usual process by directing an actor to enter reading and later defining the onstage space as "the study." Thus, in Heywood's *2 Edward IV* Doctor Shaw enters "*pensively reading on his book*" (as opposed to "*in his study*") and is subsequently accosted by Friar Anselm's ghost who tells Shaw: "Here in thy study shalt thou starve thyself, / And from this hour not taste one bit of food" (I, 162, 164).

11 In an early scene in *The Two Noble Ladies*, the foolish Barebones, fleeing from a battle, seeks refuge with his master, the conjuror Cyprian, who is "*discovered at his book*" (83); Cyprian is protected by his art, but Barebones nonetheless "Hides him under the table" (98–9). Cyprian's powerful magic, however, does not work against Justina late in the play: "*Justina is discovered in a chair asleep, in her hands a prayer book, devils about her*" (1752–4). To Cyprian's amazement ("has this weak woman pow'r to make hell shake?" – 1798), Justina and her book prove equal to the powers of Hell: "*She looks in her book, and the Spirits fly from her*" (1796–7). A chastened Cyprian subsequently rejects his magic ("*Throws his charmed rod, and his books under the stage. A flame riseth*") and accepts in its place "*The Angel's book*," saying: "This sacred truth alone – / shall be my study" (1899–1903).

12 Of the eighty-two uses of *study–studying–studies* in the canon, thirty are to be found in *Love's Labor's Lost*. As to overall usage, various Shakespeare figures refer to a study not seen by the playgoer: thus, Friar Laurence tells Romeo "run to my study" (3.3.76); Brutus tells Lucius "get me a taper in my study" (2.1.7); Beatrice says she'll "burn my study" (1.1.69). *Study* as a verb, however, is far more common: for example, Miranda tells Ferdinand that Prospero is "hard at study" (3.1.20) in a play with at least one distinctive book. Twice in 1 *Henry VI* Shakespeare sets up a strong link between study and books. First, the lawyer who decides the debate in the Temple Garden states: "Unless my study and my books be false, / The argument you held was wrong in you" (2.4.56–7); later, the young king comments on the prospect of marriage: "And fitter is my study and my books / Than wanton dalliance with a paramour" (5.1.22–3).

13 *The Comedy of Errors* provides the best-known Elizabethan example of such "houses" as seen from the outside. In *The Wit of a Woman* three figures set up tables in front of their houses (as represented by the stage doors) to advertise their wares; the subsequent signals

include: "*Exit to his house*" (386–7); two figures entering "*from Balia's house*" (421–2); and "*Exeunt into his house*" (547). In *A Warning for Fair Women*: "*Enter Anne Sanders with her little son, and sit at her door*"; Browne then comments: "Yonder she sits to light this obscure street" (B2V). In Heywood's *The English Traveller* (IV, 62–4), old Lionel is given a tour of his neighbor's house that starts outside with Ricot "*walking before the gate.*" In the dialogue, Lionel describes for the auditor the gate and its "brave carv'd posts," the "goodly fair Bay windows," and eventually various "inside" details (e.g., "And what a Gallery, How costly Ceiled; / What painting round about?").

14 Typical are such signals as "*two Chairs set out*" (Fletcher, *The Lover's Progress*, V, 104); "*Chair and stools out*"; "*The Table set out and stools*" (Fletcher, *The Spanish Curate*, II, 128, 133); "*A Table set forth, Jewels and Bags upon it*" (Massinger, *The Renegado*, 2.4.0.s.d.); "*A Table with a Book and Papers set out*" (Alexander Brome, *The Cunning Lovers*, 5.1.0.s.d.). More picturesque are "*Enter Lopez at a Table with Jewels and Money upon it, an Egg roasting by a Candle*" (Fletcher, *Women Pleased*, VII, 242); and "*Enter Novall Junior, as newly dressed, a Tailor, Barber, Perfumer, Liladam, Aymer, Page. Novall sits in a chair, Barber orders his Hair, Perfumer gives powder, Tailor sets his clothes*" (Massinger, *The Fatal Dowry*, 4.1.0.s.d.). For an ensemble scene, "*Enter two or three setting three or four Chairs, and four or five stools*" (Field, *A Woman is a Weathercock*, 5.2.0.s.d.).

15 For other examples of women sewing see Greene, *James IV*, 724–5; *Sir Giles Goosecap*, 2.1.16.s.d.; Chapman, *All Fools*, 2.1.221.s.d., 229.s.d.; and *Woodstock* where the queen and other ladies enter "*with shirts and bands and other lining*" (1014–15). In a few instances the women sewing are sitting in front of the house rather than in it. In *A Knack to Know an Honest Man*, "*Enter Annetta and Lucida with their work in their hands*" (660–1); when a procession comes, Sempronio says "get you in" (738) and the stage direction reads: "*Here put them in at door*" (739).

16 For evidence linking keys and gaolers see Dessen, *Elizabethan Stage Conventions*, p. 100. Thus, in three different plays (*Richard III*, *2 Edward IV*, *The True Tragedy of Richard III*) a hapless Brackenbury hands over his keys to figures about to murder a prisoner in his charge. Within the house, the lady or wife usually controls the domestic keys – as when Lady Capulet orders: "Hold, take these keys and fetch more spices, nurse" (*Romeo*, 4.4.1).

17 For complex romance intrigues that involve one or more keys see such diverse works as *A Knack to Know an Honest Man*, Fletcher's *The Coxcomb*, Middleton's *The Witch*, Rowley's *All's Lost by Lust*,

Massinger's *The Renegado*, Brome's *The Novella*, and Davenant's *Love and Honour*.

18 For typical examples see such diverse plays as Marlowe's *The Jew of Malta*, Munday's *The Death of Robert Earl of Huntingdon*, Jonson's *Volpone* and *The Alchemist*, Heywood's *The English Traveller*, May's *The Old Couple*, and *The Late Witches of Lancashire*.

19 At least two plays, both of them postdating *The Merchant of Venice* (and the second in the repertory of the King's Men), include golden keys. In Heywood's *The Royal King and the Loyal Subject*, when the Lord Martial is stripped of his offices by the king, he is first forced to give up his staff and then: "Command yon fellow give his golden Key / To the Lord Clinton; henceforth we debar him / Access unto our Chamber" (VI, 27). Similarly, in Barnes's *The Devil's Charter*, Pope Alexander (under siege by King Charles) is forced to throw down his golden keys to symbolize his capitulation ("*He throws his keys*" – D4r).

20 *The Geneva Bible: A Facsimile of the 1560 Edition*, ed. Lloyd E. Berry (Madison, Milwaukee, and London: University of Wisconsin Press, 1969).

9 "ROMEO OPENS THE TOMB"

1 Ample evidence does exist about tombs, monuments, and funeral practices outside the professional repertory theatre. For an excellent summary of such materials along with discussion of a host of relevant scenes see Michael Neill, "'*Exeunt with a Dead March*': Funeral Pageantry on the Shakespearean Stage," in *Pageantry in the Shakespearean Theater*, ed. David M. Bergeron (Athens: University of Georgia Press, 1985), pp. 153–93.

2 For another apparent equation of tomb and coffin roughly contemporary to *Apius*, see the dumb show before Act 2 in George Gascoigne and Francis Kinwelmersh's *Jocasta* (p. 86) in which a procession of mourners brings in two coffins; then, "after they had carried the coffins about the stage, there opened and appeared a Grave, wherein they buried the coffins and put fire to them: but the flames did sever and part in twain, signifying discord by the history of two brethren, whose discord in their life was not only to be wondered at, but being buried both in one Tomb (as some writers affirm) the flames of their funerals did yet part the one from the other in like manner, and would in no wise join into one flame." In this explanation of the fiction, two coffins placed in the ground can epitomize "one Tomb."

3 See *Henslowe's Diary*, ed. R. A. Foakes and R. T. Rickert

(Cambridge University Press, 1961), p. 319, lines 56–7. The editors note lost plays of *Guido* and *Dido and Aeneas* in 1597–8. Henslowe notes a range of items linked to specific plays (e.g., a cauldron for *The Jew of Malta*, a frame for the beheading in *Black Joan*, a wheel and frame in *The Siege of London*, a pair of stairs for Phaeton), but also includes (apparently) unattached items (e.g., a rock, a cage, a hell-mouth, a bedstead, a wooden canopy, a wooden mattock, two moss-banks).

4 The opening stage direction of *The Valiant Welshman* (pr. 1615) reads: "*Fortune descends down from heaven to the Stage, and then she calls forth four Harpers, that by the sound of their Music they might awake the ancient Bardh, a kind of Welsh Poet, who long ago was there entombed*" (A4r); so Fortune speaks, "*The Harpers play, and the Bardh riseth from his Tomb*" (A4v). The Bardh appears again in 2.2 to explain a dumb show (so, although not a Gower, he does have some narrative functions) and at the end to tell us that if we like the story, he will give us more, but if not, "then go I to my silent Tomb" (I4v). Does this Bardh rise from a verisimilar tomb structure or from a coffin conveniently placed on the stage, in the discovery space, or in a trap door? This play does present some action "below" with the clownish Morion and also invokes a cave and temple, magicians and serpents (all of which could be accommodated by means of stage doors). If then (as in *James IV*) a verisimilar or fictional tomb is the starting point of a play, an initial image (for whatever reason), does that "tomb" remain a presence to be seen by the playgoer or is it removed? Would such a "tomb" structure-pavilion house something else as well? For a recent (and shrewd) argument in behalf of the presence and repeated use of such an onstage pavilion, see Scott McMillin, *The Elizabethan Theatre and* "*The Book of Sir Thomas More*" (Ithaca and London: Cornell University, 1987), pp. 96–112.

5 This tomb is not mentioned again in the play proper, but a tomb does turn up in a subsequent dumb show wherein Cyrus of Persia is "*laid in a marble tomb*" and Alexander reads the inscription. Oberon explains: "Cyrus of Persia, / Mighty in life, within a marble grave, / Was laid to rot, whom Alexander once / Beheld entombed, and weeping did confess / Nothing in life could scape from wretchedness: / Why then boast men?" (687–92). Bohan responds: "What reck I then of life, / Who makes the grave my tomb, the earth my wife" (693–4). Given the textual muddle created by the lumping together of these dumb shows, moreover, Bohan's last speech here could be an epilogue (to be placed at the very end) before Oberon's last word and departure; his "jig" has

shown "the loath of sins, and where corruption dwells" (714) so "Hail me no more with shows of goodly sights: / My grave is mine, that rids me from despites. / Accept my jig good King, and let me rest, / The grave with good men, is a gay built nest" (715–18). Conceivably, then, a tomb could remain visible onstage throughout the entire show to be associated with Bohan, used in one of the dumb shows, and linked to the final moments, especially if the final word comes from Bohan rather than from the romance reconciliation in the play proper. Or, just as likely, the tomb–coffin–sarcophagus could have been introduced ("*conveniently*") as needed and then removed so as not to be juxtaposed with the romance plot.

6 In *Fidele and Fortunio*, at the outset of an extended tomb–temple scene, Captain Crackstone announces: "I'll slip into the Temple, / and hide me in the Tomb that standeth here" (410–11); as various figures come and go, "*Crackstone lifts up his head out of the Tomb, and ducks down again*" (494–5). Subsequently, as part of a conjuring, Medusa has the women "*throw their candles into the Tomb where Crackstone lieth*" (590–1) or "Into this Tomb that as you see, hard by us here doth stand" (593), with the result: "*Crackstone riseth out of the Tomb with one candle in his mouth, and in each hand one. The Women and Pedant fly, crying the devil the devil*" (598–600). Crackstone then comments at length upon "Such sights, as among the bones of the dead in this Tomb I have seen" (604). The fiction requires a tomb into which figures can throw candles and out of which Crackstone can lift his head, duck back, and then rise up bearing candles in his mouth and hands, so that "this Tomb" could have been either a coffin–sarcophagus or the area under a trap door. For other possible links between the trap door below and a tomb, see the dumb show in *Jocasta* (note 3) and Mason's *The Turk* (note 11).

7 The *Titus* stage directions read: "*Sound Drums and Trumpets, and then enter two of Titus' sons, and then two men bearing a Coffin covered with black*" (A4r); "*then set down the Coffin*"; "*They open the Tomb*" (A4v); after the sacrifice of Alarbus, "*Sound Trumpets, and lay the Coffin in the Tomb*" (B1v); after the death of Mutius, "*they put him in the tomb*" (C1r). This tomb can therefore be opened so that coffins can be placed in it, but either a trap door or stage door could suffice. Indeed, in terms of the theatrical fiction "the tomb" is wherever the coffins are placed.

8 The "tomb" reappears in the final scene (as part of a sequence that, without any clearing of the stage, started indoors – e.g., with a figure discovered in his study). Thus, the Countess appears

briefly as a supposed ghost to accuse her poisoners, who then confess. The duke then decrees: "You shall be clos'd alive in her dead tomb" (2260), so he orders: "Close them into that grave, that dead man's Inn" (2271). After four lines from the two condemned men comes a centered stage direction: "*Countess in the Tomb*" (2277), so that, with her appearance alive, all is resolved. As opposed to the earlier tomb scene, however (in which the locale and atmosphere were carefully set up by means of dialogue, torches, and other details), this "tomb" is suddenly there in what had been (apparently) an interior scene. Such a shorthand approach to the tomb is puzzling (and, to my knowledge, unique) and suggests to me that exigencies of plot and immediacy of effect here take precedence over verisimilitude or our sense of place–locale. Again, a coffin in a designated area (the trap, a stage door) could suffice.

9 Also from Fletcher but less demanding is a much briefer scene in *A Wife for a Month* where Act 3 begins with the sick king Alphonso and monks "*going to the Tomb*"; two monks "*discover the Tomb and a Chair*"; the opening line is then "lead softly to the Tomb" (v, 26). The speechless Alphonso sits in the chair and "points to'th' Tomb" (27), a gesture explained as "That is the place he honours, / A house I fear he will not be long out of. / He will to th' Tomb." This tomb (with or without a visible coffin) is then an object or space that can be discovered; whatever it is, it is defined by Alphonso's gesture and the accompanying commentary, so that whatever he points to while sitting dumbly in his chair is, according to the fiction, the tomb. Especially for such a brief, one-shot tomb scene, such "tombness" seems a product more of the playgoer's imagination than the property master.

10 Cambridge editors Jackson and Neill (p. 139) suggest "that the Ghost is meant to emerge from the tomb"; they assume, however, that the "tomb" is a structure, not a hearse. The ghost, moreover, exits and comes back, so would the tomb–hearse be open and empty? The editors also see the King's Men having "a tomb equipped for discoveries of this kind" and cite *The Second Maiden's Tragedy* (a possibility) and *The Duchess of Malfi*, 5.3 (the echo scene, where the tomb–vault is almost certainly fictional). But how different need the staging of the church–tomb scene in *Antonio's Revenge* be from Antonio in his coffin–tomb in the previous play?

11 The same kinds of evidence and attendant problems are to be found in other plays in this category.

A In Massinger's *The Fatal Dowry*, the importance of an appropriate burial is a central issue. Thus, Charalois offers himself as prisoner for debt so that his father shall have "a place in that fair monument, / In which our noble Ancestors lie entomb'd" (1.2.212–13), for this son "had rather die alive for debt / Of the old man in prison, than he should / Rob him of Sepulture" (2.1.24–6). For the actual burial at the monument, "*Enter Funeral. Body borne by four Captains and Soldiers. Mourners*, [*Priest*]. *Scutcheons, and very good order*" (2.1.47.s.d.); Charalois adds: "Rest, rest in peace, dear earth" (54). The fiction of a tomb–monument is central to the plot, but Massinger only specifies a funeral, a body, "*very good order*," and various accoutrements. What (or how much more) would the playgoer have seen?

B In Chettle's *The Tragedy of Hoffman*, figures "*open a curtain*" and then kneel before "the black dormitory, / Where Austria and Prince Lodowick are laid / On the cold bed of earth" (1411–16). Ferdinand asks the mourners to "give your partners leave to kneel, / And make their offertory on this tomb" (1419–20); another figure asks "Is Lucibella in this monument?" (1425) This "tomb scene" therefore involves kneeling, mourning figures and a curtain to be opened, but what the playgoer actually saw (whether hearses–coffins or a more elaborate structure) is not specified.

C The final sequence of Lodowick Carlell's *The Fool Would Be a Favorite* is centered around the tomb of the supposedly dead Philanthus, with repeated reference to "this sacred ground, that does contain / The body of my friend" (80); "his Tomb" (six times – 81, 83, 84, 86); "this hard / And unkind Marble" (83); "the Tomb / Of Philanthus" (84); "Come from the Tomb" (85); and the body that "lies here in this Tomb" (85). Once Philanthus reveals himself to be alive, the Moor notes "how easy 'twas / To cozen you ... by filling / The Coffin with some trash" (86). Dialogue references to a "tomb" abound, but an unopened coffin would suffice to sustain the fiction.

D In both the Manuscript and Folio version of William Berkeley's *The Lost Lady*, a misplaced stage direction reads: "*The Tomb discovered*" (Folio, p. 6; MS, 240); the actual scene begins (p. 9; 383–4): "*Enter Lysicles, kneels to the Tomb, and then speaks.*" Later, Lysicles returns to the tomb, so a marginal stage direction reads: "*Milesia riseth like a ghost*" (p. 34, 1768 – again, the beloved is not dead as supposed). At the end of this scene (4.1, p. 37, K2r) the Folio provides only an *Exeunt*, but the Manuscript (1908) has "([*hide the Tomb*])." Apparently, this tomb is *discovered* (with the stage direction misplaced in both texts) and later hidden (presumably by means of the same curtain or door), but the ghost *riseth* or *ariseth*, presumably from a coffin rather than from a trap.

E In John Mason's *The Turk* (pr. 1610), an early tomb scene (1.3) starts with a procession that (according to the dialogue) includes a hearse; the hearse–coffin is closed because the body inside is not Julia's (as everyone thinks) owing to Borgia's plot. References follow in the dialogue to honoring the hearse, then closing the tomb (611), so presumably the hearse–coffin is interred by means of a trap door or stage door. No *tomb* stage directions are provided in this scene, but the importance of such a "place" for the fiction is clear as is the sense of interment.

12 I have chosen not to include in this category the monument sequence of *Antony and Cleopatra* which seems to me a special case. For an excellent review of the problem and an ingenious solution (that Antony is raised by the men below to a leaning Cleopatra but remains held in that position), see Leslie Thomson, "*Antony and Cleopatra*, Act 4 Scene 16: 'A Heavy Sight'," *Shakespeare Survey 41* (1989): 77–90.

10 *VANISH* AND VANISHING

1 Some insight into the "quaint device" may be provided by other plays. In Lupton's *All for Money*, a moral play from the 1570s, to act out Money's giving birth to Pleasure, Money sits in a chair and "*feigneth himself to be sick*" (A4v); "*Here Money shall make as though he would vomit, and with some fine conveyance Pleasure shall appear from beneath and lie there apparelled*" (B1r). In the induction to *Wily Beguiled*, a juggler, who specializes in "tricks of Legerdemain, sleight of hand, cleanly conveyance, or *deceptio visus*," provides "a trick of cleanly conveyance" for the Prologue by adroitly switching the title of the play to follow; the stage direction reads: "'*Spectrum*' *is conveyed away: and* '*Wily Beguiled,*' *stands in the place of it*" (24–5, 41–2, 46–7). Most reminiscent of the vanishing banquet in *The Tempest* is the denouement of *The Wasp*, a manuscript play from the 1630s, where a sumptuous banquet of "Viands" is suddenly transformed into something horrible to look at ("snakes toads and newts" – 2220–1) and then, later in the scene, reverts to its original condition ("these comfortable viands" – 2325). The stage direction for the first moment reads: "*the table turns and such things appear*" (2220–1); and for the second: "*Table turns*" (2324). With or without a harpy, a reversible table (and perhaps some misdirection of the playgoer's attention) can yield the desired effect. Without reference to *The Wasp* Andrew Gurr also suggests "a kind of reversible table-top with dishes fastened to one surface and the other bare – in which case the banquet would certainly

have been brought out already fastened to the table." See *The Shakespearean Stage 1574–1642*, Second Edition (Cambridge, 1980), p. 176.

2 Although *heavily* is not a recurring term in stage directions of the period, it does turn up in one theatrical document, the "plot" of 2 *The Seven Deadly Sins*, where, after the two sons of Gorboduc quarrel, "*The Queen and Lords Depart Heavily*" (24–5). Here *heavily* sounds like *sadly*.

3 For example, at the end of Massinger's *The Unnatural Combat*, Malefort, tormented by the appearance of two ghosts, asks: "Can any penance expiate my guilt? / Or can repentance save me? they are vanish'd" (5.2.298–9). As in *Caesar* 4.3, from Malefort's point of view the two figures vanish, but the script provides an *Exeunt* rather than any evidence for a verisimilar effect for the playgoer. In addition, Brutus' quizzing of figures after the ghost's departure or vanishing is a recurring element in many comparable scenes. Along with *Macbeth*, 4.1.135–7 and *Henry VIII*, 4.2.86–9, see Dekker, *The Virgin Martyr*, 5.1.66–75; Munday, *The Death of Robert Earl of Huntingdon*, 961–72; Heywood, *1 If you know not me you know nobody*, I, 228; Middleton, *A Mad World My Masters*, 4.1.76–95; and Brome, *The Love-sick Court*, II, 128–9.

4 At the ghost's first exit in this scene Bernardo (1.1.50) says "See, it stalks away," so no fading or vanishing is called for here, in 1.4, in 1.5, or in the closet scene where Hamlet says: "Look how it steals away!... Look where he goes even now out at the portal!" (3.4.135, 137). Yet the second exit in 1.1 *is* given special emphasis both in the dialogue and in the stage business with the partisans.

5 William J. Lawrence offers as his rule-of-thumb that "iterative references to any phenomenon generally mean that the effect was left to the imagination" (*Pre-Restoration Studies*, Cambridge, Mass.: Harvard University Press, 1927, p. 226). Such reinforcement after the event recurs in *vanish* situations – as with Horatio's report to Hamlet that the ghost "vanished from our sight" (1.2.220) or Macbeth's letter that stresses that the witches "made themselves air, into which they vanish'd" (1.5.5). Typical is Heywood and Brome's *The Late Lancashire Witches* where, at the end of a wedding dance "*Mal vanishes, and the piper*," followed by the comment: "Vanish'd, she and the Piper both vanish'd, nobody knows how" (IV, 217). Curiously, the only such reinforcement in *The Tempest*, 3.3 is not for the disappearing banquet or harpy; rather, after the figures who bear in the banquet "*depart*," a courtier notes that "they vanish'd strangely" (17.s.d., 40).

6 As Herbert Berry remarks, although brief contemporary comments

about Elizabethan plays do survive, "we have had nothing that we might reasonably describe as a review of an actual production." As a result, "we study the plays of Shakespeare's time in chambers deaf to chatter about how those plays were played and received." For Berry, that silence "is one of the most important ways in which our understanding of the drama of that time is sadly inferior to our understanding of the drama of later times" ("The Globe Bewitched and *El Hombre Fiel*," *Medieval and Renaissance Drama in England* 1 [1984]: 211). In this essay Berry provides and comments upon Nathaniel Tomkyns' account of Heywood and Brome's *The Late Lancashire Witches* (seen in August 1634) in which Tomkyns describes many of the magical events and provides some details not available in the printed play. Tomkyns does not, however, mention the one onstage *vanish* effect specified in the script ("*Mal vanishes, and the piper*" – see note 5). If this disappearance was verisimilar, it did not impress Tomkyns, for he does not include it in his long and otherwise inclusive list of witchly events in this play.

7 A. R. Braunmuller, "'To the Globe I rowed': John Holles Sees *A Game at Chess*," *English Literary Renaissance* 20 (1990): 342. Holles has his limitations as an observer – e.g., he does not identify Error here – and overall provides a fictional account of the narrative that accepts the illusion rather than describing what he actually sees. Similarly, Simon Forman provides plot summary descriptions of two of the Shakespeare plays with *vanish* stage directions – *Macbeth* and *Cymbeline* – without any reference to witches or ghosts that *vanish*. Indeed, Forman fails to mention at all two of the three relevant scenes (the cauldron scene, Posthumus' vision). For some shrewd comments on the limitations of such playgoer reactions, see Andrew Gurr, *Playgoing in Shakespeare's London* (Cambridge, 1987), pp. 105–14. For example, Gurr notes that John Manningham, in his brief account of a 1602 performance of *Twelfth Night* at the Middle Temple, singles out the gulling of Malvolio as "a good practise" but mistakes Olivia's mourning for her brother as widowhood (*The Diary of John Manningham of the Middle Temple, 1602–1603*, ed. Robert Parker Sorlien [Hanover, N.H.: University Press of New England, 1976], p. 48). Gurr, however, does not use Willis (an account not linked to London) and did not have access to Holles.

8 R. Willis, *Mount Tabor* (1639) in *Records of Early English Drama: Cumberland, Westmorland, Gloucestershire*, ed. Audrey Douglas and Peter Greenfield (Toronto, Buffalo, London: University of Toronto Press, 1986), p. 363.

9 Such a distinction between an object (that can *vanish*) and an actor

may (perhaps) be teased out of a scene in *The White Devil* where Bracchiano's ghost appears to Flamineo and "*throws earth upon him and shows him the skull*" (5.4.135.s.d.). When the ghost departs ("*Exit ghost*" – 141.s.d.), Flamineo comments: "He's gone; and see, the skull and earth are vanish'd" (5.4.142). If indeed the terms are to be taken literally, the ghost exits or is "gone," but the two objects, the skull and the earth, "are vanish'd."

10 In *Histriomastix* three named figures along with "*other Nobles and Gentles*" (C3r) are onstage when: "*Enter Pride, Vainglory, Hypocrisy, and Contempt: Pride casts a mist, wherein Mavortius and his company vanish off the Stage, and Pride and her attendants remain*" (D1r). A large group of figures (five or more) therefore "*vanish off the Stage*" in connection with "*a mist.*" No such mist, however, is signaled in the final sequence: "*Enter Peace, Bacchus, Ceres, and Plenty, bearing the Cornucopiae, at the one door: At the other Poverty, with her attendants; who beholding Peace approach, vanish*" (H2r). Poverty's attendants are Famine, Sickness, Bondage, and Sluttishness, so that five figures *vanish* here, with no mist specified. The mists or fogs called for in other plays seem to me mostly fictional rather than verisimilar. See, for example, *Edward III* (H4v); *Arden of Feversham* (1721–1805); and Heywood, *2 If you know not me* (I, 302–3). Possible exceptions might include the dumb show in Fletcher's *The Prophetess* (V, 363) in which "*Delphia raises a mist*" (an effect, however, that is spelled out by the Chorus' – 364); the bogus supernatural effect provided by Valerius in Fletcher's *Four Plays in One* (X, 307); and the masque in *The Maid's Tragedy* in which "*Night rises in mists*" (I, 8). Atypical plays (such as Jonson's *The Sad Shepherd* – see H & S, VII, 39), masques, and other special entertainments are more likely to include such a special effect (e.g., mists of perfumes).

11 For some typical trap door sinkings or leaps, in Gascoigne and Kinwelmersh's *Jocasta*, the dumb show to Act 3 starts with the appearance of "*a great Gulf*" into which an armed knight "*suddenly leapt*" (p. 111). In Peele's *Edward I* Queen Elinor cries out "Oh Joan, help Joan / Thy mother sinks" to which Joan responds: "oh she is sunk, / And here the earth is new closed up again" (2198–2201). In Greene's *Alphonsus of Aragon*, the spirit of Calchas conjured up by Medea is forced to "haste to hell"; the stage direction reads: "*Calchas sink down where you came up*" (969–70). In Quarto *2 Henry VI*, after Bolingbroke orders the spirit down "unto the damned pool," "*He sinks down again*" (C1r). In *Grim the Collier of Croydon*: "*The Ground opens, and he* [Belphagor, a devil] *falls down into it*" (I4v); an observer comments: "Was there a Quagmire,

that he sunk so soon?" (K1r – so here the earth opens up and a figure sinks in, but no *vanish* is specified). In Marston's *Sophonisba*, the demon "*Erictho slips into the ground as Syphax offers his sword to her*" (5.1.21.s.d.). In *Poetaster* Envy, who arose "*in the midst of the stage*" is ready to "down, sink again" (Induction, o.s.d, 58), but the armed prologue prevents him with: "Stay, Monster, ere thou sink, thus on thy head / Set we our bolder foot" (Prologue, 1–2); Envy's sinking is therefore not so sudden that it cannot be prevented. In *The Virgin Martyr* (in which an angelic figure does *vanish*) the devil Harpax "*sinks*" twice (5.1.152.s.d., 5.2.238.s.d.) and is clearly linked to Hell below, though editor Fredson Bowers would have him *vanish* (see 5.1.156.s.d.). At the other extreme from the suddenness or evanescence implicit in *vanish* are two Caroline plays that provide elaborate sinkings that are clearly not vanishings. Thus, in Shirley's *St. Patrick for Ireland* the wicked Archimagus takes over a dozen blank verse lines to sink (5.3.124–37); in Nathaniel Richards' *Messalina*, the stage direction for the demise of three villains reads: "*Earth gapes and swallows the three murderers by degrees*" (2149–51), with one of the three taking over forty lines to complete his descent.

12 For some Shakespeare examples of the imperative *vanish*, Falstaff tells Pistol and Nym: "Rogues, hence, avaunt! Vanish like hailstones, go" (*Merry Wives*, 1.3.74); Holofernes tells Moth-Hercules: "Keep some state in thy exit, and vanish" (*Love's Labor's*, 5.2.587); the clown in *Othello* tells the musicians: "Go, vanish into air, away!" (3.1.20). The imperative *vanish* is used repeatedly by Dekker's Simon Eyre in *The Shoemakers' Holiday* (see, for example, 1.1.163; 2.3.43–4; 5.1.30–1, 36; 5.4.26, 35–6, 49–50) and by other dramatists. See, for example, *The Jew of Malta*, 1796; *Doctor Faustus*, A-text, 1021–2; *Cynthia's Revels*, 5.11.89; Dekker, *Satiromastix*, 3.1.154; Brome, *The City Wit*, 1, 284. The most unusual imperative *vanish* occurs at the end of the magic contest in Greene's *Friar Bacon*, where Bacon tells Hercules: "Vanish the tree and thou away with him" (1279) wherein (1) *vanish* is used as an imperative–transitive verb, but (2) the actual stage direction ("*Exit the spirit with Vandermast and the Tree*" – 1280) calls for an *Exit* not a *vanish*, with apparently the mighty Hercules carrying off both a tree and the actor playing Vandermast. Here neither the stage direction nor the dialogue (e.g., "Transport the German unto Hapsburg straight" – 1276) provides any further evidence for a verisimilar *vanish*. For typical non-imperative usages, in *Julius Caesar*, Flavius describes the exiting plebeians who "vanish tongue-tied in their guiltiness" (1.1.62); in *Dream* after Snug's exit

Lysander comments: "and so the lion vanish'd" (5.1.271). See also Fletcher, *Monsieur Thomas*, IV, 160; Davenport, *King John and Matilda*, p. 7.

13 For example: "I do vanish, wife" (Jonson, *Poetaster*, 2.1.139); "Sir we vanish" (Fletcher, *The Fair Maid of the Inn*, IX, 202); "I am gone, I am vanish'd" (*Every Woman in Her Humour*, B4v); "and so I vanish" (Massinger, *The Picture*, 2.1.171); "I vanish" (Massinger, *The Renegado*, 3.2.60); "We are vanish'd sir" (Davenport, *The City Night-cap*, 152); and "We do obey / Great Priest, and vanish" (Shirley, *St. Patrick for Ireland*, 4.2.137–8).

14 For other rapid exits described as vanishings, in Shirley's *The Grateful Servant*, in a bogus supernatural sequence, after "*the Nymphs suddenly leave him*," Lodowick reacts: "Vanished like Fairies?" (p. 59). In Sharpham's *Cupid's Whirligig*, after an angry speech and exit, two figures respond: "Yea, are ye vanished?" and "what is she gone?" (3.3.51–2). In Shirley's *The Wedding*, a figure in disguise reunites two lovers and then exits; one of the lovers asks: "But where's the youth / Brought me this blessing? Vanish'd?... Gone? Sure, it was some angel, was he not, / Or do I dream this happiness?" (4.4.218–23) Such a supernatural framework *is* to be found in other plays (e.g., *The Virgin Martyr*), but here the playgoer sees only a "real" boy who brings something desirable, apparently miraculous, and then surreptitiously departs.

15 I have omitted several curious examples that lack a *vanish* stage direction. Consider *The Maid's Metamorphosis* where a sleeping Ascanio is addressed by his beloved Eurymine (actually a spirit); as an onstage observer notes: "See how he catches to embrace the shade." After "Eurymine" and the observers have exited, "*Ascanio starting, says. / Eurymine*: Ah my good Angel stay: / O vanish not so suddenly away. / O stay my Goddess, whither dost thou fly?" (C3r). Ascanio therefore describes a *vanish* from his perspective, but the playgoer has seen three figures *exeunt* with no such special effect. Rather, the *vanish* point for Ascanio is when he tries to embrace his "Eurymine," but the observers stay onstage for ten lines after that moment, so this *vanish* is clearly fictional rather than theatrical. For comparable effects where figures have dreams or visions that vanish (though without any *vanish* stage directions or dialogue) see Munday, *The Death of Robert, Earl of Huntingdon*, 961–8, 996–1000 and Thomas Rawlins, *The Rebellion*, F2r. In Lyly's *Love's Metamorphosis*, to save her lover Petulius from a Siren, Protea transforms herself into an old man, the ghost of Ulysses, and tells Petulius: "Follow me at this door, and out at the other." Although the original text provides no subsequent *exeunt* or *re-enter*,

Petulius' next line is: "How am I delivered! The old man is vanished, and here for him stands Protea!" to which she responds: "Here standeth Protea, that hath saved thy life" (4.2, p. 306). A combination of a *vanish* and a protean transformation from old man to young woman is central to the narrative fiction, but no information whatsoever is provided on how such effects are to be achieved. The most likely theatrical solution would be a quick exit through one stage door (hence a non-verisimilar *vanish*) and an equally swift reappearance by two figures at another door; given two separate actors to play the "old man" and Protea, an offstage substitution rather than a costume change could enable protean Protea to reappear quickly in her original shape.

16 For several reasons, to trust in Barnes and the printed text of *The Devil's Charter* as theatrical evidence requires a leap of faith. First, according to the title page the play has been "*reviewed, corrected, and augmented*" by the author since its performance by the King's Men. Perhaps more important, the unusual *vanish* stage direction is but one of several odd or even unique bits of stage business. For example, this text provides two or three times as many discoveries as any other play of the period; it also calls for an unusually wide array of spectacular effects.

17 For more *vanish* stage directions (none of them particularly instructive about the actual staging) see Lodge, *The Wounds of Civil War*, 2527 (Sylla's Genius "*Evanescit subito*"); Fletcher, *Four Plays in One*, x, 352 (a spirit "*Sings, and vanishes*"); and Henry Shirley, *The Martyred Soldier*, p. 209 (an angel "*writes, and vanishes as it* [a song] *ends*"). Also uninstructive is the use of *vanish* in one of the theatrical plots; in *2 The Seven Deadly Sins* "*Enter Progne with the Sampler to her Tereus from Hunting . with his Lords to them Philomele with Itis' head in a dish . Mercury comes and all vanish. to him 3 Lords*" (81–4).

18 Presumably the effect was achieved by a combination of the Bellizarius actor's reaction and some expansive gesture by the angel (e.g., a spreading wide, then closing of its arms). As noted in chapter 3, such a gesture by a supernatural figure *may* be indicated in the Q2 version of *Hamlet* where (apparently in response to Horatio's "stay illusion") the marginal stage direction reads: "*It spreads his arms*" (B3r). At the crowing of the cock, this ghost then could reposition its arms so as to fade from sight and be invulnerable to the sentinels' partisans. As demonstrated by the interaction between Bellizarius and the angel, we do not know enough about Elizabethan theatrical vocabulary to dismiss "*It spreads his arms.*"

19 See also Shadwell's opera version of *The Tempest* where: "*In the midst of the Shower of Fire the Scene changes. The Cloudy Sky, Rocks, and Sea vanish; and when the Lights return, discover that Beautiful part of the Island...*" (II, 202); later in the same play, "*Devils vanish*" (223) and "*The Dance ended, the Bottles vanish, and the Table sinks again*" (249). In Aphra Behn's *The Dutch Lover* (I, 281) nymphs and shepherds are onstage with another figure when "*The Scene changes to a fine Arbour, they leave her and vanish.*"

20 I borrow these terms from Barbara Mowat's useful essay, "Prospero, Agrippa, and Hocus Pocus," *English Literary Renaissance* 11 (1981): 281–303 – and Mowat also finds in Prospero elements of the performing magician–juggler–Hocus Pocus. For good summaries of the controversy see Mowat, pp. 281–2 and John S. Mebane, *Renaissance Magic and the Return of the Golden Age: The Occult Tradition and Marlowe, Jonson, and Shakespeare* (Lincoln and London: University of Nebraska Press, 1989), pp. 178–80, 245–6. Most recent scholars have argued for the ambivalent nature of this magic, with Mebane (who sees Prospero as "benevolent artist") a notable exception. In her chapter Barbara Traister provides a revealing comparison between Prospero and other Elizabethan–Jacobean stage magicians or enchanters (*Heavenly Necromancers: The Magician in English Renaissance Drama* [Columbia: University of Missouri Press, 1984]).

21 This potential tug-of-war between storm noise and the spoken words can also be seen in *Julius Caesar* 1.3, *Pericles* 3.1, and especially *King Lear* 3.2. In the latter, the ragged rhythms of Lear's speeches contribute significantly to a playgoer's sense of the storm and, if successfully enacted, can set up a link between the outer storm and "the tempest in my mind" (3.4.12). Two of the most successful scenes in the ACTER five-actor productions of *The Tempest* (spring 1987) and *King Lear* (spring 1989) were therefore these two storm scenes, for both sets of actors were forced to rely solely upon their voices and bodies rather than upon special effects involving lighting, sound, and water.

22 "Prospero's Wife," *Representations* 8 (Fall 1984): 10.

23 Philip McGuire, who treats Ariel's departure as one of three key "open silences" in this play, provides a range of other suggestions and performance choices for this moment. See *Speechless Dialect: Shakespeare's Open Silences* (Berkeley and Los Angeles: University of California Press, 1985), especially pp. 43–7, 55.

Plays and editions cited

ABBREVIATIONS

Garland: Renaissance Drama: A Collection of Critical Editions, edited by Stephen Orgel, published by Garland Publishing, Inc.

MSR: Malone Society Reprints, published by Oxford University Press

Revels: The Revels Plays, published by Manchester University Press and The Johns Hopkins University Press

RRD: Regents Renaissance Drama Series, published by University of Nebraska Press

STC: A. W. Pollard and G. R. Redgrave, *Short-Title Catalogue*, 2nd edition, 2 vols. (London, 1976–86), followed by the number and date of publication

TFT: Tudor Facsimile Texts, edited by John S. Farmer

Wing: Number designated in Donald Wing's *Short-Title Catalogue*, revised edition, 3 vols. (New York, 1972–88), followed by the date of publication

Apius and Virginia, ed. Ronald B. McKerrow (MSR, 1911)

Arden of Feversham, ed. Hugh Macdonald (MSR, 1947)

Armin, Robert, *The Two Maids of More-Clacke* (TFT, 1913)

Barnes, Barnabe, *The Devil's Charter* (TFT, 1913)

Barry, Lording, *Ram Alley*, ed. Claude E. Jones (Louvain, 1952)

Behn, Aphra, *The Works*, ed. Montague Summers, 6 vols. (London, 1915)

Berkeley, William, *The Lost Lady*, ed. D. F. Rowan (MSR, 1987)
The Lost Lady, *STC* 1901.5 (1638)

The Bloody Banquet, ed. S. Schoenbaum (MSR, 1962)

Blurt, Master Constable, ed. Thomas L. Berger (Salzburg, 1979)

Brewer, Anthony, *The Country Girl*, Wing B-4425 (1647)

Brome, Alexander, *The Cunning Lovers*, Wing B-4850 (1654)

Brome, Richard, *The Dramatic Works*, 3 vols. (London, 1873) [*The*

Antipodes, *The City Wit*, *The Court Beggar*, *The Damoiselle*, *The English Moor*, *The Lovesick Court*, *A Mad Couple Well Matched*, *The Novella*, *The Queen and Concubine*, *The Queen's Exchange*]

Captain Thomas Stukeley, ed. Judith C. Levinson (MSR, 1975)

Carlell, Lodowick, *1* and *2 Arviragus and Philicia*, *STC* 4627 (1639)

The Fool Would Be a Favourit, ed. Allardyce Nicoll (Waltham Saint Lawrence, 1926)

Cartwright, William, *The Ordinary*, in *A Select Collection of Old English Plays Originally Published by Robert Dodsley in the Year* 1744, 4th edition, ed. W. Carew Hazlitt, 15 vols. (London, 1874–6), XII, 203–318

Chamberlain, Robert, *The Swaggering Damsell*, *STC* 4946 (1649)

Chapman, George, *The Plays of George Chapman: The Comedies*, gen. ed. Allan Holaday (Urbana, Chicago, London, 1970) [*All Fools*, *The Gentleman Usher*, *The Widow's Tears*]

The Plays of George Chapman: The Tragedies with Sir Gyles Goosecappe, gen. ed. Allan Holaday (Cambridge: D. S. Brewer, 1987) [*Bussy D'Ambois*, *Caesar and Pompey*, *Sir Giles Goosecap*, *The Tragedy of Byron*]

The Chester Mystery Cycle, ed. R. M. Lumiansky and David Mills, EETS (Oxford, 1974)

Chettle, Henry, *The Tragedy of Hoffman*, ed. Harold Jenkins (MSR, 1951)

Claudius Tiberius Nero (*The Tragedy of Tiberius*), ed. W. W. Greg (MSR, 1915)

Clyomon and Clamydes (TFT, 1913)

Cooke, John, *Greene's Tu Quoque* (TFT, 1913)

Davenant, William, *The Dramatic Works*, 5 vols. (Edinburgh, 1872) [*The Fair Favourite*, *Love and Honour*, *News from Plymouth*, *The Platonic Lovers*, *The Playhouse to Be Let*, *The Rivals*, *The Wits*]

Davenport, Robert, *The Works*, in *A Collection of Old English Plays*, ed. A. H. Bullen, 4 vols. (London, 1882–9), vol. 3 [*The City Night-cap*, *King John and Matilda*]

Day, John, *Law Tricks*, ed. John Crow (MSR, 1950)

The Works, ed. A. H. Bullen (London, 1881) [*The Travels of the Three English Brothers*]

Dekker, Thomas, *The Dramatic Works*, ed. Fredson Bowers, 4 vols. (Cambridge, 1953–61) [*1 The Honest Whore*, *2 The Honest Whore*, *If this be a good play the devil is in it*, *Match Me in London*, *Old Fortunatus*, *The Roaring Girl*, *Satiromastix*, *The Shoemakers' Holiday*, *The Virgin Martyr*, *Westward Ho*, *The Witch of Edmonton*]

Denham, Sir John, *The Sophy*, Wing D-1009 (1642)

Dick of Devonshire, ed. James G. and Mary R. McManaway (MSR, 1955)

Drue, Thomas, *The Duchess of Suffolk*, *STC* 7242 (1631)
Dryden, John, *Works*, vols. 8–11, 13, 15 (Berkeley and Los Angeles, 1962–84)
Early English Classical Tragedies, ed. John W. Cunliffe (Oxford, 1912) [*Gorboduc*, *Jocasta*]
Eastward Ho (TFT, 1914)
Edmond Ironside, ed. Eleanore Boswell (MSR, 1928)
Edward III (TFT, 1910)
Etherege, George, *The Plays*, ed. Michael Cordner (Cambridge, 1982)
Every Woman In Her Humour (TFT, 1913)
Fair Em, ed. W. W. Greg (MSR, 1928)
The Faithful Friends, ed. G. M. Pincuss and G. R. Proudfoot (MSR, 1975)
Fidele and Fortunio (*Two Italian Gentlemen*), ed. Percy Simpson (MSR, 1910)
Field, Nathan, *The Plays*, ed. William Peery (Austin, 1950) [*Amends for Ladies*, *A Woman is a Weathercock*]
Fletcher, John (and Francis Beaumont), *The Works*, ed. Arnold Glover and A. R. Waller, 10 vols. (Cambridge, 1905–12) [*The Coxcomb*, *The Double Marriage*, *The Fair Maid of the Inn*, *Four Plays in One*, *The Humourous Lieutenant*, *The Island Princess*, *The Knight of the Burning Pestle*, *The Knight of Malta*, *The Little French Lawyer*, *Love's Cure*, *Love's Pilgrimage*, *The Lover's Progress*, *The Maid in the Mill*, *The Maid's Tragedy*, *Monsieur Thomas*, *The Pilgrim*, *The Prophetess*, *The Queen of Corinth*, *The Scornful Lady*, *The Spanish Curate*, *Thierry and Theodoret*, *Valentinian*, *A Wife for a Month*, *The Woman Hater*, *The Woman's Prize*, *Women Pleased*]
and Philip Massinger, *Sir John van Olden Barnavelt*, ed. T. H. Howard-Hill (MSR, 1980)
Ford, John, *The Broken Heart*, ed. T. J. B. Spencer (Revels, 1980)
The Lover's Melancholy, ed. R. F. Hill (Revels, 1985)
Love's Sacrifice, *STC* 11164 (1633)
The Queen, ed. W. Bang (Louvain, 1906)
'Tis Pity She's a Whore, ed. Derek Roper (Revels, 1975)
Fulwell, Ulpian, *Like Will to Like*, ed. Peter Happe (MSR, 1991)
Garter, Thomas, *The Virtuous and Godly Susanna*, ed. B. Ifor Evans (MSR, 1937)
George a Greene, ed. F. W. Clarke (MSR, 1911)
Glapthorne, Henry, *The Plays and Poems*, 2 vols. (London, 1874) [*Wit in a Constable*]
Goffe, Thomas, *The Raging Turk*, ed. David Carnegie (MSR, 1974)
The Tragedy of Orestes, *STC* 11982 (1633)
Greene, Robert, *Alphonsus King of Aragon*, ed. W. W. Greg (MSR, 1926)

Friar Bacon and Friar Bungay, ed. W. W. Greg (MSR, 1926)
James IV, ed. A. E. H. Swaen and W. W. Greg (MSR, 1921)
Greg, W. W., *Dramatic Documents from the Elizabethan Playhouses*, 2 vols. (Oxford: Clarendon Press, 1931) ["plots" for *The Dead Man's Fortune*, *Frederick and Basilea*, *2 The Seven Deadly Sins*, *Troilus and Cressida*]
Grim the Collier of Croydon (TFT, 1912)
Haughton, William, *Englishmen for My Money*, ed. W. W. Greg (MSR, 1913)
Heywood, Thomas, *The Captives*, ed. Arthur Brown (MSR, 1953)
The Dramatic Works, 6 vols. (London, 1874) [*The Brazen Age*, *A Challenge for Beauty*, *1 Edward IV*, *2 Edward IV*, *The English Traveller*, *The Fair Maid of the Exchange*, *Fortune by Land and Sea*, *The Four Prentices of London*, *The Golden Age*, *1 If you know not me you know nobody*, *2 If you know not me you know nobody*, *1 The Iron Age*, *2 The Iron Age*, *The Late Lancashire Witches*, *The Rape of Lucrece*, *The Royal King and the Loyal Subject*, *The Silver Age*, *The Wise Woman of Hogsdon*, *A Woman Killed With Kindness*]
Histriomastix (TFT, 1912)
The Honest Lawyer (TFT, 1914)
How a Man may Choose a Good Wife from a Bad (TFT, 1912)
Jacob and Esau, in *Six Anonymous Plays*, 2nd Series, ed. John Farmer (London, 1906)
Jonson, Ben, *Ben Jonson*, ed. C. H. Herford and Percy and Evelyn Simpson, 11 vols. (Oxford, 1925–52) [*The Alchemist*, *The Case is Altered*, *Catiline*, *Cynthia's Revels*, *The Devil is an Ass*, *Epicoene*, *Every Man Out of His Humour*, *The Magnetic Lady*, *Poetaster*, *The Sad Shepherd*, *The Staple of News*, *Volpone*]
Killigrew, Henry, *The Conspiracy*, *STC* 14958 (1638)
King Leir, ed. W. W. Greg (MSR, 1908)
A Knack to Know an Honest Man, ed. H. De Vocht (MSR, 1910)
The Knave in Grain, ed. R. C. Bald (MSR, 1961)
Kyd, Thomas, *The First Part of Hieronimo* and *The Spanish Tragedy*, ed. Andrew S. Cairncross (RRD, 1967)
The Spanish Tragedy, ed. Philip Edwards (Revels, 1959)
A Larum for London (TFT, 1912)
The Late Medieval Religious Plays of Bodleian MSS Digby 133 *and E Museo* 160, ed. Donald C. Baker, John L. Murphy, and Louis B. Hall Jr., EETS (Oxford, 1982) [*The Conversion of St. Paul*, *Mary Magdalen*]
Locrine, ed. Ronald B. McKerrow (MSR, 1908)
Lodge, Thomas, *The Wounds of Civil War*, ed. J. Dover Wilson (MSR, 1910)

and Robert Greene, *A Looking Glass for London and England*, ed. W. W. Greg (MSR, 1932)
Love's Changelings' Change, ed. John P. Cutts (Fennimore, Wisconsin, 1974)
Ludus Coventriae: The Corpus Christi Play of the English Middle Ages, ed. R. T. Davies (London, 1972)
Lupton, Thomas, *All for Money* (TFT, 1910)
Lyly, John, *The Plays of John Lyly*, ed. Carter A. Daniel (Lewisburg, 1988) [*Gallathea*, *Love's Metamorphosis*]
The Maid's Metamorphosis (TFT, 1912)
Markham, Gervaise and William Sampson, *Herod and Antipater*, *STC* 17401 (1622)
Marlowe, Christopher, *Marlowe's "Doctor Faustus" 1604–1616*, ed. W. W. Greg (Oxford, 1950)
The Works, ed. C. F. Tucker Brooke (Oxford, 1910) [*Edward II*, *The Jew of Malta*, *The Massacre at Paris*, *2 Tamburlaine*]
Marston, John, *The Fawn*, ed. David A. Blostein (Revels, 1978)
The Insatiate Countess, ed. Giorgio Melchiori (Revels, 1984)
The Selected Plays, ed. Macdonald P. Jackson and Michael Neill (Cambridge, 1986) [*Antonio and Mellida*, *Antonio's Revenge*, *The Dutch Courtesan*, *Sophonisba*]
Mason, John, *The Turk*, ed. Joseph Q. Adams (Louvain, 1913)
Massinger, Philip, *Believe as You List*, ed. Charles J. Sisson (MSR, 1928)
The Plays and Poems, ed. Philip Edwards and Colin Gibson, 5 vols. (Oxford, 1976) [*The Bashful Lover*, *The City Madam*, *The Emperor of the East*, *The Fatal Dowry*, *The Great Duke of Florence*, *The Guardian*, *A New Way to Pay Old Debts*, *The Picture*, *The Renegado*, *The Unnatural Combat*]
May, Thomas, *The Old Couple* in *A Select Collection of Old English Plays Originally Published by Robert Dodsley in the Year* 1744, 4th edition, ed. W. Carew Hazlitt, 15 vols. (London, 1874–6), XII, 1–83
Mayne, Jasper, *The Amorous War*, Wing M-1463 (1648)
The Merry Devil of Edmonton (TFT, 1911)
Middleton, Thomas, *A Chaste Maid in Cheapside*, ed. R. B. Parker (Revels, 1969)
A Game at Chess, ed. T. H. Howard-Hill, Trinity manuscript (MSR, 1990)
Hengist, King of Kent, ed. R. C. Bald (New York and London, 1938)
A Mad World My Masters, ed. Standish Henning (RRD, 1965)
The Phoenix, *STC* 17892 (1607)
The Witch, ed. W. W. Greg and F. P. Wilson (MSR, 1950)
The Widow, Wing J-1015 (1652)

Women Beware Women, ed. J. R. Mulryne (Revels, 1975)
and William Rowley, *The Changeling*, ed. N. W. Bawcutt (Revels, 1958)
Mucedorus (TFT, 1910)
Munday, Anthony, *The Death of Robert Earl of Huntingdon*, ed. John C. Meagher (MSR, 1967)
The Downfall of Robert Earl of Huntingdon, ed. John C. Meagher (MSR, 1965)
John a Kent and John a Cumber, ed. Muriel St. Clare Byrne (MSR, 1923)
Sir Thomas More, ed. Vittorio Gabrieli and Giorgio Melchiori (Revels, 1990)
Nabbes, Thomas, *The Works*, ed. A. H. Bullen, 2 vols. (London, 1887) [*Tottenham Court*]
The Noble Spanish Soldier, in *A Collection of Old English Plays*, 4 vols., ed. A. H. Bullen (London, 1882–9), I, 257–334
Peele, George, *The Dramatic Works*, ed. Frank S. Hook, John Yoklavich, R. Mark Benbow, and Elmer Blistein, 2 vols. (New Haven and London, 1961–70) [*The Arraignment of Paris*, *The Battle of Alcazar*, *Edward I*, *The Old Wives Tale*]
Porter, Henry, *The Two Angry Women of Abington*, ed. W. W. Greg (MSR, 1913)
Preston, Thomas, *Cambises* (TFT, 1910)
The Puritan (TFT, 1911)
Rawlins, Thomas, *The Rebellion*, *STC* 20770 (1640)
2 The Return from Parnassus (TFT, 1912).
Richards, Nathaniel, *Messalina*, ed. A. R. Skemp (Louvain, 1910)
Rider, William, *The Twins*, Wing R-1446 (1655)
Rowley, Samuel, *When You See Me You Know Me*, ed. F. P. Wilson (MSR, 1952)
Rowley, William, *All's Lost by Lust* and *A Shoemaker, a Gentlemen*, ed. Charles Wharton Stork (Philadelphia, 1910)
A Match at Midnight, ed. Stephen Blase Young (Garland, 1980)
The Second Maiden's Tragedy, ed. W. W. Greg (MSR, 1910)
Sedley, Sir Charles, *The Poetical and Dramatic Works*, ed. V. De Sola Pinto, 2 vols. (London, 1928)
Shadwell, Thomas, *The Complete Works*, ed. Montague Summers, 5 vols. (London, 1927)
Shakespeare, William, *The Complete Pelican Shakespeare*, gen. ed. Alfred Harbage (Baltimore, 1969)
The History of King Henry the Fourth, as revised by Sir Edward Dering, Bart., ed. George Walton Williams and Gwynne Blakemore Evans, the Folger Facsimiles (Charlottesville, 1974)

The Norton Facsimile: The First Folio of Shakespeare, ed. Charlton Hinman (New York and London, 1968)

Shakespeare's Plays in Quarto, ed. Michael J. B. Allen and Kenneth Muir (Berkeley and Los Angeles, 1982) [includes *The Two Noble Kinsmen*]

and John Fletcher, *The Two Noble Kinsmen*, ed. G. R. Proudfoot (RRD, 1970)

Sharpe, Lewis, *The Noble Stranger, STC* 22377 (1640)

Sharpham, Edward, *A Critical Old Spelling Edition of the Words of Edward Sharpham*, ed. Christopher Gordon Petter (Garland, 1986) [*Cupid's Whirligig, The Fleer*]

Shirley, Henry, *The Martyred Soldier*, in *A Collection of Old English Plays*, 4 vols., ed. A. H. Bullen (London, 1882–9), I, 165–256

Shirley, James, *The Cardinal*, ed. E. M. Yearling (Revels, 1986)

Changes, or Love in a Maze, STC 22437 (1632)

The Dramatic Works and Poems, ed. William Gifford and Alexander Dyce, 6 vols. (London, 1833) [*The Maid's Revenge, The Witty Fair One*]

The Example, ed. William F. Jones (Garland, 1987)

The Gentleman of Venice, ed. Wilson F. Engel (Salzburg, 1976)

The Grateful Servant, STC 22444 (1630)

Love's Cruelty, ed. John Frederick Nims (Garland, 1980)

The Politician, ed. Robert J. Fehrenbach (Garland, 1980)

St. Patrick for Ireland, ed. John P. Turner Jr. (Garland, 1979)

The Wedding, ed. Sister Martin Flavin (Garland, 1980)

Skelton, John, *Magnificence*, ed. Paula Neuss (Revels, 1980)

Smith, Wentworth, *The Hector of Germany*, ed. Leonidas Warren Payne, Jr. (Philadelphia, 1906)

The Soddered Citizen, ed. J. H. P. Pafford (MSR, 1936)

Suckling, Sir John, *The Plays*, ed. L. A. Beaurline (Oxford, 1971) [*Aglaura, Brennoralt, The Goblins, The Sad One*]

Tailor, Robert, *The Hog Hath Lost His Pearl*, ed. D. F. MacKenzie (MSR, 1972)

The Taming of a Shrew (TFT, 1912)

The Telltale, ed. R. A. Foakes and J. C. Gibson (MSR, 1960)

Thomas Lord Cromwell (TFT, 1911)

The Thracian Wonder, Wing T-1078A (1661)

Tom a Lincoln, ed. G. R. Proudfoot (MSR, 1992)

Tourneur, Cyril, *The Atheist's Tragedy*, ed. Irving Ribner (Revels, 1964)

The Revenger's Tragedy, ed. R. A. Foakes (Revels, 1966)

The Towneley Plays, ed. George England and Alfred W. Pollard, EETS (London, 1897)

The Second Part of the Troublesome Reign of John, King of England (TFT, 1911)
The True Tragedy of Richard III, ed. W. W. Greg (MSR, 1929)
The Two Merry Milkmaids (TFT, 1914)
The Two Noble Ladies, ed. Rebecca G. Rhoads (MSR, 1930)
The Valiant Welshman (TFT, 1913)
Vanbrugh, Sir John, *The Complete Works*, ed. Bonamy Dobree and Geoffrey Webb, 4 vols. (London, 1927)
Wager, W., *The Longer Thou Livest* and *Enough is as Good as a Feast*, ed. R. Mark Benbow (RRD, 1967)
Wapull, George, *The Tide Tarrieth No Man* (TFT, 1910)
A Warning for Fair Women (TFT, 1912)
The Wasp, ed. J. W. Lever (MSR, 1976)
The Weakest Goeth to the Wall, ed. W. W. Greg (MSR, 1912)
Wealth and Health, ed. W. W. Greg (MSR, 1907).
Webster, John, *The Devil's Law-Case*, ed. Frances A. Shirley (RRD, 1972)
The Duchess of Malfi, ed. John Russell Brown (Revels, 1964)
The White Devil, ed. John Russell Brown (Revels, 1960)
The Welsh Embassador, ed. H. Littledale and W. W. Greg (MSR, 1921)
Whetstone, George, *Promos and Cassandra* (TFT, 1910)
Wilson, Arthur, *The Swisser*, ed. Linda V. Itzoe (Garland, 1984)
Wilson, Robert, *The Cobbler's Prophecy* (TFT, 1911)
The Three Lords and Three Ladies of London (TFT, 1912)
Wily Beguiled, ed. W. W. Greg (MSR, 1913)
The Wit of a Woman, ed. W. W. Greg (MSR, 1913)
Woodstock (*1 Richard II*), ed. Wilhelmina P. Frijlinck (MSR, 1929)
Wycherley, William, *The Plays*, ed. Peter Holland (Cambridge, 1981)
Yarington, Robert, *Two Lamentable Tragedies* (TFT, 1913)
A Yorkshire Tragedy, ed. Sylvia D. Feldman (MSR, 1973)

Index

Apius and Virginia, 133, 178, 249
Arden of Feversham, 166, 264
Armin, Robert, *The Two Maids of More-Clacke*, 180, 232, 247
Armstrong, Paul, 88–9

Barnes, Barnabe, *The Devil's Charter*, 138, 143, 160, 206–7, 253, 256, 267
Barry, Lording, *Ram Alley*, 160, 235
Beckerman, Bernard, 25–6, 41, 48, 53, 60, 127–8, 251
Behn, Aphra, 248, 268
Berkeley, William, *The Lost Lady*, 260
Berry, Herbert, 262–3
Bloody Banquet, The, 247, 254
Blurt, Master Constable, 138
Brewer, Anthony, *The Country Girl*, 139
Brome, Alexander, *The Cunning Lovers*, 255
Brome, Richard
  The Antipodes, 138
  The City Wit, 157, 235, 245, 247, 265
  The Court Beggar, 244
  The Damoiselle, 235, 247
  The English Moor, 204
  The Love-sick Court, 262
  A Mad Couple Well Matched, 139, 235, 252
  The Novella, 160, 256
  The Queen and Concubine, 139, 245
  The Queen's Exchange, 138, 247

Campion, Thomas, 228
Captain Thomas Stukeley, 139, 250, 252
Carlell, Lodowick
  1 *Arviragus and Philicia*, 139
  2 *Arviragus and Philicia*, 139
  The Fool Would Be a Favorite, 260
Cartwright, William, *The Ordinary*, 247
Chamberlain, Robert, *The Swaggering Damsel*, 136
Chapman, George
  All Fools, 255
  Bussy D'Ambois, 250
  Caesar and Pompey, 253
  The Gentleman Usher, 245
  Sir Giles Goosecap, 255
  The Tragedy of Byron, 56
  The Widow's Tears, 42, 182–3, 189, 234
Chester Mystery Cycle, 131–2, 209
Chettle, Henry, *The Tragedy of Hoffman*, 42, 260
Claudius Tiberius Nero, 138
Clyomon and Clamydes, 247
Common Conditions, 61
Conversion of St. Paul, The, 209
Cooke, John, *Greene's Tu Quoque*, 138, 141, 156, 161, 230
Cradle of Security, The, 201–2

Daley, A. Stuart, 153
Davenant, William
  The Fair Favourite, 135
  Love and Honour, 256
  News from Plymouth, 160
  The Platonic Lovers, 112, 247, 251
  The Playhouse to Be Let, 208–9
  The Rivals, 248
  The Wits, 114, 189, 247
Davenport, Robert
  The City Nightcap, 135, 139, 254, 266
  King John and Matilda, 58, 249, 266
Day, John
  Law Tricks, 167–8, 184–5, 234, 235, 252, 258–9

The Travels of the Three English Brothers, 250
Dekker, Thomas
1 The Honest Whore, 156
2 The Honest Whore, 156
If this be a good play the devil is in it, 62, 157
Match Me in London, 252
Old Fortunatus, 61, 207
The Roaring Girl, 135, 156
Satiromastix, 135, 160, 245, 265
The Shoemakers' Holiday, 135, 265
The Virgin Martyr, 147, 160, 206, 250, 253, 262, 265, 266
Westward Ho, 114
The Witch of Edmonton, 137, 146, 205–6, 232, 247, 250
Denham, Sir John, *The Sophy*, 58, 134, 247, 248
designer's theatre, 148–9
Dick of Devonshire, 29, 43, 249
Drue, Thomas, *The Duchess of Suffolk*, 245
Dryden, John, 248

Eastward Ho, 156
Edmond Ironside, 234
Edward III, 264
Etherege, George, 248
Every Woman in Her Humour, 266

Fair Em, 113, 233, 245
Faithful Friends, The, 231
Fidele and Fortunio, 180, 258
Field, Nathan
Amends for Ladies, 140, 156, 166
A Woman is a Weathercock, 138, 166, 255
Fletcher, John, 245
The Beggar's Bush, 61
The Coxcomb, 61, 136, 255
The Double Marriage, 112, 135
The Fair Maid of the Inn, 141, 161, 247, 266
Four Plays in One, 247, 264, 267
The Humourous Lieutenant, 253
The Island Princess, 250
The Knight of Malta, 185–6
The Knight of the Burning Pestle, 156
The Little French Lawyer, 139, 247
Love's Cure, 56
Love's Pilgrimage, 134
The Lover's Progress, 136, 255
The Maid in the the Mill, 165, 230
The Maid's Tragedy, 264
Monsieur Thomas, 244, 245, 266
The Pilgrim, 44
The Prophetess, 264
The Queen of Corinth, 134, 230
The Scornful Lady, 247
Sir John van Olden Barnavelt, 160–1, 250
The Spanish Curate, 255
Thierry and Theodoret, 136, 244
Valentinian, 244, 248
A Wife for a Month, 259
The Woman Hater, 56, 252
The Woman's Prize, 137
Women Pleased, 255
Ford, John
The Broken Heart, 245
The Lover's Melancholy, 253
Love's Sacrifice, 135, 178–9
The Queen, 146, 147
'Tis Pity She's a Whore, 136, 160, 161–3, 254
Forman, Simon, 263
Fulwell, Ulpian, *Like Will to Like*, 111, 132–3

Garter, Thomas, *The Virtuous and Godly Susanna*, 133
Gaskell, Philip, 7, 226
George a Greene, 157
Glapthorne, Henry, *Wit in a Constable*, 140
Goffe, Thomas
The Raging Turk, 204–5
The Tragedy of Orestes, 135, 136
Gorboduc, 133
Greenblatt, Stephen, 2, 242
Greene, Robert
Alphonsus King of Aragon, 264
Friar Bacon and Friar Bungay, 61, 111, 160, 234, 265
James IV, 113, 180, 255, 257–8
Grim the Collier of Croydon, 264–5
Gurr, Andrew, 5, 40, 230, 261, 263

Hapgood, Robert, 242
Haughton, William, *Englishmen for My Money*, 245
Henslowe's Diary, 60–1, 179, 256–7

Heywood, Thomas
The Brazen Age, 223–4, 231
The Captives, 134, 137
A Challenge for Beauty, 146
1 Edward IV, 146, 157, 231, 248
2 Edward IV, 146, 245, 253, 254, 255
The English Traveller, 43, 134, 136, 138, 165, 255, 256
The Fair Maid of the Exchange, 156, 229
Fortune by Land and Sea, 34
The Four Prentices of London, 137, 233, 234
The Golden Age, 139, 145
1 If you know not me you know nobody, 112, 114, 262
2 If you know not me you know nobody, 156, 264
1 The Iron Age, 134, 143, 236
2 The Iron Age, 42, 136, 139, 206, 246
The Late Lancashire Witches, 138, 256, 262, 263
The Rape of Lucrece, 139, 145
The Royal King and the Loyal Subject, 136, 161, 256
The Silver Age, 137
The Wise Woman of Hogsdon, 57, 134, 135, 136, 138, 156
A Woman Killed With Kindness, 29, 136, 161, 166, 169, 246, 249
Hickscorner, 108
1 Hieronimo, 204, 208
Histriomastix, 111, 234, 253, 264
Holles, John, 201, 263
Honest Lawyer, The, 62
Honigmann, E. A. J., 54–5, 85–6
Hosley, Richard, 55–6
How a Man may Choose a Good Wife from a Bad, 135, 145, 184

Jacob and Esau, 132
Jocasta, 235, 256, 264
Jonson, Ben, 7
The Alchemist, 249, 256
The Case is Altered, 62, 252
Catiline, 252
Cynthia's Revels, 265
The Devil is an Ass, 111, 134, 141–2
Epicoene, 134
Every Man Out of His Humour, 165
The Magnetic Lady, 245
Poetaster, 265, 266
The Sad Shepherd, 264
The Staple of News, 244, 252
Volpone, 54, 114, 245, 256
Killigrew, Henry, *The Conspiracy*, 140, 142, 246
King Leir, 233, 244
Knack to Know an Honest Man, A, 243, 255
Knave in Grain, The, 139, 231
Kolve, V. A., 130
Kyd, Thomas, *The Spanish Tragedy*, 95, 234, 235–6, 253

Larum for London, A, 180
Lawrence, William J., 44, 230, 262
Levin, Richard, 2, 15
Locrine, 133, 157, 233, 243–4, 245
Lodge, Thomas
The Wounds of Civil War, 57, 267
A Looking Glass for London and England, 61, 137, 205
Long, William, 227–8, 241, 252
Love's Changelings' Change, 137
Ludus Coventriae, 131, 138, 209, 246
Lupton, Thomas, *All for Money*, 132, 261
Lyly, John
Gallathea, 60
Love's Metamorphosis, 266–7

McGann, Jerome J., 10
Maid's Metamorphosis, The, 266
Manningham, John, 263
Markham, Gervaise and William Sampson, *Herod and Antipater*, 245
Marlowe, Christopher
Doctor Faustus, 42, 99, 125, 137, 163, 265
Edward II, 232
The Jew of Malta, 167, 233, 256, 265
The Massacre at Paris, 61, 114, 253
2 Tamburlaine, 112, 143
Marston, John
Antonio and Mellida, 180
Antonio's Revenge, 134, 186–7, 250, 259
The Dutch Courtesan, 232
The Fawn, 62
The Insatiate Countess, 137, 146–7, 250, 252
Sophonisba, 245, 265
Mary Magdalen, 209
Mason, John, *The Turk*, 261
masques, 14, 228

Massinger, Philip, 233
The Bashful Lover, 136, 253
Believe as You List, 56
The City Madam, 56, 134, 135, 168
The Emperor of the East, 112, 245
The Fatal Dowry, 250, 255, 259–60
The Great Duke of Florence, 247
The Guardian, 231
A New Way to Pay Old Debts, 135
The Picture, 266
The Renegado, 252, 253, 255, 256, 266
The Unnatural Combat, 43, 262
May, Thomas, *The Old Couple*, 245, 256
Mayne, Jasper, *The Amorous War*, 140, 247
Merry Devil of Edmonton, The, 43
Middleton, Thomas
The Changeling, 169, 234
A Chaste Maid in Cheapside, 112, 252
A Game at Chess, 134, 201
Hengist, King of Kent, 245, 250
A Mad World My Masters, 114, 253, 262
The Phoenix, 145
The Widow, 252
The Witch, 255
Women Beware Women, 138
Mucedorus, 27–8
Munday, Anthony
The Death of Robert Earl of Huntingdon, 233, 251, 256, 262, 266
The Downfall of Robert Earl of Huntingdon, 60, 136, 246
John a Kent and John a Cumber, 61–2, 232, 241
Sir Thomas More, 134, 140, 166

Nabbes, Thomas, *Tottenham Court*, 247
Noble Spanish Soldier, The, 137

Orgel, Stephen, 213, 226–7

Peacham drawing, 232, 250
Peele, George
The Arraignment of Paris, 61
The Battle of Alcazar, 245
Edward I, 43, 113, 133, 137, 142, 146, 245, 264
The Old Wives Tale, 253
"plots," 12
The Dead Man's Fortune, 147, 232
Frederick and Basilea, 249
2 The Seven Deadly Sins, 142, 143, 262, 267
Troilus and Cressida, 142, 249
Porter, Henry, *The Two Angry Women of Abington*, 138
Preston, Thomas, *Cambises*, 132
Puritan, The, 56, 137, 231

Rawlins, Thomas, *The Rebellion*, 266
2 Return from Parnassus, The, 113
Rhodes, Ernest L., 53, 60
Richards, Nathaniel, *Messalina*, 204, 265
Rider, William, *The Twins*, 140, 166, 254
Rowley, Samuel, *When You See Me You Know Me*, 138
Rowley, William
All's Lost by Lust, 255
A Shoemaker, a Gentlemen, 113, 134, 155
A Match at Midnight, 166, 247

Second Maiden's Tragedy, The, 181–2, 189–90, 231, 245, 259
Sedley, Sir Charles, 248
Shadwell, Thomas, 267–8
Shakespeare, William
All's Well That Ends Well, 45, 56, 70–1, 112, 124, 147, 232, 238
Antony and Cleopatra, 58, 124, 203, 232, 234, 247, 261
As You Like It, 33, 65, 67–8, 77–8, 80–1, 105–7, 153–5, 232, 237
The Comedy of Errors, 135, 238, 254
Coriolanus, 51, 56, 73–4, 78, 135, 144, 145, 166, 238, 239
Cymbeline, 135, 147, 169, 170, 197–8, 240, 244, 263
Hamlet, 22–3, 43, 45–6, 54–5, 180, 200, 236, 238, 239–40, 250, 262, 267
1 Henry IV, 33, 71–2, 78–9, 83–4, 91–2, 110–11, 133, 232, 239, 242
2 Henry IV, 30–2, 43, 44, 113, 120–1, 145, 172, 232, 236, 239
Henry V, 78, 200, 236
1 Henry VI, 28, 79, 99–102, 114, 118–19, 234, 239, 240, 241, 254
2 Henry VI, 43, 45, 57–8, 79, 114, 119–20, 133, 135, 138, 142, 231–2, 234, 240, 264
3 Henry VI, 22, 52, 116, 142, 168–9, 232, 233, 234

Henry VIII, 58, 112, 114, 122–3, 135, 146, 147–8, 198, 232, 234, 248, 250, 262
Julius Caesar, 26, 43, 44, 79, 113, 114–15, 147, 198–9, 232, 234, 238, 254, 265, 268
King John, 33–5, 66–7, 113, 117, 145, 234, 237
King Lear, 61, 74–6, 79, 107–8, 114, 123–4, 240, 245, 268
Love's Labor's Lost, 51, 164, 232, 238, 254, 265
Macbeth, 33, 48–9, 52, 55, 76–7, 78, 82, 93–4, 103–5, 197, 199–200, 230, 238, 239, 249, 262, 263
Measure for Measure, 79, 169–70, 231, 232, 238
The Merchant of Venice, 52, 149, 170–4
The Merry Wives of Windsor, 51, 135, 234, 265
A Midsummer Night's Dream, 20–1, 47–8, 90, 199, 232, 238, 239, 265–6
Much Ado About Nothing, 35–8, 68–70, 80, 82–3, 148–9, 158, 179, 188, 232, 237, 254
Othello, 28–30, 58, 79, 114, 123, 166–7, 239, 265
Pericles, 51, 138, 177, 188, 238, 268
Richard II, 21, 58, 112, 121–2, 238, 241, 247, 250
Richard III, 43, 47, 52, 58, 112, 117, 143–4, 146, 168, 204, 232, 234, 239, 240, 255
Romeo and Juliet, 61, 65–6, 92–3, 113, 158–9, 176–7, 190–5, 232, 234, 236–7, 254
The Taming of the Shrew, 68, 135, 232, 240
The Tempest, 42, 44, 81–2, 136, 137, 164, 197, 198, 210–15, 233, 236, 238, 254, 262
Timon of Athens, 57, 59, 135, 188, 232, 239
Titus Andronicus, 43, 61, 94–9, 135, 141, 146, 164, 181, 236, 242–3, 250, 258
Troilus and Cressida, 43, 72–3, 144, 238, 239
Twelfth Night, 23–4, 79–80, 149, 232, 238, 240–1, 263
The Two Gentlemen of Verona, 232
The Two Noble Kinsmen, 61, 114, 135, 197, 233, 238
The Winter's Tale, 232, 247, 250
Sharpe, Lewis, *The Noble Stranger*, 135
Sharpham, Edward
Cupid's Whirligig, 266
The Fleer, 156
Shirley, Henry, *The Martyred Soldier*, 114, 208, 244, 267
Shirley, James
The Cardinal, 58, 247
Changes, 204
The Example, 135, 247
The Gentleman of Venice, 140–1
The Grateful Servant, 266
The Imposture, 61
Love's Cruelty, 251
The Maid's Revenge, 252
The Politician, 245
St. Patrick for Ireland, 265, 266
The Wedding, 266
The Witty Fair One, 114, 244, 247
Skelton, John, *Magnificence*, 132, 246
Smith, Bruce, 235
Smith, Wentworth, *The Hector of Germany*, 112, 113, 114, 137
Soddered Citizen, The, 137, 244, 245
Sophocles, *Oedipus Rex*, 39–40
stage effects:
beheadings, 249–50
conceptual casting, 26–8, 229
corpses, 83–4
council-Parliament scenes, 57–9
disappearing objects, 197, 261–2, 263–4
early entrances, 23–4, 65–77, 103–5, 236–40
execution scenes, 145–7, 249–50
inside the house, 164–8, 255
interval-intermission, 32–3
keys, 168–74, 255–6
late exits, 77–81, 240–1
mists, 203, 264
night-darkness, 35–8, 106–8, 128, 139
overlapping images, 81–5, 105–7, 243–4
place-locale, 30–2, 105–8, 148–9, 150–75
prison scenes, 139–40, 151, 255
sewing, 166, 255
shop scenes, 155–9, 252
sickness, 112–16

sick-chair, 114, 116–26, 245
sinking through a trap-door, 203, 264–5
stage doors, use of, 25–6
study scenes, 160–4, 252–4
tent scenes, 142–4
theatrical *italics*, 88–108, 154–5
tomb scenes, 35–8, 176–95, 256–61
trees and forest scenes, 59–63, 151, 152–5, 235–6
See also Vocabulary
Suckling, Sir John
Aglaura, 136, 231
Brennoralt, 139, 247
The Goblins, 135, 139, 231, 247
The Sad One, 247
Swander, Homer, 21, 84

Tailor, Robert, *The Hog Hath Lost His Pearl*, 59, 168, 204, 230
Taming of a Shrew, The, 54
Taylor, Gary, 9–11, 20
Telltale, The, 112, 245
Thomas Lord Cromwell, 252, 253
Thracian Wonder, The, 134, 137
Tom a Lincoln, 138
Tomkyns, Nathaniel, 263
Tourneur, Cyril
The Atheist's Tragedy, 187, 230, 234
The Revenger's Tragedy, 234
Towneley Plays, 209
Troublesome Reign of King John, The, 33–4, 117
True Tragedy of Richard III, The, 147, 255
Two Merry Milkmaids, The, 160, 253
Two Noble Ladies, The, 50, 112, 163, 203, 205, 252, 254
Twycross, Meg, 130–1

Valiant Welshman, The, 180, 257
Vanbrugh, Sir John, 248
Visitatio Sepulchri of St. Ethelwold, 129–30, 246
vocabulary:
as from ..., 134–9, 141
as if-though ..., 57–9, 129–49
as in ..., 139–44, 158–9, 161, 163, 166, 192
as in medieval and Tudor drama, 129–33
as in the Restoration, 248
as to ..., 247
aside, 49–55, 232–5
discover, 42, 155–7, 160, 252–3
"*enter a gentle astringer*," 45
enter booted, 43
enter in a chair, 114, 116–26, 245
enter in a nightgown, 28–30, 43–4
enter in a shop, 155–7
enter in his study, 160–4, 253
enter muffled, 43, 231
enter sick, 112–16, 244–5
enter to council, 57–9
enter to execution, 145–7
enter to him, 42
enter with a halter, 43
enter with halberds, 47, 231–2, 250
enter with her hair disheveled, 43
exeunt, 42, 77–8
fictional vs. theatrical stage directions, 55–7, 62–3, 142, 145, 152, 176–7, 202, 249, 252
"*It spreads his arms*," 45–6, 267
offers to go, 42
seems, 250–1
speaks to himself, 52, 233
vanish in dialogue, 203–5, 208, 262, 265–6
vanish in eye witness accounts, 201–2, 263
vanish in Shakespeare, 197–201, 210–15
vanish in stage directions, 205–7, 208–9, 267
vanish in *The Tempest*, 197, 198, 210–15
whispers, 52, 233–4
within, 72–3, 238–9
See also stage effects

Wager, W.
Enough is as Good as a Feast, 111
The Longer Thou Livest, 111
Wapull, George, *The Tide Tarrieth No Man*, 132
Warning for Fair Women, A, 57, 146, 232, 235, 243, 245, 250, 255
Warren, Michael, 240
Wasp, The, 261
Weakest Goeth to the Wall, The, 234
Wealth and Health, 113
Webster, John
The Devil's Law-Case, 251
The Duchess of Malfi, 169, 259

The White Devil, 43–4, 134, 247, 248, 264
Welsh Embassador, The, 253
Whetstone, George, *Promos and Cassandra*, 60, 135, 141
Willis, R., *Mount Tabor*, 201–2
Wilson, Arthur, *The Swisser*, 43, 253
Wilson, Robert
The Cobbler's Prophecy, 133
The Three Lords and Three Ladies of London, 133
Wily Beguiled, 261
Wit of a Woman, The, 245, 253, 254–5
Woodstock, 136, 255
Wycherley, William, 248

Yarington, Robert, *Two Lamentable Tragedies*, 147, 232, 233
Yorkshire Tragedy, A, 134, 245
Youth, The Interlude of, 108